American Public Life and the Historical Imagination

American Public Life

AND THE

Historical Imagination

WENDY GAMBER

MICHAEL GROSSBERG

HENDRIK HARTOG

EDITORS

University of Notre Dame Press
Notre Dame, Indiana

Library of Congress Cataloging-in-Publication Data
American public life and the historical imagination / edited by
Wendy Gamber, Michael Grossberg, and Hendrik Hartog.
p.   cm.
Includes bibliographical references and index.
ISBN 0-268-02017-5 (alk. paper)
ISBN 0-268-02018-3 (pbk. : alk. paper)
1. United States—Politics and government.   2. Political culture—
United States—History.   3. Social movements—United
States—History.   4. United States—Historiography.   I. Gamber, Wendy, 1958–
II. Grossberg, Michael, 1950–   III. Hartog, Hendrik, 1948–
E183.A495   2003
973—dc21
2003009068

For Mickey

CONTENTS

CONTRIBUTORS

RAYMOND ARSENAULT is the John Hope Franklin Professor of Southern History and director of the University Honors College at the University of South Florida, St. Petersburg. He is the author of *The Wild Ass of the Ozarks* (1984) and "The End of the Long Hot Summer: The Air Conditioner and Southern Culture," *Journal of Southern History* (1984). His most recent book, coedited with Roy Peter Clark, is *The Changing South of Gene Patterson: Journalism and Civil Rights, 1960–1968* (2002).

CHARLES W. CHEAPE is professor of history at Loyola College in Baltimore, Maryland. He is the author of *Strictly Business: Walter S. Carpenter at Du Pont and General Motors* (1995), and *Family Firm to Modern Multinational: Norton Company, a New England Enterprise* (1985).

JAMES J. CONNOLLY is associate professor of history at Ball State University. He is the author of *The Triumph of Ethnic Progressivism: Urban Political Culture in Boston, 1900–1925* (1998) and is currently working on a book entitled *The Idea of the Machine: A Cultural History of Party Politics in Industrializing America*.

ELLEN FITZPATRICK is professor of history at the University of New Hampshire. She is the author of *Endless Crusade: Women Socialist Scientists and Progressive Reform* (1990) and *History's Memory: Writing America's Past* (2002).

ALLON GAL is professor of modern Jewish history, senior fellow at Ben-Gurion Research Institute, founder and director of North American Jewry Center, Ben Gurion University of the Negev, Israel. He specializes in Zionism, American Jewish history, history of the Yishuv and the State of Israel, ethnicity, and nationalism.

J. MATTHEW GALLMAN is professor of history at the University of Florida. His publications include *Mastering Wartime: A Social History of Philadelphia During the Civil War* (1990), *The North Fights the Civil War: The Home Front* (1996), and *Receiving Erin's Children: Philadelphia, Liverpool, and the Irish Famine Migration* (2000). He is currently writing a biography of Anna Elizabeth Dickinson, the nineteenth-century orator and author.

WENDY GAMBER is an associate professor at Indiana University. She is the author of *The Female Economy: The Millinery and Dressmaking Trades, 1860–1930* (1997) and is currently at work on *An American Institution: Boardinghouses in Nineteenth-Century America* (forthcoming, Johns Hopkins University Press).

MICHAEL GROSSBERG is professor of history and law at Indiana University and editor of the *American Historical Review*. He is the author of *A Judgment for Solomon: The d'Hauteville Case and Legal Experience in Antebellum America* (1995) and is currently coediting *The Cambridge History of Law in the United States*. He is working on a history of child protection in America.

HENDRIK HARTOG is the Class of 1921 Bicentennial Professor of the History of American Law and Liberty at Princeton University. He is the author of *Man and Wife in America: A History* (2000).

FREDERICK E. HOXIE is Swanlund Professor of History at the University of Illinois, Urbana/Champaign. He is the author *Parading through History: The Making of the Crow Nation in America* (1995) and coauthor of *The People: A History of Native Americans* (2003). He is a former vice president of the Newberry Library in Chicago and director of the Newberry's Center for American Indian History.

BETH LaDOW is a historian and author of *The Medicine Line: Life and Death on a North American Borderland* (2001).

WILLIAM J. NOVAK is associate professor of history at the University of Chicago and Research Fellow at the American Bar Foundation. He is the author of *The People's Welfare: Law and Regulation in Nineteenth-Century America* (1996).

THOMAS R. PEGRAM is professor of American history at Loyola College in Maryland. He is the author of *Battling Demon Rum: The Struggle for a Dry America, 1800–1933* (1998) and *Partisans and Progressives: Private Interest and Public Policy in Illinois, 1870–1922* (1992).

Particulars and Perspectives

Rethinking the History of American Public Life

Wendy Gamber, Michael Grossberg, and Hendrik Hartog

The history of "public life" is not yet a standard category in the writing of American history. It has not yet supplanted "political history" or "legal/constitutional history" or "institutional history" or the history of "political economy" or the "cultural study of politics" or any of the more conventional demarcations within the output of the profession. Tellingly, the authoritative "Recent Scholarship" section of the *Journal of American History* does not yet collect work under the heading "public life," nor does the *American Historical Association Guide to Historical Literature*.

Still, "public life" is a particularly apt way to describe the subject matter of much of what is new, exciting, and significant in recent American historiography. In the last few years, scholars have explored how social movements and political events transformed constitutionalism; they have revealed new features of the long history of struggles over economic power and public regulation; they have unpacked how gender and race shaped apparently neutral legal doctrines. Others study the roles trials have played as encapsulations of cultural conflicts, the ways pluralism has continued to shape politics, how various media—including newspapers, radio, television, social science works, and book clubs—have shaped and been shaped by the changing political culture, and how citizenship has been lived across the nineteenth and twentieth centuries. Recent work teaches us much about how the categories of private life—of marriage, family life, intimate caretaking, and "privacy" itself—became matters of public debate and struggle throughout American history. Such work has obviously not languished uncategorized. The books and articles that have resulted have found homes elsewhere, within the conventional and old-fashioned demarcations found, for example, in the *JAH* or the AHA *Guide*. But such work also points to the emergence of a newer understanding of the American polity that resists the traditional separations of historical writing—of politics not law, of culture not politics, of economics not race, of women's history not legal history, and similar exclusions. Instead, such work draws attention to the continuities and slippages between apparently distinct categories of historical experience, and it reminds us that such demarcations are usually products of the historian's limited imagination. And such work also seems to us best identified as belonging to the broader inquiry that we think of as the history of American public life.

The essays in this volume apply a variety of critical historical strategies and methodologies to the study of American public life, even as they also share a common commitment to the complexity and plurality of American experience. Readers of the pages that follow will find rich descriptions, odd viewpoints, and a diverse landscape of public and private institutions, all mobilized to challenge dominant and monotonal pictures of American history. Phenomena that historical conventional wisdom suggests should not belong together—the Anti-Saloon League and the Ku Klux Klan, for example, or nineteenth-century women and business life, for another—are here joined. Readers will discover Native Americans as historians of the United States, the interrelated lives of Montanans and their Canadian neighbors, the difficulties that an early twentieth-century legal theorist found in describing the functions of marriage, the legal and political foundations of voluntarism, hurricane control as a paradigm of twentieth-century institutional life, and the surprising centrality of child savers and elite lawyers as agents of twentieth-century historical change.

The essays collected here challenge recent approaches to American institutional and public life. In the past generation political scientists, political economists, and law professors have had a major influence on the study of American public life. Books by Theda Skocpol, Rogers Smith, Karen Orren, Stephen Skrowonek, Bruce Ackerman, and Richard Posner, among others, have transformed and reconfigured our understanding of American history. And all American historians have much to learn from their work.

And yet, most historians sense a disciplinary divide that such books have not crossed. From the traditional standpoint of the social sciences, these authors exhibit a newfound commitment to historicity and temporal change, a gratifying new commitment from the historian's standpoint. In a few cases the social scientists have engaged in intensive archival historical research of a sort that historians admire deeply. Still, the political scientists and political economists remain bound to longstanding social science conventions, in particular to a desire to generalize beyond the immediate research subject and to the faith that the right method is at least as important as immersion in sources. For them, the particulars of the past typically remain sites for generalization and theorizing. For them, careers and scholarly significance are measured less by the quantity of research and the quality of the historical imagination than by the "power" of the categories introduced and the capacity of those categories to cross temporal and spatial boundaries.

The authors of the essays in this book are all historians. Indeed, we are all students of Morton Keller, who introduced us to the study of American public life and whose own writings exemplify the historical enterprise that this book means to illustrate. The wide-ranging subjects of these essays reflect the breadth of Keller's scholarship and his expansive vision of public life, a vision that encompasses all the institutions that constitute and maintain American society, politics, and economy. All of us have had to confront the newer writings on institutional and public life; and yet, as a result of our training, all of us retain a historian's traditional commitment to the critical significance of the counterexample, to the distinctive voice, to the complexity and difficulty in coming to generalizations about the past. As historians, we are less concerned with supplanting one "covering" explanation with another, and more interested in complicating dominant narratives with particular, situated voices or with telling "smaller" narratives that reflect back critically on the dominant narratives. For us, pluralism is less a theoretical construct, more a descriptive conclusion drawn out of our historical research. The common commitment found throughout this volume is to a complicated and multilayered conception of American public life. Our historical work challenges the easy assumption that the past is directly accessible to the present, and that one can theorize past and present into continuity with one another. For us, the hard work of history is to enter into imagined dialogue with those who came before. In our writings, we have struggled to convey the distinctive practices and habits and cultures of those who came into our historical field of view. And for us, that struggle epitomizes the enterprise of "doing history," far more so than the construction of simplifying theories and generalizations.

These essays exemplify methodology as well as historiography; they model how evidence is mobilized in pursuit of historiographical critique and the reimagining of American history. These approaches are evident in the categories that divide the book. Each presents essays that confront conventional understandings of the American past. Part one, "Pluralist Methods and Contexts," disputes presumptions of unity and challenges the power of "covering explanations." Rather than proposing a new pluralistic "master narrative," the essays in this section offer concrete examples of pluralistic interventions into the telling of American history. Part two, "Identities," probes the analytical struggles between those committed to strong understandings of identity founded in gender, color, ethnicity, sexuality, or similar characteristics and those committed to fracturing those identities. In much recent writing, such struggles are set against a backdrop of stable identities imagined as existing "once upon a time." Not here. Instead the essays in this section explore a set of ironic discoveries about the contingent significance of historically situated individuals. And finally, part three, "Institutional Experiences," demonstrates how historians are interested in institutional practices throughout American history. In contrast to political scientists' tendency to study "the problem of institutions" and their concern with identifying "key" institutions, these essays pay careful attention to placing specific institutions in their particular historical contexts.

As the essays that follow attest, the history of American public life is complex, multilayered, and far from exhausted. No single methodology or overarching synthesis emerges from these pages. This is not cause for lamentation. Rather, it is testimony to the scholarly potential of public life and the richness of the historical imagination.

PART ONE

Pluralist Methods and Contexts

"Thinking Like an Indian"

Exploring American Indian Views of American History

Frederick E. Hoxie

In a recent essay, Native American historian Donald Fixico declared that "obtaining a tribal viewpoint, a Native feeling, and the other side of history, and then thinking like an Indian and putting yourself in that other position, is mandatory for teaching and writing a balanced history of Indian-white relations."[1] This is a familiar admonition. For at least half a century, American historians have been engaged with the problem of constructing a national history that accurately reflects the social diversity of the United States. Spurred on by the global process of decolonization and its American echoes—the civil rights movement, immigration reform, and the women's movement—scholars have been busy reexamining conventional understandings of the national past. Instead of assuming the existence of a national ideology or a set of common experiences (such as social mobility) that all groups have shared, historians have focused attention on individual communities and at the varieties of experiences that have taken place within them. Rather than presuming to know the outlook of ethnic, racial, or occupational groups because they were "American," or confidently predicting the peaceful resolution of conflicts among them, scholars have turned to examining how individual communities have perceived and acted upon their historical circumstances. In the course of this reexamination the objects of American history-making have become the subjects of a rich new history.

Many of the giants of mid-twentieth-century American history writing, such as W. E. B. Du Bois and Oscar Handlin, pioneered the creation of this plural past by exploring the historical experience of African Americans and immigrants, in the process demolishing the inherited truisms formerly applied to each group.[2] Thanks to the work of these historians and their heirs, easy assumptions regarding the assimilation of ethnic minorities into an American "mainstream" or the power of market forces or political ideology to dissolve group loyalty were gradually replaced with more dynamic models. Historians today imagine American society as the product of a variety of influences that emerge from—and act on—individual communities.[3]

It would seem logical, then, to extend this inquiry to American Indians. But how might one respond to Fixico's statement? How exactly does "an Indian" think? What links this Indian "thinking" to a "tribal viewpoint" and a "balanced view" of history? Several features of the Native American experience make answering these questions difficult. First, American Indians have resisted incorporation into the national culture for five centuries. Opposing American settlement from the sixteenth century onward, Indians have struggled to remain outside the national institutions that grew up around them and played such a destructive role in their lives. Native Americans typically have viewed themselves as people who belong to two "nations," the United States and their own indigenous community. It would seem unlikely that there would be much of a record of Indians "thinking" about history—particularly the history of the United States.

Second, with origins deep in the continent's past, Native American cultures hardly resemble other racial and ethnic groups in the United States. Indeed an entire discipline, anthropology, began as the study of these distinct (and distinctly nonwestern) communities and traditions. These cultures maintain an array of historical traditions. "History," one Navajo scholar has noted, is not a tree called "history" with Navajo history represented by one of its branches. Instead, she argues, history "is a forest of many and varied trees."[4] The effort to "think like an Indian" may carry with it the flawed assumption that researchers can recover a distinct historical viewpoint from diverse and culturally distant peoples whose concerns rarely intersect with those of non-Indian scholars. Of course each tree in the Indian "forest" of history may represent a meaningful approach to the past, but the traditional Native American focus on tribal origins, the interaction of human and "other than human" actors, and events occurring solely in a local setting undermines their utility for historians seeking to construct a plural vision of the national past. It may turn out that "thinking like an Indian" will leave us in despair with Old Lodge Skins, Thomas Berger's character in *Little Big Man*. The fictional Cheyenne elder reflected on the history he had seen in his lifetime and declared, "White people are crazy."[5]

Third, with a population that has suffered more demographic disruption and has intermarried more extensively with outsiders than any other racial minority in the United States, American Indians may be too diverse to "think" one way. Native Americans belong to a widely scattered community. Stretched across every corner of the United States and crosscut by tribal, religious, and socioeconomic differences, native people might well exceed the boundaries of what any social scientist could conclude with respect to a single group. It may be no more possible to "think like an Indian" than it would be to think like a "worker," a "father," or a "left-handed person."

Finally, the category "Indian," like the term itself, is rooted in romance and misconception. Is the "Indian" one imagines "thinking" in history a distinct individual or a compilation of Leatherstocking heroes who themselves have been constructed from white fantasy and nostalgia? Which Indian's thoughts should we compile? And what is the process by which we should make that decision? Should historians employ the federal government's "blood" standards that admit only those with the proper genetic makeup to tribal membership and historical consideration? Or should they accept all self-proclaimed "Indians" at their word, treating the historical experience of each as if it were equivalent to all the rest?

"Thinking like an Indian," then, is not a simple task. But there is a historical literature that would encourage us to press on. In recent years historians have extended earlier scholarship to explore the diversity within racial and ethnic groups, the relationships these groups have had to one another, and the many ways in which the concerns of different actors and categories of people have overlapped with one another through time.[6] This literature suggests that what the "thinking" historians might find most useful for obtaining a "tribal viewpoint" is not the self-contained literature of creation stories and other traditional chronicles favored by anthropologists but the record of those occasions when Native Americans have looked beyond local affairs to comment explicitly on the history of the United States. Just as a plural society is defined by the transactions that occur within public institutions and public places, so the effort to understand and encompass the perspectives of multiple groups requires us to look for places where different people are engaged in a common conversation. To understand what it means for historians to "think like an Indian" requires that we focus on those occasions when native people have examined and spoken out about the history of the wider society. Exploring Indians "thinking" in that arena should provide both a wider view of the American past and a sharper understanding of the dynamics of plural societies themselves. In the process we will witness Native American "thinkers" accomplishing an essential task: using the historical imagination to overcome boundaries of race, culture, and time.

The first extended indigenous historical narrative regarding the encounter between Euro-Americans and Native Americans emerged from the religious and political upheavals of the late eighteenth century, when a series of visionary prophets mobilized their communities to resist Anglo-American expansion into the Ohio valley. Neolin, a Delaware teacher whose home lay in eastern Ohio not far from the frontier trading post of Pittsburgh, was the first of these prophets whose careers can be documented. Described in accounts from the 1760s as a young man, Neolin based his preaching on a vision that had convinced him that Indian people should separate themselves from all trappings of European culture. As part of his ministry, Neolin distributed a pictographic chart to his followers that represented white people in the form of a black box that stood between earth-bound Indians and the heavenly realm above them. The box symbolized the white man's evil gifts: drink, avarice, and over hunting. According to Neolin, whites were a disruptive and dangerous presence in an otherwise harmonious world.[7]

Neolin's chart made it clear that he and his followers believed white people and Indians represented separate orders of being. Searching for native allies in the struggle to resist the English and the Americans, and eager to identify common ground among divided and competing groups of Delawares, Miamis, Iroquois, Ojibwes, Ottawas, Shawnees, and others, Neolin called for Indian unity. He argued that despite tribal and linguistic differences, Native Americans had more in common with each other than they could ever have with the alien and evil race that had come from east of the mountains. Neolin called on his followers to reject European technology and trade goods (especially alcohol) and to make that renunciation public by participating in a ceremony that involved taking a special emetic that caused participants to vomit up any white poisons that remained within them.

A generation later, Tecumseh's brother, the Shawnee prophet Tenskwatawa, carried Neolin's message and the call for pan-Indian resistance to a confederacy of tribes gathered in Indiana. Tenskwatawa shared Neolin's view that whites and Indians had been created separately. He told his followers that the

Master of Life had assured him during a great vision, "The Americans I did not make. They are not my children but the children of the Evil Spirit. . . . They grew from the scum of the great water when it was troubled by the Evil Spirit. And the froth was driven into the woods by a strong east wind. They are numerous, but I hate them." [8] His message would be a crucial element in forging the anti-American alliance that fought valiantly but unsuccessfully alongside the British in the War of 1812. (A version of the Shawnee's teaching was carried to the Creeks of Georgia and Alabama and probably played a role in the Red Stick rebellion which took place shortly thereafter.)[9]

The message of these visionaries was clear: Indian people and white people shared no common history. European culture was the birthplace of sorcery and evil; those who preached the goodness of Christianity or European culture were the victims of a devilish deception. Citizens of the United States were therefore defined as incomprehensible and evil; there were no points at which the lives of the two races overlapped. Native American history, on the other hand, rested on a set of common origins and a set of common values. This outlook, which historian Gregory Evans Dowd has called "Nativist," characterized much of the prophetic teaching that emerged from the violent border conflicts of the early nineteenth century. It was central to the militant appeal of Tecumseh and the Red Sticks, and it was an element in the peaceful message of renewal enunciated by the Seneca prophet, Handsome Lake. The leaders of these movements believed that the newcomers from Europe were like the black cloud that blocked the pathway from earth to heaven; their "tribal viewpoint" was that Americans and their history were alien and evil.

In 1831, while Handsome Lake's teachings were finding receptive audiences among the Iroquois peoples of western New York and Tenskwatawa (forced west by the Americans) was settling into a new home near modern Kansas City, another American Indian visionary told his life story and embarked on a similar campaign of teaching and conversion. William Apess's autobiography, *A Son of the Forest,* contained his "thinking" about history. It contained a stinging indictment of American avarice and deception. Nevertheless, Apess viewed both himself and his white tormenters from a remarkably different perspective than the nativist prophets of the Ohio and Alabama frontiers. Apess grew up in a world where the borders between whites and Indians could not be drawn with clarity. His father was the son of a white man and an Indian woman and his childhood was spent with his Pequot kin, traveling between Indian and white settlements in southern New England. Apess was also the victim of abuse in a violent, alcoholic family; he was bound out to a white man at an early age. As a consequence he did not separate the worlds of virtue and evil along tribal or racial lines. When he "thought like an Indian" he did not necessarily define himself in opposition to the cultures of Europe. Unlike the nativist prophets, Apess declared that all people shared a common origin. For him, ancestry meant nothing. "I consider myself nothing more than a worm of the earth," he declared.[10]

But the Apess revealed in *A Son of the Forest* was no less a visionary than Neolin or Handsome Lake. Growing up as an indentured servant in white households, the young Pequot was curious about Christianity and increasingly preoccupied with his own shortcomings. He was drawn to what he referred to as the "noisy Methodists," both because of their emotional services—"people shouted for joy while sinners wept"—and because they were persecuted by his upper-class employers.[11] The Methodists' democratic culture and lack of formal doctrine finally won him over. For a lonely, frightened child separated from his parents and their traditions, the promise of Christian redemption provided a way of ordering the world. "I felt convinced that Christ died for all mankind," Apess wrote, "that age, sect, color, country, or situation made no difference. I felt an assurance that I was included in the plan of redemption with all my brethren. No one can conceive with what joy I hailed this new doctrine."[12]

Apess's story follows the pattern of a formulaic nineteenth-century conversion narrative—a young man lost and then found through faith—but the "peace of mind" he described in his autobiography was not the smug satisfaction of a pious Christian convert. He went on to detail his conversion. It involved a number of almost Indian rituals—participatory, emotional worship with the Methodists, individual wandering not unlike a vision quest, and a culminating personal event: a visionary journey where he was shown the two paths that lay before him. Methodism became for Apess, Barry O'Connell has written, "a place to join being Christian and Native American."[13]

Echoing the antislavery voices of his day, Apess used what he took to be the central message of Christianity—"Christ died for all mankind"—to establish a moral yardstick against which he could measure the behavior of his fellow Americans. His conversion armed him with a moral language he used to think about himself as a Native American in a world ruled by outsiders. Cut off from his own tribal traditions, and engulfed by an indifferent white community, Apess shared many of the conditions facing the Senecas or Shawnees. But he did not take the nativist path of Neolin or Tenskwatawa. He didn't think of whites as inscrutable devils; he thought they were sinners. So he condemned them in their own tongue. "How much better it would be if the whites would act like civilized people," he declared.[14]

William Apess offered his most sustained commentary on American history in his "Eulogy on King Philip," a widely reprinted speech he delivered in Boston in 1836 at the height of the controversy surrounding the removal of the Cherokees from Georgia. The "Eulogy" was a defense of the seventeenth-century Pokanoket-Wampanoag leader's patriotism and, by implication, an attack on the patriotic hero—Andrew Jackson—who now stood poised to dispossess thousands of southeastern Indians from their homes in Georgia, Alabama, and Florida. Apess mocked the president's self-serving statements that stressed his concern for the tribes' welfare. According to the Pequot preacher, Jackson was really saying to the Indians, "You must go, even if the lions devour you, for we promised the land you have to somebody else long ago . . . and we did it without your consent, it is true. But this has been the way our fathers first brought us up."[15]

Apess's moralistic reading of history led him to an apocalyptic conclusion. The evil of racial hatred must be eradicated from the nation so that everyone—Indian and white—might be free. "We want trumpets that sound like thunder," Apess declared, calling people to "go to war with those corrupt and degrading principles that rob one of all rights merely because he is ignorant and of a little different color. Let us have principles that will give everyone his due; and then shall wars cease. . . . What do the Indians want?" he asked rhetorically, "you have only to look at the unjust laws made for them and say, 'they want what I want.'"[16]

The nativist and moralist views of American history dominated Native American thinking and writing about the national past for a century after William Apess's speech. Community leaders like Tecumseh and Neolin, who sought to forge multitribal alliances, frequently resorted to the nativist view. They argued that Indians and whites had nothing in common and that American behavior could not be explained or altered. Sitting Bull represents the most dramatic example of a nineteenth-century intertribal leader who employed these nativist ideas to explain his predicament and inspire his followers. Relying on visionary experiences that indicated spiritual helpers would deliver them from the Americans' relentless advance, the Hunkpapa holy man rallied a collection of northern plains hunting peoples to his cause. His rhetorical and religious stance lay behind his military prowess and played a central role in his victories over American forces in the 1870s.[17]

Similarly, Wovoka, the Northern Paiute religious leader who triggered the Ghost Dance in 1889, preached a message of religious separatism and self-reliance that resembled Handsome Lake's message a century earlier. Wovoka received his knowledge in a visionary journey to heaven. Like the Seneca prophet he returned to earth to rescue all Indians from the effects of white conquest, not to lead them into battle. The Paiute leader declared that peaceful coexistence was possible because Indian salvation required its own ceremonies; there was no need to follow white instructions other than to remain at peace. Wovoka's authority came from the creator whom he encountered in his vision and who had appointed Wovoka co-president of the United States. In the prophet's words, the creator had made him his "deputy, to take charge of affairs in the West, while Governor Harrison [President Benjamin Harrison] would tend to matters in the East and he, God, would look after matters above." This division of authority reflected Wovoka's conviction that, following the fulfillment of his vision, Native Americans would live apart from the rest of the nation's people.[18]

Despite the continuing nativist tradition in American Indian life, few nativist leaders expressed themselves in print. Nativist interpretations of tribal experience and American history remained within Indian communities, communicated orally to enlist new followers and to extend the influence of visionary leaders. They entered the printed literature through the efforts of anthropologists who began conducting field work in the late nineteenth century. James Mooney sought out Wovoka only a few years after his initial vision and at a time when his followers were still active in Oklahoma and on the Plains. His record of the Paiute prophet's vision was the first such account to be published. Handsome Lake's teachings, although actively studied and celebrated among Iroquois people, were not compiled and published until 1913 through the efforts of the Seneca anthropologist Arthur C. Parker. These texts were gradually joined over the next several decades by scholarly studies of other visionary leaders.

Until well into the twentieth century, when Native American thinking about American history found its way into print it generally followed the moralistic model established by Willam Apess. Examples of this moralist outlook appeared in the widely reprinted speeches and statements of Black Hawk, Geronimo, Red Cloud, Sarah Winnemucca, and Chief Joseph. Speaking generally in the wake of a military defeat, these leaders called on white Americans to view their nation's history in moral rather than racial terms, and to see American Indians as fellow human beings rather than as backward savages who blocked the path to civilization.[19]

The writer who developed this moralistic view of American history most fully in the century after Apess was Charles Eastman, a Santee Sioux physician who became a popular author and lecturer in the decades surrounding World War I. Eastman published ten books of stories and autobiographical sketches between 1902 and 1920 while operating a popular summer camp and travelling widely on behalf of the YMCA and the Society of American Indians. The product of mission schools, Eastman shared Apess's view that Indians and whites shared a common humanity. Far less doctrinaire than the Pequot preacher, however, Eastman referred to the creator in general terms and he avoided linking his message to the cause of Christian missionaries.

Eastman's thinking about American history was most clearly evident in *From the Deep Woods to Civilization,* an autobiography published in 1916. The book purported to describe a young man's "rise" from a boyhood in the wilderness to the author's prosperous adulthood as a member of civilized society. On the surface this is the case: a young boy is called from the woods by his relatives who have converted to Christianity. He becomes a star pupil, a college student, a physician, an important public figure. But Eastman's narrative voice makes clear that his journey marked the passage from faith to disillusionment. Civilization, he discovered, had no moral compass. As a physician, Eastman treated survivors of the massacre at Wounded Knee, South Dakota; as a lobbyist for his tribe, he witnessed corruption in Washington, D.C.; as a civil servant, he experienced the cruelty of the Indian Office bureaucracy; and as an educated Native American, he felt the racism white Americans routinely displayed toward nonwhite people. The message of his journey was clear: Indian culture was more virtuous than white civilization. He wrote that "morality and spirituality are found to thrive better under the simplest conditions than in a highly organized society." Consequently, the "democracy and community life" of American Indians was traditionally "much nearer the ideal than ours to-day. . . . Behind the material and intellectual splendor of our civilization," Eastman argued, "primitive savagery and cruelty and lust hold sway."[20]

Eastman's moralistic perspective reflected the progressive political activism of his day. His critical but ultimately reformist view—that Indian values could inspire humanistic reforms of industrial American society—was picked up by other writers of his generation. Arthur Parker, Francis La Flesche, and Carlos Montezuma differed with Eastman on various policy issues, but they shared his belief that Native Americans had something to teach the American majority. Perhaps most outspoken was Zitkala Ša, a Yankton Sioux writer who published short stories in *Atlantic Monthly* and other popular magazines, and who criticized missionaries and school masters for their failure to appreciate Indian traditions. In one of her most outspoken stories, she describes a pious Indian convert to Christianity who called at her home and scolded her for not attending services. The stiff-necked visitor was oblivious to the beautiful spring day that glowed outside her window, focusing instead on church gossip. The author commented, "I prefer to their dogma my excursions into the natural gardens where the voice of the Great Spirit is heard . . . If this is Paganism, then at present, at least, I am a Pagan."[21]

A final view of American history emerged in aftermath of World War I, when two intellectual trajectories crossed paths. First, social theorists—anthropologists, sociologists, educators, and legal scholars—began to dismantle the progressive ideology that had dominated thinking about American nationalism since the first days of the republic. Rather than envisioning society as a homogeneous collection of individuals, each one protected by a set of legal rights, these new "social scientists" began to describe society as a collection of communities shaped by tradition, economic structure, ethnicity, and social institutions. At the same time, the first generation of American Indians began to emerge from American colleges and universities. Although often products of a missionary education, this self-conscious cohort looked beyond a religious or moralistic explanation for American events.

D'Arcy McNickle reflected both of these trends. McNickle's grandparents were Canadian Crees who fled south to the Flathead reservation in Montana in the aftermath of the 1885 Riel rebellion. Raised on the Flathead, McNickle attended the University of Montana before leaving in 1925 to study in Europe and, later, to seek his fortune as a freelance writer and novelist in New York City. In 1936 McNickle published his autobiographical novel, *The Surrounded*, and joined the Bureau of Indian Affairs, working as a liaison officer between an ambitious group of New Deal reformers in Washington, D.C., and tribal leaders on the reservations. He continued to write as his work carried him across the United States, teaching him in the process how poorly Indians and whites understood each other's cultures. The experience convinced McNickle that the barriers between Indians and whites were not racial or moral, but cultural. After World War II he witnessed the onset of decolonization and began to understand the experiences of Native Americans in global terms. "Indians saw their history extending beyond tribal limits," he wrote, "sharing the world experience of other native peoples subjected to colonial domination." The solution to this situation, the way to narrow the gap between Indians and whites, was to extend the process of decolonization to the United States: to give Native American communities the right to function as independent entities. McNickle put it this way: "Return the right of decision to the tribes—restore their power to hold the dominant society at arm's length, and to bargain again in peace and friendship. Only by possessing such power can the tribes make useful choices within the social environment encompassing them." [22]

In 1949 McNickle published a history of American Indians in the United States, the first comprehensive history written by a Native American. *They Came Here First* began with a compelling portrait of the diverse and ingenious peoples who had lived in the Americas before 1492. McNickle described native legal systems and religious beliefs and reviewed the history of contact and European expansion. "What the Europeans could not appreciate," he noted, "was that they had come face to face with customs, beliefs, habits—cultures—which had been some thousands of years in the forming. Whether these were inferior or superior was inconsequential; they had grown out of an antiquity of their own."[23] This ignorance produced what he called, "The Indian War That Never Ends."

D'Arcy McNickle's thinking about history followed an anti-colonial point of view. Writing from a secular perspective rather than a religious or moralistic one, McNickle and those who followed his lead identified a number of American characteristics that defined the national experience: cultural chauvinism, environmental exploitation, and bureaucratic inertia. Rooted in cultural misunderstanding and political ambition, American behavior must be altered, McNickle argued, so that native people might govern themselves like other citizens. In a manifesto drafted for a national Indian congress in 1961 McNickle brought this point home by connecting Native American concerns to the concerns of the then-emerging Third World: "What we ask is not charity, not paternalism, even when benevolent. We ask only that the nature of our situation be recognized and made the basis of policy and action.... the Indians ask for assistance, technical and financial, ... to regain in the America of the space age some measure of the adjustment they enjoyed as the original possessors of their native land."[24] Like Apess and Eastman, McNickle saw a future for American Indians within the United States, but that future would require more than the acceptance of native morality by Christian whites. It would require a restructuring of American democracy.

By the 1970s, when Indian activists protesting federal inaction began commandeering television screens while small armies of white and Native American lawyers launched assaults on the nation's antiquated policy apparatus, there were three distinctive strains of historical writing from which Indian analysts could draw as they sought to make sense of the national past. There has been such an explosion of creative scholarship in the past generation that it would be foolish to claim that all of it follows neatly the patterns established over the previous two centuries. Nevertheless, if one focuses on the writing of Native Americans alone, there is a striking congruence between these three inherited perspectives—nativist, moralist, and anticolonial—and a great deal of contemporary writing. Three examples will have to make this case.

Ward Churchill, who describes himself as a member of the American Indian Movement and a member of the Keetowah Band of the Cherokee Tribe, is both a political activist and an academic historian (he is a professor at the University of Colorado). While ranging over many topics, from environmental destruction to the antiradical programs of the FBI, he has been an insistent advocate of labeling American Indian history as the story of a holocaust. "From most of the history of what has happened," he writes, "the perpetrators, from aristocrats like Jeffrey Amherst to the lowliest private in his army, from the highest elected officials to the humblest of farmers, openly described America's indigenous peoples as vermin, launched literally hundreds of campaigns to effect their extermination, and then reveled in the carnage which resulted." As a consequence of this sustained effort, he concludes, "The American holocaust was and remains unparalleled."[25]

Like the nativist leaders of the nineteenth century, Churchill insists his historical conclusions support his political commitment. He declares that "American Indians, demonstrably one of the most victimized groups in the history of humanity, are entitled to every ounce of moral authority we can get." In addition, Churchill charges that American leaders have been perpetrators of a holocaust and deniers of its reality. Officials have denied their guilt and manipulated government agencies to shield them from prosecution for their crimes. Americans, he asserts, have created a "New World Order" which "promises to institutionalize genocide as an instrument of state power." Using heavily footnoted texts rather than visionary journeys, Churchill offers a relentless indictment of American action that one can nevertheless imagine as a black image on Neolin's drawing of the road to heaven. The enemies of indigenous people share nothing with native communities; loyal Indians should join with each other under a single leadership, rejecting compromise with white leaders or involvement with American institutions.

Second, during the course of the past twenty-five years an energetic community of Native American scholars has entered the American academy; many of them are historians. Within the group are specialists in women's history, colonial America, federal Indian policy, Indian law, and western history. Like William Apess and Charles Eastman, these authors speak from within American society. Teaching and writing for non-Indians as well as Native Americans, these scholars do not draw the dividing lines that are so evident in the work of more radical figures. They are also reluctant—as most historians are—to embrace the larger theoretical framework of colonialism (and its modern incarnation, subaltern studies). Their work falls into the moralistic-progressive vein. Anti-Indian actions are the result of avaricious land-grabbers, legal schemers, misguided policymakers, and moralizing charlatans. Donald Fixico, for example, quoted at the outset of this essay, has written an account of the exploitation of tribal natural resources in the twentieth century. In his view, the story of the fate of Native American resources is part of the story of American greed. "Greed has become the driving force in seizing land and using its natural resources without regard to the consequences, he writes. "The tragic outcome of this ethic can be seen in the brutal exploitation that Indians have experienced."[26]

Jean O'Brien's *Dispossession by Degrees* is a richly detailed study of the Massachusetts "Praying Town" of Natick, a community settled initially by Christian Indians seeking refuge from colonial dislocation and violence. In her book O'Brien traces the threads of community connection and loyalty that held Indian people to Natick as they gradually lost their grip on their lands and political power. The book has a great deal to say about the nature of New England Indian communities, but operating throughout the narrative is the relentless acquisitiveness of New England's white settlers. Gradually they shift Natick's Indian residents to the margins of the town; ultimately they push them out altogether. Different conceptions of land and identity lay beneath the struggle over Natick: "English ideas about fixity on the land and its connection to the impulse to assign everyone a proper place in the social order informed their interpretations of Indian ways of life, and . . . provided them with justifications for dispossessing Indians."[27]

Here is a moral stance not unlike that of Apess and Eastman. Americans have fallen short of their ideal of fairness. European settlers refused to recognize native people as human beings with an equal claim to the land. Persistent native traditions and land use practices suggest that Indian people in Natick were neither mindless savages nor passive victims. They were fellow colonists, dispossessed by American expansion. In this sense, O'Brien's monograph, like Fixico's, shares the moralist-progressive agenda of Winnemucca, Eastman, and Apess.

Finally, the most dominant Native American intellectual of the past generation has been Vine Deloria Jr., author of the bestselling *Custer Died for Your Sins*, first published in 1969, and more than a dozen other works of history and commentary. Deloria's attention has shifted successively from white misconceptions and stereotypes to radical activism to moral philosophy to the value of traditional native epistemology; it is therefore quite difficult (and probably unwise) to characterize neatly his complex point of view. Yet when one isolates his historical writing, his anticolonial approach comes sharply into view.

From the outset of his career as a public figure, Deloria insisted that non-Indians understand that Native Americans were not interested in "civil rights." Instead, "The modern Indian movement for national recognition has its roots in the tireless resistance of generations of unknown Indians who have refused to melt into homogeneity of American life and accept American citizenship." The goal of this movement was not to win acceptance from the white majority but to restore treaties as the basis for relations between tribes and the government. Such a restoration would involve recognizing American Indian communities as independent, political sovereigns. In Deloria's view, the revival of political activism that he had witnessed and participated in during the 1960s and 1970s was an American version of the anticolonial struggle that swept the globe in the generation after World War II: "The Third World ideology which proved so useful to Europeans in interpreting the events of the world . . . seemed to be fulfilling itself in North America as well as in Africa and Asia."[28]

Although not among the Indian radicals who occupied the Bureau of Indian Affairs offices in 1972 or took over the crossroads settlement of Wounded Knee in 1973, Deloria defended those actions because they demonstrated that Native Americans sought more than "fairness" or cultural sensitivity. "The pressing need today," Deloria wrote in 1974, "is that the United States not only recognize the international status of the Indian tribes, . . . but that it also authorize the creation of a special court to settle treaty violations." As political passions cooled in the 1980s and 1990s, Deloria continued to insist that sovereignty, not civil rights, should be the objective of Indian leaders. "A change in perception by both Indians and federal and state officials who deal with Indians is imperative if any substantial progress is to be achieved in the future. . . . It is probably too late," Deloria concluded, "to put the Indian genie back into the bottle."[29]

From Deloria's perspective, the history of the United States resembled the history of any other imperial power. Gradually expanding its power over native communities, the federal government had implemented a series of authoritarian policies designed to justify and defend its seizure of Indian land and resources. American officials were not particularly immoral or especially unusual. "Exploration and settlement required a good deal of intellectual effort," Deloria wrote with his tongue fixed firmly in his cheek. "The Europeans were equal to the occasion" and they developed an approach "which, naturally, gave them all the advantages." American expansion, then, was carried out for selfish reasons and the treaties tribes signed in the eighteenth and nineteenth centuries are an artifact of that process. But despite their colonial heritage, to Deloria these treaties are an important badge of Indian sovereignty, for they carry with them a recognition of the Indians' "residual right of political existence." It is this link between American history and contemporary treaty rights that defines Deloria's anticolonial stance.[30]

What has this review taught us about what it has meant to "think like an Indian" about American history? First, Native American historical perspectives vary over time and space. Influenced by political motivation, individual life experience, and historical context, these perspectives suggest that "thinking like an Indian" requires more than extrapolating from a set of ethnographic descriptors to create a checklist of tribal (or Indian) beliefs. Clearly, there is no single "Indian" approach to events in the national past.

Second, none of these major interpretive approaches traces itself to pre-contact Native American cultures. Pointing out their postcontact origins does not, of course, lessen their claim to authority as "Indian" perspectives, but it does suggest that Native American perspectives on the past are products of history as well as of cultural inheritance. In particular, just as the Indian label itself is a white invention, "thinking like an Indian" about the encounter is an outgrowth of contact with Europeans. The visionary prophets spoke from an indigenous tradition, but both the timing of their message and its emphasis on intertribal collaboration were responses to eighteenth-century military realities. Similarly, the moralist and anticolonial approaches explored by other Native American thinkers emerged from confrontations with whites as well as from contact with Christian missionaries, reformers, and academic scholars.

Finally, the approaches to "thinking like an Indian" described here emerged most clearly during the twentieth century, just as the general American public was wrestling with the demands of an increasingly pluralist society. As issues of race relations, economic justice, immigration reform, and women's rights repeatedly entered the public arena, politicians sought ways to resolve them. They produced a variety of policies, from segregation to women's suffrage to controls on immigration based on the "scientific" study of ethnic groups. Ongoing debate over these policies made discussions of American pluralism a part of public life. As a part of that discussion, non-Indians and Native Americans themselves asserted what they believed Indians were "thinking" about history and public policy. This "thinking," in turn, became a key element in policy reforms.[31] The modern Native American advocates of nativist, moralist, and anticolonial approaches to Indian history are representative of this contentious milieu.

As we search for what it means to "think like an Indian" we confront the fact that the historical experience of American Indians is deeply intertwined with the history of the United States. While arising from distinctive indigenous traditions that continue to shape community life, native people have been locked in a contest with outsiders that has affected every aspect of their lives.[32] It appears that "thinking like an Indian," is not so much a function of a distinctive cultural tradition as it is a product of a shared history. Where then, does this leave us in our quest? Can historians hope to answer Fixico's call that we "think like an Indian?"

Literary scholar Kathryn Shanley has recently urged her fellow Native American academics to assert a "strategic essentialism, a positing of an essential difference for the sake of shifting the center of power." The assertion that Indian people by their nature have an essentially different point of view from non-Indians should be the foundation on which to build "respect for indigenous difference in a range of arenas from philosophy to law." Shanley rejects racial essentialism—the notion that members of particular races naturally share particular ways of thinking—but she insists that native scholars must "redefine space" within the academy.[33] Like Fixico's invitation to "think like an Indian," Shanley's proposal has a familiar ring. People who have been marginalized and excluded need to be heard and to be taken seriously. A worthy sentiment, but our discussion of the many ways Indians have "thought" about the past suggests her goal is futile. There is no essential "Indian" quality that functions across real time and circumstances.

It would be tempting to end this essay on that anti-essentialist note. But there is another way to view the diverse community of historians that begins with Neolin and ends with Vine Deloria. Although shifting widely in their cultural outlooks, attitudes, and assessments of American culture, each of these historians speaks as an American Indian, a historical person struggling to understand his or her surroundings and attempting to communicate beyond a local community. Variety within the group reveals not the weakness of Native American culture but its flexibility, adaptability, and complexity. "Thinking like an Indian" has proved not to be as singular or static as Donald Fixico implied it would be. Instead, it is something changing and unpredictable. Striving to uncover how and what Native Americans were thinking is futile only if one sets out expecting to find the same outlook at the end of each search.

If we accept the diversity of Native American historical experience, Shanley's "strategic essentialism" carries a different meaning. To assert one's "Indianness" as a literary critic or historian need not mean asserting a single identity or point of view. It can mean instead asserting a distinctive historical experience. Discovering that the Native American community encompasses a variety of historical perspectives should encourage us to imagine a plural past as encompassing a variety of conversations both within groups and between them and the larger society. Plural histories should reflect that complex and shifting reality, resembling cacophonous public meetings more than they do well-staged festivals of culture, where each group shows up in its native costume and dances its assigned folk dance.[34]

Historian Richard White has observed that "there have been few peoples as culturally, politically, and socially complicated as Indians."[35] This being true, as this essay underscores, focusing seriously on the experience of Native Americans cannot be a simple or predictable task, just as writing a plural history cannot be accomplished by allotting groups of homogeneous communities their assigned space in an ideologically or theoretically driven narrative. Understanding the complexity of native life, we cannot know in advance what "Indianness" will be, just as we cannot predict the future of any dynamic and diverse society. As historians we should know that we cannot predict what an Indian will think.

NOTES

1. Donald L. Fixico, "Ethics and Responsibilities in Writing American Indian History," in *Natives and Academics: Researching and Writing about Native Americans,* ed. Devon Mihesuah (Lincoln: University of Nebraska Press, 1998), 93. I am grateful to Colin Calloway, Betty Bell, and Brenda Farnell for reading and commenting on an earlier draft of this essay and to the members of the University of Illinois Social History Workshop for their candid and helpful suggestions.

2. See W. E. B. Du Bois, *Black Reconstruction in America,* 1935 ed. (New York: Atheneum, 1992); Oscar Handlin, *Boston's Immigrants: A Study in Acculturation,* rev. ed. (Cambridge: Harvard University Press, 1979).

3. For a sampling of this movement, see Eric Foner, ed., *The New American History* (Philadelphia: Temple University Press, 1990); Lawrence H. Fuchs, *The American Kaleidoscope* (Hanover: University Press of New England, 1990); and a multiauthor reference work: Stephan Thernstrom, ed., *Harvard Encyclopedia of American Ethnic Groups* (Cambridge: Harvard University Press, 1980).

4. Ruth Roessel, quoted in Peter Nabokov, "Native Views of History," in *The Cambridge History of the Native Peoples of the Americas,* ed. Bruce Trigger and Wilcomb Washburn (New York: Cambridge University Press, 1996), vol. 1 (North America), part 1, 55.

5. The divide between traditional Native American views of history and contemporary academic history is illustrated by two recent essays that attempt to bridge it. Peter Nabokov's wonderful essay in the *Cambridge History of the Native Peoples of the Americas* (cited in n. 4) offers insights into the historical nature of traditional

"myths and legends" and defends the value of these elements of tribal culture. But nowhere in the essay does Nabokov explore how and where Indians have "thought" about the larger historical enterprise or how Indian "thinking" might affect historical scholarship. Second, Peter Iverson's opening chapter for *The Oxford History of the American West* (New York: Oxford University Press, 1994), 13–43, offers an excellent summary of native and non-native views of the West before the nineteenth century but does not link these two points of view. We are left to speculate about how Indians might "think" about the historical chronology that follows.

6. The broadest discussion of this complex process can be found in David Hollinger's *Postethnic America*, rev. ed. (New York: Basic Books, 2000). For more focused studies of this phenomenon, see James R. Barrett and David Roediger, "Inbetween Peoples: Race, Nationality and the 'New Immigrant' Working Class," *Journal of American Ethnic History* 16, 3 (spring 1997): 3–44; Hasia Diner, *Erin's Daughters in America: Irish Immigrant Women in the Nineteenth Century* (Baltimore: Johns Hopkins University Press, 1983); Herbert G. Gutman, *The Black Family in Slavery and Freedom, 1750–1925* (New York: Vintage, 1977); David R. Roediger, *The Wages of Whiteness: Race and the Making of the American Working Class* (London: Verso, 1991); Werner Sollers, *Beyond Ethnicity: Consent and Descent in American Culture* (New York: Oxford University Press, 1986); and Alexander Saxton, *The Rise and Fall of the White Republic: Class Politics and Mass Culture in Nineteenth Century America* (London: Verso, 1990).

7. Gregory Evans Dowd, *A Spirited Resistance: The North American Indian Struggle for Unity, 1745–1815* (Baltimore: Johns Hopkins University Press, 1992), 33.

8. R. David Edmunds, *The Shawnee Prophet* (Lincoln: University of Nebraska Press, 1983), 38.

9. See Joel Martin, *Sacred Revolt: The Muscogees' Struggle for a New World* (Boston: Beacon Press, 1991), chap. 5.

10. William Apess, *On Our Own Ground: The Complete Writings of William Apess, A Pequot,* ed. Barry O'Connell (Amherst: University of Massachusetts Press, 1992), 4.

11. Ibid., 18.

12. Ibid., 19.

13. Ibid., lix.

14. Ibid., 33.

15. Ibid., 307.

16. Ibid., 307, 310.

17. See Robert M. Utley, *The Lance and the Shield: The Life and Times of Sitting Bull* (New York: Henry Holt, 1993), chap. 11, esp. p. 138.

18. See James Mooney, *The Ghost Dance Religion* (1896; Chicago: University of Chicago Press, 1965), 14.

19. See Donald Jackson, ed., *Black Hawk: An Autobiography* (1833; Urbana: University of Illinois Press, 1955); S. M. Barrett, ed., *Geronimo: His Own Story* (1906; New York: Ballantine Books, 1970); for Red Cloud and Chief Joseph as public speakers, see

F. P. Prucha, *American Indian Policy in Crisis* (Norman: University of Oklahoma Press, 1976), 126, 196.

20. Charles Eastman, *From the Deep Woods to Civilization* (Boston: Little, Brown, 1916), 188, 194.

21. Zitkala Ša, "Why I Am a Pagan," *Atlantic Monthly* 90 (December 1902): 803.

22. D'Arcy McNickle, *They Came Here First: The Epic of the American Indian* (1949; New York: Harper & Row, Perennial, 1975), 285.

23. Ibid., 93.

24. Quoted in Francis P. Prucha, ed., *Documents of United States Indian Policy*, 2d ed. (Lincoln: University of Nebraska Press, 1990), 246.

25. Ward Churchill, *A Little Matter of Genocide* (San Francisco: City Lights Books, 1997), 2, 4.

26. Donald L. Fixico, *The Invasion of Indian Country in the Twentieth Century* (Niwot: University Press of Colorado, 1998), xix.

27. Jean O'Brien, *Dispossession by Degrees: Indian Land and Identity in Natick, Massachusetts, 1650–1790* (New York: Cambridge University Press, 1997), 26.

28. Vine Deloria Jr., *Behind the Trail of Broken Treaties: An Indian Declaration of Independence* (New York: Delacorte Press, 1974), 20, 82. For biographical background, see Robert Allen Warrior, *Tribal Secrets: Recovering American Indian Intellectual Traditions* (Minneapolis: University of Minnesota Press, 1995), 30–41.

29. Deloria, *Behind the Trail of Broken Treaties*, 228; Vine Deloria and Clifford Lytle, *The Nations Within: The Past and Future of American Indian Sovereignty* (New York: Pantheon, 1984), 264.

30. Deloria, *Behind the Trail of Broken Treaties*, 85, 115.

31. For a description of this public debate and its effect on policymaking, see Morton Keller, *Regulating a New Society: Public Policy and Social Change in America, 1900–1933* (Cambridge: Harvard University Press, 1994), chap. 9. For an example of how public debate shaped Indian policy in that era, see Lawrence C. Kelly, *The Assault on Assimilation: John Collier and the Origins of Indian Policy Reform* (Albuquerque: University of New Mexico Press, 1983).

32. Mia Bay makes a similar point in the conclusion of her recent book on African American writings about whites. See *The White Image in the Black Mind: African American Ideas about White People, 1830–1925* (New York: Oxford University Press, 2000), 223.

33. Kathryn W. Shanley, "Writing Indian: American Indian Literature and the Future of Native American Studies," in *Studying Native America: Problems and Prospects*, ed. Russell Thornton (Madison: University of Wisconsin Press, 1998), 132, 146.

34. This pluralistic sense of contemporary Native American identity is not too distant from the provocative position outlined by Paul Gilroy in *The Black Atlantic: Modernity and Double Consciousness* (Cambridge: Harvard University Press, 1993). Like Gilroy, Shanley and her contemporaries acknowledge the hybrid and shifting—

yet distinctive—nature of Native American identity. For them, the many cultural homelands spread across the North American landscape provide a terrestrial equivalent to the world of Gilroy's black diaspora. Modern Native American culture is both indigenous and diasporic.

35. Richard White, "Using the Past: History and Native American Studies," in Thornton, *Studying Native America*, 237.

The Pluralist State

The Convergence of Public and Private Power in America

William J. Novak

> In our world everything is political, the state is everywhere, and public
> responsibility is interwoven in the whole fabric of society.
>
> *—Karl Mannheim*

Over the past decade, the state has certainly come back as an important research topic in the social sciences. After a generation devoted primarily to social and cultural models of historical explanation, the history of politics, governance, law, public policy, and political thought has returned in an exciting
way. The new institutionalism and studies in the history of political development among scholars like Stephen Skowronek and Karen Orren have turned
politics and history into one of the most vigorous fields in political science. In
sociology, Theda Skocpol and her numerous collaborators have made the
question of the origin and nature of modern welfare states central to historical-
sociological inquiry.[1] In the field of history, the question of the American state
was never really out, kept alive as a pivotal area of research by the likes of
Samuel Hays, Ellis Hawley, Barry Karl, Morton Keller, Louis Galambos, and
Harry Scheiber, and recently reinvigorated by new interest in the gendered

origins of the American welfare state, the rise and fall of the New Deal order, and labor governance and industrial democracy.[2] In social theory, the later grand theories of Michel Foucault on governmentality and Jürgen Habermas on the public sphere and legal liberalism have powerfully recentered questions of politics, law, and statecraft.[3] Finally, in contemporary politics, the resurgence of issues of global political economy and domestic political institutions (like impeachment procedures and local election laws) have piqued academic energies. Together these developments have created a stimulating public atmosphere for returning problems of political economy and political power to the center of historical and social scientific inquiry.

On a more pessimistic note, much newer work on the American state remains hamstrung by an age-old interpretive tendency in political analysis— a tendency to force discussion of American governmental development into one of two dominant counternarratives. Those counternarratives have deep ideological and political roots in American history. For the purposes of this essay, it is useful to refer to them as the *classical liberal* and the *reform liberal* interpretations of American politics.

The classical liberal tradition is epitomized across the twentieth century by writers as diverse as Edward Corwin, Louis Hartz, and Richard Epstein. For the most part, classical liberals locate the essence of American political life in ideas and ideology—in a few broad and foundational political principles that demarcate the exceptional distinctiveness of American political experience. Their traditional interpretation usually takes the form of an intellectual or constitutional history highlighting the linear, continuous, and relatively consensual unfolding of classical liberal ideals in the United States. What are these ideals? Hartz, Corwin, and Epstein are suggestive when they powerfully reduce American politics to Lockean possessive individualism, negative constitutional liberty, and antistatist laissez-faire. For Hartz the "master assumption of American political thought" is "the reality of atomistic social freedom." Consequently, only in America could the pure "individualist norms of John Locke" produce the unchallenged conclusion that "the power of the state must be limited." In variations on that theme, Corwin and Epstein argue that the "basic doctrine of American constitutional law" is the protection of that atomistic individual liberty against government through explicit legal doctrines like vested rights, due process of law, and the takings clause. Despite its variety, the overarching constant in the classical liberal tradition of American political history is an emphasis on a fundamental and immutable individualism at the heart of American politics and law. As Carl Swisher once noted on the cover of Corwin's volume *The "Higher Law" Back-*

ground of American Constitutional Law, that was the tradition "from Demosthenes to Calvin Coolidge and beyond."[4]

In addition to its interpretive focus on the individual, the classical liberal tradition also emphasizes the overweening significance of the *private* in American political life—the supremacy of private property, private rights, private interests, and the private markets of neoclassical economics. For the classical liberal, the predominance of the private sphere holds the key to the American experiment in democratic governance. And classical liberals spend much time describing the mechanisms that protect the private sphere of American civil society from the public coercions and interventions of the state. Despite the efforts of many historians and social scientists to contest exceptional myths of possessive individualism, vested rights, and laissez-faire, the classical liberal interpretation of American politics remains one of the most resilient tropes for explaining America to itself.[5]

Not surprisingly, the interpretive power and persistence of the classical liberal tradition has spawned a vigorous counter explanation of American political life. The reform liberal tradition contests the classical understanding at virtually every point. Originating in the political and economic reforms of the Progressive era and represented through the twentieth century by scholars as diverse as Charles Beard, Arthur Schlesinger Jr., and Sean Wilentz, the reform liberal tradition holds that the key to American politics lies not in the higher ideals of individual rights, liberty of contract, or constitutional limitations, but in the gritty material reality of the social organization of political and economic power.[6] In contrast to the liberal emphasis on the abstracted, decontextualized individual, reform liberals tend to focus on the collective, on the situated and interested social group. Working often from a socioeconomic perspective, the reform liberal tradition charts the episodes of political conflict through which the people or a particular class or social movement attempt to redress the perennial imbalance of power that they see as the defining feature of American progressive democracy. Decentering the constitutional ideals of individualism and private rights, the new liberals identify the particular socioeconomic struggles for social justice and the general welfare as the hallmark of American political history.

In place of the classical liberal emphasis on the preeminence of the American private sphere, reform liberals stress the importance of the *public* in American political life—the role of the state and the bureaucracy in reigning in renegade private interests for the greater good of the whole. Reform liberals thus spend much more time elaborating the structure of American government and charting historical periods of public activism in the United

States. In place of the rather linear story of the teleological evolution of classical liberal ideals, reform liberals stress the more episodic development of public responsibility and positive liberty through highly charged periodic contests between private interest and the common good. In the twentieth century the high points of the reform liberal story have been the great eras of governmental activism: Progressivism, the New Deal, the Great Society, and the civil rights revolution.

The most important thing to notice about these two master narratives of American politics is that despite their seemingly diametrical emphases on private interest and public power, they are both liberal interpretations of American public life. Both are concerned fundamentally with what John Dewey described as the hallmark of liberalism: the claim of every person to "the full development of his [or her] capacities."[7] They differ primarily on means rather than ends: classical liberals favor an absolutist, negative defense of private rights against the state as the best means of securing personal creative development, whereas reform liberals see a crucial role for the state in producing actual rather than merely formal legal freedom. And since Dewey, many commentators have attempted to reconcile these two competing versions of liberalism in American history. The usual method of reconciliation is a neat teleological periodization of American political development *from* classical *to* reform liberalism. The typical account highlights a single, seismic historical shift in American liberalism between the nineteenth and twentieth centuries—a shift prompted by the rise of industrial corporate capitalism and characterized variously as a shift from old liberalism to new liberalism (Dewey's language), from individualism to collectivism, from negative liberty to positive liberty, or more generally, from laissez-faire to the general-welfare state.[8]

An alternative mode of reconciling classical and reform liberalism posits a more constant, cyclical struggle between private interest and public power that dominates almost all eras of American history. Here, too, a variety of different labels and languages is frequently used to describe the same recurring political tension: for example, the interests vs. the people, conservatism vs. liberalism, individualism vs. communitarianism, liberalism vs. republicanism, Democrats vs. Republicans. The most famous rendering is perhaps Arthur Schlesinger Sr.'s demarcation of eleven cycles of political change along a single liberal/conservative oscillation: Liberal 1776, followed by Conservative 1787; the Age of Jefferson, followed by retreat after 1812; the Age of Jackson to the rule of slaveholders; radical Reconstruction followed by the Gilded Age; the Progressive era to Republican normalcy; and the New Deal.[9] A final method of reconciling the two tropes is a simple redescription of one of the liberalisms (usually reform liberalism) as but a new bottle for old wine. The efforts of Gabriel Kolko, James Weinstein, and Martin Sklar to redefine progressive statecraft as in reality but a new set of defenses for the private interests of corporate capitalism is perhaps the best example of that strategy.[10] The proliferation of attempts to reconcile the two liberal traditions across time testifies to the powerful hold of those categories on general interpretations of American political history.

For the purposes of this essay, however, the most striking aspect of these two powerful master narratives of American political development is how *little* of the work of the major commentators on American politics can be captured by them. Despite the persistent use and popularity of the classical liberal/ reform liberal formulations among generalists and synthesists, most of the breakthrough social-scientific commentaries on the American state resist such categorization. The great mass of the best analyses of American politics—the work of Alexis de Tocqueville, Francis Lieber, James Bryce, Ernst Freund, Roscoe Pound, John Commons, Morris Cohen, Robert Hale, Harold Laski, Adolf A. Berle, V. O. Key, Grant McConnell, Charles McIlwain, Robert Dahl, Joseph Schumpeter, John Kenneth Galbraith, Oscar and Mary Handlin, Willard Hurst, Morton Keller, Theodore Lowi, and Theda Skocpol—cannot be described as fitting easily into either the old liberal or the new liberal camp. The question arises: Is there a third major tradition of American political interpretation?

I believe there is. The authors listed above do form the core of an alternative interpretation of American politics. They are well known—indeed, together they have produced some of the most lasting investigations into the basic mechanisms of American public life. They are a diverse group, respected individually for their distinctive and independent theses. But collectively they also share a general perspective on American politics that cannot be reduced to liberalism, old or new. Labeling such a perspective (or grouping such a diverse set of scholars) is, of course, always a risky enterprise. Nonetheless, I think this third interpretation of American politics is best called pluralism. It has five defining features.

First, pluralism is a critical approach to American politics. That may seem surprising, as pluralism is frequently misinterpreted as a celebratory theory of American exceptionalism. Pluralism's critics often portray it as something of a soothing American alternative to Marxist or social-democratic theories of politics, wherein fundamental contests over the distribution of politico-economic resources dissolve in the mild vapors of American consensus, contentment, and relative social commensurability. Nothing could be further from the truth. For the heart of the pluralist project and the essence of its critical capacity is its emphasis on *power* in American history. All of the authors listed above are concerned with a realistic interrogation of the location, organization, and distribution of power. And though they illuminate and emphasize multiple sites of powerholding in America, that power is the subject of almost continuous conflict and contest.

As its name implies, the second and third features of pluralism are intertwined in the idea that the problem of power in American is complex (or plural) not simple (or singular), especially as it concerns the relationship of public and private. In contradistinction to the classical and reform liberal interpretations, pluralists avoid splitting the problem of power—the relationship of individual and state, right and sovereignty, market and regulation, interest and well-being—along a single private-public binary. In place of the either-or quality of the reigning liberal paradigms, pluralism holds that one of the defining features of the American polity over time is the intersection or convergence of public and private power. The hallmark of American politics from this perspective is the distinctive way in which power is distributed along an exceedingly complex array of persons, associations, and institutions that are not easily categorized private or public. Highlighting the everyday nexus of the legal-political and the socioeconomic, the pluralist is interested in the interplay in actual social and economic life of forces often separated out in more polemical forms of inquiry: right and power, contract and coercion, autonomy and solidarity.

Impatience with the public-private distinction suggests the fourth feature of pluralism: the importance of particularity and specificity. Pluralists are for the most part empirical and realistic in their approach to power. Rather than spending time endlessly debating the essence of American politics, the pluralist method concentrates instead on the particular governmental structures and everyday practices that constitute American public life. Like John Commons, who (along with other sociological jurists and legal realists) defined "the state" in terms of "what its officials do," the pluralist perspective prefers action-oriented "how" questions—how American government actually operates over time—to more essentialist questions of the meaning or prime mover of American politics.[11] In place of theoretical and ideological emphasis on transcendent political abstractions like "the state," "the people," "liberalism," or "democracy," pluralism emphasizes the actual day-to-day practice and conduct of governance in all of its guises, from the enforcement of local by-laws to the bureaucratic articulation of policy alternatives to the formal geopolitical relations of nation-states. Rather than restrict analysis of government to the formal realm of political theory or the highly visible actions of parties, movements, and states, the pluralist instead follows the insight of Michael Oakeshott who broadly defined "governing" as "an activity which is apt to appear whenever men are associated together or even whenever, in the course of their activities, they habitually cross one another's paths."[12]

As one might expect, then, this pluralist preference for particularity and specificity also leads to a rather intense dissatisfaction with the sweeping generalizations and periodizations of classical and reform liberalism. And one problem with pluralism is that its overarching storylines—its narratives of American political development—lack the singular simplicity of "the evolution of liberalism since Demosthenes" or the political drama of "cyclical battles between interest and reform." Pluralists do put forward their own distinctive chronologies and periodizations of American political history. But true to their method, pluralist narratives tend to focus more on theories of the middle-range, usually built around quite specific transformations in the locus and use of power in America. Such alternative chronologies constitute the fifth and final feature of American pluralism.

These five features—power, plurality, the relationship of public and private, particularity, and the issue of periodization—do suggest the broad outlines of a pluralist approach to American politics. But almost by definition, the actual interpretive possibilities of pluralism evade abstract delineation. The method's power lies in its application and demonstration across the diverse range of fact situations in American social and economic history. The pluralist mantra is perhaps found in Stendahl: "All the truth, and all the pleasure, lies in the details."[13] Accordingly, a full appreciation requires a more concrete if necessarily brief survey of pluralism in practice.

One of the more intriguing aspects of the pluralist approach to American politics is its longevity, its persistence. Whereas nationalist, classical liberal, and reform liberal interpretations seem to be primarily identified with one era or another, pluralism is well-represented across the sweep of American history. Indeed, many pluralists, most notably Robert Dahl, insist on starting any discussion of pluralism with the original American constitutional moment. And that point of departure nicely illustrates the first feature of the pluralist perspective, the focus on power.

The pluralist reading of the American constitution downplays the significance of abstract theories of private right and public sovereignty in favor of a more realistic and practical discussion of the problem of power and the question of its distribution. In place of Locke and Blackstone, pluralists look to Montesquieu and Madison for insights into the complicated intersection and interdependence of private and public power in the founding structure of

American constitutionalism. That power was the framing concern is never doubted by pluralists. As Montesquieu noted: "Political liberty is to be found only . . . when there is no abuse of power. But constant experience shows us that every man invested with power is apt to abuse it. . . . To prevent this abuse, it is necessary from the very nature of things that power should be a check to power."[14] Madison's classic discussion in Federalist #10 of the inevitable struggles for power in civil society among factions and interests echoed this sentiment. This founding concern about the abuse of power (private as well as public) yielded an original governmental structure ordered around a complex separation of competing powers and multiple jurisdictions.[15]

But pluralism involves more than Montesquieu and Madison, more than a recognition of the original constitutional significance of the problem of power. During the nineteenth century, a group of social and political thinkers pushed pluralist analyses further in an attempt to locate an alternative to the seemingly inevitable trajectory of modern governments toward absolutism and centralization. Avoiding the either-or approaches of liberal rights and contract theories, on the one hand, and nascent theories of socialism and state sovereignty, on the other, these thinkers worked toward a more realistic understanding of the practical diffusion of power in society and the blending of private and public in everyday governance. The main focus of their interpretive energies was not the formal structure of the state or the nature of political factionalism, but the real power of the social group or association.

Otto von Gierke's *Das Deutsche Genossenschaftsrecht* (The German Law of Fellowship) was perhaps the most well-developed version of this mid-nineteenth-century structural pluralism.[16] But in the United States it was Alexis de Tocqueville's observations about the power of American associationalism as distinct from European models of administrative statecraft that had the greatest effect on the development of pluralist ideas about the diffusion of power. As Tocqueville described, "Americans of all ages, all stations in life, and all types of disposition are forever forming associations. . . . In every case, at the head of any new undertaking, where in France you would find the government or in England some territorial magnate, in the United States you are sure to find an association."[17] Though at times Tocqueville seemed to imply that American associations were a simple, private, civil-society alternative to public statecraft, the most interesting parts of his analysis were those in which he explored the convergence of public and private in associational action. He gives a classic example: "If some obstacle blocks the public road halting the circulation of traffic, the neighbors at once form a deliberative body; this improvised assembly produces an executive authority which remedies the trouble before anyone has thought of the possibility of some previously constituted authority beyond that of those concerned." What Tocqueville is talking about here is not some innocuous private group activity but an extremely powerful legal and governmental process known as the summary abatement of a public nuisance. Public nuisance law in the nineteenth century was the foundation of early American state police power.[18] The point is that pluralism is not simply a theory of the diffusion of power or an endorsement of private over public authority. Rather, pluralists insist on investigating those crucial points of overlap where state powers are wielded by seemingly private entities (e.g., the nineteenth-century law of railroads and eminent domain), or where private entities are constituted or underwritten by state authority (the nineteenth-century law of corporations), or where public and private are so intertwined as to become unhelpful categories (the nineteenth-century law of officeholding).

But even more than Tocqueville, it was Francis Lieber who most fully elaborated the convergence of public and private power in American associationalism. Lieber's pluralism began with a critique of statist (or what he termed Gallican) theories of politics, wherein an absorbing paternal power in the central government culminated in "a vast hierarchy of officers, forming a class of mandarins for themselves, and acting as though they formed and were the state, and the people only the substratum on which the state is founded." But Lieber refused to locate a solution to the political problem of despotic centralization in an apolitical realm of private civil society. Instead, Lieber endorsed the particular Anglo-American legal-political practices that he denoted in his magnum opus as *Civil Liberty and Self-Government.*[19] Civil liberty and self-government consisted of the active exercise of public power through a set of self-ruling associations—"a vast system of institutions, whose number supports the whole, as the many pillars support the rotunda of our capital." There were many kinds of institutions beneath the state in which power was exercised,[20] but it was the self-governing institution—the one most resembling associations, corporations, and local bodies politic—that most held Lieber's attention. The self-governing association was not concerned with "vague or theoretical liberty," but with the regulated and relative "civil" liberty ("within the social system and political organism") that engaged the practical "realities of life." Indeed, the essence of such associations was the by-law (the law of the place or community)—the right of institutions and associations to pass the laws and regulations "necessary for its own government" which "shall stand good in the courts of law, and shall be as binding upon every one concerned as any statute or law."[21] This merger of society and state, private and public in Lieber's pluralist theory opened American political investigation to the whole range of corporative, rule-making associations from the formal institutions of national and local governments to voluntary social groups and economic partnerships.

The late nineteenth and early twentieth centuries witnessed an explosion of interest in the kinds of socioeconomic associations and institutions delimited by Gierke, Tocqueville, and Lieber. The transformative role of corporations, trusts, farm alliances, labor unions, and powerful new national associations like the YMCA and the WCTU focused attention on the legal and political identity of such collectives and the extraordinary powers they seemed to wield in an industrializing American society. Following the lead of Frederic William Maitland (who introduced many English speakers to the work of Otto von Gierke),[22] numerous philosophers, historians, and legal and political thinkers began to carefully investigate the nature and power of the corporation and the union, from the more abstract dissections of Harold Laski and John Dewey to the politico-economic treatments of Richard T. Ely, John Commons, and Adolf Berle.[23] Their findings seriously challenged simple demarcations of public and private power in modern America.

The sociological jurisprudence of Roscoe Pound, Morris Cohen, and Robert Hale took the challenge of unmasking the public powers of seemingly private organizations and actors furthest. In "Liberty of Contract," Pound exposed the fallacies of overly individualistic, private, and antistatist conceptions of justice. Abstract fictions like liberty of contract and the free market, he argued, theoretically masked the deeper mobilizations of political and economic power that suppressed the actual realization of liberty at the turn of the century. For example: "insanitary housing, exorbitant rent, payment in advance, subjection to shop regulations, fixing of the method and the duration of work, fines, the sweating system."[24] In "Property and Sovereignty," Cohen extended Pound's implicit critique of the separation of the private and the public, the civil and the political, *dominium* and *imperium*—a separation that Cohen saw at the heart of the reactionary jurisprudence of the late nineteenth century. Cohen brilliantly deconstructed the naturalistic distinction between private property and public sovereignty by demonstrating their deep historical and legal interdependence. His article was an extended proof of the "character of property as sovereign power compelling service and obedience" and the "fact that dominion over things is also *imperium* over our fellow human beings."[25] Robert Hale continued this critical examination of the way in which law conferred "sovereign power on our captains of industry" in "Coercion and Distribution in a Supposedly Non-Coercive State," a title which captures the essence of a pluralist approach to power. Hale took direct aim at the classical liberal philosophies of his time, arguing that "the systems advocated by professed upholders of laissez-faire are in reality permeated with coercive restrictions of individual freedom."[26] Hale contended that a sharp theoretical separation of public and private obscured the actual proactive role of public power in structuring the so-called private bargains that had such an immense effect on the distribution of wealth and power in American society. As Hale summarized in his pluralist text *Freedom through Law: Public Control of Private Governing Power,* because of the obvious power of governmental coercions, "we are apt to think of liberty narrowly in terms of freedom from restrictions imposed by those official bodies (national, state, or local) which are conventionally regarded as 'governmental' and to overlook the existence of private government, which, unless restrained by law, is as capable . . . of destroying individual liberty as is public government itself."[27]

Although this interrogation of the public nature of private economic power was crucial to the development of progressive pluralism, just as significant was the way some of these same thinkers turned their critical energies on the problem of official state power. In an era when formalist theories of state and sovereignty reached something of an apex (thanks to the work of scholars like J. K. Bluntschli, John W. Burgess, and Woodrow Wilson), pluralist scholars mounted an impressive sociological and realist critique.[28] Most famously, Harold Laski for the first time utilized the label "pluralism" in synthesizing a heterogeneous assemblage of thought opposed to unitary ideas about the sovereign state. Following the lead of Leon Duguit, he outlined a more sociological definition of the state based on realistically asking what the state is actually doing: "Its function is to provide for certain public needs. . . . The whole theory of the state, indeed, is contained in the idea of public need. It is the performance by the mass of officials of [that] social function."[29] John Commons, in a less well known but important tract, "A Sociological View of Sovereignty," elaborated this pluralist and functional approach to the state by emphasizing its institutional and developmental qualities. He argued that the sociologist should not be primarily concerned with "the moral end of the state," but rather "with its actual qualities, and its concrete relations to other institutions." Viewed sociologically, the state was an institution not an idea, and it had to be understood in *context,* through its interactions with other institutions, and in *sequence,* through its multifaceted development in historical time. And, as Commons noted simply, "Development is differentiation."[30]

The sociological critique of sovereignty enabled scholars to look realistically at state power not as a unitary public authority but as a highly differentiated historical institution interacting in different ways with a whole range of other social institutions: the family, the church, political parties, corporations, unions, municipalities, schools, and civic associations. Consequently, analyses and periodizations of American politics could become far more nuanced, detailed, and multidimensional than the classical and reform liberal syntheses. Ernst Freund's pioneering empirical studies of American law and legislation began with a recognition that the American state was a complex and multifaceted legal entity. In contrast to simple liberal models of state intervention or public intrusion into the private sphere, Freund made the finer analytical point that not all state actions were created equal. Rather, a radical difference in kind distinguished the level at which governmental power was exercised (e.g., international, national, state, or local), the branch of government exercising the power (executive, legislative, judicial, or administrative), and, just as important, the kind of power being exercised (levying property taxes, distributing public lands, delegating eminent domain, regulating corporations, or prohibiting the sale of liquor). Freund demarcated at least four substantively different "manifestations" of governance: justice, police regulation, taxation, and the management of public resources and personnel.[31] It was precisely that kind of finer-grained analysis of state power that allowed contemporary scholars like Theodore Lowi to experiment with new ways of dividing American political development into periods. Lowi reduced Freund's four manifestations of statecraft to three techniques of governmental power: patronage (the distribution of public resources), regulation (stricter state police controls), and redistribution (the fiscal shifting of resources from one group to another). In place of linear stories of liberal evolution or cyclical contests between reform and reaction, Lowi was then able to think about the history of the American state in terms of structural shifts in basic governmental functions: from the distributive and promotional policies of the nineteenth century to the regulatory regime of the progressives to the macroeconomic redistributions of the post–New Deal era.[32]

As Lowi's work exemplifies, in some ways the golden age for the pluralistic perspective on American politics was the post–World War II period. Despite persistent fascination with central elite politics (along the lines developed by Gaetano Mosca, Karl Mannheim, and C. Wright Mills) and the arrival of powerful new defenses of private right (along the lines developed by Isaiah Berlin, Friedrich von Hayek, and Leo Strauss), American social scientists continued to flesh out the sociological and pluralistic approach to politics and government outlined above.[33] The work of scholars like V. O. Key on the powers of pressure groups and parties and Robert Dahl on political theory turned pluralism into a fixture of postwar American political science.[34] In economics Joseph Schumpeter and John Kenneth Galbraith made major contributions on the centrality of the distribution of power to the development of American capitalism and democracy.[35] Perhaps the best work on the specific pluralist theme of the convergence of public and private power came from the field of history. There the so-called commonwealth school of American historians began a wide-ranging, and still on-going, set of inquiries into the origins, structures, and changing functions of governmental power in the United States from the Revolution to the present.

One of the major accomplishments of the commonwealth school was a devastating historical critique of classical liberal ideas about laissez-faire as scholars like Oscar and Mary Handlin, Carter Goodrich, and Harry Scheiber demonstrated the multilayered involvement of states (e.g., the promotion of banks, canals, and railroads; the distribution of public lands; the regulation of nascent corporations) that underwrote early American economic growth.[36] Inspired by the accomplishments of the commonwealth school in reinterpreting American history before the Civil War, two other historians generalized the pluralist theme of the complex intermingling of public and private across the whole of American governmental history.

One was the legal historian Willard Hurst. At the heart of Hurst's legal histories was the question of the balance and dispersion of power. Indeed, Hurst formally located American constitutionalism in the idea that "any kind of organized power ought to measured against criteria of ends and means which are not defined or enforced by the immediate power holders themselves. It is as simple as that: We don't want to trust any group of power holders to be their own judges upon the ends for which they use the power or the ways in which they use it."[37] The power that was Hurst's main concern came in many guises, private as well as public, practically economic as well as formally political. One of his main accomplishments was an extension of the sociological and pluralist analysis of the state to include the capacious power of law:

> In deciding what to include as "law" I do not find it profitable to distinguish "law" from "government" or from "policy." The heart of the matter is that we formed organizations for collective action characterized by their own distinctive bases of legitimacy. . . . In order to see law in its relations to society as a whole, one must appraise all formal and informal aspects of political organized power—observe the functions of all legal agencies (legislative, executive, administrative, or judicial) and take account of the interplay of such agencies with voters and nonvoters, lobbyists and

interest groups, politicians and political parties. This definition overruns traditional boundaries dividing the study of law from study of political history, political science, and sociology.[38]

For Hurst, law was fundamentally intertwined with public policymaking—the general economic and social policies that connected governmental institutions to the people and to everyday life.

The other contemporary historian who adopted this broad, pluralistic understanding of power, politics, and policymaking is Morton Keller. Keller begins the sequel to his monumental *Affairs of State* with a self-conscious, pragmatic, and pluralist critique of the usefulness of theory in historical inquiry. To William James's skeptical observation that "the trouble with all social theories is that they leak at every joint," Keller adds Turgenev's wise counsel: "The only people who treasure systems are those whom the whole truth evades, who want to catch it by the tail; a system is like truth's tail, but the truth is like a lizard; it will leave the tail in your hand and escape: it knows that it will soon grow another tail." For Keller, historical understanding emerges not from a "predetermined theoretical pattern" but from the "rich, complex texture of social experience."[39] It should come as no surprise then that Morton Keller makes little use of either of the two great liberal schools of writing about American politics. One searches in vain in Keller's legal and political histories for paeans to the glittering generalities of classical liberal constitutionalism: individual rights, private property, due process of law. Equally hard to find are the bottom-up depictions of social and political power struggles that are the stock in trade of the reform tradition. Neither the liberal individual nor the democratic people are the main characters in Keller's American political history. Rather, rejecting what he calls the "celebratory historical" approach and "tendentious adversary" style, Keller calls for a more disciplined and empirical analysis of American politics. In his delineation of the "polity" ("the general or fundamental system of organization of a government" and "its relation to the people") as the appropriate unit for political study, Keller advocates making political analysis as systematic and comprehensive as analyses of the American economy.[40]

In pursuit of this goal throughout his work, Keller relies on some well-established pluralistic models to avoid the traps of classical liberal and reform liberal history. One of the most salient is historical institutionalism. Though political scientists have spent much ink defining and defending a "new" institutionalist methodology,[41] historical institutionalist analysis is perhaps the oldest form of social-scientific inquiry with roots in Montesquieu, the Scottish

Enlightenment, the historical jurisprudence of Maine and Maitland, and the advent of modern historical and political sciences at Johns Hopkins and Columbia University at the turn of the twentieth century. Two of Keller's favorite institutionalists are Alexis de Tocqueville and James Bryce. Though *Democracy in America* was concerned with political ideas and ideology (Bryce even called it a "deductive" text), Tocqueville's original emphasis on laws, constitutional structure, and the political practices of free institutions like townships and civil associations made it, along with the *Federalist Papers,* a founding text in American political institutional history.[42] Bryce began his investigation into the *American Commonwealth* with the omnipresent American political question: "What do you think of our institutions?" He proceeded to amass the most compendious survey of the institutional workings of American government in society until Herbert Hoover commissioned his President's Research Committee on Social Trends in 1929.[43] What Keller locates in these classic pluralist political inquiries is an understanding of modern American statecraft best approached not through abstract ideology or particular social and electoral contests, but through "political, legal, and governmental institutions . . . and the public policies that emerged from them." Following Matthew Arnold's insight that "[t]he more I see of America, the more I find myself led to treat 'institutions' with increased respect," Keller seeks the key to American public life in painstakingly thick descriptions of the multiple institutional practices and policies that composed the American polity.[44]

From his close analysis of the structure of corporate power in the turn-of-the-century insurance industry to his wide-ranging catalog of affairs of state in his most recent volumes, Morton Keller's pluralism runs close to the surface.[45] One of its central elements is a broad conception of the political as more than ideas, elections, and movements—the political as the complex totality of governance, law, and social and economic policymaking. Just as Willard Hurst moved our conception of legal power well beyond a concern with the occasional naysaying doctrines of famous U.S. Supreme Court cases, Morton Keller challenges us to expand our conception of political power beyond the actions of national elites and professional interest groups, beyond the formal constructs of liberal theory, and beyond the interpretive limitations of the public-private distinction.

No doubt much American political commentary will continue to remain trapped by the ideological constructions of the classical liberal and reform liberal traditions—and the simple attractiveness of thinking about American politics in terms of the routine binaries: the individual vs. the state, private interest vs. public welfare, and conservative reaction vs. liberal reform. But there is an alternative. The pluralist interpretation of power in America has deep roots in political and social-scientific inquiry since the Revolution. It suggests that one of the distinctive and constant features of American political history has been the odd convergence of public and private power, from state subsidization of economic development to the governmental policing of social status to the almost invisible role of modern fiscal policy in structuring everyday social and economic relations. Pluralism, broadly construed and properly understood, holds out the promise of a critical and sociological approach to politics capable of capturing and interrogating the full plurality of power in America.

NOTES

1. Karen Orren and Stephen Skowronek, eds., *Studies in American Political Development* (New York: Cambridge University Press, 1986–); Stephen Skowronek, *Building a New American State: The Expansion of National Administrative Capacities, 1877–1920* (New York: Cambridge University Press, 1982); Karen Orren, *Belated Feudalism: Labor, the Law, and Liberal Development in the United States* (New York: Cambridge University Press, 1991); Peter B. Evans, Dietrich Rueschemeyer, and Theda Skocpol, eds., *Bringing the State Back In* (New York: Cambridge University Press, 1985); Theda Skocpol, *Protecting Soldiers and Mothers: The Political Origins of Social Policy in the United States* (Cambridge: Harvard University Press, 1992).

2. See, e.g., Samuel P. Hays, *American Political History as Social Analysis* (Knoxville: University of Tennessee Press, 1980); Ellis Hawley, *The New Deal and the Problem of Monopoly* (Princeton, N.J.: Princeton University Press, 1966); Barry Karl, *The Uneasy State: The United States from 1915 to 1945* (Chicago: University of Chicago Press, 1983); Morton Keller, *Affairs of State: Public Life in Late Nineteenth Century America* (Cambridge: Harvard University Press, 1977); Louis Galambos, ed., *The New American State: Bureaucracies and Policies since World War II* (Baltimore: Johns Hopkins University Press, 1987); Harry N. Scheiber, *Ohio Canal Era: A Case Study of Government and the Economy, 1820–1861* (Athens: Ohio University Press, 1969); Linda Gordon, ed., *Women, the State and Welfare* (Madison: University of Wisconsin Press, 1990); Steve Fraser and Gary Gerstle, eds., *The Rise and Fall of the New Deal Order, 1930–1980* (Princeton, N.J.: Princeton University Press, 1989); Nelson Lichtenstein and Howell John Harris, eds., *Industrial Democracy in America: The Ambiguous Promise* (New York: Cambridge University Press, 1993).

3. Graham Burchell, Colin Gordon, and Peter Miller, eds., *The Foucault Effect: Studies in Governmentality* (Chicago: University of Chicago Press, 1991); Jürgen Habermas, *The Structural Transformation of the Public Sphere: An Inquiry into a Category of Bourgeois Society*, trans. Thomas Burger (Cambridge: MIT Press, 1991); Habermas, *Be-

tween Facts and Norms: Contributions to a Discourse Theory of Law and Democracy,
trans. William Rehg (Cambridge: MIT Press, 1996).

4. See, e.g.. Edward S. Corwin, *Liberty Against Government: The Rise, Flowering
and Decline of a Famous Juridical Concept* (Baton Rouge: Louisiana State University
Press, 1948); Corwin, "The Basic Doctrine of American Constitutional Law," *Michigan Law Review* 12 (1914): 247–76, 538–72; Corwin, *The "Higher Law" Background of
American Constitutional Law* (Ithaca, N.Y.: Cornell University Press, 1955); Louis
Hartz, *The Liberal Tradition in America: An Interpretation of American Political Thought
since the Revolution* (New York: Harcourt, Brace, 1955), 60–62; Richard A. Epstein:
Takings: Private Property and the Power of Eminent Domain (Cambridge: Harvard University Press, 1985). Though never fully developed, Hartz was quite aware of the legal
ramifications of his argument about the "fixed, dogmatic liberalism" of American
life, offering up "the unusual power of the Supreme Court and the cult of constitution worship" in the United States as direct outgrowths of classical liberalism: "Judicial review as it has worked in America would be inconceivable without the national
acceptance of the Lockian [*sic*] creed." Hartz, *Liberal Tradition*, 9.

5. For the best recent critique, see James T. Kloppenberg, *The Virtues of Liberalism* (New York: Oxford University Press, 1998).

6. See, e.g., Charles A. Beard, *An Economic Interpretation of the Constitution of the
United States* (New York: Macmillan, 1919); Arthur M. Schlesinger Jr., *The Age of Jackson*
(Boston: Little, Brown, 1945); Sean Wilentz, *Chants Democratic: New York City and the
Rise of the American Working Class, 1788–1850* (New York: Oxford University Press, 1984).

7. John Dewey, *Liberalism and Social Action* (1935), in vol. 11 of *The Later Works,
1925–1953,* ed. Jo Ann Boydston (Carbondale: Southern Illinois University Press,
1987), 20.

8. A. V. Dicey, *Lectures on the Relation Between Law & Public Opinion in England
During the Nineteenth Century* (New York: Macmillan, 1914); Sidney Fine, *Laissez Faire
and the General-Welfare State: A Study of Conflict in American Thought, 1865–1901* (Ann
Arbor: University of Michigan Press, 1956).

9. Schlesinger quite carefully determined the average length of these periods to
be 16.5 years. And his cyclical model has some predictive capacity. In 1924 Schlesinger
predicted the end of Coolidge-style conservatism by 1932. In 1939 he suggested that
the New Deal era would run its course by 1947. In 1949 Schlesinger posited a revival of
reform about 1962, followed by a period of conservatism beginning about 1978.
Arthur M. Schlesinger, "The Tides of National Politics," in *Paths to the Present* (New
York: Macmillan, 1949), 89–103. See also Arthur M. Schlesinger Jr., *The Cycles of
American History* (Boston: Houghton Mifflin, 1986).

10. Gabriel Kolko, *The Triumph of Conservatism: A Reinterpretation of American
History, 1900–1916* (Glencoe, Ill.: Free Press, 1963); James Weinstein, *The Corporate
Ideal in the Liberal State, 1900–1918* (Boston: Beacon Press, 1968); Martin J. Sklar, *The
Corporate Reconstruction of American Capitalism, 1890–1916: The Market, Law, and Politics* (New York: Cambridge University Press, 1988). See also some of the New Deal

histories, e.g., Paul K. Conkin, *The New Deal* (New York: Crowell, 1967); and Barton J. Bernstein, "The New Deal," in Bernstein, ed., *Towards a New Past: Dissenting Essays in American History* (New York: Pantheon Books, 1968), 263–88.

11. John R. Commons, *Legal Foundations of Capitalism* (1924; Madison: University of Wisconsin Press, 1957), 122. Also see Karl Llewellyn's realist definition of law: "This doing of something about disputes, this doing of it reasonably, is the business of law. And the people who have the doing in charge, whether they be judges or sheriffs or clerks or jailers or lawyers, are officials of the law. What these officials do about disputes is, to my mind, the law itself." Karl N. Llewellyn, *The Bramble Bush: On Our Law and Its Study* (1930; New York: Oceana, 1960), 12.

12. Michael Oakeshott, *Morality and Politics in Modern Europe: The Harvard Lectures,* ed. Shirley Robin Letwin (New Haven, Conn.: Yale University Press, 1993), 7.

13. Quoted in Morton Keller, *Regulating a New Economy: Public Policy and Economic Change in America, 1900–1933* (Cambridge: Harvard University Press, 1990), xi. "The proof is in the pudding" might also suffice, but it would overdo the alliteration.

14. Baron de Montesquieu, *The Spirit of the Laws,* trans. Thomas Nugent (New York: Hafner Press, 1949), 150.

15. Federalist #10, *The Federalist Papers,* ed. Clinton Rossiter (New York: Mentor Books, 1961), 77–84. The classic contemporary pluralist discussion of this "Madisonian" pluralism is Robert A. Dahl, *A Preface to Democratic Theory* (Chicago: University of Chicago Press, 1956).

16. Otto von Gierke, *Das Deutsche Genossenschaftsrecht* (The German Law of Fellowship), 4 vols. (Berlin, 1868–1913). Substantial parts of Gierke's treatise are available in English. See Frederic William Maitland, *Political Theories of the Middle Age* (Cambridge: Cambridge University Press, 1900); Ernest Barker, *Natural Law and the Theory of Society 1500 to 1800* (Cambridge: Cambridge University Press, 1958); Antony Black, *Community in Historical Perspective* (Cambridge: Cambridge University Press, 1990); and G. Heiman, *Associations and the Law: The Classical and Early Christian Stages* (Toronto: University of Toronto Press, 1977).

17. Alexis de Tocqueville, *Democracy in America,* ed. J. P. Mayer (Garden City, N. Y.: Doubleday, 1969), 513.

18. Tocqueville, *Democracy in America,* 189. For a discussion of the relationship of nuisance law to American state regulatory authority, see William J. Novak, *The People's Welfare: Law and Regulation in Nineteenth-Century America* (Chapel Hill: University of North Carolina Press, 1996), esp. chap. 3. For an interpretation of Tocqueville and American associationalism that misses this point about the convergence of public and private power, see Arthur M. Schlesinger Sr.'s "Biography of a Nation of Joiners," in *Paths to the Present* (Boston: Houghton Mifflin, 1964), 24–50: "Traditionally, Americans have distrusted collective organization as embodied in government while insisting upon their own untrammeled right to form voluntary associations. This conception of a state of minimal powers actually made it necessary for private citizens to organize for undertakings too large for a single person. By re-

verse effect the success of such enterprises hindered the enlargement of governmental authority" (24).

19. Francis Lieber, *On Civil Liberty and Self-Government*, 3d ed., rev. (1853; Philadelphia: Lippincott, 1891), 248–49. A good personal biography of Lieber (though inadequate on his jurisprudence) is Frank Freidel, *Francis Lieber: Nineteenth-Century Liberal* (Baton Rouge: Louisiana State University Press, 1947).

20. Lieber enumerated a range of institutions, past and present, good and bad, expedient, and unwise, human and divine: a bank, parliament, a court of justice, the bar, the church, the mail, a state, the Lord's supper, a university, the Inquisition, property, the sabbath, the feudal system, the Roman triumph, the Hindu castes, the bill of exchange, the French Institute, our presidency, the New York tract society, the Areopagus, the Olympic games, an insurance company, the janizaries, the English common law, the episcopate, the tribunate, the captainship of a fishing fleet, the crown, the German book-trade, the Goldsmiths' Company, our senate, our representatives, our congress, our state legislatures, courts of conciliation, the justiceship of the peace, the priesthood, a confederacy, the patent, the copyright, hospitals for lunatics, estates, the East India Company. Lieber, *On Civil Liberty*, 301–2.

21. Ibid., 300, 319, 322.

22. Maitland, *Political Theories of the Middle Age*. Maitland's pioneering essays on corporation, trust, legal personality, and body politic are collected in H. D. Hazeltine, G. Lapsley, and P. H. Winfield, eds., *Maitland: Selected Essays* (Cambridge: Cambridge University Press, 1936).

23. Harold J. Laski, "The Personality of Associations," *Harvard Law Review* 29 (1915–16): 404–26; John Dewey, "The Historical Background of Corporate Legal Personality," *Yale Law Journal* 35 (1926): 655; Richard T. Ely, *Property and Contract in Their Relations to the Distribution of Wealth*, 2 vols. (New York: Macmillan, 1914); John R. Commons, *Legal Foundations of Capitalism* (New York: Macmillan, 1924); Adolf A. Berle and Gardiner C. Means, *The Modern Corporation and Private Property* (New York: Macmillan, 1932).

24. Roscoe Pound, "Liberty of Contract," *Yale Law Journal* 18 (1909): 454–87, 454–55 (quotation); Pound, "Scope and Purpose of Sociological Jurisprudence," *Harvard Law Review* 24 (1911): 591–619; 25 (1912): 140–168, 489–516, 502 (quotation).

25. Morris R. Cohen, "Property and Sovereignty," *Cornell Law Quarterly* 13 (1927): 8–30, 12–13 (quotation). As Cohen elaborated more specifically: "The extent of the power over the life of others which the legal order confers on those called owners is not fully appreciated by those who think of the law as merely protecting men in their possession. Property law does more. It determines what men shall acquire. Thus, protecting the property rights of a landlord means giving him the right to collect rent, protecting the property of a railroad or a public service corporation means giving it the right to make certain charges. . . . Thus not only medieval landlords but the owners of all revenue-producing property are in fact granted by the law certain powers to tax the future social product. When to this power of taxation there is

added the power to command the services of large numbers who are not economically independent, we have the essence of what historically has constituted political sovereignty."

26. Cohen, "Property and Sovereignty," 29. Robert L. Hale, "Coercion and Distribution in a Supposedly Non-Coercive State," *Political Science Quarterly* 38 (1923): 470–94, 470 (quotation).

27. Robert L. Hale, *Freedom through Law: Public Control of Private Governing Power* (New York: Columbia University Press, 1952).

28. J. K. Bluntschli, *The Theory of the State,* trans. D. G. Ritchie et al. (London: Oxford University Press, 1895); John W. Burgess, *Political Science and Comparative Constitutional Law,* 2 vols. (Boston: Ginn, 1890); Woodrow Wilson, *The State: Elements of Historical and Practical Politics* (Boston: D.C. Heath, 1890).

29. Harold J. Laski, *Studies in the Problem of Sovereignty* (New Haven: Yale University Press, 1917); Laski, *The Foundations of Sovereignty* (New York: Harcourt Brace, 1921); Laski, "The Pluralistic State," *Philosophical Review* 28 (1919): 562–75; Leon Duguit, *Law in the Modern State,* trans. Harold J. Laski (London: George Allen & Unwin, 1921), xx. See generally David Runciman, *Pluralism and the Personality of the State* (Cambridge: Cambridge University Press, 1997).

30. John R. Commons, *A Sociological View of Sovereignty* (New York: Augustus M. Kelley, 1965), 2–3.

31. Ernst Freund, *Legislative Regulation: A Study of the Ways and Means of Written Law* (New York: Commonwealth Fund, 1932), 53; Freund, *Standards of American Legislation: An Estimate of Restrictive and Constructive Factors* (Chicago: University of Chicago Press, 1917); Freund, *The Police Power: Public Policy and Constitutional Rights* (Chicago: Callaghan, 1904).

32. Theodore J. Lowi, "American Business, Public Policy, Case-Studies, and Political Theory," *World Politics* 16 (1964): 677. For a historian's deployment of these basic categories, see Richard L. McCormick, "The Party Period and Public Policy: An Exploratory Hypothesis," *Journal of American History* 66 (1979): 279.

33. See, e.g., Gaetano Mosca, *The Ruling Class,* trans. Hannah D. Kahn (New York: McGraw-Hill, 1939); Karl Mannheim, *Freedom, Power, and Democratic Planning* (New York: Oxford University Press, 1950); C. Wright Mills, *The Power Elite* (New York: Oxford University Press, 1956). The founding text in this tradition is, of course, Robert Michels, *Political Parties: A Sociological Study of the Oligarchical Tendencies of Modern Democracy,* trans. Eden and Cedar Paul (London: Jarrold & Sons, 1916). Isaiah Berlin, "Two Concepts of Liberty," in *Four Essays on Liberty* (Oxford: Oxford University Press, 1969), 118–72; Friedrich A. von Hayek, *The Road to Serfdom* (London: Routledge, 1944); Leo Strauss, *Natural Right and History* (Chicago: University of Chicago Press, 1953).

34. V. O. Key Jr., *Politics, Parties, and Pressure Groups* (New York: Thomas Y. Crowell, 1942); Robert A. Dahl, *Pluralist Democracy in the United States: Conflict and Consent* (Chicago: Rand McNally, 1967).

35. Joseph A. Schumpeter, *Capitalism, Socialism, and Democracy* (New York: Harper & Bros., 1942); John Kenneth Galbraith, *American Capitalism: The Concept of Countervailing Power* (Boston: Houghton Mifflin, 1952); Galbraith, *The New Industrial State* (Boston: Houghton Mifflin, 1967).

36. Oscar and Mary Flug Handlin, *Commonwealth: A Study of the Role of Government in the American Economy: Massachusetts, 1774–1861* (New York: Oxford University Press, 1947); Oscar and Mary Handlin, *The Dimensions of Liberty* (Cambridge: Harvard University Press, 1961); Carter Goodrich, *Government Promotion of American Canals and Railroads, 1800–1890* (New York: Columbia University Press, 1960); Scheiber, *Ohio Canal Era*. Of course, the influence of the commonwealth school runs much further than these scholars. One must first add Louis Hartz's early study of Pennsylvania, *Economic Policy and Democratic Thought: Pennsylvania, 1776–1860* (Cambridge: Harvard University Press, 1948)—a study difficult to square with his *Liberal Tradition in America*—as well as the work of Milton Heath, Bray Hammond, James Neal Primm, George Miller, Paul Gates, and Edwin M. Dodd. For a fuller discussion and bibliography, see Robert A. Lively, "The American System: A Review Article," *Business History Review* 29 (1955): 91–96; and Harry N. Scheiber, "Government and the Economy: Studies of the 'Commonwealth' Policy in Nineteenth-Century America," *Journal of Interdisciplinary History* 3 (1972): 135–51; Novak, *People's Welfare*.

37. James Willard Hurst, "Problems of Legitimacy in the Contemporary Legal Order," *Oklahoma Law Review* 24 (1971): 224–38, 225 (quotation). Hurst's approach to power also came with a full appreciation of the complexity of historical generalization: "There can be no single point of view from which all United States legal history falls into a coherent sequence. Rather, the subject must be turned this way and that, to catch different but relevant aspects of a complex reality." Hurst, *Law and Social Order in the United States* (Ithaca, N.Y.: Cornell University Press, 1977), 25. Hurst's most complete portrait of the depth of the complex relationships between legal power and the economy was contained in his densely researched *Law and Economic Growth: The Legal History of the Lumber Industry in Wisconsin, 1836–1915* (Cambridge: Harvard University Press, 1964).

38. Hurst, *Law and Social Order*, 25. Like Lowi, Hurst's sociological and pluralistic approach to legal power and policymaking allowed him to divide American history into periods according to changes in the structure of policymaking, from an emphasis on the release of economic energy (1800–70) to struggles over the balance of political power (1840–1900) to the rise of modern administrative statecraft (1900–present). Hurst, *Law and the Conditions of Freedom in the Nineteenth-Century United States* (Madison: University of Wisconsin Press, 1956), 40. For a more complete discussion of Hurst's historical sociology of law, see William J. Novak, "Law, Capitalism, and the Liberal State: The Historical Sociology of James Willard Hurst," *Law and History Review* 18 (2000): 97–145.

39. Like Charles Beard, Keller likens the task of pulling a semblance of order from the dense, complex, and variegated experiences of history to "pulling a tomcat by its tail across a Brussels carpet." Keller, *Regulating a New Economy*, xi, 6.

40. Morton Keller, *Affairs of State: Public Life in Late Nineteenth Century America* (Cambridge: Harvard University Press, 1977), vii–viii.

41. See, e.g., James G. March and Johan P. Olsen, "The New Institutionalism: Organizational Factors in Political Life," *American Political Science Review* 78 (1984): 734–49; Rogers M. Smith, "Political Jurisprudence, the 'New Institutionalism,' and the Future of Public Law," *American Political Science Review* 82 (1988): 89–108; Sven Steinmo, Kathleen Thelen, and Frank Longstreth, *Structuring Politics: Historical Institutionalism in Comparative Analysis* (Cambridge: Cambridge University Press, 1992).

42. Tocqueville, *Democracy in America*. For Bryce's critique, see James Bryce, *The American Commonwealth*, 2 vols., 2d rev. ed. (London: Macmillan, 1891), 1:3–4; and James Bryce, "The United States Constitution as Seen in the Past: The Predictions of Hamilton and Tocqueville," in Bryce, *Studies in History and Jurisprudence* (New York: Oxford University Press, 1901), 301–58.

43. Bryce, *American Commonwealth*, 1:1; President's Research Committee on Social Trends, *Recent Social Trends in the United States* (New York: McGraw-Hill, 1933).

44. Morton Keller, "(Jerry-)Building a New American State," *Reviews in American History* 11 (1983): 248–52, 248 (quotation); Matthew Arnold, *Civilization in the United States: First and Last Impressions of America* (Boston: Cupples and Hurd, 1888) quoted in Keller, *Affairs of State*, vi.

45. Morton Keller, *The Life Insurance Enterprise, 1885–1910: A Study in the Limits of Corporate Power* (Cambridge: Harvard University Press, 1963); Keller, *Regulating a New Society: Public Policy and Social Change in America, 1900–1933* (Cambridge: Harvard University Press, 1994).

THREE

Progressivism and Pluralism

James J. Connolly

Historical consideration of Progressivism has revived in recent years. Journalists, political scientists, and social philosophers have turned to the reform wave of the early twentieth century to understand the problems and the possibilities of twenty-first-century American civic life. They see it as a source of the key characteristics of modern politics in the United States: a more active state, a powerful mass media, and a plethora of interest groups. Many on both the right and left also see Progressive reform as a model for the renewal of a politics that places the public interest ahead of individual or group interests.[1]

Although these analysts have appropriated Progressivism for different political projects, they share the idea that it was characterized by concern for the common good. Conservatives perceive in this emphasis on unity a counterforce to multiculturalism and the special interest pleading that fed the expansion of the welfare state. Liberals, looking back longingly to the unabashedly activist governing style of Theodore Roosevelt and Woodrow Wilson, detect an antidote to rising corporate power and an example of aggressive advocacy on behalf of the people. Both sets of observers acknowledge—and pledge to avoid—the centralization of power and concomitant decline in the influence of ordinary citizens described by many students of the period. But the nationalist politics they each extract from the ferment of the early-twentieth-century public life has proven too seductive to deter them from an embrace of Progressivism.

In seizing the mantle of TR and Woodrow Wilson for themselves, contemporary commentators have sidestepped the debates that one reviewer recently described as the American historical profession's version of the proverbial "snipe hunt."[2] Historians have accumulated mountains of evidence and shelves full of articles and monographs documenting the varieties of Progressives and Progressive reform. Where they once found a relatively coherent ideology of the Anglo–middle class, most now see a proliferation of Progressivisms among an ever-widening set of interests. Corporations, middle-class women, urban machine politicians, labor activists, and a host of other groups advocated reform in one context or another. More recent work argues that spokespersons for ethnics, African Americans, and others also employed Progressivism to further the collective interests of the groups they claimed to represent. This historical complexity is lost in the rush to claim Progressivism's legacy in contemporary political discussion.

In ignoring this diversity, current observers have overlooked Progressivism's most enduring irony. The same insistence on a politics devoted to the common good that helped build a national state also splintered the American body politic. Early-twentieth-century reform advocates worked furiously to place the ideal of the public good ahead of individual or group interest. Most of them were so wedded to this idea that they failed to consider the possibility that people with different values, backgrounds, and desires could define the public and its interests in different, often contradictory, ways. When prominent voices speaking on behalf of various communities appropriated Progressive rhetoric and concepts for their own purposes, they laid the groundwork for collective action outside of party lines. As this range of activism developed during and after the Progressive era, the plural character of American public life intensified.

Progressivism's multiplicity becomes evident when we treat it as a rhetorical framework for public action rather than as the ideology of a particular group. The image of a united community arising to battle selfish interests linked a variety of otherwise divergent endeavors. Drawing from this traditional motif of American political culture, civic and political leaders (or those seeking such roles) depicted themselves at the head of united efforts to battle selfish interests and address the problems of urban-industrial life. Who the interests were and what "the people" meant varied according to the context and the political goals of Progressivism's purveyors. It was possible for a wide range of activists to speak for a growing number of different, often overlapping, communities, defined in racial, ethnic, geographic, or political terms. The result was many specific Progressivisms, each with distinctive meanings, active simultaneously.

This essay documents the pluralizing impact of Progressivism by examining recent scholarship on ethnics and African Americans. It shows how men and women in immigrant and black communities employed Progressivism to depict themselves at the head of communal efforts to battle selfish interests and address the problems of urban-industrial life. Their definitions of the people and the interests varied according to the context in which they operated, as did their capacity to act on these representations. But the language of Progressivism was loose and flexible enough to serve as a vehicle for political action along widely divergent lines. The result was the mobilization—or at least the purported mobilization—of many communities, each defined in distinctly ethnic and racial terms.

The unfolding of this process is best grasped at the grassroots. It may be possible to define precisely a "Progressive tradition" or to revive a "Progressive public doctrine" created by a small group of intellectuals and self-conscious reformers, a project that contemporary critics continue to find irresistible.[3] But studies of famous reformers and high politics often miss the ways leaders of different groups purposefully seized upon the image of the people battling the interests and invested it with idiosyncratic meanings. The best way to grasp the distinctive meanings various people attached to Progressivism is through careful attention to specific contexts. As a review of recent historical accounts of black and immigrant activism shows, Progressivism is best viewed as something looser and more open than an ideology, as a recurrent theme that fostered a range of political projects.

That historians have provided the basis for this reassessment is no coincidence. Devoted to recovering historical context in a way that theory-driven social scientists and present-minded journalists are not, the practice of history is best suited to grasping the specific understandings people developed of the world around them. This concern has manifested itself in the large number of community studies that historians have produced. Beyond their concern for particularities, historians since the 1960s have also displayed greater concern for the experiences of marginal groups and for the process of group identity formation. Those focusing on women's experience have persuaded researchers to broaden their definition of politics beyond the traditional emphasis on parties and elections. These predispositions have encouraged historians to explore the ways in which different groups of people employed Progressivism. In doing so they helped us understand how Progressivism's language of unity unexpectedly sharpened group identities and made pluralism an even more salient feature of modern American public life.[4]

The work of contemporary historians has set the stage for a new, more plural view of Progressivism and its consequences. This vision does not rely so much on overarching generalization as it does on a descriptive approach that encourages us to treat Progressive reform as a coherent, national phenomenon, yet allows for a multiplicity of specific meanings and experiences. Many of the scholars whose research has provided the basis for a more subtle and more ironic account of Progressivism have not set for themselves the task of redefining the term. Rather, capitalizing on the freedom created by the absence of a consensus on its character, these scholars have been able to approach it as they see fit. Their central concern has not been to resolve the "essence of Progressivism" debate, but to understand the particular experiences and perspectives of specific communities or groups. In the process they have laid the foundation for a portrayal of Progressive-era public life that encompasses its extraordinary diversity.

Progressivism as Discourse

A new approach to Progressivism is possible because historians have disagreed on the term's meaning. Almost from the time the study of the reform wave of the early twentieth century became a topic of serious scholarly consideration, analysts have disagreed about its origins, character, and consequences. No sooner had Richard Hofstadter argued that Progressivism was the product of the status anxiety of a traditional middle class than others countered with claims that a "new" middle class, workers, ethnic, white southerners, or big businessmen were the true force behind Progressive reform. The dissatisfaction this revisionism engendered received full expression in Peter Filene's 1970 "obituary for the Progressive Movement," which argued forcefully against the notion that there was a coherent ideology or program that defined reform activism before World War I. Although historians hardly abandoned Progressivism as a useful category, they began to load their discussions with caveats designed to protect them from hostile reviewers and skeptical colleagues.[5]

The logjam surrounding Progressivism appears to have broken during the last two decades. Historians have begun to approach it is as something looser and more abstract than a social movement. Although they disagree on the particulars, proponents of this method share an emphasis on treating Progressivism as discourse. Daniel Rodgers initiated this tactic in his 1982 essay "In Search of Progressivism," which treated Progressivism as three "social languages" constructed around opposition to monopoly power, the importance of social bonds, and the idea of efficiency. Later he suggested that the vocabulary of "the people" battling "the interests" provided the "rhetorical skin" of the Progressive era, a language that linked otherwise disparate reform campaigns. More recently Steven Diner has proposed the existence of a common "Progressive discourse" that filled the era's public life with expressions of concern over the power of "trusts" and "special interests," calls for efficiency, and pledges of fealty to "the will of the people."[6]

This language grew increasingly powerful over the two decades leading to World War I. Beginning with the muckrakers' call to action, reform activists called for a politics that placed the public interest ahead of the special interests.[7] Politicians of all parties scrambled to place themselves at the head of this imagined public. Urban reformers such as Cleveland's Tom Johnson and Detroit's Hazen Pingree worked to improve social conditions and make city government more democratic and efficient in the public's name. State level reformers such as Wisconsin's Robert LaFollette and California's Hiram Johnson rose to national prominence with anticorporate campaigns and pledges to serve the interests of "the people." The presidential campaign of 1912 marked the zenith of Progressive discourse in American politics. Democratic nominee Woodrow Wilson declared that "the business of government is to organize the common interest against the special interests," while Progressive Party nominee Theodore Roosevelt breathlessly placed himself at the head of "a movement of truth, sincerity and wisdom, a movement which proposes to put at the service of all our people the collective power of the people." Even Republican nominee and purported "conservative" William Howard Taft could with some credibility describe himself as a reformer working for the public good.[8]

Reformers also placed virtually every reform campaign in this context. Antitrust battles easily and obviously fell within the Progressive framework. Municipal reformers sought to reorganize city politics to remove impediments to achieving the public good. Settlement residents, municipal housekeepers, and suffragists insisted that women, through their experiences as wives and mothers, were better equipped to recognize and pursue the public interest on a range of social issues. Environmental activism, efficiency drives, Americanization campaigns, antivice crusades, and dozens of other reform programs came packaged as attempts to implement the people's will, testimony to both the prevailing faith in the language of the public good and to its flexibility.

Approaching Progressivism as discourse has allowed scholars to treat it as a coherent phenomenon while also acknowledging its heterogeneity. Although proponents of a discursive approach to Progressivism have not themselves explored the ways in which it could take on a specific, often group-based, local character, they have left open the possibility that others might. Historians concerned with the experiences of marginal groups and sensitive to the distinctive meanings they gave to broader social phenomena have been able to treat Progressivism as something shaped by particular people acting in particular social and political contexts. They have made it possible to imagine many Progressivisms instead of arguing about the definition of just one.

African Americans and Progressivism

C. Vann Woodward and others once reserved Progressivism for "whites only," at least in the South. With the exception of W. E. B. DuBois and a handful of activists, African Americans found little place for themselves in the annals of early twentieth-century reform. But in recent years, a number of scholars have begun to explore the ways that blacks created Progressivisms of their own. They argue that middle-class African Americans found in the nonpartisan style of Progressive reform a way to act on behalf of their communities, even in the face of the strictures of Jim Crow.

Although this research is revising Woodward's view of southern Progressivism, they are honoring its spirit. In *The Origins of the New South,* he challenged the notion that Progressivism emanated strictly from the urban north and the agrarian west. "The southern counterpart to Northern Progressivism developed nearly all the traits familiar to the genus," he noted, "but it was in no sense derivative. It was a pretty strictly indigenous growth." Woodward described how white southern politicians arrayed the collective interest of "the people" against northern "plutocrats" and the corporations allied with them, creating a logic for a range of reforms, including railroad regulation, trust busting, consumer safety laws, and many social welfare measures. The people in this instance meant whites, which also allowed the disenfranchisement of black voters and the erection of Jim Crow to be presented as reforms.[9]

Woodward's ability to see southern Progressivism as an "indigenous growth" stemmed from his desire to place a broader phenomenon within a specific historical context. A southerner himself, Woodward sought to help both Americans and his fellow southerners understand "the collective experience and distinctive character of the South." But he also sought to present the region as something more than a racist backwater cut off from the experiences of the rest of the nation. "The South is obviously American as well as Southern," he wrote in 1960, and it was this duality that he sought to portray. Showing how southerners in the early twentieth century participated in the broad sweep of Progressive reform on their own terms, he integrated their history with the rest of the country's, while remaining acutely aware of the region's idiosyncrasy.[10]

Recent work on African Americans and Progressive reform in the South has demonstrated a similar sensibility. Displaying careful attention to local, state, and regional contexts, as well as a concern for connecting marginal groups to mainstream public life, this research has expanded the definition of Progressivism and made historical understanding of the region's politics far richer and more complex. Much of this work has concentrated on middle-class black women, who were best equipped to draw on Progressivism to frame their forays into public life for two reasons. The first was the implementation of Jim Crow itself, especially the policy of disfranchisement, which removed black men from the electoral sphere. Second was the growth of women's activism in the Progressive era, which created opportunities for African American women to represent their community in what Glenda Gilmore has called "a nonpolitical guise." As this history takes shape, it is substantially altering our view of Progressivism in the South and throughout the nation.[11]

Gender and Jim Crow, Gilmore's study of race and women's activism in North Carolina is the best example of this work. A native of the state, she brought to her research the concerns and sensibilities of women's history and a strong sense of place. Immersing herself in a rich but obscure body of primary sources, Gilmore produced "a study of North Carolina politics with black women at its center," one that illuminated the heretofore "invisible" actions of a group supposedly marginalized by gender and race. The ways in which these women used Progressivism is central to understanding this history.[12]

Gilmore's account of the African American appropriation of Progressivism centers on the Salisbury (N.C.) Colored Women's League. Formed in 1910, the league declared its purpose to be "the general civic interest of our people" and began engaging in various social reform activities. It worked for playground construction, improved public health conditions, better educational facilities, and greater social assistance for the poor. In doing so it established interracial contact with local white women's reform organizations, a connection the league could exploit in its efforts to win concessions from local government. Its members also lobbied local government directly seeking better services for their community. White authorities accepted their efforts because as nonpartisan women they did appear to represent a direct assertion of black political power.[13]

These clearly political efforts attracted little in the way of white backlash, despite the careful patrolling of racial boundaries in southern public life. This was possible in part because of the cautious way African American women used Progressivism. They could not attack "the interests" aggressively because in this Progressive scenario the villains were powerful white men. Instead they stressed the nonpartisan, communal dimensions of their activism. In one instance, the Salisbury Colored Women's Club staged "community cleanup days" but avoided direct attacks on white slumlords in the fashion that characterized similar campaigns in other parts of the country so as not to provoke powerful whites. Black clubwomen also used gender to their advantage. They cooperated with white women's groups, despite having to take a subordinate role in joint efforts, to cultivate an image of respectability and moderation. African American women could aspire to only modest accomplishments amid the violence of Jim Crow, but as Gilmore's sensitive exploration of this heretofore hidden activism shows, they were able to adapt Progressivism to their purposes.[14]

Studies with similar agendas have unearthed evidence of comparable efforts in other southern settings. In a 1992 essay collection, *Gender, Class, Race, and Reform in the Progressive Era,* a group of women's historians turned their attention to the public participation of women of various racial, ethnic, and class backgrounds. Arguing in favor of "the centrality of women to progressivism," they moved beyond the usual focus on middle-class clubwomen to document the politicization of women from a variety of racial, ethnic, and class groups.[15]

Two of the essays in the book, both focused on specific communities, show how southern black women used Progressivism to create a public platform for themselves. Jacqueline Rouse examined the work of the Women's Civic and Social Improvement Committee in Atlanta, an organization that allowed black women to lobby local government on behalf of their community and to attack the worst aspects of segregation in the city. They held "mass meetings," petitioned city government on behalf of "residents and taxpayers of the City of Atlanta," and "spoke in the interests of the civic and social welfare of our Negro boys and girls." The committee pushed for free kindergarten and childcare for black children, pressed the local school board to increase teacher salaries and reduce overcrowding in African American schools, and demanded numerous other measures, with a surprising degree of success. Nancy Hewitt described how black women in Tampa created schools, clubs, and voluntary organizations that worked for "the autonomy and dignity of their people." Eventually, she noted, these institutions helped create a sense of solidarity among the city's African Americans that gave them "leverage" in local public life.[16]

The discovery of a black women's Progressivism in so inhospitable a climate suggests that other African Americans were in position to exploit this language of communal action as well. Historians exploring the vibrant institutional life rooted in the churches, schools, and voluntary groups of African American communities have begun to develop a "new synthesis" on the relationship between blacks and the Progressive movement. As in the South, they have found that middle-class women spearheaded many of these campaigns. A variety of church leaders and activists engaged in a range of social gospel-based campaigns designed to benefit growing black communities in urban settings. Some of these endeavors—the founding of the NAACP and the Urban League—are well known, but many local appropriations of Progressivism remain unexplored.[17]

In a suggestive essay, Douglas Flamming has examined how African Americans in Los Angeles adapted Progressivism to their ends. He found that African American civic and political leaders there used the same language employed by Hiram Johnson against the Southern Pacific Railroad to encourage an independent black insurgency. These men and women broke with the Republican Party in local affairs and positioned themselves as spokespersons for a united black community instead of as cogs in the Republican machine. This gambit not only gave them greater independence from the dictates of white party leaders but also helped them solidify their role as the voice of the African American community in the city. African American women in Los Angeles also grew more publicly active, engaging in social reform work and campaigning for suffrage in a fashion similar to that of their white counterparts.[18]

Flamming's research shows how the rich institutional life of black Los Angeles provided the public platform necessary for using Progressivism. Several organizations, including the Forum, a church-sponsored discussion group, the Los Angeles branch of the Afro-American Council, and the Evangelical Ministers Conference offered settings in which to define and assert community interests. The local press, particularly the Republican-leaning but reform-minded *California Eagle* and the independent *Liberator,* also provided the means to speak on behalf of an African American public. And the local branch of the State Federation of Colored Women's Clubs provided women with access to the public sphere as well.[19]

The Progressive-style rhetoric of black Los Angelinos leaps off the pages of Flamming's essay. African American activists enthusiastically endorsed various reform measures and expressed a desire "to put government entirely in the hands of the people." At least some black leaders aligned themselves with the "fight to overthrow predatory forces" promoted by Progressive governor

Hiram Johnson and Teddy Roosevelt's 1912 campaign. The *Liberator* declared itself "Devoted to the Cause of Good Government and the Advancement of the American Negro," principles it found entirely compatible.

This language placed them outside of the Republican Party and put them in a position to speak for the collective interests of the entire black community. Increasingly they pressed local officials for fairer treatment and greater respect for their civil rights. They were able to exercise a degree of power this way, cultivating a "black vote" outside the control of the Republican Party and helping defeat a racist mayoral candidate in 1913. As Flamming argues, the use of the Progressive formula helped Los Angeles' black leaders create "an ethnic political culture" that allowed them to "strike a balance between race consciousness and American consciousness" in their public enterprises.[20]

That Progressivism could foster such a mentality in Los Angeles, as it did in the South, implies that it was useful tool for African Americans throughout the country. Much more work needs to be done to document the ways black Americans used the language of reform for their own purposes, particularly in the urban north. Doing so can add to the historical understanding of the development African American communities in large cities on the eve of the great migrations of the twentieth century. It can also help us better understand the way in which Progressivism's emphasis on unity bred diversity in modern American public life.

Ethnics and Progressivism

Just as African Americans have most often been overlooked in the chronicles of Progressive reform, so have immigrants. Richard Hofstadter's claim that they were "a potent mass that limited the range and achievement of Progressivism" carried the day for many scholars. But this neglect often led to improbable conclusions. When David Thelen described the formation of Wisconsin Progressivism, he argued that it involved the creation of a common popular identity as citizens and taxpayers. He also noted that many of the Wisconsinites who supported LaFollette were Germans and Scandinavians. It is difficult to imagine that they simply stopped thinking of themselves as ethnics and began to conceive of themselves entirely as citizens and taxpayers. It is far more realistic to assume that they combined a sense of new citizenship with their ethnic identities.[21]

J. Joseph Huthmacher took the first step in reconciling immigrants and Progressivism a generation ago. Rejecting Hoftstadter's argument, he insisted that immigrant politicians supported and even initiated social welfare reforms and some political changes. He documented this reform activism through careful examination of Massachusetts politics before the New Deal and a review of the career of New York's Robert Wagner. John Buenker and others elaborated on his argument, although neither Huthmacher nor his successors went so far as to call these groups Progressives, choosing instead the label urban liberalism. Nevertheless, they opened the way for historians to consider the Progressive credentials of urban groups other than the Anglo-Protestant middle class.[22]

Huthmacher's revisionism followed the best practices of historical scholarship. The son of immigrants himself, he not only displayed an interest in ethnic groups supposedly outside the mainstream of early-twentieth-century life, he also insisted on careful documentation of the urban liberal tradition. He urged historians to "devote more attention to exploring hitherto neglected elements of the American social structure." They would have to conduct "tedious research" on local communities, in "unalluring source materials such as local and foreign language newspapers, out of the way manuscript collections, and the correlations between the make-up and voting records of small-scale election districts." Some of the best recent research has followed this advice to demonstrate the many ways supposedly marginalized groups participated in the surge of civic activism that characterized the Progressive era.[23]

One study that began to move in this direction was Maureen Flanagan's 1987 monograph *Charter Reform in Chicago*. Although she shied away from addressing the Progressivism issue head on, Flanagan was able to document how Chicago's ethnics were able to develop a distinctive reform vision of their own. Flanagan's study displayed two key virtues: an awareness of the importance of local context and a concern for documenting the political ideas and activism of groups usually left out of political history, particularly women and working-class immigrants. She rejected the customary labels that linked Progressivism to the native-born middle class and presented immigrants as the mindless dupes of political machines. The history of charter reform in Chicago thus emerges as a competition among varied visions of the public good rather than as an attempt by the middle class to impose order on unruly urban society.[24]

Chicago's United Societies for Local Self Government served as the vehicle for expressing the ethnic reform vision Flanagan documented. Organized in 1906 to mobilize opposition to a new city charter designed to increase municipal control over city finances and to restructure city government, the United Societies brought together more than 350 nationality- and neighborhood-based ethnic clubs with more than 60,000 members. Their dissatisfaction with the charter did not stem from a desire to preserve machine politics but rather from its failure to provide sufficient home rule for the city. In particular, it allowed rural Illinois legislators too much power over cosmopolitan Chicago. Ethnic dissenters were especially concerned by the absence of a local option for Chicago, which would give downstate politicians the power to regulate the drinking habits of the city's immigrants. Their opposition—and their efforts to mobilize ethnic voters against it—contributed substantially to the defeat of the charter and the failure of municipal reform in Chicago. Both contemporary observers and historians have interpreted this position as an expression of an ethnic group's desire to maintain cultural differences and thus as antagonism to the Progressive idea of a single public interest.[25]

Flanagan's study provides evidence of how the United Societies used Progressivism to position itself as the voice of the people—whom it defined in ethnic terms. Its position was not opposition to reform in the abstract, but rather support for even more democracy than the charter revision proposed. Flanagan, though she eschewed the label Progressivism, described how the United Societies expressed a larger reform vision rooted in the notion of popular control of all aspects of local affairs, including cultural practices. In their public statements against the charter, its leaders insisted the liquor issue was just one of many concerns and declared their support for civil service reform, more efficient schools, and more equitable taxation. They also insisted that the people of Chicago shared their desire for full home rule. The problem was far broader, the ethnic organization asserted, because the proposed charter reduces "the people's representation in the city council, thereby making it easier for privilege-seeking corporations to attain their ends." The charter's taxation provisions "deprived the masses for the benefit of the few." Even when the question of alcohol came to the fore, as it often did, it was frequently expressed as something more than naked group interest, as a battle against the "tyranny" of rural forces seeking to deny the people of Chicago the right to rule themselves.[26]

In the wake of the charter's defeat, the United Societies continued its political activism and continued to employ Progressive rhetoric. According to Flanagan, the groups saw the reform proposal's failure as "a victory for the people and independent politics," and it renewed its insistence on democratic elections, fair taxation, and home rule. In these and subsequent reform efforts, one leader warned, "the rights of the majority should be considered instead of the arrogant demands of private interests and political bosses." The United Societies remained a nonpartisan force in Chicago public life into the 1930s, framing its hostility to prohibition as a defense of the interests and power of the people. This Progressive language and style lent legitimacy to the organization's positions and helped establish it as a persistent political voice on behalf of ethnic Chicago over the next two decades.[27]

Flanagan missed an opportunity when she chose not to enter the debates over the character of Progressivism. She did not label the United Societies' reform vision—or any of the other groups she describes—as "Progressive." The term itself does not even appear in the book's index and was never directly discussed. This may have been intentional; the historiography of Progressivism was at its most tangled at the time and it was probably simpler and less controversial simply to avoid it. Yet in doing so, she overlooked a way to start untying the knot. The United Societies' clearly drew on the words and images that animated so many reform campaigns during the early twentieth century. Presenting Progressivism as a tool for explicitly ethnic mobilization would have helped us see more clearly that it was not the ideology of a single group but a political style open to many.

A close look at ethnic politics in Boston reveals this flexibility. As I have argued elsewhere, that city's immigrants seized upon Progressivism during the first decade of the twentieth century to frame political action outside the bounds of traditional party politics. A simple tally of mayoral election results or a scan of citywide dailies leaves this process undetected; it only becomes evident through ground-level research using the "unalluring source materials" Huthmacher described. In the tenement-filled North End, a small set of middle-class Italians established an insurgent movement directed against Democratic boss John Fitzgerald and on behalf of the "Italian people" of the district. A few of their Jewish neighbors in the nearby West End organized themselves in similar fashion to do battle against Irish ward leader Martin Lomasney and his powerful machine. Although initially these efforts bore little electoral fruit, they provided the groundwork for a fuller mobilization of both groups in subsequent decades.[28]

The Boston Irish, the largest ethnic group in the city, found its own uses for the Progressive style. Politicians and activists at all levels used it to circumvent unsympathetic party organizations and seek power in new ways. The most successful was four-time Mayor James Michael Curley. Most historians have classified Curley as one of the last of the classic city bosses—outrageous, generous, and corrupt. He was all that, but he was also a master manipulator of language and imagery who began his career at a moment when the political environment began to place a premium on those skills. First elected mayor in 1914, Curley cast himself as a reformer, pushing for fiscal economy, woman suffrage, urban planning, revision of the city charter, and a host of social reforms. He also pledged himself to "the welfare of the entire community" over the "wishes and welfare of a particular element of the community." Yet most scholars overlook or dismiss such proposals as mere talk because they do not fit the preconception that immigrants were hostile to Progressive reform. They overlook the resonance such language had in ethnic neighborhoods and the specific meanings Curley invested in his language. When Curley spoke of the "entire community" or "a particular element," Irish Bostonians recognized the ethnic significance of the phrases—an understanding the flamboyant Curley made clear when he carved shamrocks in his Jamaica Plain mansion or mocked the city's Brahmin elite. This distinctly ethnic Progressivism helped shape the clannish outlook that distinguished the twentieth-century Boston Irish.[29]

Research on non-European groups has begun to provide tantalizing hints of even more exotic Progressivisms. Judy Yung has argued that Chinese American women in San Francisco developed their own variation of reform activism. Yung's book explored the adaptation of Chinese women to American life and the ways they combined ethnic and American cultural materials to forge distinctive identities. In a brief section of the book she describes how a small group of educated, middle-class women combined "Chinese nationalism and Western progressivism," to enter San Francisco's public life. These women formed the Chinese Women's Jeleab [Self-Reliance] Association in 1913, choosing a Chinese term to express the combination of independence, social unity, and public activism that animated the organization. The group's 200 members conducted language courses and taught "American sewing patterns," pushed for women's rights and self-improvement, and engaged in volunteer work and political discussion during its short-lived existence. Although a small segment of her study, Yung's suggestive account of the Jeleab Association demonstrates the extraordinary reach of the Progressive style beyond the confines of white, Anglo-Protestant, middle-class America.[30]

In another history of California immigrants, George Sanchez has argued that middle-class Mexicans in Southern California developed their own idiosyncratic Progressivism. His Becoming Mexican-American explores the formation of a distinctive group identity among Chicano immigrants in early-twentieth-century Los Angeles. Sanchez's concerns are those of the ethnic historian—he aimed to refute the traditional dichotomy between immigrants rooted entirely in an old-world mentality and fully assimilated Americans. Looking for ways that Mexicans participated in yet remade American culture for their own purposes, he was able to envision the Mexicanization of Progressivism.

What Sanchez found was a broad "impulse" for social order that Mexican leaders used in Los Angeles to define and to speak for their community.

But in the hands of local Mexican leaders, many with ties to the Mexican consulate, this Progressivism served to cement the loyalty of working-class Chicanos to their mother country and even to encourage return migration. Through public celebrations and educational projects, these Mexican Progressives countered Anglo efforts at Americanization with their own campaign of Mexicanization. It was in this form, Sanchez claims, rather than as a way to enter American political life that Mexicans used Progressivism.[31]

Sanchez's treatment of Progressivism is problematic but nevertheless suggests how flexible it could be. He deals almost exclusively with the period after World War I, when popular enthusiasm for the Progressive style had waned. There is little in his study that considers how or whether middle-class Mexicans used Progressivism when it most clearly prevailed in American public discourse. He also portrays Anglo Progressivism primarily as an Americanization drive, a fragment of the full range of early-twentieth-century reform activism. Even with these limitations, the push for Mexicanization described by Sanchez shows how thoroughly Mexican leaders redesigned Progressivism, using it to create a stronger public presence for Mexicans in Los Angeles, but steering them away from greater participation in American civic life.

Juxtaposing the singularly Mexican use of Progressivism described by Sanchez with its European American counterparts throws into sharp relief the value reform rhetoric had as a vehicle for political assimilation. Unlike Los Angeles Mexican leaders, most middle-class ethnics sought fuller inclusion in American public life. Progressivism provided a way to present ethnic claims as the desire of a united community, a public manner more likely to win mainstream respect than would a simple assertion of group interest. It also offered a mechanism for circumventing party machines, which represented ethnic interests unevenly at best. Finally, it demonstrated the civic patriotism of these groups by placing them within the broader Progressive-era campaign to eliminate political corruption and create more responsive governing institutions and processes.

The Uses of Progressivism

Not all Progressivisms were equal but they all mattered. Theodore Roosevelt was in far better position to act on his version of Progressivism than most blacks and immigrants. African Americans in the Jim Crow South obviously had far less power to achieve their goals than did white supremacists. The capacity of Los Angeles Mexicans to make their Progressive visions real paled in comparison to that of Chicago's ethnics. But prominent voices within each of these "publics" encouraged independent collective action based on communal concerns. In the short term some of these movements accomplished more than others did. But in the long run each fueled a sense of collective identity and interest that would expand in later years, accentuating the plural, group-driven character of twentieth-century American public life.

Arguing that the modern American public sphere grew more plural does not mean it grew more equitable. Studies of African Americans and immigrants indicate that middle-class activists of varying racial and ethnic backgrounds most often used Progressivism to speak for a specific community. These local leaders had greater access to the press and to organizations that gave them a public platform from which to act as the voice of the people. Progressivism's emphasis on unified action also appeared to fit poorly with political action driven by a sense of class conflict. There is, however, a developing body of work that finds working-class groups fashioned a useful political tool from Progressivism. This analysis suggests, in Richard Schneirov's words, "Progressivism was capable of containing, including, and transcending labor populism as well as opposing it."[32] Much research on this issue remains to be done, as is the case for the question of Progressivism's relationship to other groups. But as this works develops, the manner in which Progressivism bred diversity will grow clearer.

Scholars and contemporary critics looking to Progressivism as a model for a politics devoted to the common good might well take note of this fragmentation. In search of a remedy to the civic balkanization so evident at the start of the twentieth-first century, they have turned to the early twentieth century for guidance and inspiration. Uprooting the rhetoric of the era from its context, they envision Progressivism as an example of a politics that transcended particular interests to serve the nation as a whole. Historians have created a far more paradoxical story than this generalization can encompass through their careful inspections of grassroots politics. They have shown how Progressivism's rhetoric of unity intensified the pluralism of American public life, an irony that scholars and present-day reformers ignore at their peril.

NOTES

1. See, e.g., Eldon Eisenach, *The Lost Promise of Progressivism* (Lawrence: Kansas University Press, 1994); Michael Lind, *The Next American Nation: The New Nationalism and the Fourth American Revolution* (New York: Free Press, 1995); E. J. Dionne, *They*

Only Look Dead: Why Progressives Will Dominate the Next Political Era (New York: Simon and Schuster, 1996); Peter Beinart, "The Pride of the Cities: The New Breed of Progressive Mayors," *New Republic* 216, 26 (June 30, 1997): 16–23; Sidney M. Milkis and Jerome M. Mileur, eds., *Progressivism and the New Democracy* (Amherst: University of Massachusetts Press, 1999).

2. Colin Gordon, "Still Searching for Progressivism," *Reviews in American History* 23, 4 (1995): 669.

3. See, e.g., Eisenach, *Lost Promise of Progressivism.*

4. For a discussion of the importance of pluralism for understanding the public life of the Progressive era, see Morton Keller, *Regulating a New Economy: Public Policy and Economic Change in America, 1900–1933* (Cambridge: Harvard University Press, 1990), esp. pp. 1–6, and idem, *Regulating a New Society: Public Policy and Social Change in America, 1900–1933* (Cambridge: Harvard University Press, 1994).

5. Peter Filene, "An Obituary for the Progressive Movement," *American Quarterly* 22 (1970): 20–34;

6. Daniel T. Rodgers, "In Search of Progressivism," *Reviews in American History* 10 (1982): 113–32; Daniel T. Rodgers, *Contested Truths: Keywords in American Politics Since Independence* (New York: Basic Books, 1987), 187; Steven J. Diner, *A Very Different Age: Americans of the Progressive Era* (New York: Hill and Wang, 1998), 232.

7. Richard L. McCormick, "The Discovery That Business Corrupts Politics: A Reappraisal of the Origins of Progressivism," in *The Party Period and Public Policy: American Politics from the Age of Jackson to the Progressive Era* (New York: Oxford University Press, 1986), 311–56.

8. Rodgers, *Contested Truths,* 178; "Provisional National Committee Minutes," 5–6, in Theodore Roosevelt Collection, Harvard College Library, Cambridge, Massachusetts.

9. C. Vann Woodward, *Origins of the New South, 1877–1913* (Baton Rouge: Louisiana State University Press), 369–95. For additional discussions of southern Progressivism and its racial dimensions, see J. Morgan Kousser, "Progressivism—For Middle-Class Whites Only: North Carolina Education, 1880–1910," *Journal of Southern History* 46 (May 1980): 168–94, and Dewey W. Grantham, *Southern Progressivism: The Reconciliation of Progress and Tradition* (Knoxville: University of Tennessee Press, 1985).

10. C. Vann Woodward, *The Burden of Southern History,* rev. ed. (Baton Rouge: Louisiana State University Press, 1968), xii.

11. Glenda Elizabeth Gilmore, *Gender and Jim Crow: Women and the Politics of White Supremacy* (Chapel Hill: University of North Carolina Press, 1996), 148. I do not wish to imply that scholars have not linked Progressive reform and civil rights activism before. Nancy Weiss, for instance, in *The National Urban League, 1910–1940* (New York: Oxford University Press, 1974), notes the connection between Progressivism and campaigns for racial equality but still makes a distinction between "Progressives" and "racial reformers" (e.g., p. 69). What distinguishes recent work is its emphasis on how African Americans invested Progressivism with new meanings.

12. Gilmore, *Gender and Jim Crow*, xvi.

13. Ibid., 165–72.

14. Ibid., 169, 177–202.

15. Nancy S. Dye, "Introduction," in *Gender, Class, Race, and Reform in the Progressive Era*, ed. Noralee Frankel and Nancy S. Dye (Lexington: University of Kentucky Press, 1991), 4.

16. Jacqueline A. Rouse, "Atlanta's African-American Women's Attack on Segregation, 1900–1920," in Frankel and Dye, *Gender, Class, Race, and Reform*, 16, 20; Nancy Hewitt, "Politicizing Domesticity: Anglo, Black, and Latin Women in Tampa's Progressive Movements," in Frankel and Dye, *Gender, Class, Race, and Reform*, 35–36.

17. Jimmie Franklin, "Blacks and the Progressive Movement: Emergence of a New Synthesis," *OAH Magazine of History* 13, 3 (spring 1999): 20–23.

18. Douglas Flamming, "African-Americans and the Politics of Race in Progressive-Era Los Angeles," in *California Progressivism Revisited*, ed. William Deverell and Tom Sitton (Berkeley: University of California Press, 1994), 203–28.

19. Ibid., 205–8.

20. Ibid., 214, 211, 215, 223, 207.

21. Richard Hofstadter, *The Age of Reform: From Bryan to F. D. R.* (New York: Vintage Books, 1955), 182; David Thelen, *The New Citizenship: Origins of Progressivism in Wisconsin, 1885–1900* (Columbia: University of Missouri Press, 1972).

22. J. Joseph Huthmacher, *Massachusetts People and Politics, 1919–1933* (Cambridge: Harvard University Press, 1959; Huthmacher, *Senator Robert F. Wagner and the Rise of Urban Liberalism* (New York: Atheneum, 1968); John D. Buenker, *Urban Liberalism and Progressive Reform* (New York: W. W. Norton, 1973).

23. J. Joseph Huthmacher, "Urban Liberalism and Progressive Reform," *Mississippi Valley Historical Review* 49 (1962): 241.

24. Maureen Flanagan, *Charter Reform in Chicago* (Carbondale: University of Southern Illinois Press, 1987), 1–9.

25. See, e.g., Thomas R. Pegram, *Partisans and Progressives: Private Interest and Public Policy in Illinois, 1870–1922* (Urbana: University of Illinois Press, 1992), 105–19.

26. Pegram, *Partisans and Progressives*, 257; Flanagan, *Charter Reform in Chicago*, 113–14, 134.

27. Flanagan, *Charter Reform in Chicago*, 137, 140.

28. James J. Connolly, *The Triumph of Ethnic Progressivism: Urban Political Culture in Boston, 1900–1925* (Cambridge: Harvard University Press, 1998), 56–66. See also James J. Connolly, "Beyond the Machine: Martin Lomasney and Ethnic Politics," in *Faces of Community: Immigrant Massachusetts, 1840–2000*, ed. Reed Ueda and Conrad Wright (Boston: Northeastern University Press, 2003).

29. Connolly, *Triumph of Ethnic Progressivism*, 135–89, 143 (quotation).

30. Judy Yung, *Unbound Feet: A Social History of Chinese Women in San Francisco* (Berkeley: University of California Press, 1995), 101–5.

31. George J. Sanchez, *Becoming Mexican-American: Ethnicity, Culture, and Identity in Chicano Los Angeles, 1900–1945* (New York: Oxford University Press, 1993), 108–25.

32. Richard Schneirov, *Labor and Urban Politics: Class Conflict and the Origins of Modern Liberalism in Chicago, 1864–1897* (Urbana: University of Illinois Press, 1998), 356. See also Elisabeth S. Clemens, *The People's Lobby: Organizational Innovation and the Rise of Interest Group Politics in the United States, 1890–1925* (Chicago: University of Chicago Press, 1997), and Shelton Stromquist, "The Crucible of Class: Cleveland Politics and the Origins of Municipal Reform in the Progressive Era," *Journal of Urban History* 23, 2 (January 1997): 197–220.

FOUR

Llewellyn, Divorce, and Description

Hendrik Hartog

Around several of the corners of academia where I have lived for the past two decades (among scholars of family law, family history, women's history, and feminist theory), a general but usually unarticulated discomfort with marriage as an institution is conventional, expected. Many are married; some may even be happy in their marriages. But very few ever describe marriage as a good or a necessary institution. Would we even dare to describe it as one that helps achieve important social values? Sometimes, but often not. We are uncomfortable with the sense that heterosexual marriage still remains a privileged relationship. We pay close attention to the diversity of ways that people rear children, find sexual satisfaction, and manage economic sharing. We fear identification with patriarchy or the religious right or sociobiology. We worry about the political ramifications when empirical work appears to reveal that children who grow up in single-parent households have difficulties that children in married households don't generally experience. In current writing, my own included, marriage emerges as, at best (or at most), a body of "private" practices that reflect individual freedom, in particular, rights of association and privacy. People should be free to do what they want, including marry or not marry, stay or leave. It is a matter of deep sociological and historical interest that so many have chosen and continue to choose to live within the conventions of this longstanding institution. And marriage remains significant in the construction of adult identities (some might add that divorce too has become a significant marker of adult experience). But that's as much as most of us today dare claim, and perhaps more than some would concede.[1]

Once upon a time such discomfort with claiming the significance of marriage would have seemed odd in the extreme. And indeed, much of the history of social science could be written as a narrative about the changing but constant work of explaining the emergence of monogamous (usually Christian) marriage in human history and its unquestionable moral centrality for society. Almost all that writing, whether written from conservative or radical, religious or secular perspectives, would have insisted that the institution of marriage had a central role in the constitution of public life. But it is conventional today to discount most all of the social scientific and legal writing about marriage produced in the past (that is to say, almost everything written before the 1970s) as rooted in rejected paradigms, as patriarchal and misogynist, as driven by theology, as tendentious and uninteresting. And little of it will be read today, except as a way to reveal the happily forgotten thoughts of those who worked to shore up and to justify a largely repressive institution, or who were blind to its actual effects. Such writings belong to history, only.

Among the lessons Morton Keller has taught his students, though, is to be most self-critical when one finds oneself discounting the wisdom or understanding of past voices, particularly when discounting their understandings of what mattered most to them. I haven't always respected that lesson. But it is in the spirit of Keller's admonitions that I write this essay about an idiosyncratic study of marriage and divorce by the great early-twentieth-century legal theorist Karl N. Llewellyn.

"Behind the Law of Divorce," published in two parts in the *Columbia Law Review* in 1932 and 1933, remains little remembered among the explosion of writings Llewellyn published in the late 1920s and early 1930s.[2] It has played no role in the revived study of legal realism of the past two decades. It is Llewellyn's only sustained work on family law.[3] On the other hand, it may be a mistake to call this two-part article a piece about family law, since it includes no discussion or citation to cases or statutes or conventional legal materials. Nor is it a work of actual social science. As Llewellyn emphasized early on in the article, it is based on nothing but guesses and hunches, and is dependent on "insight."

My examination of "Behind the Law of Divorce" begins by laying out Llewellyn's argument in the first half of part one, where he described marriage as an institution. By emphasizing the ways Llewellyn constantly complicated and qualified his argument, I want to show someone working to capture and evoke what it meant to be married in the late 1920s and early 1930s. Then I isolate two aspects of his descriptive enterprise: how he went about creating a description of his contemporary world and how he situated himself in historical time. I conclude with a speculation about why he wrote the piece.

Insofar as I have a methodological purpose in writing this essay, it is to defend a descriptive enterprise that I draw from Llewellyn's writings—a desire to describe law in its complexities and its contradictions. The experience of confronting Llewellyn's struggles to capture the multiplicities of marital life and to get them all in, not to exclude or to simplify, has reminded me of the oddly similar experience of diving into Morton Keller's scholarship. A reader of Llewellyn's "Behind the Law of Divorce," like a reader of Keller's histories of late-nineteenth- and early-twentieth-century American public life, comes away wondering how anyone could have read so much; more, how anyone could have engaged critically with so much obscure and intractable material. Like Keller, Llewellyn rejected monocausal portrayals and worked to avoid reductionisms. For both, the ultimate challenge was always to create coherence while celebrating and even reproducing the noisiness and messiness of life.

This reading both builds on and challenges recent considerations of Llewellyn by historians of legal thought. He remains an inescapable figure in the history of twentieth-century legal thought and, in particular, in the historiography of the intellectual movement known in the legal academy as "legal realism." In Morton Horwitz's *Transformation of American Law, 1870–1960: The Crisis of Legal Orthodoxy,* Llewellyn epitomizes the apologetic and empiricist tendencies in legal realism (leading in a straight line to late-twentieth-century law and economics). He is read through the lens of a "functionalism" that, as Laura Kalman has argued, remains legal realism's legacy to mainstream American legalism. Both Horwitz and Natalie Hull also point to Llewellyn's "poetic" side, but for both of them the label "poetic" stands in for a sentimental image of someone tortured and fuzzy in his thinking, and for Horwitz this poetic impulse seems to imply Llewellyn's bad faith in not pursuing a more critical stance. Others, including Twining, Singer, and the rest of the historiographic brigade that has reinvigorated the study of twentieth-century legal thought, all work to reduce Llewellyn to his times, to an expression of a particular mindset in the intellectual culture of the late 1920s and early 1930s.[4]

I too believe Llewellyn was of his times. Where else could he have been? But, in working through "Behind the Law of Divorce," I have come to see him as engaged consciously and critically with much more that "his times" presented, including much that conventional legal thought could not acknowledge and some things that only existed as possibilities.[5] His present, as he imagined it, incorporated a sexual and marital future and a compendious past. He was "poetic," in a way. But I wish I could reclaim the label "poetic" for him, in a different sense than how the term is mobilized by Hull and Horwitz. In my reading Llewellyn was poetic because he tried to hear and to see everything ("everything" being, of course, something different than "every thing") and because he worked so hard to find words (the right words) for experiences and situations not easily reducible to language.

In "Behind the Law of Divorce," Llewellyn reached, realistically and allusively, toward an understanding of marriage as an "institution." Reading this article forces the early-twenty-first-century reader to confront his own avoidance of institutional thinking (about marriage and much else). As in many of his other writings, Llewellyn placed the problem of how and when complex historically situated practices and understandings become "institutions" at the center of the project.[6] He did not shy away from characterizing the values that attached to "the institution." Those values and his ways of describing those values were not ones that will seem familiar to many of us today. Some of the time, he contented himself with an occasionally crude, although still useful, approach that equated an institution with "jobs" done for the society. He made occasional noises as if he believed in an evolutionary narrative of legal change. Always he looked at institutions through the lens of a functionalism learned from German sociology, from institutional economics, and from early-twentieth-century anthropology, a functionalism that satisfied his desire for a passive stance (at least rhetorically) toward whatever it was that he was studying. As Schlegel and others have noted, there is a complacency that is an inescapable presence in the Llewellyn corpus, along with his energy and imagination.[7] But in "Behind the Law of Divorce," there is something else as well: there, he approached the problem of institutional description in a way that placed his functionalism in tension with historical change and that undercut easy generalizations and evolutionary assumptions with constant reminders of countering forces and contrary facts. There we come to see "the nature" of an institution revealed in its contingent retention of a singular identity in history. As an institution, he might have written (if he could have borrowed Morton Keller's phrase), marriage would be known only by attending to its "bewildering mix of old and new," over the course of a long and uncertain history.[8]

Marriage as an Institution

Llewellyn begins both parts of "Behind the Law of Divorce" with the same short paragraph: "Divorce presupposes marriage. Without marriage it lacks all meaning. From marriage it takes origin, form, effect. Change the practices of marriage, and divorce, after due lag, will be found readjusting to suit." (27)

But what is marriage? Llewellyn dives into "perplexing confusion[s]." Marriage means both "wedding and wedlock." He isn't really interested in the "wedding" side, although divorce requires the "wedding." And he knows that both wedding and wedlock are situations of "social fact" and "legal concepts." But for starters he wants to focus on marriage-as-wedlock and on wedlock as a social institution. But doing the latter implicates at least three definitional standpoints. Wedlock describes a "social institution in the large: i.e. patterns of behavior more or less standardized throughout a society." It also means "prevailing concepts and idealizations—noble or ribald" that shape what "men" believe marriage is and ought to be. But third, and most important, wedlock must be understood as "concrete unions, recognized going concerns made up of one man plus one woman." Each standpoint has to be distinguished from the others. They have differing, although interactive, histories. Patterns of behavior change faster than concepts, but both, according to Llewellyn, stabilize individual marriages. And important changes all begin in the ways and practices of actual marriages, of "concrete single, going concerns."

Then comes what is, for me, the key sentence: "The problem before us is description." How to account for all the "divergent" yet interactive "branches" of law, of society, of collective behavior, of ideology, and of the individual case (that is, the individual marriage)? How to find the "going whole," while still respecting the distinctiveness of differing parts? Social science as such cannot answer these questions. It is too "meager," too "spotty," too "ambiguous." Llewellyn will "gamble" instead on "insight," on inferences and critical analyses and syntheses of the descriptive accounts and stories found, among other places, in social science. And he will rely on his own knowledge of the world in which he lives. (27–29)

Description is not just a methodological stance, of course. It carries political meaning itself, in the sense that he declines to provide "solutions" to the problem of divorce. Indeed, he will argue in the later pages of "Behind the Law of Divorce" that divorce is not a problem at all. Rather, it is an outcome, to be understood only through careful description of what marriage is becoming (thus the opening paragraph). Nor does he mean description as an assumption of a universalistic or omniscient standpoint. Llewellyn's generalizations will be limited to "the bourgeois marriage" in the United States, in part because his own experience is "thus" limited, and he knows that other marital situations, "say" those among "unskilled factory workers" would be different. (He does, on the other hand, claim that in the United States the category "bourgeois" is larger than elsewhere, that it includes farmers and skilled workers, unlike in Germany.) "Behind the Law of Divorce" is an essay about what he can know, both from what he has experienced and from what he has read and studied. "Nothing in the paper purports to have any guaranty more trustworthy than common sense and personal observation. Sample drillings into the available data are offered in the footnotes."(29–30)

How to describe a marriage? For a moment he shifts to very broad (today we would say sociobiological) generalizations. There are two sexes; there is sexual attraction; man (by which he seems to mean both humanity and "man") is "a creature of habit"; there is "an unceasing drive" toward permanent or semipermanent relationships; "children are not kittens" and need years of care. "One man, one woman, living permanently together, known as belonging together: the type; becoming as the type always tends to become, the norm. The way of that living we call marriage."

But immediately he steps back from the unifying generalization. There is no pattern. Thinking in terms of patterns denies the role of individual actions and variations. Each pair comes to its own solutions to the dark and pervasive problems of how two individuals can possibly live together. "(I'm going strong; your eyes need props to keep them open; well, then, do *we* go home?)" Solutions change over time; sometimes they become habits, sometimes couples learn solutions from others or from the culture. There are limits on what any particular man or woman can do within this culture, if a couple is to be known as a couple. At least in Llewellyn's world, it must be "we" who are invited, "we" who go or stay. And some choices that seem distinctive to a single couple can be understood as collective or class-based, when one looks at how individual decisions and choices "bunch" together. (At this point Llewellyn gives a long footnote analyzing available statistics on birth control use.)

"The norm is none too uniform," and ideology does nothing to unify the situation. Norms "run largely free" of practices. Yet, there are norms, notions of what marriage is or ought to be, how people ought to behave. And those norms, often articulated in law, maintain themselves stubbornly and independently of what most people do. For Llewellyn, the legal realist, the norms themselves are relatively uninteresting. More interesting to him are "the variant facts": birth control, abortion, sexual oddities, work—all of the secret or defiant ways a couple works out a "private" married life and all the ways the secret or defiant decisions of bunches of couples emerge into social and legal practices. But then he turns back to the power of the norm, of ideology. "What I concede myself I may be far from conceding to the general." And in a footnote he returns to a recent survey of 10,000 women of whom 1,000 filled out a questionnaire on their use of contraceptives: "Among the 9,000 married women who did not cooperate . . . one would expect to find a material percentage who used birth control devices but disapproved their use; i.e. whose practices were ahead of their conscious norms." For him this represents the struggle of ideology with "insurgent facts."

Together it all makes for an institution, actually "a goodly number" of contradictory institutions, contradictory "both in needs and in effects." (31–33)

But then, given all the contradictions, why marriage? For anyone concerned to show his bona fides as a consumer of early-twentieth-century social science, and particularly for someone like Llewellyn who had absorbed an anthropological sensibility, there was an inevitable answer: marriage serves societal "functions." And Llewellyn will soon carry the reader through his own idiosyncratic survey of marriage's functions. But at least for a moment, Llewellyn is not going to go quietly into the night of functionalist social science. You can feel him wavering and talking to himself as he moves toward a functionalist resolution. Irony is his opening gambit: "Old learning passes in review: the functions of this well nigh most versatile of social structures, the services it performs." Then a quick metahistorical flourish. The number of functions "grew" over time "or happened, agglomerating around the mere recurrent fact of two people and their life together." The functions seem to have no end, edging into the land of boring truisms. But then a happier thought: "Curious . . . how the social values of the institution and its services to the participant play in together. . . . two faces of a single coin." But then the quick return to ironic realism: Do the "interests" of "the whole" exist at all, save as individual interests? How do we know what society wants or needs? And finally, a moderate stance: individuals may recognize that they have long-range interests (articulated by functional description) that perhaps conflict with their immediate or short-term interests or with the long- or short-term interests of some others. In other words, perhaps a caught but unrepentant philanderer would believe in marriage in the long run, even if he feels harmed by it in the short term. (33–34)

After that paragraph, comes his listing of thirteen essential functions, grouped into four categories: sex, group perpetuation, economics, and the more personal (or psychological). It is worth noting that the "society" for which this marriage is functional seems to be largely made up of men. It is also worth mentioning, as Llewellyn himself does, that his colleague, the legal historian Julius Goebel, thought the listing of functions had been done better in the Anglican Book of Common Prayer.

Many of his "functions" are conventional, of the sort that could be found in family sociology texts then and now: Marriage provides "an astounding reduction of conflict between men over women . . . An evening in a sailor's dive will prove persuasive" (function 1). It offers a kind of old-age insurance to wives, "independent of" their "continuing sex charm" (function 4). It is within marriages that children are socialized into the culture. They become citizens, "not wild somethings"(function 5). Some husbands will be kicked by marriage toward supporting dependents, because they know "who *is* the family," and because, in theory they cannot run away (function 6). Such units offer the occasion for capital accumulation. "Love and responsibility [for wife and children] add something to self-preservation, self-furthering, even (greatest of all) to habit." By contrast, a regime of free love or "sex alone," a regime that lacked "the impending tomorrow" that encourages thrift and investment is likely to lead only to "wild-eyed wasting" (function 8). (This is followed by a long footnote describing this claim as the strongest—the only plausible—defense of the rightslessness of illegitimate children, a defense he does not regard as adequate.)

The first of his "more personal phases" of marriage is equally conventional. Marriage "both satisfies and creates" the belief in "this woman . . . not only to have her, but to have her around, to know that *she* will stay around." He follows Sumner "in one of his rare moments of sentiment." Marriage is not necessary for love, "though institutions can further the tendency or lessen it." But "conjugal affection" can only develop out of lasting life together. But then he undercuts his argument. The very nobility of the sentiment "spells risk of rarity" (function 11). And if "as seemingly today" such love is "more intensely wanted than it is achieved," then the effect of the faith in love is to break more marriages than it holds together. This marital function results in more divorce.

And then he concludes with two complementary functions: the first directed at men, the second at women. Weak egos need marriage. Marriage gives men a standpoint from which "to bear" their lonely "fate." Marriage offers "understanding treatment of individual idiocy or weakness." It offers a kind of ongoing therapy session to bear up against an ill-understood and arbitrary, bitter world (function 12). He details an odd assortment of "spiritual" needs—being the master somewhere; a shoulder to cry on; one person you can bully; some place where you are loved as is; the infinite glorious sequence of intangible buttressings of the struggling ego afflicted with the world that is. The family of birth first satisfied that need (and usually it too sprang from marriage). And if a present marriage fails to give a man what he needs, a further marriage may provide escape and cure.

On the other hand, marriage also builds strong female egos (function 13). He recognizes that people (his reference is to gynecologists) often mobilize the prescription—"what you need is to be married, and to have a baby"—as a weapon against women. Yet, marriage furthers the development of individual personality of the wife. In doing the work of marriage, including caring for frail men, women become strong adults. And as that occurs, they become less dependent on the institution. Thus this tendency stands in inevitable contradiction with the coercive and compulsory features of marriage (as it was). Stronger women can leave marriages. But, Llewellyn concludes, here as elsewhere we see new forms being created within the institution as it evolves. (34–41)

Llewellyn next turns to an exploration of the role of law in the structuring of marriage and its functions, an enterprise he justifies because other "non-monographic" "synthetic" works on marriage and divorce have either slighted or exaggerated the significance of law. As before, his claims come accompanied with qualifications and distinctions and exceptions. Here, however, his fundamental stance is clear and unqualified: Law does less than most people think. Law may facilitate aspects of marriage by recognizing social practices, but it does not create those practices.

Even when the law appears crucial, as with the patriarchal "ordering of sex-relations," there is less there than first appears. Would property-like conceptions like "possession" exist without law? Llewellyn thinks they would. "Women have been over-blind in their attacks upon the possessory conception of the wife. Possession has its weaknesses, in marriage as in property. But in both places, its drive is toward turning individual strengths that merely happen (love, fun in working) into strengths that can be counted on and last." Selfishness and jealousy are recreated as social strengths. And though, like property relations, wifely possession may result in oppressions and misuses, still Llewellyn thinks such practices have "done a better job than in property—conceding that the problems to be solved were simpler." Likewise with the apparently law-created boundary between marriage and nonmarriage. For him the law is merely reflective here of a culture that divides women into loose women and prostitutes, on the one hand, and those who can be "acquired *only* as permanencies," a culture that creates unambiguous markers for the married—"a plain third-finger band; in some circles, a diamond still will serve." His focus is on the "tabus," and on the ways children and adults are socialized to maintain those tabus. (42–44)

According to Llewellyn, the habits and ways of being—the self-knowledge—of the married do not result from law. "Are we to take the statutes against fornication and adultery seriously today? . . . Is there a need for the official license and ceremony, in order that we may know the married from the single?" Again, the strong denial forces him immediately toward qualifications and exceptions. After the second sentence of the quotation, he adds a

note acknowledging that social workers believe that a working-class man re-
gards common law marriage as an opportunity to live with a woman as long
as he wants to, whereas for a woman, the legal practice "obscures the decision
whether she wants to live with a man without being his wife." In the text he
notes that criminal punishment of bigamists may affect some marriages and
may restrain some men. But again, he expects that the primary influence of
bigamy law is to encourage secrecy by bigamists. It is not bigamy law that
keeps married men monogamous. (44–45)

For him the primary significance of law in the ordering of sex (and in
other aspects of wedlock) is as backdrop: as producer of "the Peace," of the
monopoly of legitimate violence that the state makes available to the legiti-
mately married, as it does to all who adopt legally approved identities. "Assault, kidnapping, raiding for women, poisoning or knifing of unwanted
mates (one's own or another's) are not the order of the day." (Again, though,
there is a qualifying note on "seduction," acknowledging that the seduction of
young women by men has likely been promoted by the law's role in "further-
ing and buttressing" the unequal distribution of wealth.)

As for what he here calls "the comforter-function" of marriage, law plays
little role at all, within the going marriage. The expectations of one partner
for and in the other ("not only 'love your wife,' but 'come home—five eve-
nings a week.' Not only 'keep her happy,' but 'take her to a show'") are produced by the couple itself and by the groups to which it belongs. And the efforts within the law to reinforce some expectations, as in creation of a legal
duty to cherish, do little for cherishing by anyone.

On the other hand, once there is a separation, once law has intervened as
"the exclusive authorization of divorce," then law becomes important as a
repository of ideology. It is at those moments, when marriages are no longer
permanent and going, that "Law . . . makes marriage-as-permanent easy to
see, to inculcate, to think about. . . . It . . . sets a goal, contains a threat, and
urges to a process." (46)[9]

Law does matter, Llewellyn concedes, once the relationship has been disrupted. And once he starts down that direction, he begins to think of other
situations where law matters. Soon he is arguing against the view (articulated
by the German jurisprude Ehrlich) that law does not have significance in the
shaping of the property relations within couples in ongoing marriages.
Llewellyn concedes the relatively greater power of "group-ways and norms":
"the turning over of the unopened pay envelope has as little to do with legal
rules as the despotic purse-power not infrequent with him whose every asset
stands in his wife's name." Yet it also seems to him apparent that a husband's

legal power over assets often "tip the balance" when major "policy" decisions, such as major purchases, occur. "Feet do get put down, and it is the law which provides the footing." And the patriarchal rules of marital property do shape decisions as they are made. (49–51)

Llewellyn also has an optimistic and classically Progressive faith that law can make a difference in forcing sharing of resources within marriage. An irresponsible father can be made to surrender a portion of his paycheck. And he is a strong believer in public regulation to control venereal disease. He also argues that rules defining marital property do have some significance during marriage, although only because of the need to protect third parties to the marriage.

But, in summary, law is to marriage fundamentally as it is to most other relationships: reinforcement when social patterns fail to prevent violence, irresponsibility, fraud, and cruelty, a provider of clear (or relatively clear) forms of notice and recognition, and a mobilization of power that forces a few to "alter" their ways. As with many other relationships, law usually becomes crucial for marriage only when the possibility of an ending has been raised. "What non-official society can clearly and sharply do in creating marriage, it lacks the means to do in dissolution." Then the "air" becomes "alive with assertions, accusations, "promises," "agreements," denials. It takes an official to determine what is what, and what to do." For Llewellyn the law's significance in determining endings is not a necessary result, but, rather, a contingent effect of the rules for divorce in early-twentieth-century America. Were divorce by mutual consent (which we today would call no-fault divorce) the normal form of marital closure, then law would have no more significance in the endings of marriage as in its ongoing practices. But as of 1932, that is not the case.[10] And as a result, *law's influence is felt direct when marriage ceases to be going marriage.* And so ends part one of "Behind the Law of Divorce." (51–52).

Llewellyn's World

In part two, Llewellyn situates the "divorce crisis" of his day within a long historical transition, in which an older marriage pattern (we might call it patriarchal; he doesn't) is first intensified by the isolation of frontier living and then gradually and incompletely replaced by a more companionate marital form. His polemical goal is to demonstrate that many divorces—particularly those by young people without children—do not threaten marriage's core values and functions, as described in part one. "*[W]orking wedlock in our society holds firm, and grows, and readjusts.* Divorces are the shavings that dribble from the joiner's bench." (63–64) I find this second half less compelling then the first; it carries more than a whiff of the functionalist complacency characteristic of 1970s social welfare thought, rushing to explain how no-fault divorce would not really change marriage.

Still, part two carries its own rewards. It remains unmatched as an imagined picture of how divorce becomes normalized, from "almost a crime, . . . through the stage of social outrage, of terrible misfortune, of regrettable necessity (and in the large, a menace), of a something better not alluded to, of a 'that's too bad'—till it becomes an event not too greatly different from another." Here Llewellyn stands as a then-still-isolated legal voice for the emerging view that divorces were ways of coming to terms with reality rather than means of determining legal fault.[11] And as in part one, though in somewhat more muted form, there is Llewellyn's voice, wrestling with his intuitions and his readings, searching for the illuminating description. "Take a single tiny but terrific source of strain," begins his statement of the value of marital permanence, in the face of the ordinary strains created when two people try to live together. A man believes "that you sit up till you are heavy-ripe for sleep"; his wife, on the other hand, believes "that only with lights out and the back at rest can things that need talking over really come up for speech." (80) Or, in a note a few pages earlier, after having taken apart a statistical study of divorce for being "spotty as a leopard, craftsmanship and often brilliance set off by commonplace and nonsense": "It is, I think, statistically normal for a newly wed after three months to have some real difficulty in sizing up his own prior single life as such: weddedness in the teeth of all its problems, integrates experience not only forward, *but back.*" (74)

Together, the two parts of "Behind the Law of Divorce" describe the emergence and the conditions of a world—America in the 1920s and 1930s—within which changing divorce practices will have meaning. What are the dimensions, the salient features, of that imagined world?

The first thing to notice is how full it is. Even those whom he has labeled not relevant to his project—those not of the bourgeoisie—appear regularly in the notes. It seems as if he has read and worked through every statistical study of divorce and marriage and all of the early-twentieth-century social surveys. The numbers of African American divorces, who is prosecuted for nonsupport, the work of "domestic relations courts," the National Desertion Bureau, and the working lives of prostitutes all pass in review (and for close critical commentary). Their apparent absence from his analytic portrait (above the footnote line) is both explained and challenged by his actual presentation, which demands that the reader attend to the notes in dialogue with the text.

Llewellyn uses social science studies much as he would use legal cases in other writings. They too are constituent parts of his world, and they provide much of the descriptive detail he will mobilize. But they are also texts to test and to challenge and to work with as he comes to his own conclusions. Although he admires some studies, notably the Lynds' *Middletown,* no work is ever claimed as authority.[12] Much of the time particular studies are made to embody varying positions, to represent the diversity of voices that constitute the present. And their content becomes the occasion for close statistical analysis and disaggregation. If you're not reading really closely, it all can seem a blur of numbers.

Marital "facts" never stand apart, behind institutional walls. Llewellyn constantly draws analogic connections, particularly with business practices. A note on the effects of law on third parties who have to deal with a couple where the husband manages his wife's assets recasts the problem as one of "business organization, . . . somewhat paralleled by the dominant stockholder who piles up liabilities only against the corporation, while draining off any current profits." His discussion of the role of marriage as a provider of comfort and protection to weak male egos expands into a broader frame: of how understandings of "justice" ought to take account of the "vital desire" for understanding of "individual idiocy or weakness." And to illustrate that frame he describes a "boss" who is "great because he helps out those in trouble. He helps you out first, and helps without regard to whether you have been at fault. If you have, he bawls you out—as is his function. *It does not stop this help.* You have no use for what reformers keep calling 'justice,' even-handed, and the law. You need the undeserved aid reformers will denounce as favoritism, influence, corruption." (39)

At the same time, each marriage, each couple, stands apart, creates its own history, founded in negotiations and background and wealth and habits. And in spite of his male-centered understanding of the institution in the large, he never assumes that a wife's interests or expectations are the same (or even similar) to those of her husband. Some couples hold to old ways, some challenge the old, and some skirt the line between old and new, as wives and husbands negotiate the terms of their lives together. Some couples share a worldview or a perspective, say on birth control or abortion; some couples differ. Everyone is shaped by the institution; everyone is independent of the institution; everyone constructs the institution. Marital unity is not a relevant category. Conflict and negotiated solutions and distinct interests underlie all marriages.

Almost anything identified as an emergent tendency or truth produces reactions and countertendencies. Sometimes this is indicated by nothing more than a citation. The statement that women retain a much stronger commitment to premarital chastity than men do produces a citation to Sumner's *Folkways,* which is followed by a "but cf" to the writings of the sex radical and juvenile court pioneer, Judge Ben Lindsey, who was notorious for his defense of a young woman's right to sexual experimentation. (44) More often the exceptions and variations become the subject of a textual note. After Llewellyn has insisted that wedlock can offer the opportunity for "the development of individual personality, and especially that of the wife," his note immediately acknowledges: "Among some couples, not all. The nub of the situation is the persistence of old patterns side by side with new." This particular note moves across time and spheres of activity, as Llewellyn reflects further. Side-by-sidedness is found within marriages and between different couples, and it is found in business and industry as well. Meanwhile those who make laws imagine that there must be "a single way for all," and the results are "desperate." (Here he allows himself a quick wave at specialized administrative tribunals and at Samuel Williston's conservative treatise on contracts and the desire for unification and simplicity characteristic of classical legal thought.) As to marriage in the law, there have been, he concedes, some changes that make room for greater variety. He thinks married women's property acts were one such change. But, he acknowledges, such changes often persist in denying the fact of multiplicity. They are written as if the new rules apply alike to all married women. Still, the growing number of statutes offers reason for hope. If there are enough rules, judges will be free to pick and choose, to exercise discretion and to make the rules fit the individuals they confront. Doctrinal interpretation adds more variation. And still newer institutions, like domestic relations courts, represent a new step "towards abdication of the ideal of government-by-rule." (40–41)

As I think about the thickness of Llewellyn's world, the ways it seems to burst the physical boundaries of the page, particularly as compared to the descriptive thinness of most legal writing (then and now), I begin to wonder if I am not mistaken in my characterization of his presentation as argument followed by exceptions. Formally, I am right, and Llewellyn has certainly marked the essay with headings that indicate a thesis with development. One can draw a linear outline from his text. But it is as if the burden of description pushes him toward something different and more interesting, something more like a Whitmanesque layering of multiple and contradictory voices, a simultaneity of emergent possibilities and past structures and habits, a present tense of the married and the unmarried, the once-married and the never-to-be-married, all of whom together create the conditions for divorce (and presumably for much else in the society). Apparently contradictory positions and attitudes, drawn from differing historical situations, are all present and constitutive of divorce in 1932. As he writes in his last paragraph, "Most persons live in two or more . . . [historical] stages simultaneously; which one is uppermost turns on the degree of knowledge and closeness to specific cases. Hence, when change in *legislation* is concerned, the older range of attitudes crops up peculiarly." (96)

And yet, to pose Llewellyn's sensibility as if he were simply treating the past (his past) as dead or dying practices and understandings, as over-ripe or dried up leftovers still in the refrigerator of contemporary marriage, denies what is also apparent: that he was always thinking historically. His present always sat within periods and in relation to a past.

Llewellyn's historical standpoint bears the markings of his time and of his reading. There's a lot of Sumner's *Folkways*, and a bit of Malinowski, in the imagined past that serves as backdrop to the struggle of American modernity to come to the fore. Frederick Jackson Turner's frontier hypothesis does a lot of work in part two. Still, throughout part two, a conventional perspective that defines what is "modern" and what is archaic and paints evolutionary pictures is regularly challenged by a variety of reconstructed periodizations. Strikingly, he thinks of the 130 years up to the time of his writing as one period, defined by a process and a set of concerns and issues that join the beginning of the nineteenth century to the early 1930s. Meanwhile, he also marks democratization, the rise of feminism, the passage of married women's property acts, and the beginning of the secular rise in the rate of divorce in post–Civil War America as moments of importance.

He is, not surprisingly, particularly interested in "the galloping increase" in divorce statistics after 1870. And here, as elsewhere, he attacks the numbers and the statisticians, challenging and complicating apparent conclusions and meanings.[13] How, for example, to understand the longstanding fact that more divorces had occurred in western states than elsewhere in the country? One standard source (Ogburn's *Recent Social Trends*) argued that one could not conclude that those states were models for the rest of the country, since the "spread in rate" (the differential) was growing.[14] Western states did not have the growing Catholic populations located in the east. The eastern birthrate, made up of incipient opponents of divorce, meant that the differences between east and west would widen. But Llewellyn is skeptical. He doubts that Catholicism is a permanent "barrier." And he mobilizes many sources to show growing rates of marital disruption among Catholics. "There is no reason to doubt that those factors in our civilization which tend toward divorce will over the long run reach *increasingly* any group subjected to their stress." But then he again adds "on the other hand": he would not be read as assuming that there is some tendency everywhere in the country toward a uniform rate. "Not only laws but practices and attitudes diverge, these last in ways too subtle for the unaided eye to mark." (67–68)

His historical narrative is dependent on the work of others. But again, what is striking is his critical engagement with historiographic conventional wisdom. For example, he briefly explores the perceived rise in late-nineteenth-century America of new marriage patterns that competed with an older patriarchal form, a change that many historians and sociologists identify (then and now) as the rise of companionate or egalitarian marriage. On the one hand, he is sure that there was a large social transition, marked by, among other things, the decay of a fundamentally economic understanding of a married couple as a firm or enterprise. On the other hand, he disdains most accounts of that change. Yes, men became "business-ridden, business-souled"; conversely, bourgeois wives, or at least some, became pioneers "in a region of the psyche still not thickly settled: wedlock, *on a democratic scale,* as a hearth of mutual cultural interests." But did that make marriages actually companionate? He adds another note, one that begins by contrasting the attempts by recent sociologists to describe a single marital ideal type ("companionate" or "equalitarian" or "maternal" or "emancipated") as the emergent norm. Llewellyn is quickly and predictably dismissive of that enterprise. He then shifts back to the past, to "the beginning" of the companionate ideal among the relatively wealthy urbanites of mid-nineteenth-century America. But was that ideal lived by those who claimed it? That is, were the women who formulated the ideal able to impose it on their husbands? He notes that the French commentator Auguste Carlier, who had traveled as a latter-day Alexis de Tocqueville in pre–Civil War America, thought that American wives never became the confidantes of their husbands, that there was no real intimacy or companionate relationship. He does not "trust Carlier far on such matters." But in this case, Llewellyn decides that Carlier's observation may have been correct. Early companionate marriage may have been an empty shell. And, Llewellyn concludes, "the violence of the early Women's Rights crusaders [by which he means their anger at the legal institution of marriage] is suggestive." (63)

The historicity of Llewellyn's "Behind the Law of Divorce" is marked by a familiar paradox. On the one hand, his is a story of change and of an arrow of time that can move in only one direction: "the marriage-pattern as this country knew it . . . will not within our children's lifetime come again; . . . the remnants left of it are already seized upon by dissolution. The problem is not the arresting of decay; still less is it a problem of return. Both are impossible." (62) At the same time, it is striking the extent to which he sees himself and his contemporary world in long historical view. There is a way in which even the 1840s and certainly the 1870s and 1880s remain part of his world: as baselines for modern tendencies, as formative moments, and as containers for possibilities still present in 1932.

Conclusion: Why Go Behind the Law of Divorce?

When I first thought of writing this essay, I e-mailed with Laura Kalman. I asked her why Llewellyn would have written this piece, given that he wrote little else on marriage or the family. She suggested that I think in terms of legal education, that almost everything the realists wrote was, she thought, directed at the reform of the curriculum and pedagogy of American law schools.

I dutifully reread "Behind the Law of Divorce," looking for the marks of legal education. When I didn't find them, I spent a day rereading other works of Llewellyn from the late 1920s and early 1930s, all of which did bear those marks. Unlike them, "Behind the Law of Divorce" contains no citations to the classic cases of the casebooks, no argument with Restatements, little in the way of doctrinal struggle. I learned that Llewellyn never taught domestic relations law. Indeed, everything about the essay suggests his distance from the entire subject as it would have been taught in the 1920s and 1930s.[15] He is not even critical of the enterprise. It's just not relevant to him.[16]

But if it's not the struggle for the law schools that motivated "Behind the Law of Divorce," what then was it? In her recent study of Llewellyn and Roscoe Pound, Natalie Hull reads "Behind the Law of Divorce" as the reflections of a somewhat misogynist man. In her rendition, Llewellyn, who had recently divorced his first wife, was a grumpy and angry man, a precursor of modern men's rights advocates, who used the article to lash out at an institution that had harmed him.[17]

As I hope the previous pages make clear, I find little about "Behind the Law of Divorce" that resonates with that reading. It's not an angry piece. If his own divorce was the energizing event, it was to stimulate reflection and to locate himself within a wider world and a longer history, precisely what Hull denies he had done.

But Hull's reading reminded me of her admonition throughout her study of Pound and Llewellyn to take seriously the significance of a private life. There is something to the enterprise of locating "Behind the Law of Divorce" within the events of Llewellyn's life. But the salient facts are not just that Llewellyn had recently been divorced by Elizabeth Sanford but also that he would soon marry again, to Emma Corstvet, a social statistician and sociologist teaching at Yale Law School. All I know about Corstvet I know from Schlegel's study of social science in American legal education, and that is, unfortunately, too little to do more than speculate.[18] But it occurs to me that one might read "Behind the Law of Divorce" as a peculiar piece of courtship. Corstvet, a woman with a career, would not be quick to marry (at a time when professional women were told to choose between marriage and careers). She would need convincing. And so Llewellyn proceeded to show that marriage was still a worthy institution, in spite of its past, that it responded and changed with the times and that it could accommodate new practices and that it could be good for a woman.

Of course, if he was courting her, he needed to prove himself worthy of her. And it was thus important that he demonstrate that his past as a divorcé was not disabling or corrupting of his capacity for lasting matrimony. And so he did, insisting that early divorce was in fact structurally homologous with a commitment to marriage for life. More, he needed to show that he was interested in what was most important to her. Thus this essay, more than others he wrote at the time, showed his direct immersion in the statistics that were central to Corstvet's professional identity: critical analyses of social surveys as a love offering. Of course, he should not be seen as competing with her, and so he argued he was merely synthesizing, not doing social science. And he would want to show how their mutual gifts and interests were complementary. Thus "Behind the Law of Divorce" took as its apparent subject the problem of the relative significance of "the legal aspects."

If I am right in my speculation about the purpose behind the piece, then it seems that he got his wish, that his courtship was successful. For he and Emma Corstvet soon married. Of course, once one starts down this road, once one begins to think of Llewellyn's life as context for this essay, one confronts the later unhappiness of his marriage to Corstvet and his later divorce from her to marry Soia Mentschikoff.[19] All of which suggests that Llewellyn's stated belief that early divorce was not inconsistent with long-term marriage was belied (or at least challenged) by his own later experiences. Llewellyn, the institutional theorist, would not have been surprised.

NOTES

This essay was first drafted for presentation at a conference in Stockholm comparing Swedish and American legal realism. Later drafts were presented at faculty colloquia at the Georgetown University School of Law, the Columbia Law School, and the Indiana University (Bloomington) School of Law. At a session of the 2000 annual meeting of the American Society for Legal History, I benefited from the comments of Jack Schlegel and Mary Anne Case. Dan Rodgers, Carol Sanger, and Sarah Igo also offered helpful comments on early drafts.

1. Clearly, there are many who do not share this understanding of marriage, a point brought home forcefully when I presented this paper to a faculty colloquium at Columbia Law School. But see Martha Fineman, *The Neutered Mother, the Sexual Family, and Other Twentieth-Century Tragedies* (New York: Routledge, 1995); Nancy F. Cott, *Public Vows: A History of Marriage and the Nation* (Cambridge: Harvard University Press, 2001).

2. Karl N. Llewellyn, "Behind the Law of Divorce," *Columbia Law Review* 32 (1932): 1281–1308; ibid. 33 (1933): 249–94. The essays were reprinted in Association of American Law Schools, *Selected Essays in Family Law* (New York: AALS, 1950), 27–96. Page references throughout will be to the reprinted version.

3. But see Karl N. Llewellyn, "The Limits of Sexual Law," in *About the Kinsey Report*, ed. Donald Porter Geddes and Enid Curie (New York: New American Library, 1948).

4. Morton J. Horwitz, *The Transformation of American Law, 1870–1960: The Crisis of Legal Orthodoxy* (New York: Oxford University Press, 1992), 169–212; Laura Kalman, *Legal Realism at Yale, 1927–1960*, Studies in Legal History (Chapel Hill: University of North Carolina Press, 1986); N. E. H. Hull, *Roscoe Pound and Karl Llewellyn: Searching for an American Jurisprudence* (Chicago: University of Chicago Press, 1997); William Twining, *Karl Llewellyn and the Realist Movement* (Norman: University of Oklahoma Press, 1985); Joseph Singer, "Legal Realism Now," *California Law Review* 76 (1988): 465. Schlegel's work on legal realism stands apart from this generalization. See John Henry Schlegel, *American Legal Realism and Empirical Social Science*, Studies in Legal History (Chapel Hill: University of North Carolina Press, 1995).

5. He thought his "biases" had effectively "reworked" all the facts he had read or absorbed over an eighteen-year period. The "effective forces" lying behind his biases included "a conservatively acting, radically thinking mother," in combination with a reading after college of both the writings (translated into French) of the Swedish feminist Ellen Key and of William Graham Sumner's *Folkways: A Study of the Sociological Importance of Usages, Manners, Customs, Mores, and Morals* (Boston: Ginn, 1906). See "Behind the Law of Divorce," 55.

6. See, e.g., Karl N. Llewellyn and E. Adamson Hoebel, *The Cheyenne Way: Conflict and Case Law in Primitive Jurisprudence* (Norman: University of Oklahoma

Press, 1941); Karl. N. Llewellyn, *Jurisprudence* (Chicago: University of Chicago Press, 1962), 233–42, 352–71.

7. This was the gist of Schlegel's comment at the ASLH session.

8. Morton Keller, *Regulating a New Society* (Cambridge: Harvard University Press, 1994), 18. Keller, more than the Llewellyn of "Behind the Law of Divorce," emphasizes the "persistence" of traditions.

9. See Hendrik Hartog, *Man and Wife in America: A History* (Cambridge: Harvard University Press, 2000).

10. It is, of course, a matter of continuing debate what role no-fault divorce plays today in the continuing conflicts and negotiations, involving child custody, child support, and marital property, that are a part of the modern lore of family law with regard to marital endings. It has also become conventional, certainly in the family law literature, to view marriage through the lens of divorce, that is, to assume that the institution of marriage is constituted through the legal conditions and availability of divorce. In that sense, the late-twentieth- and early-twenty-first-century understanding of the relationship of marriage to divorce is precisely the reverse of what Llewellyn posited in his opening passage.

11. See Keller, *Regulating a New Society*, 25–26. In many ways, Llewellyn's perspective continues the legal "project" first articulated in formal legal terms by the nineteenth-century treatise writer Joel Prentiss Bishop, who worked to make marriage and divorce law take account of the "reality" of marital unhappiness. See Hartog, *Man and Wife in America*, 269–72.

12. Robert S. Lynd and Helen Merrell Lynd, *Middletown: A Study in American Culture* (New York: n.p., 1929). On the public reaction to the Lynds' work, see Sarah N. Igo, "America Surveyed: The Making of a Social Scientific Public, 1920–1960" (Ph. D. diss., Princeton University, 2001).

13. On the near meaninglessness of such statistics until the postwar era, see Katherine L. Caldwell, "Not Ozzie and Harriet: Postwar Divorce and the American Liberal Welfare State," *Law and Social Inquiry* 23, 1 (winter 1998): 1–54.

14. *Recent Social Trends in the United States; Report of the President's Research Committee on Social Trends, with a Foreword by Herbert Hoover* (New York, 1934).

15. I base this statement on my work with twentieth-century domestic relations casebooks. See Hartog, *Man and Wife in America*, 287–309.

16. At the same time, the voice Llewellyn develops in "Behind the Law of Divorce" might represent the voice of his conception of the ideal law professor: complicating, contesting, challenging generalizations, working through available data looking for usable meanings, making sure his students have confronted all the possible materials that go in to legal life, making sure they approach those materials with the same critical but not dismissive perspective that they mobilize for conventional legal sources. It is a skeptical voice; yet it is also one that believes in the reality of institutional structures. And it is also one that asks students to imagine how people actually

live within the institution of marriage. In that sense, one can understand his goals here by thinking about the pedagogical and educational ambitions described more explicitly in works like *The Bramble Bush*, "What Price Contract?" and his exchanges with Pound over legal realism. In that sense, Laura Kalman was surely right.

17. Hull, *Roscoe Pound & Karl Llewellyn*, 228–32.

18. Schlegel, *American Legal Realism*.

19. On Llewellyn's second divorce and remarriage, see Twining, *Karl Llewellyn and the Realist Movement.*

PART TWO

Identities

Anna Dickinson, America's Joan of Arc

Public Discourse and Gendered Rhetoric during the Civil War

J. Matthew Gallman

In January 1864 Anna Elizabeth Dickinson, a twenty-one-year-old Philadelphia Quaker, entered the hall of the House of Representatives, with the speaker of the house and the vice president flanking her on the makeshift platform, and President Abraham Lincoln and Mary Todd Lincoln in the audience.[1] Two months earlier Dickinson had journeyed to Chicago, where she delivered two lectures—for a substantial fee of $600—at the Northwest Sanitary Fair. Some Chicago newspapers questioned the propriety of Dickinson's accepting money for a charitable event, but the *Chicago Tribune* celebrated Dickinson's appearance: "Anna Dickinson is a born orator. She has a mind that can grapple with the most subtle arguments—a voice of rare sweetness, strength and endurance—and a combination of powers that never fails to magnetize the most careless audience. . . . And yet amid all this, she is still a woman—has a woman's way of thinking, and a very womanly way of saying what she thinks."[2]

By the time she appeared in Chicago, Dickinson was one of America's leading orators and one of the nation's most celebrated women. This fame had come quickly. Dickinson delivered her first invited lecture before the

— 91 —

Pennsylvania Anti-Slavery Society in the fall of 1860. The following February the teenage prodigy addressed a large audience at Philadelphia's Concert Hall where she spoke on "The Rights and Wrongs of Women." In early 1862 William Lloyd Garrison arranged for her to deliver a series of lectures in the Boston area. The next year the secretary of New Hampshire's Republican State Committee invited her to visit the Granite State to speak for the party's candidates. Although much of her early reputation was built on abolitionist and women's rights speaking, Dickinson proved to be an exceptionally effective partisan stump speaker, attracting enthusiastic Republican audiences in Maine, Connecticut, Pennsylvania, and New York.

As a wartime orator, Dickinson stands at the confluence of two major streams in the recent scholarship in women's history. One considers the various ways in which women entered the public arena. Central to that literature has been a reexamination of the notion of rigidly dichotomized separate gender spheres in antebellum America as well as a rethinking of what we mean by "public" activity. Despite a host of cultural messages and legal restrictions emphasizing that a woman's proper place was in the home, there is ample evidence that middle-class white women ventured into the public arena in various ways: organizing voluntary societies, publishing books and articles, running small businesses, pursuing reform agendas, appearing in civic rituals, and engaging in public discourse.[3] Moreover, recent scholarship has demonstrated that the concept of public and private spheres had less clear resonance beyond the white middle classes.[4] Still, there remains a kernel of truth, encoded in northern society's prescriptions about the proper roles of women in public life, and enforced through both law and custom. Although some northern antebellum women were actively engaged in the crucial reform debates of the time, and some leading figures stepped to the podium before mixed audiences, the rough and tumble world of partisan politics remained a male-dominated world. Anna Dickinson, it would appear, transgressed that line with impunity.[5]

The second scholarly stream concerns the history of women during the Civil War. Immediately after the conflict various tomes celebrated the contributions of the "noble women" on both sides.[6] More recently, scholars have examined the wartime experiences of women in both the North and South.[7] Some of this work has emphasized the underexplored experiences of women who served as soldiers, spies, and the like, but nineteenth-century women's historians have fairly recently discovered the war years as an important episode in the history of women's public activism.[8] Thus, the two interpretive streams come together in the war years.

In her study of women's "warwork," Jeanie Attie examined the activities of women in northern voluntary societies and their tensions with the male leadership of the United States Sanitary Commission. Attie observed that "Although legal and social codes prevented women from performing their loyalties in the same manner as men, war mobilization nevertheless presented women with ways of exploiting the very structures of gender inequality to demonstrate their loyalties." Wartime women, Attie argues, supported the war effort while chafing at the constraints imposed by a cultural world that limited their public actions and a male leadership intent on circumscribing their role to a largely symbolic, passive, form of patriotic support and fund-raising.[9]

Anna Dickinson moved in this same world, but she hardly seems of that world at all. Dickinson's "war work" does not fit under Attie's umbrella in that she worked completely outside the normal constraints defined by her gender. Dickinson has received some scholarly attention as an outspoken abolitionist and advocate for women's rights, but such an iconoclastic nonjoiner does not fit well into analyses of organizational developments or emerging ideological debates. Could it be that she was so distinctive that her wartime experiences are only of limited historic significance? One might reasonably set aside the highly idiosyncratic diarist or the obscure author, but Anna Dickinson was the most public of gender transgressors. If she truly violated accepted gender norms, she did so before hundreds of wartime audiences, often speaking in halls of a thousand or more paying customers.

This essay examines how those audiences made sense of this charismatic female orator. The analysis is really doubly about public discourse. On the one hand, the focus will be on Dickinson as a public orator and contemporary responses to those appearances. And, on the other hand, the evidence is from a wide array of newspaper accounts, which taken together suggest an ongoing public discussion on the propriety of women entering the partisan political arena, and of course a public discourse constructed to shape—and not merely reflect—popular opinion. The reporters and editors who participated in that discourse fell along a spectrum generally reflecting each newspaper's perspective on Dickinson's politics. Although some commentators celebrated Dickinson as a pioneer for women's entrance into the public arena, far more adopted some stance that allowed for no such transforming legacy. Although Anna Dickinson was celebrated as a woman in the public arena, the responses to her celebrity had within them the seeds for future constraints.

Of course these published accounts and editorial comments must be read with care, rather than being accepted as literal depictions of contemporary gender norms. They certainly reflect an ongoing dialogue between newspapers and their readers, with the partisan press endeavoring to simultaneously reflect, exploit, and shape readers' responses about gender roles *and* political policy. In highly competitive publishing markets (even in the smaller cities where Dickinson spoke there were commonly two or even three competing local journalists in the audience), the press could ill afford to offend readers' sensibilities about gender while trying to maintain a political following and an economic base. Mid-nineteenth-century Americans certainly had no universal notion of the proper role for women in public life, but the responses to Dickinson's appearances, and the language of those responses, provide a telling sketch of the parameters of popular thought.

In his magisterial study of the postwar American polity Morton Keller underscored the "ambiguous inheritance of the Civil War." The powerful forces of change unleashed by the Civil War, Keller argues, soon gave way to the more enduring values of racism, localism, and laissez-faire. This essay will argue that the political rhetoric surrounding Anna Dickinson's wartime career suggests a similar ideological conservativism organized around gender roles. As is commonly the case, the crisis of war opened the door for a woman to go beyond familiar practices, but the responses to Dickinson's wartime efforts helped limit their broader impact.[10]

"*She* has a right to speak in public"

Although already a celebrated public speaker, Dickinson emerged as a Republican force during the 1863 and 1864 campaigns. Pundits acknowledged that her performances played an important role in the party's successes; Connecticut Republicans dubbed her "the heroine of the triumph."[11] Rather than only praising the party (she was in fact highly critical of the moderate Lincoln administration), Dickinson specialized in biting attacks on Democratic candidates and Copperhead newspapers, interwoven with discussions of rebel misdeeds, critical analyses of unsuccessful Union generals, and calls for uncompromising patriotism. Observers found that Dickinson speeches were grand performances. She paced the stage like a caged tiger, speaking for an hour or more without notes. Although working from carefully constructed texts, she was at her best responding to a heckler or taking on a local editor, thus ensuring that each appearance had its own unique quality.

Whatever their political perspective, the nation's newspapers took Dickinson's lectures quite seriously, publishing extended summaries of her texts. Even those accounts that did not expressly discuss women in public routinely

included detailed, highly gendered discussions of Dickinson's clothing, appearance, mannerisms, and rhetorical style. After her first appearance before the
Pennsylvania Anti-Slavery Society, one Philadelphia paper made much of the
seventeen-year-old's age and appearance as well as her speaking ability, concluding "the beauty and talent of the young woman exercised a talismanic effect upon even the rudest."[12] Later the examinations of Dickinson's appearance
became more clinical, as observers seemed to look for clues to her great success.
Following a March 1862 "Lecture on Behalf of the Contrabands," The *Philadelphia Press* reported, "In person, she is rather under the medium height,
with a fine, intellectual-looking countenance, large nose, with distended nos-
trils, which, as she spoke, moved with a sort of nervous twitching. Her mouth
is rather large, with arching lips, which gives it an expression of firmness, and,
although we cannot say that the general contour of her face is pretty, we must
say that, in her general appearance, she is rather prepossessing." Another reporter concluded that "Miss Dickinson, unlike most ladies who speak in public, is young, and made a narrow escape from being pretty."[13]

The *New York Herald* attributed Dickinson's success to her "youth and
good looks" as well as her oratorical skills, noting that "[s]he has a full, gracefully rounded figure, is of the medium size of women, has a well balanced,
firmly set head, round oval face, a fresh, healthy complexion, inclining to
the hue of the brunette, and wears her dark hair in full, heavy clusters about
her neck." The *Chicago Tribune* adopted a phrenological approach, reporting,
"Her head seems to be perfectly well made, and balanced in all of its parts.
The forehead, however, is upon a closer examination capacious, and of a fine
intellectual architecture; broad in the regions of ideality, and, what the phre-
nologists call 'the top head,' is grandly developed. The back of the head is pro-
portionally large, and the whole physique, so far, gives to a careful observer
the assurance of a vigorous intellect and a high moral nature, based upon a
splendid animal background."

Such detailed physical descriptions, even when accompanied by glowing
accounts of her rhetoric, established Dickinson as a physical object whose appeal was not purely about oratorical skill.[14] As she became more financially
successful and began abandoning her staid Quaker roots, Dickinson took to
wearing custom made dresses and pieces of jewelry. By the end of the war the
newspaper accounts began including detailed examinations of her clothing
and ornaments, as well as her short-cropped curls and physical appearance.

This emphasis on Anna Dickinson's appearance suggests that she was
dismissed by some as little more than a charmingly attractive curiosity, but
other reporters—even while noting her appearance—celebrated Dickinson

as a woman in public. As early as April 1862 the *Providence Press* was applauding Dickinson as an orator in the abolitionist tradition of William Lloyd Garrison and Horace Greeley, who "with the tongue of *a dozen women* . . . combines the boldness of forty men."[15] Following Dickinson's "A Plea for Women" in late 1862, a New Hampshire newspaper declared, "There has been and still is great prejudice against female lecturers, but all reformers in all ages of the world have met with opposition. Fair minded men and women are willing to listen to all, and then act their pleasure."[16] The radical *Independent* celebrated Dickinson's April 1863 appearance at New York's Cooper Institution as a great display of women's abilities. "Those who have prejudices against women who speak in public ought not to see Miss Anna E Dickinson of Philadelphia, if they mean to keep those prejudices," the paper warned. "*She* has a right to speak in public. . . . Miss Dickinson is not a woman speaking like a man. She is a woman. She thinks and feels like a woman. And she proves beyond all controversy that there are elements of truth, and phases of public affairs, important to be known, that can be given from no other stand-point than the heart of a true woman."[17]

In June 1863, while working for the *Cincinnati Gazette,* Whitelaw Reid ventured to Philadelphia to meet the popular young orator. "Of course she is radical," Reid told his readers, "as all women of culture are likely to be . . . and, of course, like all other women, she sometimes jumps to illogical conclusions without any bother of reasoning on the road. . . . But enough! This young girl, so brilliant, so magnetic, so wonderfully gifted, is a real Genius; and God gives us so few of these, we may be pardoned the rudeness of talking about them in the newspapers."[18] Reid's comments are characteristic of many supportive responses to Dickinson's public role. On the one hand, her allies often embraced the notion of women tackling political issues at public podiums, but, on the other hand, many evaluated her performances through a distinctly gendered lens. In Reid's eyes Dickinson was both "brilliant" and "gifted" but also typically "illogical" and thus "amusing."

These efforts to place Dickinson into some received gender paradigm periodically yielded contradictory results. The *Republican* approved of her public appearances, finding that "Miss Dickinson is preeminently a woman, with nothing but a woman's artillery to conduct and propel electric forces."[19] A Philadelphia paper agreed that Dickinson's skills were distinctly feminine. She was, "[a] perfect mistress of her art, a modulated voice—no declamation, that's schoolboyish—no gesture, that's mannish—for the most part with clasped hands, clenched at times, pacing the stage when the words came too fast for her—with an occasional impatient tap of her foot—a most womanly way of rendering a speech, and, just because it is womanly, utterly incomprehensible to masculine critics."[20] And a correspondent to a San Francisco newspaper added that "Miss D. is a good reasoner . . . but still apparently delighted to leap from the slow approximations of reasoning to the swifter flights, and perhaps truer results, of a keen, womanly intuition."[21]

But other favorable accounts used distinctly masculine language to describe—and praise—her rhetorical powers. A correspondent to the *Philadelphia Press* reported that "[s]he handled her subject in a most masterly, and, I might add, statesmanlike manner, giving facts, figures and dates in such a compact and harmonious whole as to impress all with her wonderful power of memory, and intelligent comprehension of her subject."[22] Claremont, New Hampshire's *National Eagle* added that "[t]o the true woman's natural wit and readiness, she adds a masculine vigor of thought and generalization, [and] a memory never at fault."[23] A letter to another New England newspaper concluded, "She is evidently a *masculine* mind."[24] And a Pennsylvania newspaper found Dickinson "[q]uite passably handsome, with short curling hair, large and expressive eyes, a loud, ringing, masculine voice, a distinctive and forcible enunciation" but concluded that "[h]er address was *womanly* as far as logic and accuracy were concerned."[25]

Some reporters seemed to disagree about whether Dickinson's gender was a strength or a liability. The Rochester *Evening Express* declared that "Miss Dickinson has far more of this real womanhood than the thousands of Fiora McFlimseys, who would affect to despise or sneer at her for violating their rules of false delicacy in publicly laboring for human welfare."[26] Dickinson's February 1865 appearance in Portland, Maine, provided the local press with "the strongest illustration of woman's power on the platform—and the *power* carries with it the *right* to be there—that we ever witnessed," but the account added, "Her faults as a speaker are characteristic of the feminine mind . . . a propensity to use the tongue *as a lash*" and "the feminine propensity to run to extremes."[27]

These stories all shared the conviction that Anna Dickinson was an effective speaker who had every right to a public audience, and they all measured her strengths and shortcomings in gendered terms. But they shared no consensus about whether Dickinson was distinctly feminine or some masculine-like gender-transgressor who had the ability to apply male logic and masculine oratorical skills to the political problems of the day.

Although Dickinson's supporters were divided on this topic, they seemed to agree that she was unique, perhaps even Heaven-sent. Following a triumphal appearance in Hartford the *Daily Post* announced that she was "[n]ot a woman but a girl 20 years of age, a Joan of Arc that God sent into the field, as many half believed, to maintain the cause of the country at this dreadful and last crisis." The neighboring *Courant* found that Dickinson was "a noble, patriotic woman—a woman who is using the great talents given her by God for the salvation of her country in its day of trial."[28]

These themes persisted throughout her wartime career. No normal process of education and intellectual development could have produced such a young woman. Instead, her supporters seemed certain that Dickinson was sent by God to attend to the nation's urgent needs. "When the country was in its darkest," one report began, "when occupied with an infuriate foe in front, a craven, treacherous band 'assailed her in the back.' A Philadelphia woman, another maid of Orleans in youth, in chivalric daring and grave forecast, in sweet womanly grace and lambent genius . . . went forth with . . . her country-loving and God fearing womanhood—and stood among the people." In so doing Dickinson was following long established patterns: "Ever since the nation had life, women here and there, in different stations, periods and crises, have broken conventional shell or crust, peeped and piped their little hour, and disappeared."[29]

The *Chicago Tribune* adopted a similar historical perspective. "Society at large has an honest horror of the assumption by women of the functions which belong strictly to men," the paper explained. "The feeling is laudable, and ought to be respected." In recent years this concern for gender differences had taken on a new urgency "because of the dissemination amongst us of exaggerated notions concerning woman's sphere, rights and duties, and in consequence of which many good but mistaken women were induced to make very unwomanly exhibitions, much to the scandal of the sex." Nonetheless, the *Tribune* acknowledged, "Nature has endowed some women with genius and power equal to those qualities which are the chief pride of the male sex; and it will not do to shut our eyes and allow our prejudices to entirely overcome us." Anna Dickinson, the Chicago newspaper concluded, was just such a woman, capable of answering the great national need.[30]

In a similar vein, a San Francisco correspondent admitted, "I must acknowledge that I am not, in theory, predisposed to favor female oratory. We cannot afford to let the finer edge of the female character be dulled by the collisions of public life; and yet when a lady can speak as Miss Dickinson does, why, it seems to me her gift is proof of her mission."[31] So many found parallels between young Anna's great success (and combative flair) and Joan of Arc that it became commonplace for reporters to compare her with "the Maid of Orleans," thus underscoring the notion that she was some sort of spiritual, sainted phenomenon rather than merely a young woman speaking her mind.[32]

These responses to Dickinson's public appearances suggest preliminary answers to our central question. True, a radical handful witnessed Anna Dickinson's public appearances and concluded that they illustrated what women could accomplish, but far more of her political supporters selected language which seemed to explain away Dickinson's larger significance. Some attributed her fame to her physical charms, despite feminine shortcomings of logic; others explained her success as evidence that she successfully aped masculine traits. But for many Dickinson was simply a unique aberration, whose appearance on the scene reflected divine will but no larger challenge to contemporary gender roles. In this fashion Dickinson's political supporters were able to profit from her popularity without challenging their essential patriarchal world view.

The Female Termagant

Anna Dickinson's adversaries faced a different task in coming to terms with her popularity. Both her controversial words, and the fact that they were delivered by a woman, produced widespread outrage among northern Democrats. And the resulting rhetorical battles in the press were only fueled by Dickinson's fondness for selecting targets in the local media.

The early Democratic responses to Dickinson's lectures were dismissive but generally not too biting. After she called General George McClellan "either a traitor or a doughface," one reporter sheepishly acknowledged that "we have seldom heard a more eloquent speaker" whose "musical voice . . . together with her youthful appearance and winning address, make it a pleasure to listen, even though she advanced the most unwelcome sentiments."[33] Or, as a New Jersey newspaper summed up a March 1862 lecture: "It was the words of mediocrity spoken through the lips of genius."[34]

Others opted for the paternalistic assumption that Dickinson was merely a mouthpiece for the abolitionist male leadership, or worse, that the radical Republicans were shamelessly swept up by Dickinson's beauty and charm and thus unable to discern her true mediocrity.[35] These critics commonly blamed the Republicans for leading the innocent Dickinson astray. Following her 1863 appearances in Hartford, where Dickinson had received top billing at the party's election eve rally, several local papers reprinted an editorial from the *Journal of Commerce* which noted that "[p]olitical partisanship sometimes blinds men to the most ordinary rules of common sense. . . . our Republican friends . . . have forgotten the purity and delicacy that attaches to the female character."[36] The following month the *New York Herald* essentially absolved Dickinson from blame for her own actions: "The pretty face, tuneful voice and pleasant manners of the new Joan of Arc contrast ludicrously with the bloodthirsty sentiments she expresses and the reckless vituperations in which she indulges. For a young Quakeress to make such orations might be considered strange, did we not know that she is only the sweet mouthpiece through which the abolition politicians, reverend and irreverend, address the President and the public."[37]

Two years later the *Herald* was singing a very similar tune, with a bit more bite. The "gaseous matter" of Dickinson's latest speech, the James Gordon Bennett newspaper proclaimed, "from masculine lips would be dreadful enough; but coming from a woman's lips, formed only for kisses, smiles and sweet, sympathizing speech, they strike us with a nameless horror. . . . The war has produced many revolutions; but we had no idea that it could so revolutionize a woman's holy nature." But once again the *Herald* concluded that "Miss Dickinson is really much more to be pitied than blamed [whereas] . . . those contemptible cowards who hide behind her petticoats and bid her utter the black and bloody sentences which their craven tongues, less defiant than their reckless minds, dare not frame in public" were the true villains.[38] In this fashion Dickinson's political adversaries used her gender to dismiss her, while also calling into question the manhood of those supporters who had thrust her into the public eye.

The language selected to belittle Dickinson is quite telling. In addition to claiming that she merely rehashed the words of her male Republican handlers, several commentators tried to portray Dickinson as a mentally unstable spiritualist.[39] The highly partisan *World* dubbed Dickinson the "Political Witch," claiming that she was the latest in a recent proliferation of practitioners of "feminine astrology."[40] Such comments on Dickinson's otherworldly nature present an interesting parallel to those of her supporters who contended that she was sent by God. Either perspective implicitly dismissed Dickinson's significance as a pathbreaking woman in the public sphere.

Others openly attacked Dickinson as a gender transgressor. Many joined the *West Jersey Pioneer* in opining that "[t]he young lady in question cannot do better than exchange the harassing duties of public life for those serener and domestic walks so befitting her sex."[41] Or, as another paper took pains to point out: "The province of woman is too well understood to need explanation now. She is the home angel, not the politician. . . . we should disgrace the gentle and noble character of our American women if we encourage them to the public exhibition of political preferences."[42] Even observers who were sympathetic to Dickinson's positions expressed reservations at her actions. A correspondent to the *New York Evangelist* admitted, "We have no patience for the twaddle for 'woman's rights,' and no especial liking for the itinerant Amazons who have gone crusading through the land." Still, within minutes after Dickinson begins speaking "you forget whether it were a man, or a woman, or one of Mary Wollstonecraft's 'third sex' who was pulling at your heartstrings." Nevertheless, after much back and forth about women in public, the author declared his fervid hope that Dickinson's actions would not be duplicated: "We are no more anxious to hear a woman's voice in our Church-meetings, or on the political rostrum, than we ever were. We are fully persuaded that 'woman's mission' is quite in another direction."[43]

By the time she appeared at the Cooper Institute in 1863, Anna Dickinson's fiercest Copperhead adversaries were ready to take the gloves off. "Someone has said that a woman's name should appear in print but twice—when she is married and when she dies," declared the *World* in a lengthy editorial. "Miss Anna E Dickinson, of Philadelphia, is evidently of the contrary opinion, as likewise are Henry Ward Beecher and Senator Morgan, who countenanced a female of that name, night before last, in indecencies of speech which would have disgraced a pot-house brawler of the other sex."[44] Many of the *World's* critiques mined familiar veins. Dickinson had merely offered "the hack arguments of male politicians reiterated in tones an octave higher." But the New York paper went much further in attacking Dickinson's womanhood and the masculinity of her supporters: "Mirrors, it is said, are unlike women, inasmuch as they reflect without speaking, while women are apt to speak without reflecting; but Miss Dickinson in speaking mirrored her audience. Divested of the grace of her sex, as they of the humanity of theirs, stripped of the gentleness and charity and puremindedness of woman as they of the dignity and sobriety and wisdom of men, she unsexed and they without sense, the exhibition was one which no woman of refinement and no man of good sense could witness without blushing for her kind."[45]

These attacks proved too much for Dickinson's supporters to swallow. The *Philadelphia Press* charged the editor of the *World* with having sunk to new lows by "abusing a woman" thus "relinquish[ing] all claim to the consideration of gentlemen." The *Press* admitted some discomfort with "the propriety of Miss Dickinson's appearance before the public as a speaker" but concluded that "she has followed what seemed to her to be a holy and conscientious mission." The essence of the *Press*'s defense was that the *World* had treated a lady in an "unmanly manner." Thus, even her political supporters in the press—presumably mirroring the sensibilities of their readers—fell back on gender paradigms in defending Dickinson.[46]

This sort of highly gendered rhetorical battle between Democratic and Republican newspapers, often involving bitter rivals within the same city, followed Dickinson wherever she traveled. After the *Hartford Times* published a particularly unflattering account of her March 1863 lecture, the *Courant* responded, "We had supposed that the editor of the *Times* had some little spark of manliness left in him, and that when he found he had been convicted of grossly maligning a woman he would have had the decency to retract, and make the apology due from a gentleman."[47] When the Portland *Argus* criticized the orator for accepting a fee for her Chicago performances, the Portland *Press* declared that its adversary had "cowardly and ruffian-like, *dealt a blow at a woman*, whose only shield is her virtue; whose only defense is her spotless purity and good works."[48]

Following an appearance in upstate New York, the Copperhead *Courier and Union* published a particularly virulent attack on "Short Haired Anna." The report, full of explicit gendered imagery, is worth extensive quotation:

> "SHORT HAIRED" ANNA—The female lecture termagant, who is now doing the dirty work for the Radicals, in the usual 'spread eagle' style of the strong-minded, brazen-faced sex who eschew womanly dignity, and make the rostrum take the place of the cradle and baby-jumper, is just now in great favor with the admirers of the unsexed; and, as a natural consequence, she flutters her plumage of feathers in the face of the community, and in this way makes a very pitiable effort to bedaub a certain class whom she is hired to abuse, with the slime from her unclean nest. The strong-minded of her sex applaud her when she says anything remarkably smutty and out of place in a woman.

The *Courier and Union* paid particular attention to "the notices which Miss Dickinson has received from that portion of the admiring press that best appreciates her mental capabilities." The Copperhead paper quoted extensively from a detailed physical description in the admiring *Standard* which praised "the 'symmetrical young creature'" and her "'well knit agility of frame'" all the way down to "the *lower fold* of her plain, Quaker-brown dress, which was so intently gazed upon by the stripling reporter of the *Standard*, whose craven and lasivious [*sic*] tastes rivited [*sic*] his huge owlish eyes in that direction!" These attacks followed familiar lines, with special barbs aimed at Dickinson's supporters in the press, but notice how the editorial has sexualized the young orator, both in its physical description of her "'spread eagle' style" and in the detailed characterization of the *Standard's* fawning portrayal. Moreover, this account is free with condemnation of Dickinson's "slime," "filth-throwing," and general vulgarity. By way of explanation, the author noted, "We are not ordinarily in the habit of criticizing women; but when leaving the sanctity of their home retirement and the privacy of womanly pursuits, they assume manhood's tasks and enter the political arena" where rough and tumble debate was the norm. "For ourselves," the editorial continued, "we believe that woman in her household sphere, discharging faithfully its duties of love, training, sympathy and protection, and purifying and ennobling her home and social circle, has a diviner mission and a nobler and brighter, if a more humble sphere." Dickinson's male supporters, the newspaper concluded, should "consult the New Testament and see what it says as to women talking in public meetings."[49]

Anna Dickinson's triumphant appearance before Congress in January 1864 pushed some of her most dedicated critics to new heights of outrage. The *New York World's* response was particularly inflamed:

> There is really nothing remarkable about this young woman. She is a very ordinary-looking person, with a harsh voice, an unfeminine manner, and a parrot-like flow of words. What she says is merely a rehash of the loose and violent assertions of the extreme radical journalists and orators. She attracts crowds when she speaks, by appealing to the same love of the marvelous and monstrous which Barnum has made his fortune in exhibiting woolly horses, dwarfs, Feejee mermaids, and other queer fish. Yet this silly young person was allowed the use of the hall of Representatives last Saturday to make one of her unwomanly displays.

This critique combines many of the Copperhead strategies for marginalizing Dickinson: as unfeminine, as a "parrot" for the opinions of others, and as little more than a sideshow. After Dickinson repeated her Washington lecture in New York, the *Rochester Union* suggested that "she ought to be pointed to the famous woman order of Gen. Butler, whom she so much admires, and be made to understand that with suitable variations it meets her case exactly. So long as she mounts the political stump so long she will be treated as 'a woman plying her vocation.'"[50]

The *Geneva (N.Y.) Gazette* ran a long essay attacking "Anna E. Dickinson and the Gynaekokracy." This extended diatribe built on the established theme that Dickinson represented a larger evil in social development. Applying a fascinating variant on familiar anatomical metaphors for political life, the *Gazette* argued that periodically "idiosyncracies . . . originate and throw to the surface certain manifestations of disease more or less loathsome and distressing; just as in a morbid state of the human body, boils and carbuncles are produced upon the surface by insidious causes seated perhaps in the vital forces of the system."

"Among the excrescences upon the body politic," the article continued, "is one which may be best described by its Greek name Gynaekokracy, which manifests itself in the absurd endeavors of women to usurp the places and execute the functions of the male sex. It is a moral and social monstrosity— an inversion, bouleversement of the laws of nature, which have assigned to each sex its appropriate relations and duties; and a subversion, so far as it prevails, of some of the fundamental principles of morality and social order." The author—who apparently had never heard Dickinson speak—summarized her lectures as "entirely political, intensely partisan and objugatory, made up chiefly of extracts from Wendell Phillips, Charles Sumner and Horace Greeley, loosely put together, and delivered with great self-possession, flippancy and boldness." Her successes had encouraged "many rivals" to "[spring] up from among the young girls of the country" but the article was pleased to note that "to the credit of the sex . . . so far as is known to the writer, she has not been encouraged in this career by respectable ladies. Her sphere is with the men, and all sensible and modest women, who have a regard for the proprieties of the sex, will be content to leave it there."[51]

By early 1865, as the war was winding down, the venom of the attacks on Dickinson seemed to increase. In February, only days after the *New York Herald* had attacked her "gaseous" performance at the Cooper Institute, the *New York Daily News* added further reflections on the Dickinson phenomenon:

> The war has, in fact, rallied to its support all the social radicalisms of the country, and from Abolition to miscegenation, free love and woman's rights, they have been let loose to rush shrieking through the land to the horror of all decency and common sense. Miss Anna Dickenson [*sic*] is . . . one of the illustrations of the revolution that rules the hour. As a woman she would command the charity of our silence; but in discharge of our duty as a journalist we are bound, very sorely against our will, to deal with her as an advocate and example of a dangerous system of ethics.

Dismissing her, like many of its Democratic colleagues, as a mere "parrot" to abolitionist ideas, the *Daily News* concluded, "The factionists by whom the lady is thrust into a position so false are evil counselors for a woman, and, we can assure Miss Dickinson, have placed her outside the sphere proper to a true woman. This blunt speaking is not only a duty to society in her case, but is a duty of manly frankness to the lady herself."[52] A few days later the *Providence Daily Post* concluded that "Miss Dickinson is a good specimen of a very useless sort of woman."[53]

Conclusion

Only a few weeks before the end of the war Dickinson traveled to Lawrence, Massachusetts, to deliver her new lecture on "Women's Work and Wages." Both local papers praised the performer and the performance, but the *Lawrence Sentinel* still concluded that "[w]e trust she will refrain from political discussion. There are other softer and more womanly themes in the intellectual storehouse—that sit more gracefully on her lips."[54] That is, the newspaper was perfectly willing to grant that Dickinson had earned her place at the public rostrum, but it still wished that she would maintain ladylike decorum by steering clear of partisan political topics, thus suggesting a different take on separate spheres, defined by topic rather than place.

Throughout the Civil War, northern newspapers had divided over Anna Dickinson's political messages, and, to a lesser extent, over the propriety of her public appearances. Many of Dickinson's supporters joined the *Sentinel* in admitting that they were happiest when she steered clear of the masculine world of partisan politics. During the crisis Republicans needed Dickinson to support their cause, but only the radical minority suggested that Dickinson's public appearances should be viewed as evidence of woman's larger capacity. Others, at least implicitly, marginalized Dickinson and thus minimized her gender significance by emphasizing her physical characteristics or her masculine oratorical skills, or by linking her to the sainted Joan of Arc or some other otherworldly imagery. In so doing, Dickinson's political allies could profit from her celebrity and oratorical power while avoiding the taint of woman's rights.

In the meantime, Dickinson's adversaries grew bold in attacking her femininity as a means of dismissing her message. They portrayed Dickinson as the worst sort of "unsexed" gender transgressor, thoroughly beyond the bounds of proper human discourse. Her supporters were happy to fight the battle along gendered lines, blasting Copperhead editors as unmanly for their crude comments about the lady orator. In this fashion they were able to set themselves up as the defenders of womanhood—and separate gender spheres—while at least implicitly supporting Dickinson's political content.

Although today largely forgotten, or historically marginalized, Anna Dickinson's wartime career sheds new light on the two intertwined issues that shaped this essay: the role of women in nineteenth-century public life and the Civil War experiences of American women. Dickinson's stump-speaking career dramatically exceeded the midcentury public political appearances of her most celebrated female contemporaries, suggesting, on the one hand, the breadth of possibilities for Civil War–era public women, and, on the other hand, demonstrating the rule that is best illustrated through the exception. My emphasis here has been less on the activities of this exceptional woman than on what can be learned by examining the range of responses to her public oratory.[55] These responses demonstrate that midcentury gender assumptions were neither fixed nor universally held. The various newspaper reports show that there was a commonly accepted notion of separate gender spheres, but that the shape and rigidity of those spheres was subject to continual negotiation. By pushing at the edges of what was familiar and—to many—acceptable, Dickinson provided the context for an ongoing examination of the proper roles for both women and men. And as I have argued, those who favored her opinions but were uncomfortable with her public role found various strategies to circumscribe the enduring effect of her gender transgressions.

It is perhaps fitting that Dickinson emerged as a public figure in the midst of the Civil War. After all, the demands of war drew thousands of women into unaccustomed roles in both the North and the South. It may even be the case, as some reports suggested, that the sectional crisis made some listeners particularly receptive to the wisdom of a woman's perspective. Dickinson's own wartime correspondence and speeches do not provide much support for the idea that she felt called, *as a woman,* to enter the public arena in this time of crisis. In other guises Dickinson was a strong public advocate for women, both during and after the war, supporting suffrage and delivering powerful speeches defending the interests of working women, prostitutes, and Morman wives. But in her wartime political stump speeches Dickinson did not suggest that she was offering a woman's perspective on politics, nor in any sense advance the idea that she was bringing the domestic sphere into political discourse. Dickinson's motivations for becoming a Republican stump speaker appear to have been threefold: She felt a deep passion for the war effort in general, and the interests of African Americans in particular; she was under tremendous financial pressure to support herself, her older sister, and her widowed mother, and lecturing promised excellent financial returns; and she clearly loved public speaking and national celebrity.[56]

Dickinson's own motivations and sense of self further complicate our understanding of nineteenth-century gender assumptions. Although a public advocate for women, Dickinson did not go onto the Republican stump as part of that agenda and apparently did not claim, either in her public statements or in her private correspondence, that her gender identity gave her a distinctive voice. In no sense was she claiming to bring a domestic perspective to the political platform.[57] But regardless of her own sense of identity, Dickinson's audiences observed her performances through a gendered lens, absorbing her words in the context of her appearance, clothing, haircut, and mannerisms. And the press—friend and foe alike—refracted her words through their own version of that lens as well. Thus, the public discourse about her lectures commonly devolved into debates predicated on gender distinctiveness, even while Dickinson asserted no such claim to a particular woman's voice.

Following the war Dickinson became one of the nation's most active, and best paid, lyceum speakers. When the support for the lyceum circuit waned, she turned to the theater, as both an actress and playwright. She also published three books, including a controversial novel about miscegenation.[58] In 1872 Dickinson returned to the political arena to campaign for Horace Greeley and the Liberal Republicans. Sixteen years later she made a brief, ill-fated, venture back into the political arena as a Republican stump speaker. In 1891 her sister, Susan, had Anna committed to an asylum for the insane. Dickinson eventually won her freedom and then sued those responsible for her incarceration—and the newspapers that had reported her insanity—in a series of celebrated legal battles, before retiring to obscurity in upstate New York.

Although she remained in the public eye for nearly three decades after the war, Dickinson's reduced political voice supports Morton Keller's argument that there was a conservative process of postwar retrenchment: Public activity that was accepted in 1864 was no longer as permissible in peacetime, leading Dickinson to turn to the popular lyceum circuit. But Dickinson's brief return to the stump during the unusual election of 1872 does suggest a postwar political world in flux. Once again political crisis opened the door for an expanded role for women. With the Republicans divided, and the notorious Victoria Woodhull throwing her own hat in the ring, the Greeley and Grant forces competed mightily for Dickinson's support. But this time Dickinson was hardly alone as a partisan public woman. Grant, ostensibly an advocate of women's suffrage, lined up an impressive list of female orators and public figures on his side, while Greeley only succeeded in garnering the support of his old friend and ally Anna Dickinson.

The contrast between the campaigns of 1864 and 1872 was striking. Although women were still disenfranchised and would remain so for another half century, in this election both major parties were anxious to trumpet endorsements from the nation's leading public women. Between Woodhull's flamboyant campaign and Susan B. Anthony's arrest and trial for voting in the presidential election, 1872 is recognized as an important benchmark in the history of women in public.[59] But too often forgotten is the role that Anna Dickinson played two elections earlier when she campaigned for Lincoln and other Republican candidates while most of her peers in the woman's rights movement remained on the sidelines or behind the scenes.[60] Dickinson's unpopular decision to support Greeley, who died shortly after losing the election, cost her quite a bit in political friendships, in future lecture fees, and perhaps in her place in historic memory. But one wonders how much her bold political speech during the Civil War paved the way for the modest gains of the next decades.[61]

NOTES

1. This essay is part of an ongoing biographical study of the life of Anna Dickinson. The only published biography of Dickinson is Giraud Chester, *Embattled Maiden: The Life of Anna Dickinson* (New York: Putnam, 1951). James Harvey Young, who also wrote a dissertation on Dickinson's wartime career, authored a biography that has never been published. I am indebted to Dr. Young for permission to inspect both this manuscript ("Anna Elizabeth Dickinson") and his extensive research notes in the James Harvey Young Papers, Special Collections, Emory University, Atlanta, Georgia (hereafter JHY Papers). For brief treatments of Dickinson's war years see Elizabeth Cady Stanton et al., eds., *History of Woman Suffrage*, 3 vols. (1881; New York: Arno Press, 1969), 2:40–50; Young, "Anna Elizabeth Dickinson and the Civil War: For and Against Lincoln," *Mississippi Valley Historical Review* 31 (June 1944): 59–80; and Wendy Hamand Venet, *Neither Ballots nor Bullets: Women Abolitionists and the Civil War* (Charlottesville: University Press of Virginia, 1991), 37–56 and passim. For my own overview of "Anna E. Dickinson's Civil War," see Steven E. Woodworth, ed., *The Human Tradition in the Civil War and Reconstruction* (Wilmington, Del.: SR Books, 2000), 93–110. For Dickinson's personal responses to her wartime career, see J. Matthew Gallman, "An Inspiration to Work: Anna Elizabeth Dickinson, Public Orator," in *The War Was You and Me: Civilians in the American Civil War*, ed. Joan E. Cashin (Princeton, N.J.: Princeton University Press, 2002).

2. *Chicago Tribune,* November 18, 1863, Dickinson Scrapbook, art. 125, Anna Elizabeth Dickinson Papers, microfilm reel 25, Library of Congress, Washington, D.C. Hereafter, Dickinson Scrapbook.

3. The literature on women in public is vast. See Mary P. Ryan, *Women in Public: Between Banners and Ballots, 1825–1880* (Baltimore: Johns Hopkins University Press, 1990); Lori Ginzberg, *Women and the Work of Benevolence: Morality, Politics, and Class in the Nineteenth-Century United States* (New Haven, Conn.: Yale University Press, 1990); Glenna Matthews, *The Rise of Public Woman: Woman's Power and Woman's Place in the United States, 1630–1970* (New York: Oxford University Press, 1992); Mary Ryan, "Gender and Public Access: Women's Politics in Nineteenth-Century America," in *Habermas and the Public Sphere,* ed. Craig Calhoun (Cambridge: Harvard University Press, 1992), 259–88 and note 4.

4. For an excellent overview of the discussion, see Linda K. Kerber, "Separate Spheres, Female Worlds, Woman's Place: The Rhetoric of Women's History," *Journal of American History* (June 1988): 9–39.

5. There are scattered examples of women giving political speeches during the 1850s and into the war years. Elizabeth Varon has uncovered cases of Whigs inviting women to speak before mixed audience in antebellum Virginia. Abolitionist Clarina Nichols spoke for Kansas Republicans in 1856. As Dickinson's wartime popularity grew, Democrats periodically countered with female orators to support their own candidates. Nevertheless, no wartime (or antebellum) woman approached Dickinson's fame as a political orator. Elizabeth R. Varon, "Tippecanoe and the Ladies, Too: White Women and Party Politics in Antebellum Virginia," *Journal of American History* 82 (1995): 494–521; Varon, *We Mean to Be Counted: White Women and Politics in Antebellum Virginia* (Chapel Hill: University of North Carolina Press, 1998); Robert J. Dinkin, *Before Equal Suffrage: Women in Partisan Politics from Colonial Times to 1920* (Westport, Conn.: Greenwood Press, 1995); Rebecca Edwards, *Angels in the Machinery: Gender in American Party Politics from the Civil War to the Progressive Era* (New York: Oxford University Press, 1997). See also Janet L. Coryell, "Superseding Gender: The Role of the Woman Politico in Antebellum Partisan Politics," in *Women and the Unstable State in Nineteenth-Century America,* ed. Alison M. Parker and Stephanie Cole (College Station: Texas A&M Press, 2000), 84–112.

6. Frank Moore, *Women of the War; Their Heroism and Self-Sacrifice* (Hartford, Conn.: S. S. Scranton, 1866); Linus Pierpoint Brockett and Mary C. Vaughan, *Woman's Work in the Civil War: A Record of Heroism, Patriotism and Patience* (Boston: R. H. Curran, 1867).

7. For a recent summary of this scholarship, see Drew Gilpin Faust, "'Ours as Well as That of the Men': Women and Gender in the Civil War," in *Writing the Civil War: The Quest to Understand,* ed. James M. McPherson and William J. Cooper Jr. (Columbia: University of South Carolina Press, 1998), 228–40. A few important books have appeared since that essay was published: Jeanie Attie, *Patriotic Toil: Northern Women and the American Civil War* (Ithaca, N.Y.: Cornell University Press, 1998); Elizabeth D.

Leonard, *All the Daring of the Soldier: Women of the Civil War Armies* (New York: W.W. Norton, 1999); Judith Ann Giesberg, *Civil War Sisterhood: The U.S. Sanitary Commission and Women's Politics in Transition* (Boston: Northeastern University Press, 2000).

8. See Venet, *Neither Ballots nor Bullets;* Attie, *Patriotic Toil;* Giesberg, *Civil War Sisterhood.*

9. Attie, *Patriotic Toil,* 25.

10. Morton Keller, *Affairs of State: Public Life in Late Nineteenth Century America* (Cambridge: Harvard University Press, 1977).

11. *Springfield Republican,* June ?, 1863, Dickinson Scrapbook, art. 79.

12. Unknown newspaper, n.d. [October 1860?], Dickinson Scrapbook, art. 19. Of course, contemporary accounts of male orators also reported on their appearance and physical bearing.

13. *United States Gazette?* [handwritten notation], n.d. [roughly March 26, 1862], Dickinson Scrapbook, art. 11.

14. *Press,* March 26, 1862, Dickinson Scrapbook, art. 10; *New York Herald,* n.d., quoted in *National Anti-Slavery Standard,* April 25, 1863; *Chicago Tribune,* November 5, 1863.

15. *Providence Press,* [April 1862], reprinted in unknown newspaper, n.d., Dickinson Scrapbook, art. 20.

16. Unknown newspaper, December 15, 1862, Dickinson Scrapbook, art. 98.

17. *Independent,* [April 1863], reprinted in unknown newspaper, n.d., Dickinson Scrapbook, art. 76

18. *Cincinnati Gazette?* June 22, 1863, Dickinson Scrapbook, art. 92. The newspaper is unlabeled but the story is identified as from a correspondent to the *Gazette.* The story is signed by "Agate," a name used by Reid. A letter from Judge William D. Kelley to Dickinson confirms that this letter was written by Reid. Kelley to AED, August 20, 1863, container 9, Dickinson Papers.

19. *Republican,* April 23, 1863, Dickinson Scrapbook, art. 84.

20. Unknown Philadelphia newspaper [May 1863], Dickinson Scrapbook, art. 116.

21. Unknown San Francisco newspaper [October 1864?], Dickinson Scrapbook, art. 154–55.

22. "Correspondent to the *Philadelphia Press,*" reprinted in several unknown papers, October 29, 1864, Dickinson Scrapbook, arts. 87, 163, 168.

23. *National Eagle,* March 10, 1863, Dickinson Scrapbook, art. 29.

24. *Greenfield Gazette?* January 4, 1864, Dickinson Scrapbook, art. 157.

25. *Luzerne Union,* n.d. [October 3, 1863?], Dickinson Scrapbook, art. 148.

26. Rochester *Evening Express,* March 15, 1864, Dickinson Scrapbook, art. 210.

27. [*Portland, Maine?*] *Transcript,* February 18, 1865, Dickinson Scrapbook, art. 227.

28. *Hartford Daily Post,* March 24, 1863; *Hartford Courant,* March 25, 1863.

29. *Republican,* April 23, 1863, Dickinson Scrapbook, art. 84.

30. *Chicago Tribune,* November 11, 1863.

31. Unknown San Francisco newspaper, [October 1864?], Dickinson Scrapbook, art. 154–55.

32. See *Springfield Republican,* April 22, 1863, Dickinson Scrapbook, art. 76; "Correspondent to the *Missouri Democrat,*" January 18, 1864, Dickinson Scrapbook, art. 166.

33. Unknown newspaper [late 1862], Dickinson Scrapbook, art. 8. For similar sentiments, see *Luzerne Union,* n.d. [October 3, 1863?], Dickinson Scrapbook, art. 148.

34. Unknown newspaper ["for the *West Jersey Pioneer*"], n.d. [March 1862], Dickinson Scrapbook, art. 23.

35. See unknown Hartford newspaper, n.d., Dickinson Scrapbook, art. 43.

36. *Hartford Times,* April 6, 1863, and unknown newspaper [April 1863], Dickinson Scrapbook, art. 111. Both reprinted an undated article from the *Journal of Commerce.*

37. *New York Herald,* n.d. [May 1863], Dickinson Scrapbook, art. 100b.

38. *New York Herald,* February 15, 1865, Dickinson Scrapbook, art. 255.

39. *Hartford Times,* March 30, 1863.

40. *World,* May 4, 1863. See also *New York Express,* n.d. [May 8, 1863?], Dickinson Scrapbook, art. 101.

41. *West Jersey Pioneer?* n.d. [March 1862?], Dickinson Scrapbook, art. 23.

42. *Journal of Commerce,* reprinted in *Hartford Times,* April 6, 1863.

43. Unknown newspaper quoting "from the *New York Evangelist,*" n.d. [April 1863], Dickinson Scrapbook, art. 164b.

44. Henry Ward Beecher was a celebrated minister and abolitionist; "Senator Morgan" presumably refers to Senator Edwin Dennison Morgan of New York.

45. *World,* n.d. [April 1863], reprinted in unknown newspaper, n.d. [April 1863], Dickinson Scrapbook, art. 72–73.

46. *Philadelphia Press,* April 18, 1863, Dickinson Scrapbook, art. 83.

47. *Hartford Courant,* March 25, 1863.

48. Unknown newspaper, n.d. [November 1863], Dickinson Scrapbook, art. 124. This art. includes a lengthy excerpt from the *Press* which included quotations from the *Argus.*

49. [*Rochester?*] *Courier and Union,* November 18, 1863, Dickinson Scrapbook, art. 161–62.

50. Unknown newspaper quoting both the *World* and the *Union,* Dickinson Scrapbook, art. 168. The author was referring to General Benjamin Butler's infamous Order Number 28 which he issued while in command of occupied New Orleans. The order threatened to treat the ladies of New Orleans like "women of the streets" if they persisted in insulting the Union soldiers. This comment is particularly interesting given that the women of New Orleans had prompted General Butler's ire by their actions within the public arena. See Ryan, *Women in Public,* 143–45.

51. *Geneva (N.Y.) Gazette* [March 1864?], reprinted in *National Anti-Slavery Gazette,* April 2, 1864.

52. *New York Daily News,* February 20, 1865, Dickinson Scrapbook, art. 256.

53. *Providence Daily Post*, March 16, 1865, Dickinson Scrapbook, art. 245.

54. *Lawrence Sentinel,* April 1, 1865, Dickinson Scrapbook, art. 249; *Lawrence American,* April 1, 1865, Dickinson Scrapbook, art. 389.

55. For some thoughts on the other side of the equation, on how Dickinson navigated the war years herself, see Gallman, "An Inspiration to Work."

56. Ibid.

57. My argument here is not that Dickinson was somehow unaware that her audiences saw her as a woman and therefore distinctive, but that she asserted her right to speak on the implicit grounds of gender equality and not gender distinctiveness. For early analyses of the links between an ideology of domesticity and various aspects of public activism, see Cott, *Bonds of Womanhood;* Kathryn Kish Sklar, *Catherine Beecher: A Study in American Domesticity* (New York: Norton, 1976); and Nancy A. Hewitt, *Women's Activism and Social Change: Rochester, New York, 1822–1872* (Ithaca, N.Y.: Cornell University Press, 1984). In her study of nine women authors, Lyde Cullen Sizer examines how these writers used their prose to engage in political discourse, often from a standpoint of gender difference. *The Political Work of Northern Women Writers and the Civil War, 1850–1872* (Chapel Hill: University of North Carolina Press, 2000).

58. *What Answer?* (1868; Amherst, N.Y.: Humanity Books, 2003); *A Paying Investment* (Boston: R. Osgood, 1876); *A Ragged Register: Of People, Places and Opinions* (1879; Estes Park, Colo.: Temporal Mechanical Press, 2000).

59. See Kathleen Barry, *Susan B. Anthony: A Biography of a Singular Feminist* (New York: New York University Press, 1988), 249–74; Barbara Goldsmith, *Other Powers: The Age of Suffrage, Spiritualism, and the Scandalous Victoria Woodhull* (New York: A. A. Knopf, 1998).

60. Melanie Susan Gustafson, *Women and the Republican Party, 1854–1924* (Urbana: University of Illinois Press, 2001). This is not to say that women were silent or entirely ignored during the election of 1864. For evidence to the contrary, see Faye Dudden, "New York Strategy: The New York Women's Movement and the Civil War," in *Votes for Women: The Struggle for Suffrage Revisited,* ed. Jean H. Baker (New York: Oxford University Press, 2002), 68–72.

61. For an analysis of the 1872 campaign, and particularly of Dickinson's efforts to recast public memories of the war, see J. Matthew Gallman, "Anna Dickinson and the Election of 1872," in *The Memory of the Civil War in American Culture,* ed. Alice Fahs and Joan Waugh (Chapel Hill: University of North Carolina Press, 2003); Dinkin, *Before Equal Suffrage,* 67–70.

SIX

The Cold Spring Tragedy

Murder, Money, and Women's Business in the Gilded Age

Wendy Gamber

On Sunday, September 13, 1868, the news that the bodies of a man and a woman had been discovered at Cold Spring—a popular resort northwest of Indianapolis—"electrified" the city. Those who surveyed the remains confronted a grisly sight. "The right side of the [man's] face and a portion of [his] head had been torn off," apparently by the shotgun that lay a few feet away; the woman's body had been badly burned from the chest down ("Burned to a Crisp," the Indianapolis *Journal* delicately put it), so badly "that the intestines were uncovered, the flesh had been burned from the thighs, and the bones partially calcined."[1]

Subsequent revelations did little to diminish the sensational nature of what became known as the "Cold Spring Tragedy." Members of the "great crowd" that gathered at the scene identified the bodies as those of "Mr. Jacob Young and his wife, Nancy J. Young, well known and highly respectable residents of Indianapolis." The Youngs' reputations and forensic evidence dismissed initial suppositions of murder-suicide. By every indication, they had been happily married. More convincingly, the position of Jacob Young's body relative to the shotgun and the discovery that Nancy Young had been shot with a different weapon—a pistol—and dealt a blow to the head with a blunt instrument argued that both husband and wife were victims of foul play. Additional evidence only further inflamed a public reeling from the news that two "harmless and respected people" had been murdered. Investigators at the scene discovered a footprint that did not match the shoes of the victims, "the print of a neat little lady's gaiter in the yielding soil. Who *could* she be?" asked the *Journal?* "A woman in such a crime. . . . We sickened as we thought of it."[2]

The woman who allegedly fired the shot that killed Nancy Young was Nancy E. Clem, the wife of William F. Clem, "a man of excellent character" who ran a "flourishing" grocery business.[3] Unbeknownst to her adoring husband, Clem was engaged in a flourishing business of another sort; subsequent discussions would revolve around the meaning of her economic adventures. As the *Journal*'s outburst suggests, Clem's sex does much to explain the extraordinary attention the case attracted. Indeed, it occupied local newspapers for months—even years—and received national attention.[4] More than a sensational murder case—or perhaps, precisely because it aroused considerable notoriety—the "Cold Spring Tragedy" suggests ways in which gender infiltrated public discussions of crime and punishment.

In broadest terms, the "tragedy" reveals competing conceptions of women's place in late-nineteenth-century public life. It illuminates, I should make clear, women's relation to a particular *kind* of public life, their position in a rapidly expanding and increasing corrupt economy. As Edith Sparks has perceptively argued, scholarship concerned with women in public rarely considers commercial publics. Influenced by the Habermasian notion of a public sphere, it instead focuses on women's actual or symbolic presence in civic ceremonies, urban spaces, and political campaigns. Morton Keller's more expansive conception of public life, which emphasizes the interplay between politics, society, and economy, offers a more useful entree into the controversies that animated the Cold Spring affair, controversies that centered on "women's business."[5] At the same time, however, the case complicates the very idea of public life, because it stubbornly resists clear distinctions between public and private. At stake was not simply whether women should engage in business, but the relationship between women's "public" economic activities and the "private" political economy of marriage. At stake was nothing less than patriarchy itself.

Trials, Stories, and "Women's Business"

I use the term "women's business" not merely to denote female entrepreneurial ventures but to encompass the entire range of women's economic activity and its perceived relationship to their status as wives and daughters. We know a great deal about female wage-earners; historians' efforts have yielded nuanced, often brilliant, insights into the politics of wage work, the internal dynamics of working-class families, and the individual and collective protests of working women and men. We are beginning to learn about the lives and careers of female entrepreneurs.[6] Yet scholars of the late nineteenth century have shed little light on the wider sphere of working-class and especially middle-class women's economic activity—the power, however limited, they wielded as property owners and bank depositors, the economic arrangements they negotiated with fathers and husbands, the value accorded their unpaid household labor.[7] Partly this is because the still-powerful paradigm of separate spheres dissuades us from locating women, especially those of the middle classes, in the nineteenth-century marketplace. Partly this is because our narrow definitions of labor (usually meaning wage work) and business (usually connoting the tangible solidity of the store, factory, or corporation) obscure the multiple junctures at which women (and men) entered economic life. Yet the Cold Spring case presented a referendum on women's business, broadly defined. It raised important and quite troubling questions in the process. Were women the independent economic actors that legal reforms increasingly suggested they should be? Or were husband and wife still "one" in practice, if not in the law?

The courtroom rhetoric the case generated spoke to precisely these issues. The stories that opposing attorneys told allow us to examine women's business at a particularly important juncture in American history—the immediate aftermath of the Civil War. If, as Hendrik Hartog suggests, antebellum legal transformations meant that husbands exerted less control over their wives by midcentury, the experience of modern war—which threw thousands of wives and daughters on their own resources, some temporarily, others permanently—further eroded patriarchal authority. From the vantage point of the late 1860s, the success of official and unofficial attempts to "reconstruct the family" was far from preordained. As early as the 1850s legislative opponents of an enhanced married women's property law envisioned wives who competed directly with their husbands, "becoming . . . adventurer[s] in the marts of trade." Such fears only multiplied as pecuniary necessity forced more and more women to enter the "marts."[8]

Indeed, the powerful and historically specific links the Cold Spring case forged between business and gender do much to explain the intensity with which it was received. Generalized economic uncertainty reinforced more specific concerns about the stability of the political economy of marriage. Widespread corruption, questionable currency, massive urban growth, and the specter of oligopoly indelibly marked the post–Civil War years; at the same time an individualistic vision, one that promoted the illusion that all parties to increasingly sacred contracts stood on equal footing, gradually eclipsed the once radical notion of free labor.[9] Marital instability and acquisitive individualism represented a potentially explosive combination; they raised the possibility that women might successfully navigate the economy as individuals rather than as wives and daughters, that they might enter the marketplace on their own terms. Cultural constraints—the limited number of available female employments, the paltry value women's work garnered in a supposedly rational labor market, the limited control married women exercised over their own earnings—rendered such excursions unlikely. But Nancy Clem demonstrated the advantages the Gilded Age offered less than scrupulous "adventurers" of either sex. The confidence man, in other words, might be a woman. The confidence woman might be someone's "faithful" wife.

My interest here is less with "what happened," with who "really" committed the murders, than with what trial records tell us about the larger society and culture in which they were conceived. Nor am I concerned with whether the actors in the Cold Spring case were somehow "representative" of the city, state, or nation in which they lived. Rather, I focus on the stories that the attorneys on both sides constructed to "explain" the case to successive juries. My analysis owes much to legal scholars who see trials as narratives, who examine the process of "storytelling in the courtroom." The stories that lawyers tell need to make sense in two respects. They allow jurors to make sense of inconclusive and often contradictory evidence. If they are to persuade, they also need to make cultural sense. They help their audiences—jurors, spectators, and members of the reading public—grapple with larger social issues; they may even articulate new problems—and new solutions.[10] Faced with "facts" that made little sense in light of preexisting interpretations of women and crime, prosecution and defense almost certainly drew inspiration from postwar discussions of women's uncertain economic status. In the process they fashioned new narratives of female guilt and innocence, narratives that centered on women's business. Both pledged their allegiance to a political economy based on male breadwinners and female dependents. At the same time they exposed the tensions and contradictions that such a vision embodied. The final outcome of the case suggests that Keller's claim that the postbellum period witnessed the "resurgence—and usually the triumph—of . . . assumptions of . . . sexual inferiority" is only partially correct. To the contrary, competing definitions of the "faithful wife" continued to animate debates that never were fully resolved.[11]

The "Facts" of the Case

We will never know what happened on the afternoon of September 12, 1868, when Jacob and Nancy Young—both in their early thirties—met their untimely deaths. This much is certain: neither Young nor his alleged murderers were quite the "harmless and respected" people they presented themselves to be. Originally portrayed in newspaper accounts as an "honest, industrious, thrifty citizen, respected among business men for his uprightness, and honored among his neighbors for his exemplary social qualities," Young quickly emerged as a small-time speculator and stockholder, who had abandoned his job as drayman for a hardware store for the more lucrative pursuit of "street broker."[12]

By early 1868 he had acquired several business partners, including William Abrams, whom he had known since childhood, and Nancy Clem, an elder sister of Abrams's close friend, Silas Hartman. (Nancy Young *may* have been the only "innocent victim;" the extent of her involvement remains unclear.) Common experiences as well as bonds of friendship cemented their business ties; all three had been reared in Pike Township, a farming community northwest of Indianapolis; all three had grown up in modest if not impoverished circumstances.[13] Together they launched a series of questionable, probably illegal, business transactions that relied on a system of interchangeable loans taken out at high rates of interest. The scheme ranged widely, involving not only Young, Abrams, and Clem, but also: William Duzan, a prominent Pike Township physician, who had known Clem "since she was a child"; Robert Dorsey, a prosperous Indianapolis hardware dealer and Young's former employer; Arthur L. Wright, the county treasurer; and even Ann Hottle, Clem's dressmaker, who invested her life savings of $925, hoping to attain higher interest rates than local banks offered. Rumors abounded that the Clem-Young "ring" included some of the city's most prominent businessmen; perhaps it did. Equally plausible, these unnamed—and fictitious—characters merely served to entice potential investors.[14]

Contemporary commentators never quite understood what this business aimed to accomplish, nor would the surviving participants tell. Possibly, it involved counterfeiting. Possibly, Clem, Young, and Abrams intended to gain their victims' confidence before making off with their money. A local historian's suggestion that the three co-conspirators played a version of what later became known as the "Cassie Chadwick system"—a ruse named for a confidence woman who obtained enormous loans by representing herself as the heiress of Andrew Carnegie—describes the spirit, if not necessarily the letter, of the enterprise.[15] Whatever its precise workings, the business depended on the persuasiveness of its promoters and the willingness of profit-minded solid citizens to put moral scruples aside, or at least not to ask questions. Schemes of this sort—large and small—flourished in the post–Civil War years, at a time when it was not always clear which financial practices constituted good business behavior and which a notorious lack of business ethics. Variations on the Cold Spring theme invested the "Gilded Age"—the term Mark Twain and Charles Dudley Warner later coined to describe the era— with much of its explanatory power.

The mysterious transactions proved profitable. Jacob Young retired from his job at the hardware store and purchased a horse and buggy and a house furnished with the accouterments of Victorian domesticity. William Abrams, a carpenter who "worked occasionally" suddenly began making money very fast. Nancy Clem, too, was either making or borrowing substantial sums, handling far more money than most women could expect to garner from the legitimate economy. Some of her newfound wealth financed her son Albert's enrollment at Earlham College (an education cut short by his mother's legal predicament); some, home improvements. What she did with the rest—if indeed, as rumor had it, she retained a sizeable secret reserve—remains a mystery.[16]

The scheme ended within nine months, when Jacob and Nancy Young lost their lives. Whether, as prosecutors alleged, Young threatened to reveal Clem's business dealings to her unsuspecting spouse when—unexpectedly denied a $22,000 loan from the ever-reliable Dr. Duzan—she could not repay him, or whether the murderers simply knew that he carried a large sum with him on the day that he drove to Cold Spring is unclear.[17] Whatever the motives, police investigators identified three suspects. William Abrams supposedly purchased the shotgun that lay on the sand near Jacob Young's body. Silas Hartman, Nancy Clem's ne'er-do-well younger brother, rented a buggy and sorrel mare named Pet (whose "preventive shoes" left behind another set of incriminating footprints) that allegedly transported him to the scene of the crime. There, prosecutors maintained, having accompanied the Youngs on their Saturday excursion, Nancy Clem joined him in committing "cold-blooded atrocity." Hartman allegedly killed Jacob Young with the shotgun. Clem allegedly shot Nancy Young with a pistol that was never found, striking her with a rock or the pistol itself when the bullet failed to effect her immediate demise. Analysts offered competing explanations for the grotesque condition of Nancy Young's body. Some speculated that the murderers deliberately set it alight in order to disguise her identity. Others suggested that the powder from the pistol ignited her crinoline petticoat.[18]

All three suspects faced charges of first degree murder. Abrams was convicted and sentenced to life in prison, later receiving a gubernatorial pardon. Hartman killed himself in his jail cell before he could be tried, shortly after issuing a confession that implicated himself and Abrams but exonerated his sister (that Abrams remained his cell mate after its publication in the city's newspapers casts some doubt on the official verdict of suicide).[19] Clem faced trial—indeed several trials—events that aroused enormous popular interest. The "Young Murder" regularly took up three to four columns, even entire pages, of brief, four-to-eight-page, newspapers. Mixed-sex crowds packed tiny courtrooms, first in Marion County, later in rural Boone County, after a change of venue prompted the case's relocation. Among the spectators was Indianapolis teenager Sarah Hill Fletcher, who attended the proceedings in December 1868 with her mother and aunt, having "had the good luck to get in a back window." Speaking for many, Fletcher remarked that "it was all intensely interesting."[20]

Telling the Story

Like most events that provoke substantial publicity, the Cold Spring incident touched a number of nerves.[21] As Indianapolis's first "cold-blooded" (premeditated) murder, it attracted considerable local and regional attention.[22] Extensive trial coverage in the city's newspapers sparked a public debate— and a second series of court cases—over freedom of the press.[23] The possibility of a woman who hailed from the respectable middle classes entering the state penal system added urgency to on-going discussions of prison reform, particularly those that concerned the rehabilitation and treatment of female prisoners. The case also exposed Indianapolis's seamy underside, diminishing booster's hopes of portraying it as a "moral city." Early press reports blamed the Young murders on "rascals from New York," but it soon became clear that Cold Spring was a home grown affair.[24]

But the case derived much of its power from the questions it raised about women's business, broadly defined.[25] At the time of the crime such questions had become increasingly important. The casualties of the Civil War left thousands widowed; declining numbers of eligible men reduced women's prospects for marriage or remarriage. Confronted with the temporary or permanent absence of husbands, fathers, and sons, numerous women had little choice but to manage on their own. These national trends had local consequences. Nearly 18 percent of Indianapolis's estimated 4,000 soldiers lost their lives; countless others suffered debilitating physical and mental injuries. During the course of the war usually parsimonious city officials found it necessary to construct a Ladies' Home for destitute wives and daughters of soldiers; the dire circumstances of Indianapolis's "sewing women" attracted the attention of their better-off sisters, who formed a charitable association on their behalf.[26] Women's market labor and female poverty—as Nancy Clem's own life story would demonstrate—were nothing new. But the exigencies of wartime brought these issues—and their possible consequences—into sharper relief.

Female breadwinning had political as well as pecuniary implications. Access to the franchise no longer depended on property holding by the 1860s, but the symbolic association between suffrage and economic independence remained strong. These connections were not lost on members of the woman movement, who hoped that women's wartime contributions and sacrifices would be rewarded with the vote and with access to previously "male" employments. Mary Livermore, a prominent activist and featured speaker at a Woman's Suffrage convention held in Indianapolis the summer after the murders, reiterated what she had said at earlier gatherings in New York, Boston, Syracuse, and Lowell: she considered the "closing of avenues of remunerative labor against them," like the denial of the franchise and limited access to education, a "wrong inflicted on women." Linking the political, the economic, and the marital, a "lady in the audience" expressed her hope that the vote would be granted not only to "Mrs. Livermore and other women of that class" but also "to the poor drunkard's wife, who, here in Indianapolis, spends his wife's earnings in the rum shop, and then beats her."[27] Clearly, convention participants envisioned the possibility of refashioning both women's relation to the larger economy and their position in the more intimate political economy of marriage.

No one mentioned Nancy Clem in the course of this conversation; to do so would have attached added notoriety to an already controversial cause. Nor could Clem be easily incorporated into the sentimental tales fashioned by advocates of earnings laws; unlike the "drunkard's wife," she was victim of neither a loutish husband or a heartless marketplace.[28] (This is precisely what makes her so interesting.) Nevertheless, her trials for the murder of Nancy Young anticipated many of the issues the suffrage convention considered. Given her own involvement in "business," they provided both the opportunity and the necessity for a discussion of what women's business might be.

By the post–Civil War years Americans had become accustomed to sensational narratives of violent crime, a trend that they could trace to the antebellum period, perhaps even to the late eighteenth century. Women figured prominently in this earlier tradition, almost always as victims of violent and explicitly sexual crimes.[29] Murderesses—relatively rare—appeared as sexual predators who lured unsuspecting men to their untimely deaths or as women who committed typically "female" crimes, killing unwanted infants, sexual rivals, tyrannical husbands, or faithless lovers.[30] By dubbing it a "tragedy"— a term often invoked to describe sensational crimes—Indianapolis newspapers tried to assimilate Cold Spring into predictable scenarios. But the case was an oddity. It had its female victim to be sure—but also a female perpetrator. And Cold Spring was notable for the apparent respectability of its protagonists and the virtual absence of sexual intrigue from its story; money, not sex, occupied center stage.[31] Attorneys on both sides attempted to incorporate earlier themes into their arguments. But the circumstances of the case forced them to explore new territory.

The lawyers involved were more than equal to the task; as was typical of notorious murder cases, both prosecution and defense commanded impressive arrays of legal talent.[32] Private attorneys for all practical purposes tried the case, lending their experience and expertise to 21-year-old John Duncan, the Marion County prosecutor who "won his spurs" during Cold Spring but played a limited role in the proceedings. Future president Benjamin Harrison rose to prominence prosecuting his neighbor Nancy Clem (he resided at 299 North Alabama Street, she at 266). Only 35 years old in 1868, he had already held the positions of city attorney and reporter for the state supreme court (the latter post temporarily interrupted by his wartime service as colonel of the 70th Indiana Infantry and, eventually, brevet brigadier general) before returning to private practice barely a year before the murders. If Harrison received the greatest subsequent acclaim, it was his law partner, William Pinkney Fishback, a former Marion County prosecutor and a rising star in local Republican circles, who most impressed the spectators who gathered in crowded courtrooms. John T. Dye, Fishback's friend and future partner, and another of the city's "distinguished legal lights," completed the state's team.[33]

The defense assembled an equally qualified roster, one that senior counsel John Hanna, a former U.S. district attorney and a childhood friend of William Frank Clem, may have organized. Joining Hanna were his law partner General Frederick Knefler, a Civil War hero who claimed the distinction of being the highest ranking Jewish officer in the U.S. army, and W. W. Leathers, "perhaps the best criminal lawyer at the [Indianapolis] bar." Jonathan W. Gordon, a free soil Democrat turned Republican, a former county prosecutor, and a former speaker of the Indiana General Assembly, joined the defense team at Clem's second trial and remained her counsel for the duration of her legal ordeal.[34]

Both sides made the most of their legal expertise, the prosecution citing precedent that endorsed arguments based on circumstantial evidence, the defense invoking authorities who declared their fallibility.[35] Both called expert witnesses, shoemakers and blacksmiths who offered competing professional opinions concerning the human and equine footprints pressed into the crime scene's "yielding soil."[36] But given the paucity of "hard" evidence linking the defendant to her alleged crime, both sides also had to construct stories about Clem herself. As Ann Jones has observed, "where issues are blurred, attention centers on personality, or to use the nineteenth-century term, *character*. The question becomes: Is the accused the sort of person who could have committed the crimes charged?"[37]

The initial response of the city's press hints at the confusion that Clem aroused. Neither the Republican *Journal* nor the Democratic *Sentinel* thought she looked the part. The first described her as "about thirty-five years of age, rather under the medium size, with a pleasant and intelligent countenance, of lady-like deportment and previous good character"; the second maintained that her appearance and demeanor were "such as to baffle all the usual tests of guilt." Only later, when it published a best-selling trial pamphlet, did the *Journal* revise its opinion, painting a portrait that better suited a murderess, discerning a "dangerous expression" on Clem's face, a "sinister turn of her eye," and a "resolute set of her jaws."[38]

Just as the *Journal* changed Clem's appearance to fit her alleged crime, both prosecution and defense attempted at various junctures to interpret the Cold Spring incident according to conventional wisdom. Summoning the power of earlier narratives, Harrison hinted at an illicit relationship between Clem and Jacob Young, and Fishback alluded to Clem's "nocturnal visits" to Young's house.[39] Yet these were afterthoughts, departures from the main lines of a narrative that emphasized money not sex.

Clem's lawyers also brazenly manipulated familiar cultural scripts. Seeking to place an appropriate murderess at the crime scene, they conducted a Cinderella search for a disreputable villainess whose shoe size matched the incriminating footprints at Cold Spring. They hired a detective who seized and illegally confined three likely suspects, two of them prostitutes. They paraded one, Caroline "Cal" Bowen, before potential witnesses, attempting without success to convince them that Bowen—not Clem—was the woman they had seen riding in the Youngs' carriage on the day of the murder.[40]

Others told similar stories. Silas Hartman's confession claimed that "Frank" Clark, a local prostitute, had fired the pistol shot that killed Nancy Young. Summoned by spiritualists, the ghost of Jacob Young also chose to implicate Clark and exonerate Clem; on another occasion Nancy Young pointed a spectral finger at an unidentified "strange woman."[41] The important issue here is not whether a "strange woman," Henry Ward Beecher's famous euphemism for prostitute, had been involved. Rather, the readiness of several people to invoke her presence suggests the familiar links nineteenth-century Americans forged between sexual vice, working-class status, and other, more serious, crimes. It was no coincidence that "the late Mr. Young's servant girl" was one of the first to be arrested for the murders; alas, her "shoe was much too large."[42]

In the end, sex failed to furnish an appropriate story line for narratives that explained Clem's guilt or innocence. Ultimately, both prosecution and defense told a story about women's business.

The Faithless Wife: The Prosecution's Story

How to convince jurors that a middle-class, married woman of "lady-like deportment" was capable of cold-blooded murder? In courtroom arguments universally described as brilliant, Harrison, Dye, and Fishback opted for a rhetorical strategy predicated on gender reversals, but one that departed from familiar scripts that distinguished passionless ladies from degraded prostitutes. Nor, in an era before biological explanations of female deviance gained credence, did they present Clem as physically or physiologically masculine. Instead they created a disturbing portrait of an ordinary-looking woman who seized masculine prerogatives.[43] Clem was a woman who held power, a "terrible power," a "fatal power" over all who knew her—her family, her business associates, her alleged accomplices.[44]

A story that featured a powerful woman called for commensurately powerless men. Prosecutors sought to unsex both Clem and her alleged accomplices; the more unwomanly Clem waxed in their courtroom pronouncements, the more unmanly they rendered her partners in crime. "Can the guilt of Abrams and Hartman be compared with the guilt of this woman?" John Dye asked. The answer, of course, was no, for they were "not self-reliant men," but weaklings manipulated by "a woman of brain and of power; a woman who has twirled these men around her fingers like ribbons."[45]

Prosecutorial descriptions of the murder itself underscored this rhetorical reversal of gender roles. According to Fishback's reconstruction, Clem had exhibited unwomanly courage, Silas Hartman, unmanly cowardice. Clem had coolly stopped to rob Young's coat pocket after his murder and calmly disposed of the pistol that she handled with "dexterity and precision;" the spineless

Hartman had panicked, leaving his weapon at the crime scene. Clem, Fish-back explained, "brought off her artillery from the field, while her cowardly blundering male accomplice fled, leaving his gun lying on the ground." Clem had approached her victim openly, even struggling with her; Hartman "skulked in ambush," concealed in a clump of bushes. To a populace just returned from fighting the Civil War, the implications would have been clear: Clem played the part of soldier; Hartman that of "bushwhacker"—an ambusher and unmanly coward.[46]

According to the story crafted by her legal opponents, Clem's unnatural dominance extended beyond her immediate family, encompassing not only her brother, but William Abrams, Jacob Young, and numerous gullible men (and women) who invested in her business. The *kind* of power she allegedly wielded deserves scrutiny. As descriptions of her martial bearing implied, it was not a sexual power, the sort identified with the villainesses of antebellum crime litera-ture. Clem's power, rather, was a "calculating" power, one that explained—as prosecutors saw it—her ability to commit premeditated murder.[47]

Much of the state's case hinged on a particular interpretation of Clem's personal economic history, which in turn accounted for her calculating na-ture. The former Nancy Hartman had married William Patton, a school teacher turned plasterer, some seven years her senior, at the age of 15. He died in 1858, leaving her with two house lots, a small amount of personal property, and an eight-year-old son.[48] She resorted to a common strategy to make ends meet: taking in boarders, a choice that allowed her to combine gainful em-ployment with childrearing. Clem managed well during the two years that she remained a widow, increasing her holdings and acquiring a reputation for "industry and frugality."[49]

Prosecutors argued that this experience embittered her, fueling an obses-sion with money that, as Dye put it, "turned her mother's milk to gall." By ex-tending her pecuniary concerns beyond mere subsistence, he implied, she had overstepped the boundaries of virtuous widowhood; in what became damaging testimony, her older brother, Matthew Hartman, admitted that "she might perhaps have got along without keeping boarders."[50] Such revela-tions furnished ample ammunition for Fishback's "masterly" closing argu-ment, which included "avaricious[ness]" among Clem's crimes.[51]

To Fishback, the circumstances surrounding Clem's second marriage pro-vided additional proof that she was guilty of avarice and, therefore, murder. "Upon her marriage with her present husband," he explained, "she by arrange-ment with him, took control of and managed her own business affairs." Cer-tainly Clem exercised no more than her legal right, one granted her by married women's property acts passed by the Indiana legislature in 1852 and 1853.[52] Certainly, too, this was a sensible decision for a propertied widow to make, especially when a new spouse's prospects seemed uncertain and a child's inheritance might need protecting. Although neither prosecution nor defense publicly questioned William Frank Clem's ability as provider, evidence suggests that his wife had good reason to guard her assets. Quite possibly, he held no property of his own. He did not preside over the "flourishing grocery business" but was the junior partner in a successful firm run by his older brother.[53] But Fishback imbued Clem's antenuptial arrangement with sinister meaning, insisting that "such a woman was well qualified to act a part in this tragedy."[54] That Clem had chosen money over love, economic autonomy over male protection, was evidence of a cold heart, a calculating disposition—and guilt.

Like her stint as a boardinghouse keeper and her premarital negotiations, Clem's business ventures seemed to exceed the requirements of financial necessity or even prudent foresight, a fact that disturbed her legal opponents. "It is well enough to lay up in time of health and prosperity for a rainy day," Fishback maintained, "and in so far as she exhibited the commendable virtue of economy . . . praise is merited. But that cursed passion of avarice stepped in the moment she stepped out from the plain, straightforward path of duty as a faithful wife, to enter upon the dangerous paths of financial speculation."[55] Clem had crossed an imaginary line between "industry" and "avarice," between "faithful wife" and dangerous speculator.

Clem's transgressions were gendered offenses; the problem was not avarice per se, but that her alleged greed sundered her from the moorings of an idealized family economy. To a certain extent, the Cold Spring case *was* about sex after all, for both prosecution and defense sexualized women's business, defining marital fidelity in economic terms. In Fishback's rendition, the faithless wife was not an adulteress, but one who ventured boldly into the marketplace. Clem's financial dealings violated her marriage contract, thereby rendering her capable of the worst of acts. "It is one of the happiest of the pleasures of married life," he regretfully explained, "to be able to impart to the wife the secrets of the day's transactions, and to exchange congratulations in the success of a venture; but Frank Clem knew nothing of what was transpiring between his wife and Jacob Young and William Abrams. He never knew that these business relations existed until that final settlement at Cold Spring."[56]

No one commented on the confusion Fishback's statement embodied; perhaps this apparent blunder was part of his "masterly" strategy. Wittingly or unwittingly he reversed the sexes, noting that a husband was supposed to "impart to the wife the secrets of the day's transactions." In short, he killed two birds with one stone, condemning Clem both for keeping secrets from her spouse—rather than "imparting" them—and for transacting at all. Such arguments had the added advantage of conveniently deflecting questions regarding the character of Jacob Young's dealings by defining women's business, instead of the general businesses of "street brokering" and "speculation," as illegitimate.

As Fishback's reference to the "final settlement at Cold Spring" suggested, business provided the prosecution with a metaphor for understanding Clem's actions and a mechanism by which to prove her guilt. Lacking hard evidence, Dye, Harrison, and Fishback once again had to construct a story. Several witnesses testified that Clem and Young visited each other (both diurnally and nocturnally) and that they had "business relations," but little in the way of documentary evidence linked them. Numerous promissory notes *did*, however, confirm Young's "relations" with additional business partners—as defense attorneys never tired of pointing out.

The prosecution's solution was to construct a scenario that stressed not only Clem's economic deviance and her failure to act the part of wifely dependent, but one that emphasized her "managerial" power, her ability to orchestrate the business of murder. As Fishback explained, "In commercial enterprises we find proprietors, book-keepers, salesmen, and porters. So, in this criminal enterprise, we find confederates and each one plays an appropriate part."[57] Clem's part was that of proprietor, the most unlikely position for a woman to hold, even in a "criminal enterprise." Although little evidence pointed one way or the other to the respective roles played by Clem, Abrams, and Hartman, Benjamin Harrison pronounced her "the central figure in this whole transaction—the presiding genius of the whole conspiracy, who both procured and directed all the other actors in this tragedy."[58]

Perhaps most telling, prosecutors emphasized Clem's "self-reliance," shrewdly exploiting an opportunity provided them by the bumbling Dr. Duzan. "She is a wonderful woman," Duzan insisted as he left the witness stand, "strong-minded, self-reliant, and inflexible in the pursuit of her purposes." His intended compliment backfired; as Fishback put it, "the shaft aimed at us struck the prisoner." Changing the arrow's course required careful reinterpretation of a time-honored concept. Normally a term that had positive connotations, especially in the American context, self-reliance conjured up visions of breadwinning, entrepreneurial independence, and individual responsibility. But it was also a gendered notion, one that—as the prosecution's rhetorical strategy implied—was meant to describe masculine self-making, not feminine initiative. Applied to Clem, self-reliance transformed itself into a sort of distorted Emersonianism, supplying additional evidence of her ability to plan and commit murder. "Ah! how strong-minded and self-reliant, how inflexible in the pursuit of her purpose must have been that woman who rode out with the Young and his wife that Saturday afternoon," Fishback proclaimed. Not to be outdone, his colleague John Dye pronounced her "self-reliant and God defiant."[59]

If female self-reliance explained murder, it also threatened to become a crime itself. Prosecutors condemned Clem for a particular form of gender deviancy, one by which she exchanged wifely dependence for managerial powers. When defense attorney John Hanna asked, "To handle money successfully, to be prompt, to have credit in bank, is that an evidence of crime?" his question was more than merely rhetorical. If the prosecution's case served on one level to vilify an unlikely villainess, it also expressed a nostalgia for an idealized past, one in which men whispered business secrets to wives who, for their part, carefully observed the fictive boundaries between home and marketplace.

The Faithful Wife: The Defense's Story

Of course there are at least two sides to every story. As Dr. Duzan's admiration suggested, female self-reliance had its supporters. Nevertheless, Clem's undisputed involvement in mysterious financial schemes placed considerable burdens on her defense. Worse, she refused to explain the nature of her business to her lawyers; revealing this information, she claimed, would harm the reputations of unnamed others.

Clem's attorneys resorted to predictable strategies. They pointed to weak spots in the state's largely circumstantial case. They described their client as a "weak and innocent woman." They accused their opponents of conducting a "woman hunt."[60] But they also presented a more positive, less threatening definition of self-reliance and a sunnier version of Clem's economic past. In the process they redefined—within limits—what it meant to be a faithful wife.

Linking self-reliance to moral virtue, John Hanna presented an uplifting account of his client's history, one that denied the sinister implications the prosecution ascribed to it. "She had married young, and during her widowhood was thrown upon her own resources. She took boarders, did her own work, sewed for those she boarded, and proved herself a self-reliant woman. Nothing whatever could be produced against her virtue." Appealing to class resentments, Hanna painted prosecutors as elitists who disdained manual labor (men, he implied, who would rather hire servants than suffer their wives to do "their own work") and who harbored little sympathy for women "thrown upon their own resources." His opponents condemned Clem, he complained, merely because she had once taken in boarders. Her self-reliance deserved admiration, not censure; it furnished proof of good character, not avarice; it offered evidence of innocence, not guilt. Embracing a seemingly gender-neutral definition of self-reliance, Hanna praised Clem's industry, frugality, and "great business tact."[61]

Clem's defense maintained that female self-reliance bolstered rather than threatened marriage. W. W. Leathers argued that her industriousness, frugality, and moneymaking abilities rendered her a "faithful wife" and "model woman." Making this claim meant turning a legal tale into a sentimental one. According to Hanna, it was not Nancy Clem but her future spouse, "act[ing] a better part than a mere fortune-hunter," who insisted on the infamous antenuptial agreement. In this version of events Clem possessed neither the initiative nor the legal knowledge to assert her rights; indeed, "rights" were absent from the argument. Hanna's strategy was every bit as brilliant as that of his opponents. His story preserved William Clem's husbandly authority, entitling his wife to his symbolic protection. Nancy Clem had been faithful after all; she "managed her own estate" only because her husband suggested it.[62] (Of course William Clem's patriarchal authority rested on the shakiest of foundations, for the antenuptial agreement—even if it was his idea—gave a woman of Nancy's ambition and imagination enormous latitude.) Countering the prosecution's portrait of an avaricious predator and faithless spouse, the defense depicted its client as an able manager and dependable contributor to family coffers—a vision that might well have appealed to the middling farmers who seem to have dominated successive juries.

To be sure, this vision was neither entirely new nor especially liberating. Rather, it tried to incorporate Clem's speculative ventures into older, predominantly rural traditions that viewed women's economic contributions as essential to family prosperity and survival. The fit was far from perfect; the Nancy Clem that defense attorneys fashioned exhibited little ambition, independence, or initiative. If prosecutors portrayed her as a grasping opportunist, Clem's attorneys took pains to emphasize her economic passivity. They denied that Clem was the "mastermind" behind the "ring." In neither the business of murder nor the business of business did she play a proprietary role; she was an innocent participant in a nefarious scheme organized and orchestrated by Young and other shadowy, unnamed, characters.[63] If prosecution portrayed her as an aggressive borrower, defense presented her as a naïve lender, attracted by the high rates of interest Young offered her.[64] The question of whether Clem had been a borrower or a lender involved the larger issue of motive: a lender would have wanted Young alive, not dead. But the two terms had connotations that served additional purposes. The prosecution's depiction of Clem as an aggressive borrower fit well with an argument that stressed her economic deviance and managerial powers. The defense's representation of a naïve lender, on the other hand, nicely complemented its definition of "faithful wife."

Thus the prosecution roundly condemned female "self-reliance;" the defense praised female industriousness within carefully circumscribed limits, allowing wives a limited independence and an expanded economic role, but not fundamentally threatening the political economy of marriage. To argue otherwise would have reinforced the prosecution's case. Neither side offered a particularly "feminist" reading of the situation; both, after all, spoke to juries comprised of husbands and potential husbands.

Home Women and Clever Women: Clem's Story

Nancy Clem never took the witness stand, probably because her attorneys believed that her refusal to reveal the nature of her business or the names of her associates suggested guilt rather than innocence. Nevertheless she did testify, not in the courtroom, but in the pages of local newspapers. Clem herself articulated two very different definitions of the faithful wife, images that mirrored, albeit imperfectly, the opposing interpretations of prosecution and defense. They also mirrored, again imperfectly, each paper's partisan proclivities; hence, the degree to which either interview faithfully recorded Clem's words is open to question. Of course, if she bore any resemblance to prosecutors' depictions, she was perfectly capable of manipulating political sentiments, telling successive reporters what they wanted or expected to hear.

Clem granted each of the city's major newspapers an interview during the spring of 1869, speaking to the Republican *Journal* on March 12, to the Democratic *Sentinel*, some two weeks later, on March 29. Her conversation with the first reporter conjured up images of what historian Rebecca Edwards describes as "Republican domesticity." Clem failed to mention her business dealings, emphasizing instead her love of "home," her identity as a "home woman." "She spoke very affectingly of her home and its attachments," the *Journal's* correspondent reported, ". . . in other words that it was her delight to be there, and amidst its endearments."[65]

Clem offered strikingly different sentiments to the *Sentinel*. Here she readily admitted her transactions with Jacob Young (although she denied any responsibility for his murder). "Mr. Young was very prompt in his settlements," she explained, "and my confidence in him rapidly increased in consequence. I used every effort to obtain money to lend him whenever he required it." Equally significant, Clem stated that it was Nancy Young, the supposed innocent victim of the Cold Spring affair, "who first instigated me to lend money to her husband." "I got quite intimate with Mrs. Young, as I thought her a very clever woman. . . . she came to me and said she understood I managed my own affairs, and had some money; that her husband was engaged in a business in which he could make a good deal of money, and would pay me a high rate of interest for the use of mine."

Clem prudently presented herself in this instance as a lender, not a borrower. She carefully avoided any hint of the avariciousness attributed to her; she used her profits, she explained, for "repairing and refurnishing my home, and . . . to give my son a collegiate education."[66] Yet the image she presented in her second interview deviated considerably from the "home woman" of the first. She matter-of-factly explained that she had concealed her business from her spouse; nevertheless William Clem had "proved himself a good and true husband" whose "actions are influenced by a firm belief in my innocence." Intending to persuade the reading public of the same, Clem presented herself as a faithful wife who was also a "clever" woman, a woman of "brain," if not "power." Her responses resonated with Democratic conceptions of women as productive members of family economies and anticipated later Democratic notions of women as consumers to an extent—but only to an extent. Careful readers might have noted that the home on which Clem lavished so much attention was literally *hers*, not her husband's. And like her legal opponent, William Fishback, Clem, too, shrewdly reversed the sexes, emphasizing the "true husband" as well as the faithful wife. Once again, marital and monetary metaphors mingled. Clem's definition of a "true husband" was one who did not pry into his wife's business affairs. If the story crafted by her attorneys did not quite capture Clem's active pursuit of economic opportunities outside the bonds of matrimony, neither could Democratic narratives, which cast women's economic contributions in the context of men's household mastery, quite contain her extramarital self-reliance.[67]

Sensational trials, Lawrence M. Friedman has written, "can lay bare the soul of a given society." It is tempting, then, to interpret Cold Spring as a none-too-subtle attempt to reaffirm the mythical moral and economic order of a bygone era, one in which husbands reigned supreme and wives remained firmly ensconced within family economies. But the story is not so simple. After all, prominent, decidedly nonfeminist attorneys had argued that under certain circumstances "model women" might enter the marketplace without the knowledge or approval of their husbands. Interested above all in securing their client's acquittal, they very likely said things they did not, as husbands, personally believe. But they hoped and expected that their statements would fall on sympathetic ears. Both prosecution and defense agreed that faithless wives deserved to be punished. But each proposed its own definition of fidelity. The subtle but significant differences between them created a slender continuum between wifely dependence and limited autonomy, granting women a narrow cultural space in which to maneuver, albeit within a landscape fraught with peril.

There remained the ambiguous example of Clem herself. She seems to have elicited little sympathy. Newspapers reported that public opinion was against her. "She deserves it!" Sarah Fletcher wrote upon learning that Clem had been sentenced to a life term in the state penitentiary. Not everyone agreed. A "German friend" remembered Clem as "'one of the grandest women that ever lived.' She was a money-maker, he said." She "'knew more of the business world than many of the business men in Indianapolis.'" He said nothing of Clem's husband, whom he evidently regarded as irrelevant.[68]

Perhaps the outcome of the case itself best symbolizes the late-nineteenth-century cultural stalemate regarding women's business. In the end, neither home women nor clever women prevailed, for in the end neither prosecution nor defense decisively proved its case. Clem faced five trials for the murder of Nancy Young. Two resulted in hung juries, three in convictions. Each of the latter she appealed to the Indiana Supreme Court; each time the state's highest court overturned the jury's decision and ordered a new trial. Finally, in 1873, some five years after the murder, Marion County commissioners, citing the great public expenses involved, "refused to pay any further costs of prosecution." Just as prosecutors failed in "their efforts to convict the woman and keep her convicted," the Cold Spring case failed to resolve the issues it raised.[69]

As the nineteenth century ran its course, women's business would remain the stuff of notorious crimes, as the later cases of Lizzie Borden and Belle Gunness (the "Lady Bluebeard") suggest. Questions regarding women's relation to money—and their implications for their relations to marriage and family—remained key cultural concerns.[70] The notoriety of figures like Clem, Borden, and Gunness stemmed, I suspect, not merely from the brutality of their alleged crimes, nor from their sex as alleged perpetrators. Rather, their cases revealed the continuing uncertainties surrounding the political economy of marriage and the relation of "woman" to the marketplace. They echoed a cultural conversation that took place in many arenas—in feminist demands, in statehouses, as legislators contemplated revised married women's property acts and earnings laws, and, no doubt, in myriad negotiations between husbands and wives. The politics of the Gilded Age were at least partly the politics of women's business.

The most notorious figure of the Cold Spring affair receded into relative anonymity. After serving four years in state prison for perjury (she had offered several conflicting alibis), Clem, finally divorced by her long-suffering husband, returned to Indianapolis. There she began a second career, one that once again placed her at the margins of the legitimate economy, as an itinerant peddler of patent medicines. This was a calling at which she succeeded, a pursuit that allowed her to use her legendary powers of persuasion in a more innocuous fashion.[71]

Rumors persisted that the Clem-Young scheme had involved the "best men" of the city and that Clem had hidden away large sums of money. On her deathbed in the early summer of 1897 she revealed the whereabouts of a secret bank account to her son Albert, now a building inspector for the city engineer's office. When he visited the institution she named, no record could be found.[72] The citizens who gathered outside of the house where Clem lay dying had justice, not money, on their minds; they hoped that she would finally would explain what she knew of the murders. They were disappointed. "[S]he died with her lips sealed."[73]

NOTES

A Director's Grant from the Indiana Historical Society supported the research for this essay. I would like to thank Darrell Bingham, Ellen Dwyer, Michael Grossberg, Hendrick Hartog, Steven Herbert, the members of Indiana University's Criminal Justice Brown Bag seminar, and the anonymous reviewers of this volume for their comments on previous drafts.

1. Indianapolis *Sentinel*, September 14, 1868, 4; Indianapolis *Journal*, September 14, 1868, 8. *The Cold Spring Tragedy: Trial and Conviction of Mrs. Nancy E. Clem for the Murder of Jacob Young and Wife* . . . 3d. ed. (Indianapolis: A. C. Roach, 1869), 7 [hereafter *CST*]. For an excellent summary of the case, see Leigh Darbee's entry in David J. Bodenhamer and Robert G. Barrows, eds., *The Encyclopedia of Indianapolis* (Bloomington: Indiana University Press, 1994), 456.

2. *CST*, 10; *Journal*, September 14, 1868, 8; September 15, 1868, 8.

3. *CST*, 12.

4. *New York Herald*, September 14, 1868, 4, 5; *New York Times*, September 18, 1868, 4; December 6, 1868, 11; December 24, 1868, 4; March 2, 1868, 6; March 13, 1869, 2; March 11, 1869, 8.

5. Edith Eleanor Sparks, "Capital Instincts: The Economics of Female Proprietorship in San Francisco, 1850–1920" (Ph. D. diss., UCLA, 1999); Mary P. Ryan, *Women in Public: Between Banners and Ballots, 1825–1880* (Baltimore: Johns Hopkins University Press, 1990); Nancy Fraser, "Rethinking the Public Sphere: A Contribution to the Critique of Actually Existing Democracy," and Mary P. Ryan, "Gender and Public Access: Women's Politics in Nineteenth-Century America," both in *Habermas and the Public Sphere*, ed. Craig Calhoun, (Cambridge: MIT Press, 1992), 109–42; 259–88; Morton Keller, *Affairs of State: Public Life in Late Nineteenth Century America* (Cambridge: Harvard University Press, 1977).

6. Mary H. Blewett, *Men, Women, and Work: Class, Gender, and Protest in the New England Shoe Industry, 1780–1910* (Urbana: University of Illinois Press, 1988); Carole Turbin, *Working Women of Collar City: Gender, Class, and Community in Troy, 1864–86* (Urbana: University of Illinois Press, 1992); Ardis Cameron, *Radicals of the Worst Sort: Laboring Women in Lawrence, Massachusetts, 1860–1912* (Urbana: University of Illinois Press, 1993); Thomas Dublin, *Transforming Women's Work: New England Lives in the Industrial Revolution* (Ithaca, N. Y.: Cornell University Press, 1994); Wendy Gamber, *The Female Economy: The Millinery and Dressmaking Trades, 1860–1930* (Urbana: University of Illinois Press, 1997).

7. More comprehensive studies of women's economic contributions and legal condition emphasize the antebellum period. See Suzanne Lebsock, *The Free Women of Petersburg: Status and Culture in a Southern Town* (New York: Norton, 1984); Marylynn Salmon, *Women and the Law of Property in Early America* (Chapel Hill: University of North Carolina Press, 1986); Jeanne Boydston, *Home and Work: Housework, Wages, and the Ideology of Labor in the Early Republic* (New York: Oxford University Press, 1990). See Amy Dru Stanley, *From Bondage to Contract: Wage Labor, Marriage, and the Market in the Age of Slave Emancipation* (Cambridge: Cambridge University Press, 1998), esp. 175–217; and Megan J. McClintock, "Civil War Pensions and the Reconstruction of Union Families," *Journal of American History* 83 (September 1996): 456–80, for important exceptions.

8. Cameron, *Radicals of the Worst Sort*, 17–46; Catherine Clinton and Nina Silber, eds., *Divided Houses: Gender and the Civil War* (New York: Oxford University Press, 1992); Hendrik Hartog, "Lawyering, Husbands' Rights, and 'the Unwritten Law' in Nineteenth-Century America," *Journal of American History* 84 (June 1997): 67–96; McClintock, "Civil War Pensions;" Elizabeth R. Osborn, "'I Vote No. I am Not Afraid of My Wife.': The Influences of Gender and Culture on Law-Making in Antebellum Indiana" (seminar paper, Indiana University, Bloomington, 1996), esp. 12–13; Stanley, *From Bondage to Contract*, 156–66, 197–98.

9. Eric Foner, *Reconstruction: America's Unfinished Revolution, 1863–1877* (New York: Harper and Row, 1988); Stanley, *From Bondage to Contract*.

10. W. Lance Bennett and Martha S. Feldman, *Reconstructing Reality in the Courtroom: Justice and Judgment in American Culture* (New Brunswick, N. J.: Rutgers University Press, 1981), esp. ix–10. See also Kathryn Holmes Snedaker, "Storytelling

in Opening Statements: Framing the Argumentation of the Trial," in *Narrative and the Legal Discourse: A Reader in Storytelling and the Law*, ed. David Ray Papke (Liverpool: Deborah Charles Publications, 1991), 132–57; Bernard S. Jackson, "Narrative Theories and Legal Discourse," in *Narrative in Culture: The Uses of Storytelling in the Sciences, Philosophy, and Literature*, ed. Cristopher Nash (London: Routledge, 1990), 23–50; Karen Halttunen, *Murder Most Foul: The Killer and the American Gothic Imagination* (Cambridge: Harvard University Press, 1998), 98–107; Laura Hanft Korobkin, "The Maintenance of Mutual Confidence: Sentimental Strategies at the Adultery Trial of Henry Ward Beecher," *Yale Journal of Law & the Humanities* 7 (winter 1995): 1–48, esp. 10–16; Lawrence M. Friedman, *Crime and Punishment in American History* (New York: Basic Books, 1993), esp. 254; Michael Grossberg, *A Judgment for Solomon: The D'Hauteville Case and Legal Experience in Antebellum America* (Cambridge: Cambridge University Press, 1996); Richard Wightman Fox, *Trials of Intimacy: Love and Loss in the Beecher-Tilton Scandal* (Chicago: University of Chicago Press, 1999).

11. Keller, *Affairs of State*, 161.

12. *Journal*, September 14, 1868, 8.

13. *Journal*, September 16, 1868, 8; December 12, 1868, 2. Evidence culled from the manuscript population censuses suggests—but cannot confirm—that reports of Clem's impoverished childhood may have been exaggerated. Federal Manuscript Population Census (hereafter FMPC), 1840, Pike Township, Marion County, Indiana, microcopy 704, reel 88, pp. 338–39; 1860 FMPC, Pike Township, microcopy 653, roll 279, p. 969, line 8; p. 926, lines 30–39. Testimony, Matthew Hartman, *Sentinel*, December 12, 1868, 2; testimony, Silas Hartman, *Sentinel*, December 14, 1868, 2; *News*, June 10, 1897, 8.

14. *CST*, 29–39; testimony, Ann Hottle, *Sentinel*, December 7, 1868, 2.

15. Testimony, Robert S. Dorsey, *Sentinel*, December 11, 1868, 2; *News*, June 9, 1897, 8; Indianapolis *Star*, November 11, 1971, section B, 3; Jacob Piatt Dunn, *Greater Indianapolis: The History, the Industries, the Institutions, and the People of a City of Homes*, vol. 1 (Chicago: Lewis Publishing, 1910), 60; Kathleen De Grave, *Swindler, Spy, Rebel: The Confidence Woman in Nineteenth-Century America* (Columbia: University of Missouri Press, 1995), 58–62.

16. *Journal*, September 14, 1868, 6; September 16, 1868; December 12, 1868, 3; *Sentinel*, September 15, 1868, 4; *CST*, 11; *Sentinel*, December 12, 1868, 2; March 29, 1869, 4.

17. *CST*, 30, 99–100; Indianapolis *News*, June 9, 1897, 8.

18. *CST*, 122; *Sentinel*, September 15, 1868, 4; *News*, June 2, 1910, 3.

19. Dunn, *Greater Indianapolis*, 60.

20. Sarah Hill Fletcher, diary, December 19, 1868, M479 Emily Beeler Fletcher Diaries and Papers, 1825–1918, BV2190–2191, Indiana Historical Society.

21. Joyce G. Williams, J. Eric Smithburn and M. Jeanne Peterson, *Lizzie Borden: A Case Book of Family and Crime in the 1890s* (Bloomington, Ind.: T. I. S. Publication, 1980), vii; Friedman, *Crime and Punishment*, 252–54.

22. Dunn, *Greater Indianapolis*, 60.

23. *CST,* 13–14; *Journal,* December 1, 1868, 4; December 2, 1868, 4; December 3, 1868, 4; December 4, 1868, 4, 5, 8; December 5, 1868, 5; *Sentinel,* December 4, 1868, 1, 4; December 5, 1868, 2, 4.

24. *Journal,* November 25, 1868, 5; December 1, 1868, 5; January 12, 1869, 8; January 13, 1869, 8; January 14, 1869, 6; February 2, 1869, 4; *Sentinel,* January 13, 1869, 4; May 27, 1869, 4; *Journal,* September 14, 1868, 8.

25. The analysis that follows focuses on Clem's first trial in December 1868. Attorneys on both sides introduced additional evidence in subsequent trials, but the cultural themes they emphasized and the "stories" they constructed remained much the same.

26. Richard S. Skidmore, "Civil War," in Bodenhamer and Barrows, *Encyclopedia of Indianapolis,* 441, 443; James H. Madison, *The Indiana Way: A State History* (Bloomington: Indiana University Press, 1986), 197–98; Nancy F. Gabin, "Women," in Bodenhamer and Barrows, *Encyclopedia of Indianapolis,* 218.

27. *Journal,* June 9, 1869, 5; *Sentinel,* June 10, 1869, 4; Stanley, *From Bondage to Contract,* 197–209.

28. Stanley, *From Bondage to Contract,* 197–209.

29. Karen Halttunen, *Murder Most Foul,* 35–59; Daniel Ray Papke, *Framing the Criminal: Crime, Cultural Work, and the Loss of Critical Perspective* (Hamden, Conn.: Archon Books, 1987); Amy Gilman Srebnick, *The Mysterious Death of Mary Rogers: Sex and Culture in Nineteenth-Century New York* (New York: Oxford University Press, 1995); Patricia Cline Cohen, *The Murder of Helen Jewett: The Life and Death of a Prostitute in Nineteenth-Century New York* (New York: Alfred A. Knopf, 1998); Daniel A. Cohen, "The Murder of Maria Bickford: Fashion, Passion, and the Birth of a Consumer Culture," *American Studies* 31 (fall 1990): 5–30; Daniel A. Cohen, *Pillars of Salt, Monuments of Grace: New England Crime Literature and the Origins of American Popular Culture, 1674–1860* (New York: Oxford University Press, 1993).

30. Ryan, *Women in Public,* 70–71; Ann Jones, *Women Who Kill* (New York: Holt, Rinehart, and Winston, 1980); Judith A. Allen, *Sex and Secrets: Crimes Involving Australian Women Since 1880* (Melbourne: Oxford University Press Australia, 1990); Mary S. Hartman, *Victorian Murderesses: A True History of Thirteen Respectable French and English Women Accused of Unspeakable Crimes* (New York: Schocken Books, 1977); Edward Berenson, *The Trial of Madame Caillaux* (Berkeley: University of California Press, 1992).

31. *Journal,* December 4, 1868, 8.

32. Cohen, *Pillars of Salt, Monuments of Grace,* 29–30.

33. Dunn, *Greater Indianapolis,* 60–61; *Logan's Annual Indianapolis City directory, 1868–'9* (Indianapolis: n. p., [1869]), 37, 85; Charles W. Calhoun, "Benjamin Harrison," in Bodenhamer and Barrows, *Encyclopedia of Indianapolis,* 660–61; B. R. Sulgrove, *History of Indianapolis and Marion County, Indiana* (Philadelphia: L. H. Everts, 1884), 214E; *Edwards' Indianapolis Directory, Municipal Record, and City Register* (n.p.: n.p., [1869]), 83, 150; *Journal,* September 16, 1868, 4; *Commemorative Biographical Record of Prominent and Representative Men of Indianapolis and Vicinity* (Chicago:

J. H. Beers, 1908), 148; *Proceedings of the Indianapolis Bar Association in Memory of William Pinkney Fishback* (unpaginated typescript), SC2413 William Pinckney Fishback Papers, 1852–1901, folder 2, Indiana Historical Society.

34. Sulgrove, *History of Indianapolis and Marion County*, 180–81, 214E–F; *CST*, 83; *Sentinel*, December 5, 1868; John Hanna, closing argument, *Journal*, December 21, 1868, 3; Tony L. Trimble, "Frederick Knefler," in Bodenhamer and Barrows, eds., *Encyclopedia of Indianapolis*, 873; Dunn, *Greater Indianapolis*, 60; J. W. Gordon, *Indiana Democracy Since 1854. Judged By Its Record!* speech delivered at Cumberland, July 7, 1860, pam JK2295 . I63 G6 1860, Indiana Historical Society.

35. John T. Dye, closing argument, *Journal*, December 18, 1868, 2; Fishback, closing argument, *Journal*, December 21, 1868, 1; Fishback, closing argument, *CST*, 95–98; Hanna, closing argument, *Journal*, December 21, 1868, 3; in Clem's second trial, see W. W. Leathers, opening argument, *CST*, 60.

36. Testimony, Thomas Mansfield, *Sentinel*, December 5, 1868, 4; testimony, John Patterson, David Cady, W. S. Armstrong, and Joseph D. Vinnedge, *Sentinel*, December 9, 1868, 2; testimony, John Hitchings, John J. Gates, and George Knodle, *Sentinel*, December 10, 1868, 4; testimony, Abraham Bond and William Wirt, *Sentinel*, December 12, 1868, 2; testimony, John J. Gates and David Cady, *Sentinel*, December 15, 1868, 2.

37. Jones, *Women Who Kill*, 86.

38. *Journal*, October 8, 1868; December 2, 1868, 4; *CST*, 16.

39. Benjamin Harrison, closing argument; W. P. Fishback, closing argument, *CST*, 69, 99.

40. *Journal*, December 12, 1868, 3; *Sentinel*, December 12, 1868, 2; June 21, 1869, 4; Fishback, closing argument, *CST*, 104–5.

41. *Sentinel*, June 19, 1869, 4; August 30, 1869, 4.

42. Henry Ward Beecher, *Seven Lectures to Young Men, on Various Important Subjects* (Indianapolis: Thomas B. Cutler, 1844), 143–66; *Journal*, September 16, 1868, 8.

43. Janet L. Langlois, *Belle Gunness: The Lady Bluebeard* (Bloomington: Indiana University Press, 1985), esp. 55–65.

44. Harrison, closing argument, *CST*, 69.

45. Dye, closing argument, *Journal*, December 18, 1868, 2.

46. Fishback, closing argument, *CST*, 96–97, 100; Gerald Linderman, *Embattled Courage: The Experience of Combat in the American Civil War* (New York: Free Press, 1987), 196–97.

47. Dye, closing argument, *Journal*, December 18, 1868, 2.

48. Testimony, Matthew Hartman, *Sentinel*, December 12, 1868, 2; testimony, James W. Hill and John H. Wiley, *Sentinel*, February 18, 1869, 4.

49. Fishback, closing argument, *CST*, 100.

50. John T. Dye, closing argument, *Journal*, December 18, 1868, 2; testimony, Matthew Hartman, *Sentinel*, December 12, 1868, 2.

51. *Journal*, December 19, 1868, 3; *CST*, 92; Fishback, closing argument, *CST*, 100.

52. Fishback, closing argument, *CST*, 92, 100.

53. Correspondents for R. G. Dun & Co. reported favorably on the firm of Aaron Clem & Bro, but the extent of William Frank Clem's personal assets are difficult to determine. Similar questions arise from the 1860 census, which inadvertently enumerated the Clem household—William, Nancy, and Albert—twice, once recording William as possessing no property, once as holding $1,800 in real estate and $600 in personal property. Some, possibly all, of the real property was Nancy's, although the census taker—perhaps influenced by cultural convention or by William or Nancy's own sense of propriety—left a blank space beside her name. Indiana vol. 67, p. 26, R. G. Dun & Co. Collection, Baker Library, Harvard University Graduate School of Business Administration, Boston, Massachusetts. (Microfilmed R. G. Dun & Co. records for Marion County, Indiana, are located at the Indiana Historical Society); 1860 FMPC, Indianapolis, Ward 2, p. 159, lines 25–26; Ward 2, p. 163, lines 22–23; *Buell & Williams' Indianapolis City Directory and Business Mirror, for 1864* (Indianapolis: Buell & Williams, 1864), 75; *The Indianapolis Directory for 1865* (Indianapolis: Hall & Hutchinson, 1865), 29; *Edwards' Annual Directory to the Inhabitants, Institutions, Incorporated Companies, Manufacturing Establishments, Business Firms, Etc., Etc. in the City of Indianapolis for 1865–6* (Indianapolis: Richard Edwards, 1866), 214; *Edwards' Annual Directory . . . 1867* (Indianapolis: Edwards & Boyd, [1867]), 220.

54. Fishback, closing argument, *CST*, 100.

55. Fishback, closing argument, *Journal*, December 21, 1868, 1.

56. Ibid.

57. Ibid., 101.

58. Harrison, closing argument, *CST*, 76.

59. Fishback, closing argument, *CST*, 96; Dye, closing argument, *Journal*, December 18, 1868, 2.

60. W. W. Leathers, closing argument, *Journal*, December 19, 1868, 2; *Sentinel*, February 27, 1869, 4.

61. Hanna, opening statement, *Sentinel*, February 12, 1869, 4.

62. Hanna, closing argument, *Journal*, December 21, 1868, 3; Leathers, closing argument, *Journal*, December 19, 1868.

63. Fishback, closing argument, *Journal*, December 21, 1868, 1; Leathers, closing argument, *Journal*, December 19, 1868, 2.

64. Leathers, closing argument, *Journal*, December 19, 1868, 2; Hanna, closing argument, *Journal*, December 21, 1868; Fishback, closing argument, *CST*, 99–100.

65. *Journal*, March 12, 1869, 4; Rebecca Edwards, *Angels in the Machinery: Gender in American Party Politics from the Civil War to the Progressive Era* (New York: Oxford University Press, 1997), esp. 5–7, 31–35, 76–81, 77 (quotation).

66. *Sentinel*, March 29, 1869, 4.

67. Edwards, *Angels in the Machinery*, 24, 61, 68–74.

68. *Journal,* March 2, 1869, 4, 8; Fletcher, Diary, March 1, 1869, 107; *News,* June 10, 1897, 8; Friedman, *Crime and Punishment,* 254.

69. *News,* June 9, 1897, 8.

70. Langlois, *Belle Gunness;* Williams, Smithburn, and Peterson, *Lizzie Borden;* Friedman, *Crime and Punishment,* 254.

71. *News,* June 9, 1897, 8; June 10, 1897, 8.

72. Ibid.

73. *News,* June 9, 1897, 8.

SEVEN

The Enigma of Louis Brandeis's "Zionization"

His First Public Jewish Address

Allon Gal

The enigma of how Louis D. Brandeis (1856–1941) came to be a Zionist has long been a concern of scholars and nonscholars alike. The problem has often been thus formulated: Brandeis surprised Jewish America and American society at large when he accepted the leadership of the American Zionist movement on August 30, 1914. Then fifty-eight years old, he had given no significant previous indications of Zionist ideology. How is it that a semi-assimilated Jew of Brandeis's stature, a model of Jewish integration into American life, made an about-face to advocate particularistic Jewish nationalism—Zionism?[1]

The enigma remains unresolved largely because it has often been stated unhistorically. Framing it as "Brandeis *vs.* Zionism" is an error. Instead, the historian's question should be: how does Brandeis's biography tally with the *kind* of Zionism he embraced within, as a product of, and in keeping with American society and history? The answer is important because a correct understanding of Brandeis's road to Zionism can help build a more accurate conception of mainstream American Zionism during the five decades after the outbreak of World War I, if not to this very day.

The historiography on Brandeis has largely failed to elucidate the crucial interconnection between his road to Zionism and the nature of the Zionism he pursued. I will begin by demonstrating this failure with a brief survey of the literature, followed by a statement of my interim thesis. I will then elaborate this thesis in light of a historical example—Brandeis's first public appearance as a Jewish speaker, in 1905—and go on to show the connections between this speech and the later, more comprehensive American Zionist ideology of Louis Brandeis.

1

The hagiography of Louis Brandeis ended in 1971, when sociologist Yonathan Shapiro published his *Leadership of the American Zionist Organization*. On the issue of Brandeis's Zionism, however, Shapiro is of little help. This results from his dogmatic separation between Brandeis's road to Zionism and the new Zionist ideology that, according to Shapiro, Brandeis formulated. In chapter 3 of his book, Shapiro argues that Brandeis turned to Zionism in 1913–14 so that he would be considered "a representative Jew." This, Brandeis hoped, would help him gain an appointment from President Woodrow Wilson. In Shapiro's portrayal, this ambitious and opportunist attorney had no authentic Zionist ideology when he assumed the leadership of American Zionism in August 1914. In his final chapter, Shapiro labels Brandeis's post–World War I Americanized Zionist ideology "Palestinianism." Its essence was disregard for all cultural and spiritual aspects of Zionism and the exclusive focus on the economic development of Jewish Palestine. For Shapiro, the only thing that may connect Brandeis the Zionist novice with the elder, revered (though remote) Zionist leader of the 1920s–1930s is his shallowness and disregard for "real, historic" Zionist values.[2]

The same divorce between Brandeis's "Zionization" and the nature of his Zionist ideology critically mars political scientist Philippa Strum's massive *Louis D. Brandeis: Justice for the People* (1984). In her chapter "The Making of a Zionist," she claims that the decisive factor in making Brandeis a Zionist was nothing other than a work of political science. That said, she devotes the bulk of the chapter to Alfred Zimmern's *Greek Commonwealth*, published in 1912 and first referred to by Brandeis—indirectly—as late as November 1915. Yet when, in a later chapter, Strum delves into the nature of Brandeis's Zionist ideology, Zimmern and his book totally vanish. Thus Zimmern is more *deux ex machina* than a productive explanation.[3]

In contrast, historian Melvin I. Urofsky's work synthesizes Brandeis's road to Zionism with the kind of Zionism he developed. The editor (with David W. Levy) of *Letters of Brandeis*, Urofsky consistently argues in two books and several articles that Brandeis's Zionism corresponded with his American Progressivism. Brandeis's Zionist ideas, his vision of future Israel included, were permeated by Progressive values and programs, observes Urofsky. His solution to the enigma is, then, that Brandeis's Progressive Zionism was a natural extension of his Progressivism. Yet this explanation also suffers from a metahistorical defect. First, ignoring phases in Brandeis's socioeconomic philosophy, Urofsky depicts his hero as being a perfectionist, emblematic Progressive all his life. Second, his account of Brandeis's Zionist ideology depicts a pure and consistent Progressivism, unchanging in the face of surrounding processes and events. Finally, he does not provide the concrete circumstances and specific dates of Brandeis's leap from American to Zionist Progressivism. In short, Urofsky gives us not a personality living and working in changing circumstances, but rather an archetypal Progressive-Zionist who stands beyond time and place.[4]

Another schematic approach—in this case, one that does not adequately take into account the singular nature of American civilization nor the uniqueness of American Judaism and Zionism—is that of historian Lewis J. Paper. Rather than examining Brandeis's experience in the context of Boston and New England, Paper's book attributes his subject's Zionism to a *diabolus ex machina:* anti-Semitism. Paper, without adducing any substantive documentary evidence, claims that anti-Semitism was a major factor in pushing Brandeis toward Zionism. In keeping with this, when Paper discussed the nature of Brandeis's Zionism on the basis of an address he gave in 1915 to a Reform Jewish audience, Paper dogmatically relies on the old "European formula" of anti-Semitism/the urge for independence/the goal of a Jewish state. The most instructive facts—that Brandeis sought out Reform-Jewish audiences and that he himself had a Reform-like, though nonreligious, social-ethical orientation—are a closed book for Paper.[5]

Furthermore, if one is going to investigate the role of anti-Semitism— which was part of the story, though a rather marginal one—one should also discuss *philo*-Semitism. This phenomenon, quite typical of the English-speaking world, was prevalent in Yankee New England before World War I. Virtually ignored by most biographers, it needs to be discussed as a possible factor in Brandeis's Zionization.[6]

Ignoring the pertinent sociocultural context, too many of Brandeis's biographers seek a solution to the enigma in another personality's alchemy-like influence. Thus, for example, too much is attributed to the influence of Louis Brandeis's Zionist uncle, Lewis Naphtali Dembitz, who passed away in 1907. If this were the case, how to explain that the hefty first volume of *Letters of Brandeis*, which systematically covers the years 1870–1907, does not include even one letter to or from his uncle? Similarly, too much is ascribed by some scholars to the influence of Jacob deHaas, an organizational Zionist emissary from Europe and an editor of Jewish Boston's periodical (1908–18), known to be a hero worshiper, and about twenty years younger than Brandeis. Another "our tribe" kind of explanation is employed by Sarah Schmidt, whose non-critical volume about Horace Kallen attributes the change in Brandeis to an overnight boat trip that the already-famous "people's lawyer" took with Kallen (more than twenty-five years his junior) on August 29, 1914.[7]

I do not contend that these figures played no role in Brandeis's Zioni-zation—they clearly did. Dembitz was admired by Brandeis as a lawyer; de-Haas, at a rather late stage, diligently mentored Brandeis in the history of Zionism; and, without a doubt, Kallen considerably refined Brandeisian Zionism. But the obsession with finding the influential figure seems to me historically ill-advised. To whom did Brandeis seriously chose to listen? What did he select to absorb from other personalities? How did he interpret and synthesize this new material with his prior thinking? And when did these influences have their effect? To be really explanatory, all these topics should be historically interwoven into Brandeis's life, work, and the society in which he lived.

The democratic and pluralistic nature of American civilization should always be kept in mind. Despite some scholars' insistent claims that America of the early twentieth century was characterized by a decisive socioeconomic po-larization, historian Morton Keller had proved, in his comprehensive and penetrating study of the period, that the American society and polity of the time was typified by pluralism and dynamism as great, if not greater, than in other periods. Carrie T. Bramen, in her recent exploration of the cultural sphere, complements Keller's study by proving that at that period *variety* be-came a key notion for Americans. New England was no exception to the rule; furthermore, this section of America was also known for its ethnic diversity.[8]

New England's diversity and vitality, especially in its ethnic composition, have been recently studied in depth by two historians—William A. Braver-man and James J. Connolly. Braverman provides a systematic depiction of how Boston's Jews developed into an ethnically conscious and colorfully or-ganized community at the beginning of this century, whereas Connolly rigor-ously analyzes the prevalence of ethnicity as a major factor in the Progressivism of the Irish and other groups, including the Jews, in Boston between 1900 and 1925. Their contributions are an impetus for a reexamination of the Brandeis enigma in the context of an ethnically diverse New England.[9]

It is my thesis that Brandeis developed a genuinely *American* strain of Zionism, that is, Zionism *meaningful in the context of American society at large.* Before his leadership, Zionist ideology in the United States was rather obscure. On the one hand, the movement was affiliated with the World Zionist Organization (founded in 1897) and professed European-oriented premises, such as a radical change in the political and international position of the Jewish people by immigration to Palestine, the reconstitution there of an independent Jewish entity, and a worldwide renaissance, centered in Palestine, of Hebrew civilization. On the other hand, it was clear from the beginning of the nationwide organized Zionist movement in the United States (1898) that it differed from the classic European pattern. The difference was apparent, however, mainly in a negative way—namely, in what it did *not* include. Thus, pre-Brandeis mainstream American Zionism did not negate Jewish life in the Diaspora, did not recommend immigration to Palestine (*aliya*), and did not pursue an overall Hebrew cultural renaissance. Brandeis, by way of contrast, never occupied himself with eliminating tenets from "classic Zionism"; his Zionism was American *to begin with.* Thus he *constructively* developed, from, within America, a wholesome American kind of Zionism. Historically, then his role was reshaping American Zionism (beyond traditional divisions into religious-nonreligious, socialist-nonsocialist, cultural-political trends) to respond fully to American circumstances. His personal journey toward this new ideology was a slow one, extending roughly through the decade of 1905–15, Properly understanding his personal course of Zionization would be a tremendous help, I suggest, in correctly assessing his ideological contribution.[10]

2

Naturally, first there was Louis's *familial* connection with Jewishness and Judaism. His beloved and admired mother, Fredrika Dembitz, instilled in him spiritual and religious ethical values; these values, universalist as they were, were nevertheless loosely interwoven into a Jewish historic tradition centered in Prague. In a faint way, Louis Brandeis saw himself as a Bohemian Jew.[11]

This and others of his family's Jewish contours notwithstanding, Brandeis did not publicly speak out on Jewish subjects until 1905, when he was almost fifty years old. Up to that time he apparently considered himself a sharply dissenting nonreligious Jew whose special obligations lay simply in upholding morality and improving civic life. He and his wife, Alice (also of the Bohemian Jewish subgroup), paid membership dues to the United Hebrew Benevolent Association (later, the Federation of Jewish Charities) from his first year as a lawyer in Boston (1879), but he assumed no further responsibility in the Jewish community and took care that their small donations reflected that inactivity.[12]

At the same time though, especially from 1883 onward (that is, after Jews from the rising wave of immigration from Eastern Europe began to settle in Boston), Brandeis's professional activities strengthened his structural affiliation with his ethnic group. For example, it was during this period that his law firm began to provide legal services to the Hebrew Industrial School. Moreover, Louis and his wife subscribed to the school and donated money annually. In 1902 Brandeis even joined in the American Jewish campaign to end Russia's restrictions on the entry of American Jews into its territory. And yet, despite these and other Jewish structural connections, Brandeis did not expand his communal-Jewish commitments.[13]

Until about 1905, liberal-Progressive Brandeis could hardly identify himself with his ethnic group. The Jewish elite, largely composed of German Jews, tended to be conservative in its politics. Nor was he spiritually attracted to this milieu. Years later, Brandeis would remember these Boston Jews as crude, narrow-minded materialists, alienated from educational pursuits. Their social club, the Elysium, was undoubtedly too flat and dull for him.[14] On the other hand, the German Jews were not so far toward what Brandeis thought of as the negative side of the sociopolitical spectrum that he was repelled by the Jewish community itself. First, there were but few German Jews in the ranks of the imperialists and high tariff crusaders. Furthermore, the subcommunity was not homogeneous. The Filenes, for example, were well-known liberals with a demonstrated interest in social causes. But they were hardly integrated into the local Jewish community.[15]

During Brandeis's first twenty-five business years in Boston (roughly 1879–1904), the East European Jewish subcommunity had no political appeal for him either. In their initial period in the United States, Eastern European Jews mostly fell into the hands of the established Irish ward bosses, who aided new immigrants, on the bosses' terms, through the powerful political machine they controlled. Accordingly, in the last quarter of the nineteenth century, many Eastern European Jews gave their votes to the Democratic Irish machine.[16] Like the German Jews, though, the East European subcommunity was not homogenous. Among others, it included the radical cigar union leader, Henry Abrahams, who was elected in 1888 to the presidency of the state branch of the American Federation of Labor. But, much as the Filenes were not representative of Boston's German Jews, Abrahams was not an organic part of the local Eastern European subcommunity.[17]

Estranged as he may have been from the Boston Jewish community, Louis Brandeis was still living and working in an ethnically divided city. It is only natural to ask how he fit in. It is my contention that the answer lies in Brandeis's relations with native New Englanders and their traditions. Indeed, Brandeis deeply admired the founding Protestants, esteeming their heritage of individualism, hard work, educational excellence, and tempered reform. Young Brandeis, who had identified easily with the community that incorporated these values, considered Massachusetts's legal traditions superior to all others. Characteristically, Brandeis pointed to the cooperative ventures of the old New England seafarers as the essence of the loftiest values—freedom, self-reliance, and responsibility. He also came to love New England's landscapes.[18]

Following Harold Abramson's observations, I would suggest that Brandeis's zealous fondness for New England ways well may have been a case of an outsider overidentifying with the insiders he admired. Samuel D. Warren, his Yankee friend and later law partner, once told him: "In many ways you are a better example of New England virtues than the natives." Instructively, people who worked with Brandeis tell striking stories about his Puritan-like work ethic, austerity, scrupulousness, public-mindedness, and pioneering bent.[19]

Still, admiration for and identification with the Yankees did not cause Brandeis to discard his Jewish identity. Structurally he retained his Jewishness, too, faint as it was, while culturally he fervently adopted the natives' mores and traditions.[20]

Against this background, it is understandable that of all the public struggles Brandeis was engaged in until 1905, he was most obsessed with crusades for maintaining what he believed was the tradition of good government that Boston and Massachusetts had been founded upon. He stubbornly questioned the integrity of city hall officials, exposing specific cases and boldly naming names. His style gratified many of his Yankee supporters; after all, in his speeches for the cause of good government, Brandeis consistently commended the professed ethics of the old established business community.[21]

His orientation toward the Yankees, coupled as it was with his known Jewish affiliation, at times caused *positive* ethnic responses. As historian Barbara Solomon suggests, philo-Semitism was still alive in pre–World War I Boston: "The oldest part of that tradition was intellectual; first, the admiration for the ancient Hebrew as the fountainhead of Christianity, inherited from the seventeenth-century Puritans; second, guilt and sympathy for the persecuted Jew, stimulated by the philosophy of humanitarianism in the nineteenth century." Hence, approving references to Brandeis's Jewishness were not infrequent. His good friend Elizabeth Evans described her own reaction to learning that Brandeis was a Jew: it gave an aroma to his personality. 'A Jew! He belonged then to Isaiah and the Prophets.'"[22]

But even more meaningful were the Yankee newspapers' occasional accolades adducing Brandeis's biblical-Jewish roots. For example, the *Roxbury Gazette* reminded Brandeis, who in his clean government drive until the autumn of 1905 avoided any reference to his ethnic background, that "[t]housands of years ago, on Mount Sinai, when Jehovah gave the commandments to Moses, the path to good government was blazed out in the words of that commandment which says: 'Thou shalt not steal.'" Undoubtedly, important circles of Yankee Boston expected the compassionate Jewish lawyer to conduct his good fight with some orientation to the ancient Judaic civilization they themselves honored and sometimes were quite well-versed in.[23]

Those circles notably included scholars and educators led by Charles Eliot, president of Harvard University (1869–1909), where Brandeis studied law and with which he remained meaningfully connected all his life. They also included members of the legal establishment typified by Oliver Wendell Holmes Jr., as well as sections of the old business community such as "the Mount Vernon Street Warrens," who sponsored many cultural and social endeavors in Boston, some of which Brandeis was actively involved in. It is certainly possible that these people's expectations that he should affirm his Jewish affiliation passed into Brandeis's mind, where they later subtly worked to evoke his positive view of Jewish civilization and its relevance for modern times.[24]

Furthermore, the philosophical pluralism prevalent in intellectual New England, tinged at times with interest in and respect for Jews, also was at work in Brandeis's pre-1914 environment. Actually, from the time of his Harvard days in Boston, Brandeis had been closely exposed to the pluralistic ideas of scholars and educators such as Nathaniel S. Shaler, William James, and Charles W. Eliot. His Harvard milieu, especially his constant and intensive connection with Eliot (1834–1926), were highly meaningful. Eliot himself was a great crusader for good government in Boston, and he inspired Brandeis to join him in his campaign. In addition, Eliot's deep philo-Semitic inclinations were part of a larger liberal-pluralistic view of ethnicity in the United

States. Another influence toward a concept of positive ethnic pluralism came from sophisticated circles among Boston's social workers. Some of them were associated with Brandeis in various projects, and some cultivated sincere respect for Jews and for Brandeis as a Jew. All this together subtly prepared him, during a quarter of a century or so to embrace—when circumstances made it attractive—an ethnically pluralistic America with a distinctive place for Jews within it.[25]

On September 8, 1905, Brandeis received a telephone call from Max Mitchell, the superintendent of the Federation of Jewish Charities. Mitchell was calling about a Jewish law student and resident of the West End of Boston, Robert Silverman, who had been charged with criminal libel after speaking out against corruption in the district's educational system. Silverman now reported to Brandeis that the previous June, about the time the school board was to decide on the reappointment of public school headmasters, a young teacher named Mildred Kallen had approached him with evidence of mismanagement in the Washington School (headed by Walter L. Harrington). Washington was one of the largest educational institutions in New England and enrolled many Jewish children. Silverman investigated and found Miss Kallen's accusations to be well-founded, so he drew up and circulated a petition. But on September 6 a warrant was sworn out against him and he appeared in court the following day. The hearing was continued to the nineteenth of September. Appealing for Brandeis's help he wrote: "I knew how important it was to have the Public Schools clean and under honest and upright management in that part of the city where home influence and environments of the school children were so bad. I knew that it was an outrage to find the same kind of men at the head of the schools that the little children were accustomed to see come out of the bar rooms and dives aside their very homes." Silverman gave Brandeis the names of some Jewish Bostonians who were well informed and capable of carrying on the battle. From September 14 on, Brandeis's law firm represented Robert Silverman and Mildred Kallen and thus became intimately caught up in the changes that were taking place in the local Jewish community.[26]

As the close study of William Braverman concludes, "with the influx of East European immigrants . . . the Jews of Boston began to branch out into the professions in significant numbers." This trend was exemplified by the founding of the New Century Club in 1900 and of Mt. Sinai Hospital in 1901. The historian Stephan Thernstrom has found that 25 percent of Boston's East European Jews were white-collar workers and professionals by 1910 (the parallel figures for the Irish and Italians were dramatically less). Social worker Frederick Bushée, who wrote about the situation of the Jews in the West End in 1902, observed the background to the phenomenon: "Jewish children are among the brightest in the schools, and they study with a seriousness which is foreign to their Irish and Italian mates. High School and even college attracts a large number of those whose means permit." Growing numbers of Jewish students entered institutions such as Boston University and Harvard College.[27]

Late-nineteenth-century immigration had made East European Jews a majority within the local Jewish community before the turn of the century. From 1900 to 1910, the heavy influx of Jews from East Europe changed the demographic nature of Boston Jewry even more decisively. By 1910 there were more than forty thousand East European immigrants in Boston. Furthermore, these newly arrived masses were not, like their predecessors, a largely demoralized and "soft" electorate. Rather, they were assertive, stubbornly self-reliant, and professionally ambitious.[28]

The New Century Club well reflected that historic change. The club's president and self-appointed historian, William Blatt, wrote of the organization, "It is, indirectly and unofficially, but we think potently, behind every worthy movement for welfare and progress." Indeed, though the club did not formally commit itself to any defined ideology of social progress, it did show a clear streak of militant idealism and its members were very much involved with democratic and social concerns.[29]

With its involvement in the Silverman-Kallen affair, the firm, and Brandeis personally, became concretely aligned with a cultural-political course that corresponded to the Jewish New Century Club's direction. Edward McClennen, the person in Brandeis's office best qualified for litigation, served as Robert Silverman's counsel. The array of challengers to the school committee was formidable and included James Storrow, an astute Brahmin leader in the field of education who severely censured the Washington School authorities. Among the witnesses McClennen called to the stand was Horace Kallen of Harvard University, Mildred's brother. Then, when it was revealed that Martin Lomasney, the boss of Ward 8, backed the corrupt headmaster of the Washington School, the legal struggle to exonerate Robert Silverman developed into a political fight against the ward bosses. By mid-November the trial had riveted the public's attention and was covered in great detail by the newspapers.[30]

There were obvious ethnic overtones to the conflict. The West End was being vacated by the Irish, but those who remained behind still wielded tremendous political power and controlled the school system. The Jews, who had become the majority in the West End, aspired to schools that would serve the educational ambitions they had for their children. In this struggle the Jews gradually acquired significant Protestant backing; this support represented a calculated reaction to the school committee's bitter attack on James Storrow and the Yankee-dominated Public School Association, who were trying to maintain Boston's traditionally high educational standards.[31]

On September 29, 1905 the *Boston Advocate*, the city's most important Jewish newspaper (changed to *Jewish Advocate*, May 1909), published a long editorial entitled "Is Your Child in Danger?" It was directed at hard-working, family-oriented Jews who desired to give their children a "good education . . . decent and uplifting." The *Advocate* addressed the dangers the Silverman-Kallen affair was uncovering: "If your boy at school is not in contact with men of the highest character, you may be sure that before long he will be a shadow in your life. If your boy is in daily contact with a vulgar and depraved character, he will learn things that will make for your own and his destruction. . . . A teacher, and more particularly the master of a school, must be a model citizen. He must embody the traits that make a gentleman. If he lacks these, the boy will soon imitate the worst that he displays."[32]

The *Advocate*—far from free of anti-Irish prejudice—then called on its readers to reject the bosses and destroy their hegemony. The coming elections, the newspaper claimed, could well advance these ends: "The book-loving race, whose passion for learning is one of their imperishable heritages, are in danger if they do not keep close touch with their children at school. At election time, you have an opportunity of voting for the men and women who select your teachers, directly and indirectly. . . . Stand up for the children! Destroy the enemies who would sacrifice even them for their miserably selfish ends."[33]

Whereas for the *Boston Advocate* the heart of the elections was the subject of children's education, its prominent Protestant allies had much more encompassing sociopolitical concerns. Indeed, with the death of Mayor Patrick Collins in September 1905, the established Yankees felt they had to act with determination to reconstruct their beloved liberal Boston. John Francis Fitzgerald, Collin's opponent, had moved swiftly to seize control of the Irish machine and, they felt, exemplified its evils. When Fitzgerald won the nomination of his party to run for mayor in mid-November, the *Boston Transcript* boldly confronted him; its favorite candidate was from the "better element" of Boston, Republican Louis Adams Frothingham. The *Transcript's* editorial claimed that Fitzgerald was a real danger to "our high civic heritage" and that his victory would be "hardly less than a disaster, would be the creation of a municipal machine more unscrupulous, more tyrannous, more reckless than anything which Boston has ever experienced."[34] Even more energetically than the *Transcript,* the Good Government Association worked to defeat Fitzgerald. Their choice, too, was Louis Frothingham. For them as well, the mere possibility of Fitzgerald's coming to power seemed a catastrophe.[35]

Terrified by Fitzgerald's crowd, the *Transcript* and the Republican strategists sought to enlist the crucial Jewish vote on Frothingham's behalf. They were no doubt gratified to learn of events such as the establishment in Ward 9, toward the end of October, of a Hebrew Independent Club aimed at detaching Jewish voters from the machine. Several weeks later, the Republicans scored another tactical victory: "Frothingham Their Guest: Hebrew Dinner to [*sic*] Republican Candidate," announced the *Transcript,* informing its readers that Louis Frothingham was the guest at a lunch "given in his honor by a number of the leading young Hebrews of the city."[36]

The Jewish community was sensitively, and quite early, aware of its pivotal role in the 1905 city election. Thus, by October 20, the *Boston Advocate* was already noting that there were about ten thousand Jewish voters in Boston and asked: "Do you know what it means to place the entire strength of this army of men in any one direction? The balance of power is held by the Jewish voters of this city." The *Advocate* lamented the misuse of Jewish voting power in the past and called for a new approach: "Handed out here and there in small numbers to certain party bosses; was the Jewish vote for the good of the Jews? No, but for the good of the candidate selected by the bosses who will forget their promises nearly as soon as they are made. The Jews should not seek representation as Jews, but they should seek protection for themselves and families by honest legislation which can only be given by honest fearless men." This was a policymaking article, and from that point on the *Advocate* worked hard to mobilize the community along definite pro–good government political lines.[37]

During the mayoral campaign, the law firm of Louis D. Brandeis had the upper hand in the defense of Silverman and Kallen (Walter Harrington repeatedly failed to pursue his criminal libel against them, the case was compelled to nol-pros, and Harrington left Boston, "his whereabouts unknown"). Significantly, the firm expressed its support for their case *as a public cause,* telling Silverman: "We have concluded not to present any bill to you for the services rendered for you in the matter." Silverman wrote then to Brandeis: "The City of Boston as well as my friends and I are greatly indebted to you for what is the most significant service the municipality has in the last year been rendered."[38]

By the time the struggle over the educational system in Boston broke out in the autumn of 1905, Brandeis was already a member of both the Public School Association and the Good Government Association, with which the former closely cooperated (Charles Eliot had influenced him to join the groups). Now, for Brandeis, as for the other leaders of the Good Government Association, the possible election of either John F. Fitzgerald or James Donovan, both aspiring to the Democratic nomination for mayor, represented an imminent danger to Yankee civilization. In October he signed a petition urging Louis A. Frothingham, the favorite of the GGA, to seek the Republican nomination. When asked for his reasons, Brandeis characteristically referred to Frothingham's loyalty to the values of the old New England: "He will administer the affairs of the office . . . without any posing, in a simple and modest fashion, and in a way which must commend itself to the plain, sober, thinking people of the City."[39]

Indeed, though at times Brandeis commended Frothingham for his Progressive tendencies (mainly with respect to the transportation monopoly issue in Boston), he more often called him an upholder of Puritan social values; it was chiefly the lack of these in Fitzgerald that had aroused Brandeis's hostility. In a letter to Edmund Billings, the secretary of both the GGA and the Public School Association, Brandeis insistently asked: "Can you send me a memorandum of the reasons, besides his general reputation, why men should vote for Fitzgerald? What facts have you in regard to his record?" When Billings replied that he had some information regarding graft and blackmail, but that the file was incomplete, Brandeis responded impatiently: "Men! Arms! Ammunition! We can't win without them."[40]

From mid-October to the very day of the city's elections (December 12), Brandeis was most intensively engaged in a strenuous endeavor to install a Puritan-like, reform-oriented leadership in Boston. He continually bombarded the GGA and other civic organizations with letters, memos, declarations, petitions, appeals, and warnings to do their utmost to block the sinister corrupting forces. One of Brandeis's most instructive communications was his letter of mid-November to Billings, where he desperately requested the composition of the voters in the primaries according to wards and precincts. Undoubtedly, learning the voting patterns of ethnic Boston had become a required lesson for a lawyer-prophet zealous for his cherished City Upon a Hill.[41]

On October 26, 1905, Brandeis received an invitation to address the New Century Club of Boston. He had received invitations from the club in the past but had always excused himself. This time he accepted the invitation. It was not that the theme—the commemoration of the two hundred and fiftieth anniversary of the Jewish settlement in the United States—overwhelmed him. Rather, it was chiefly something outside the immediate Jewish context that made him decide to address a Jewish organization for the first time in his life. He was resolved to persuade his Jewish brethren to join forces with the admired Yankees.[42]

Of course, the record of the host organizations had to be suitable to Brandeis's liberal-Progressive general course, and the New Century Club was indeed interested in good government, the democratic process, the merit system for selecting officials, honest administrations, and reform. Club members William Blatt, Jacob Silverman, and Edward Bromberg were Republicans who abhorred the practices associated with names such as Donovan and Fitzgerald. In the campaign of 1905 these Jewish professionals headed Jewish organizations that actively worked to defeat the Democratic machine. Thus, the New Century Club would provide an audience to whom Brandeis could speak as a Jew without undermining his liberal-Progressive credo.[43]

Important to understanding Brandeis's move is that some of the leading Yankees of Boston and New England actively participated in the American Jewish anniversary. Prominent among them was Harvard's president, Charles Eliot, who gave a talk at the major gathering at the Faneuil Hall. Eliot, who was enthusiastically received, spoke in the spirit of pluralism and warmly and loudly praised Jewish civilization and ideals. The New Century's Club event was also graced with the presence of General Nelson A. Miles, who emphasized the significant Jewish role in fighting in the Union army for the United States and its values.[44]

Since his address (delivered on November 28) was designed to defeat Fitzgerald, Brandeis meticulously sought journalists to cover his appearance, and he, indeed, made strenuous efforts to get the widest possible press coverage.[45] The Jewish *Boston Advocate* announced the New Century Club's banquet on the front page of its November 24 issue. And, notably, in the very same issue, the weekly printed a long editorial directly defending Mildred Kallen (and Robert Silverman), with the provocative headline "The Martyr to Gang Politics—A Painful But Important Lesson to Voters." Thus, public Jewish Boston as well contrived to inspire the evasive Jewish lawyer to make, for the first time, a display of ethnic allegiance.[46]

The talk itself was carefully slanted to mobilize the Jewish vote while avoiding any affirmation of autonomous Jewish cultural life in the United States. The speech was entitled "What Loyalty Demands," by which he meant "the obligation which this great privilege of American Citizenship involves—

the obligation of loyalty to American institutions and ideals." He called on his audience to avoid being hyphenated Americans, but at the same time to be aware of, and to live up to, the Jewish people's noble traditions and virtues. And the group values that Louis Brandeis called on his people to implement in Boston were "energy, perseverance, self-restraint and devotion, . . . intelligence or genius . . . power to hurl from its pedestal the Golden Calf," as well as "austerity." Rejecting the Golden Calf and adopting austerity were at the culmination of his Jewish virtues list and were most clearly linked, of course, to the mayoralty battle.[47]

In the same vein, although on a deeper level, Brandeis thoughtfully and forcefully claimed that the self-realization of essential Jewish ethical values also meant the fulfillment of the highest ideals of democratic American civilization. The pivotal idea—the congruence of the spiritual heights of the two civilizations—came to most consistently characterize Brandeis's philosophy.[48] Thus, faithful to his innermost social beliefs and to his expanding Jewish consciousness, he presented Judaism as an all-embracing spiritual force: "'Long after the Jewish state had fallen' their religion became 'that of civilized humanity,'" quoted Brandeis. The laws of the ancient Jews regarding the treatment of strangers showed that the "demands of Jewish law 'knew no restrictions of race, so its privileges were open to all.' The recognition of those high ideals of the Jewish race its members found at last in America. Loyalty to them is loyalty to true democracy—loyalty to the American ideals of Liberty, Fraternity, and Justice."[49]

This spirited speech, however, was studded with reminders to the listeners, and through them to all of Boston Jewry, that the Jewish tradition obliged them to be politically active, and that this activity meant voting. Referring to the 1905 Boston situation in public education and local government in general, Brandeis sought to raise Jewish involvement not under the banner of ideals only, but also in the name of vital Jewish interests. "The first law of nature," he preached to his listeners, is "self preservation;" and if the Jews wanted seriously to preserve themselves against the approaching chaos in Boston, they had to take up the fateful challenge ahead of them and to vote correctly. "[T]he Jews have a certain responsible position to fill during these important times," Brandeis reiterated, "and it is up to them to exercise this right."[50]

Thus in the name of both ancient-glorious Jewish ideals and present pressing Jewish interest, Brandeis hoped to mobilize the Boston Jewish vote; this forceful bid decisively overshadowed his reservations about hyphenated

Americanism. Moreover, though Brandeis was motivated by the urge to save his beloved Boston and its ancestral values, this was just one aspect of the personal drama. The other, distinctly Jewish, aspect was composed of his wakened interest in the civic virtues of Jewish polity, of his deepening sense of the ready-made potential of Jewish civilization for the reform of modern society, and, in conclusion, of the intensifying of his ethnic assertiveness.

Indeed, a few days after his eventful address, he sent to his cherished brother, Alfred, a "portrait of his old friend Judah Touro." Ellen Smith, the historian of the Jews of colonial Boston, illuminates some of the aspects of this historic Jewish figure (1775–1854) that perfectly fall in line with Brandeis's course of awakened ethnic affirmation in 1905: "New Orleans, Boston, and most of world Jewry would remember Judah Touro. . . . He founded the first free library in New Orleans. He purchased the debt-ridden Unitarian Church . . . and returned it to the congregation rent-free. . . . Staunchly opposed to slavery, Touro would purchase slaves in order to free them, often training them and setting them up in business." Touro, who was known as a "non-speculating" businessman, took interest in Jewish matters late in his life. A famed American patriot and eventually a prominent Jewish leader, Judah Touro belonged to a milieu of the first Jewish pioneers that had come to the shores of America; obviously, Brandeis was eagerly looking for, and beginning to find, suitable heroes from his own ethnic group to supplement the ranks of the founding Pilgrims.[51]

To his father, Adolph, who was more conversant with Jewish matters than Alfred, Brandeis sent the entire manuscript of the speech at the New Century Club and made this most illuminating comment: "I am inclined to think *there is more to hope for in Russian Jews* than from the Bavarian and other Germans. *The Russians have idealism and reverence*" (my emphasis).[52]

This experience, then, meaningfully worked to link Brandeis to his ethnic group. The East European Jews were Jewishly assertive and socially progressive—and they kindled in him ethnic pride and compelling interest. (Notably, Touro, like these people, was not one of the "Bavarians" and "Germans" criticized by Brandeis, but rather a Sephardic Jew from Western Europe.)

Obviously, Brandeis interpreted the political profile of the East Europeans, or of Jewish Boston for that matter, as being faithful to the basic tenets of American civilization, while simultaneously aspiring to refine and enhance this civilization. His intensified Jewish ethnic consciousness certainly did not develop in lieu of his American identity nor as substitute for his Yankee orientation (for about full two decades after 1905 Brandeis's phraseology literally mingled the Jewish ancestors with the American founding fathers, and the Jewish pioneers in Palestine with the New England Pilgrims). Rather, he then began an enriching process toward what Philip Gleason appropriately defines as "a pluralized, harmonious national identity."[53]

3

The *Boston Advocate* sustained the process of Brandeis's intensified "pluralized identity"; it time and again came back to the Silverman-Kallen libel case, even many months after the affair was over. The importance the Jewish mouthpiece attributed to that public battle, its consistent commitment to educational and civic values—as well as its repeated compliments to the role of the law firm of Mr. Brandeis—could not escape his attention.[54]

The 1905 elections concluded with the defeat of Brandeis's favorite. However, Brandeis was not the kind of personality to despair, especially since his ethnic group did work for the right candidate. Indeed, the critical element in Brandeis's ongoing change was the Jewish community's solid response to his social-ethical quest. The local Jewish community cooperated with him from 1906 on in the promotion of a growing number of liberal-Progressive issues. From about 1910 this happened to a great extent on the national level as well. And when, from 1911 on, he identified a high potential for realizing his social-ethical values in a beautifully small, democratic, exemplary Jewish Palestine, his "Judaization" became increasingly intertwined into what we may call "Zionization" (instructively, Brandeis himself never made a clear distinction between Judaism and Zionism). These developments altogether solidified the Jewish component of his now-enriched American identity. As he himself emphasized several times after assuming Zionist leadership, his way to Judaism and Zionism was through Americanism.[55]

In March 1913 Brandeis returned to the New Century Club and for the first time voiced his full support for Zionism. This was quite symbolic, because the Judaism he had professed at that club in 1905 and the kind of Zionism he now adopted were deeply interconnected. So, in striking similarity to his 1905 address's Judaic motif, he now explicitly spoke on the Zionist endeavor in Palestine as a worthy goal because it eminently reflected "the spiritual and moral" universal obligation of the Jewish people.[56]

The thread that firmly connected the two New Century Club appearances was the pursuit, by Jewish survival, of universalistic goals that were positively meaningful for society at large. Jewish activity in the Diaspora, as well as Zionist work in Palestine, Brandeis consistently claimed, should bear a message for democratic society and should testify to the highest American and Jewish shared ideals. These motifs clearly permeated his other Zionist addresses during 1913 as well as his August 1914 Zionist leadership acceptance speech.[57]

The process that Brandeis went through after his 1905 address also encompassed new and old motifs regarding ethnic pluralism in America. Whereas in 1905 Brandeis had reservations about hyphenated Americanism, his 1910 published version of this address depicting the Jews as a "Priest People" revised and softened that reservation. His 1911 Harvard Menorah Society address and later pronouncements connected with this nationally expanding collegiate Jewish movement were attuned, much in the spirit of President Charles Eliot, to ethnic pluralism in America. His important addresses after assuming American Zionist leadership in 1914 were similarly cast (and now sharpened in part under Horace Kallen's influence). All these pluralist threads were interwoven into his comprehensive "The Jewish Problem: How to Solve It" of April 1915, wherein he clearly conceived of America as made of diverse "nationalities." Still, a closer look at the values Brandeis emphatically expected the Jews to fulfill in America reveals, in this context as well, a clear similarity to his 1905 address where he called the Jews to live up to the civil and moral values shared by the two civilizations. In 1915, too, Brandeis emphasized that the culmination of Jewish activity, and for that matter of all "nationalities" in diverse America, would be their *contribution toward the fulfillment of shared democratic-universal values* (rather than particularistic cultural traditions). Following Harold Abramson I would suggest that with this ideologically systematic address Brandeis quite successfully completed the process of his "hyphenation," that is, a process of synthesizing a decisive assertion of Jewishness with "a larger loyalty to America."[58]

Thus, in 1915 Brandeis's contribution to the American Zionist ideology became distinctive and conspicuous. This ideology was composed of elements that strongly corresponded with his ethnic path since the fall of 1905. Jewish survival, whether as a community in America or as a national enterprise in Palestine, is justified by its positive meaning and its gift to democratic society at large. Jewish and American ideals are basically akin, therefore Zionism and Americanism are historically destined to cooperate. American Jewry can safely and decently develop in democratic and ethnically pluralistic America. Therefore, Zionism in Palestine is a complement to, not a substitute for, American Jewish life.[59]

NOTES

Abbreviations

AJA   American Jewish Archives, Cincinnati, Ohio
AJH   *American Jewish History* (succeeds *Publications of American Jewish Historical Society*)
BDN   Archives of Nutter, McClennen and Fish (previously Brandeis, Dunbar and Nutter), Boston
BL   Louis D. Brandeis, *Letters of Louis D. Brandeis*, ed. Melvin I. Urofsky and David W. Levy, 5 vols. (Albany: State University of New York, 1971–78)
BD   Brandeis Office Diary (in BDN)
BPL   Boston Public Library
FCA   Filene Cooperative Association
GGA   Good Government Association
HLS   Harvard Law School
LDB   Louis Dembitz Brandeis
LU   Louis D. Brandeis's MSS, University of Louisville Law School Library, Louisville, Kentucky

1. See, e.g., Philippa Strum, *Louis D. Brandeis: Justice for the People* (Cambridge: Harvard University Press, 1984), 224.

2. Yonathan Shapiro, *Leadership of the American Zionist Organization, 1897–1930* (Urbana: University of Illinois Press, 1971), 53–76, 248–61.

3. Strum, *Brandeis*, 224–47, 248–65.

4. Melvin I. Urofsky, *A Mind of One Piece: Brandeis and American Reform* (New York: Scribner, 1971), 93–116; Urofsky, *Louis D. Brandeis and the Progressive Tradition* (Boston: Little, Brown, 1981), 87–103; and see my detailed review of the latter in *Journal of American History* 68 (1981–82): 708–9.

5. Lewis J. Paper, *Brandeis* (Englewood Cliffs, N.J.: Prentice-Hall, 1983), 2–3, 198–99, 205–6.

6. William D. Rubenstein and Hilary L. Rubenstein, *Philosemitism: Admiration and Support in the English-Speaking World for Jews, 1840–1939* (New York: St. Martin's Press, 1999); this is a nonscholarly, though partly useful, work. On historic philo-Semitism, see Ellen Smith, "Strangers and Sojourners: The Jews of Colonial Boston," in *The Jews of Boston*, ed. Jonathan D. Sarna and Ellen Smith (Boston: Philanthropies, distributed by Northeastern University Press, 1995), 28–34; Smith, "'Israelites in Boston,' 1840–1880," in ibid., 49–51. For an excellent historical analysis of philo-Semitism in New England, see Barbara M. Solomon's *Ancestors and Immigrants: A Changing New England Tradition* (Cambridge: Harvard University Press, 1956), which discusses the first decades of the twentieth century in chaps. 8–10, pp. 152–209.

7. For Dembitz, see Robert A. Burt, *Two Jewish Justices: Outcasts in the Promised Land* (Berkeley: University of California Press 1988), 117–19, 155–56, and Ben Halpern, *A Clash of Heroes: Brandeis, Weizmann, and American Zionism* (New York: Oxford University Press, 1987), 66–71, 98–101; for deHaas, see Jonathan D. Sarna, "'The Greatest Jew in the World Since Jesus Christ': The Jewish Legacy of Louis D. Brandeis," *AJH* 81, 3–4 (1994): 353; for Kallen, see Sarah Schmidt, *Horace M. Kallen: Prophet of American Zionism* (Brooklyn, N.Y.: Carlson, 1995), chap. 4.

8. Morton Keller, *Affairs of State: Public Life in Late Nineteenth Century America* (Cambridge: Harvard University Press, 1977), and Keller, *Regulating a New Economy: Public Policy and Economic Change in America, 1900–1933* (Cambridge: Harvard University Press, 1990); Carrie T. Bramen, *The Uses of Variety: Modern Americanism and the Quest for National Distinctiveness* (Cambridge: Harvard University Press, 2000); for New England, note 9 infra, and notes of section 2, this article. Harold Abramson lists six attributes of "an entire ethnic group," all applied to the ethnic groups mentioned in my article, see his "Assimilation and Pluralism," in *Harvard Encyclopedia of American Ethnic Groups*, ed. Stephan Thernstrom (Cambridge: Harvard University Press, 1980), 151; see also William Peterson, "Concepts of Ethnicity," in Thernstrom, *Harvard Encyclopedia*, 234–42.

9. William A. Braverman, "The Emergence of a Unified Community, 1880–1917," in Sarna and Smith, *Boston Jews*, 69–90; James J. Connolly, *The Triumph of Ethnic Progressivism: Urban Political Culture in Boston, 1900–1925* (Cambridge: Harvard University Press, 1998), esp. 61–66. Pertinent, succinct national historical background can be found in Edward R. Kantowicz, "Politics," in Thernstrom, *Harvard Encyclopedia*, 803–13.

10. For background, see Melvin I. Urofsky, *American Zionism from Herzl to the Holocaust* (Garden City, N.Y.: Anchor Press, 1975), 81–144; Allon Gal, "Independence and Universal Mission in Modern Jewish Nationalism: A Comparative Analysis of European and American Zionism (1897–1948)," *Studies in Contemporary Jewry* 5 (1989): 242–74. For European Zionist ideology's problems in the U.S. and some adjustments in the pre-Brandeis period, see, e.g., Evyatar Friesel, "Brandeis' Role in American Zionism Reconsidered," *AJH* 69, 1 (September 1979): 34–59.

11. Fredrika Brandeis to LDB, November 2, 1884, *Reminiscences of Fredrika Dembitz Written for her Son, Louis, in 1880 to 1886*, translated by Alice G. Brandeis for her grandchildren in 1943 (privately printed), 32–34, in Goldfarb Library, Brandeis University, Waltham, Mass.; Gershom Scholem, "Jacob Frank," in *Encyclopedia Judaica* (Jerusalem, 1971), 7:55–72; Scholem, *Studies and Texts Concerning the History of Sabbatianism and Its Metamorphoses* [in Hebrew] (Jerusalem, 1974), 47–67. Section 2 of this article is partly based on my *Brandeis of Boston* (Cambridge: Harvard University Press, 1980).

12. For communal background, see Susan Ebert, "Community and Philanthropy," in Sarna and Smith, *Jews of Boston*, 211–23; *Annual Report of the United Hebrew*

Benevolent Association, 1894 (Boston, 1895); *Ninth Annual Report of the Federation . . .,* *May 1st 1904 to May 1st 1905,* p. 5, in BDN 15589.

13. For communal background only, see Ebert, "Community and Philanthropy," 213–26; Barbara M. Solomon, *Pioneers in Service: The History of the Associated Jewish Philanthropists of Boston* (Boston: n.p., 1956), 22–25, 52–53, incorporation in BDN 11591; *Report for 1901–1902, Hebrew Industrial School* [Boston, 1906], 14, in BDN 20256.

14. Interview with Richard Ehrlich (nephew of Abraham C. Ratshevsky), Brookline, Mass., February 16, 1974. The bulk of the constituency of Temple Israel did not support its liberal rabbis during 1874–1911; see Arthur Mann, ed., *Growth and Achievement: Temple Israel, 1854–1954* (Cambridge, Mass.: Riverside Press, 1954), 45, 63. On Brandeis's opinion, see LDB to Alice G. Goldmark, June 18, 1919, *BL,* 4:401.

15. Ebert, "Community and Philanthropy," 214–19; Solomon, *Pioneers in Service,* 176–79; interviews with Dorothy Dreyfus Bloomfield (widow of Daniel Bloomfield, brother of Meyer), Brookline, Mass., October 21, 1973, Carl Barnet (in the leather buisiness), Boston, October 23, 1973, and Helen Filene Ladd Jr. (daughter of A. Lincoln Filene), Wayne, Maine, September 3, 1974.

16. Geoffrey Blodgett, *The Gentle Reformers: Massachusetts Democrats in the Cleveland Era* (Cambridge: Harvard University Press, 1966), 168, 242; Jacob Neusner, "Politics, Anti-Semitism and the Jewish Community of Boston, 1880–1914," paper at the American Jewish Historical Society, 259.

17. For Abrahams, see *Jewish Advocate,* December 10, 24, 1909, 3, 8, resp.; Arthur Mann, *Yankee Reformers in the Urban Age: Social Reform in Boston, 1880–1900* (Cambridge: Harvard University Press, 1954), 187–98; Albert Ehrenfried, *Chronicle of Boston Jewry: From the Colonial Settlement to 1900* ([Boston]: n.p., 1963), 513.

18. Richard Abrams, "Introduction . . . Torchbook edition," in LDB, *Other People's Money and How the Bankers Use It* (New York: A. M. Kelley, 1971), 4–9; LDB to Fredrika Brandeis, November 12, 1888, Alpheus T. Mason, *Brandeis: A Free Man's Life* (New York: Viking, 1946), 33–38, 93–94; LDB to Amy B. Wehle, November 19, 1898, *BL,* 1:135; James M. Landis, "Mr. Justice Brandeis and the Harvard Law School," *Harvard Law Review* 55 (1941–42): 184–88. For the Protestant aspect on the national scene, see, e.g., Robert M. Crunden, *Ministers of Reform: The Progressives' Achievement in American Civilization, 1889–1920* (New York: Basic Books, 1982).

19. Abramson, "Assimilation and Pluralism," 157–58; Samuel D. Warren to LDB, September 7, 1901, Mason, *Brandeis,* 389; Dean Acheson, *Morning and Noon* (Boston: Houghton Mifflin, 1965), 55–83; Paul A. Freund, "Mr. Justice Brandeis," in *Mr. Justice,* ed. Allison Durnham and Philip B. Kurland (Chicago: University of Chicago Press, 1964), 181, 187–89.

20. For variations of "individual ethnic experience and change," see Abramson, "Assimilation and Pluralism," 155–60.

21. For background, see Mason, *Brandeis,* 119–21; *Boston Post,* March 19, April 9, 1903; and see notes 40–41, infra.

22. Solomon, *Ancestors and Immigrants*, 167; Elizabeth G. Evans, "Memoirs," Evans, MSS, Radcliffe College, Schlesinger Library, Cambridge, Mass., folder 2, p. 3. For background, see Ellen Smith, "Strangers and Sojourners: The Jews of Colonial Boston," in Sarna and Smith, *Jews of Boston*, 28–34, and passim in this volume.

23. *Roxbury Gazette*, April 25, 1903.

24. Eliot, see note 25, infra; David A. Hollinger, "The 'Tough Minded' Justice Holmes, Jewish Intellectuals, and the Making of an American Icon," in *The Legacy of Oliver Wendell Holmes, Jr.*, Robert W. Gordon (Stanford, Calif.: Stanford University Press, 1992), 216–28; Martin Green, *The Mount Vernon Street Warrens: A Boston Story, 1860–1910* (New York: Charles Scribner's Sons, 1989), esp. 112–98.

25. Gal, *Brandeis of Boston*, 7–11, 82, 153–56, and passim.

26. LDB's memo, September 8, 1905; Robert Silverman's statement [submitted between September 8–14, 1905]; Edward F. McClennon to David A. Ellis, September 14, 1905, in BDN 14846.

27. Braverman, "The Emergence of a Unified Community," in Sarna and Smith, *Jews of Boston*, 79–80; Stephan Thernstrom, The *Other Bostonians: Poverty and Progress in the American Metropolis, 1880–1970* (Cambridge: Harvard University Press, 1973), 135–38; Frederick A. Bushée, "The Invading Host," in *Americans in Process: North and West Ends*, ed. Robert A. Woods (Boston: Houghton Mifflin, 1902), 57–58; Braverman, "Emergence of a Unified Community," 80.

28. Ehrenfried, *Chronicle of Boston Jewry*, 545; Thernstrom, *Other Bostonians*, 135; Neusner, "Politics," 260.

29. William Blatt, in *New Century Club: A Brief History* (Boston: privately printed, 1947), 1, BPL; poem, idem, in *The New Century Club: 1900–1950* ([Boston]: privately printed, 1950), BPL.

30. *Boston Traveler*, October 11, 1905; *Boston Advocate*, November 17, 1905.

31. For background, see Braverman, "Emergence of a Unified Community," 74–75; Bushée, "Invading Host," 40–53.

32. *Boston Advocate*, September 29, 1905, 8.

33. Ibid.

34. Abrams, *Conservatism in a Progressive Era*, 143–47; Boston Transcript, December 4, 1905.

35. Abrams, *Conservatism in a Progressive Era*, 143–47; Boston Transcript, December 4, 1905.

36. *Boston Advocate*, October 20, 1905, p. 5; *Boston Transcript*, December 2, 1905.

37. *Boston Advocate*, October 20, 1905, p. 5; November 3, 1905, p. 8; November 24, 1905, 3, 8; December 8, 1905, 2, 8.

38. Documents in BD&N 14846; Edward F. McClennen to Robert Silverman, January 22, 1906, and R. Silverman to LDB, January 31, 1906. A summary of the case may be found in the *Boston Advocate*, June 22, 1906, front page. The public importance of the case is also demonstrated by the fact that eight years later, when Horace Kallen contacted Brandeis regarding the social structure of Jewish Palestine, he in-

troduced himself by name, and then immediately went on to say: "You will perhaps recall it [the name] in connection with the Silverman-Harrrington case of criminal libel which your firm tried so effectively for us." letter to LDB, December 20, 1913, AJA, Brandeis Collection, box 1071.

39. *Boston Transcript*, November 14, 1905; LDB to Henry Dewey, November 13, 1905, *BL*, 1:372.

40. *BL*, 1:371–90; LDB to Edmund Billings, November 21, 23, 1905, ibid., 376–77; LDB to John F. Fitzgerald, March 21, 1906, ibid., 414; LDB to George Hibbard, December 11, 1907, ibid., 2:60; *Boston Transcript*, December 8, 1905.

41. *BL*, 1:362–91; LDB to Edmund Billing, November 18, 1905, *BL*, 1:375.

42. Jacob Silverman to LDB, October 26, 1905; LDB to J. Silverman, October 27, 1905; J. Silverman to LDB, November 8, 1905, in LU, NMF 12–6. Previous invitations, J. Silverman to LDB, September 5, 1901; LDB to J. Silverman, September 10, 1901; LDB to William Blatt, October 8, 1904, in BDN 13258.

43. See note 29, supra.

44. *Boston Advocate*, December 1, 1905. The *Jewish Advocate* extensively covered Eliot's death in 1926, devoting a special editorial to praising his educational and civic qualities, including his liberal-pluralist and philo-Semitic attitudes, August 26, 1926, 1, 8; the following issue came back, on its front page, to these same themes, *Jewish Advocate*, September 9, 1926.

45. *Boston Advocate*, December 1, 1905; newspaper clippings in LU, NMF 12–6.

46. *Boston Advocate*, November 24, 1905, 1, 8.

47. LDB to Jacob Silverman, November 14, 1905, LU, NMF 12–6. *Boston Advocate*, November 24, 1905, p. 1; "What Loyalty Demands," 5 pp. Typescript in LU, NMF 12–6.

48. Gal, *Brandeis of Boston*, chaps. 4–6; Gal, "Brandeis's View on the Upbuilding of Palestine, 1914–1923," *Studies in Zionism* 6 (autumn 1982): 211–40; "Brandeis' Social Zionism," *Studies in Zionism* 8, 2 (autumn 1987): 191–209.

49. LDB, "What Loyalty Demands," 5 pp. Typescript in LU, NMF 12–6.

50. Ibid.

51. LDB to Adolph Brandeis, December 1905, *BL*, 1:387; Smith, "Strangers and Sojourners," in Sarna and Smith, *Jews of Boston*, 41–44.

52. LDB to Adolph Brandeis, November 29, 1905, *BL*, 1:386.

53. Gal, "Brandeis's View on the Upbuilding of Palestine," 216–22, 237–38. See Philip Gleason's excellent "American Identity and Americanization," in Thernstrom, *Harvard Encyclopedia*, 31–58, 46 (quotation).

54. See, e.g., the *Boston Advocate* of June 22, 1906, which rehearsed the case on its front page, concluding the story with "the greatest praise" to the firm of Brandeis, Dunbar, & Nutter: "This firm has added another important achievement to its already numerous victories in behalf of the people," the weekly concluded.

55. Connolly, *Triumph of Ethnic Progressivism*, 61–66; Gal, *Brandeis of Boston*, 96ff; Brandeis in his acceptance speech and addresses during the first months of his leadership, September–November 1914, in Barbara A. Harris, "Zionist Speeches of

Louis D. Brandeis: A Critical Edition" (Ph. D. diss., Univ. of California, Los Angeles, 1967), e.g., 96, 100, 125, 163.

56. Jacob De Haas, *Louis D. Brandeis: A Biographical Sketch, with Special References to His Contributions to Jewish and Zionist History* (New York: Bloch, 1929), 54. Anti-Semitism, especially a social one, had a rather marginal role in the 1905–15 process, Gal, *Brandeis of Boston*, 169–73, 195–97.

57. Harris, "Zionist Speeches," 80–98.

58. Harris, "Zionist Speeches," 99–204, 490–504; for shared values to fulfill in the United States, 496, 500 and passim. This idea was classically phrased later that year in Brandeis's Fourth of July oration delivered at Faneuil Hall, Boston, entitled "True Americanism," in *Brandeis on Zionism: A Collection of Addresses and Statements by Louis D. Brandeis,* introd. Louis E. Levinthal (Washington, D.C.: Zionist Organization of America, 1942), 3–11, see esp. 8–10. Abramson, "Assimilation and Pluralism," 156.

59. Sarna's systematic "The Jewish Legacy of Brandeis" (note 7, supra) artificially separates between Brandeis's "Americanizing" and "idealizing" of Zionism and thus misses the point—that the success of the first was thanks to its built-in idealistic-democratic factor (see 356–61).

EIGHT

"We Can Play Baseball on the Other Side"

The Limits of Nationalist History on a U.S.-Canada Borderland

Beth LaDow

"Lost between Harlem, Mont., and the Canadian line," read the advertisement, "grain sack marked J. H. Betz, containing piano leg for old style piano. Will finder please notify and receive reward." Betz, a Montanan, ran the ad in the Eastend, Saskatchewan, *Enterprise,* December 7, 1916. Probably the least of his concerns was that he ran it in a foreign country.[1]

From the looks of it, the Montana-Saskatchewan border is still a place where you could lose a piano leg and then hope that somebody from the other side of the line might find and return it, though finding a piano leg here would take longer now, at the turn of the twenty-first century, than it would have in 1916 at the height of the last homestead boom in the West. In Betz's time, Canada and the United States lured settlers to this high plains borderland one last time, with parallel railroads sandwiching the border by the 1890s and then enlarged homestead acts in 1908 and 1909. Until drought and hardship drove many away in mass exodus in the early 1920s, notices of cross-border visits of friends and relatives were frequent news items in the local papers. "Messrs. John Ryan, J. H. Sheetz, L. N. Bunteen and John Regan of

Chinook, Montana, arrived in town Monday," reads a typical notice of cross-border traffic in the Maple Creek, Saskatchewan, *News*. "They came across country in an automobile." "Breeds and Indians" from Canada "peddled wolf and coyote pelts" in Chinook, reported the *Chinook Opinion* in 1901, noting in another edition that Oliver Tingley attended a Maple Creek "race meeting, which opens today, with the thoroughbreds which he recently brought out from the east," and would "take in the Regina meet before his return."[2]

Borderland residents did cross-border business—in cattle, sheep, horses, land, opium, and, during prohibition, in whiskey. They shared traveling peddlers and entertainment troupes. They traveled back and forth for visits, supplies, picnics, and ball games, crossing the border freely (unless they had livestock), without stopping at a port of customs. "Settlers in southern Saskatchewan did much of their business in Montana," one homesteader wrote. "Gas and goods were cheaper, limitations on border crossings less stringent and mileage no greater." "It was not uncommon in those days," wrote another, "to find work across the Border." They settled, back and forth, on either side, or had ranches on both sides of the border. They compared race horses. They inconveniently had babies in the middle of rutted clay roads on cross-border trips. And not least, they played baseball.[3]

The forty-ninth parallel U.S.-Canada border that stretches across seven hundred miles of sparsely inhabited prairie is a seldom explained and quiet guest in North American history—a quietude that calls into question the nearly unwavering national categories into which we fit the history of North America and the West. Americans inherit from Thomas Jefferson not only the 49th parallel boundary, but his nationalistic view of the West. The United States and British Canada, after all, were rivals in building a continental empire. What is now the world's most peaceful border, its largest commercial sieve, was for more than a century the battleground of empires. Yet since 1867, when Britain withdrew its military outposts and Canada became a nation, the U.S.-Canada border has lapsed into an agreeable somnolence. History has fallen on either side of it, into the distant camps of the American Wild West and the orderly Canadian hinterland, peacefully separate national stories.

With Frederick Jackson Turner's famous 1893 speech, "The Significance of the Frontier in American History," the American story of the westward movement and frontiers became, for a time, the heart of America's essential story, at once grandly progressive and poignantly sad: a nation born on a frontier it was destined to overcome, finding greatness in a wilderness it was destined to destroy. Since the 1950s American historians have repudiated Turner's frontier as ethnocentric, misguidedly rural, naïvely cheerful, and hopelessly imprecise—a compelling parable about holy civic nationalism but a deeply flawed explanation for it.[4]

Nevertheless, one of Turner's enduring legacies is that the word "frontier" does not mean "border" in American history, because he changed its traditional European meaning. In Europe, by the seventeenth century, "frontier" had evolved from a frontline of troops facing an enemy to a zone of military defense to the external territorial outlines of a self-conscious nation.[5] Turner went them one better. "Frontier" in the United States would become a term to describe the westward-moving, national conquest of the continent. "The American frontier is sharply distinguished from the European frontier," he explained, "a fortified boundary line running through dense populations. The most significant thing about the American frontier is, that it lies at the hither edge of free land."[6] In the expansionist United States, "frontier" would signify the advancement of civilization into a wilderness, the new world environmental condition for American egalitarian democracy and individualism. It was an ingenious substitution. Old World terms yielded to words reflecting new world conditions. Fixed zones became moving zones; borders became "zones of settlement"; places became a process; republican patriotism became Manifest Destiny. Although Canadians have done without such a nationalist mythology, the new world frontier became the prop of American nationalism, a component of the civil religion. Actual borders fled to the margins of the national narrative, even as holy nationalism became the paradigm for history.[7]

Since the 1980s, the new western American history has renewed old efforts to knock our popular John Wayne mythology out of the lead horse's saddle, championing analytical categories of race, ethnicity, gender, and environment. The old uplifting tales of progressive nationalism and rugged individualism on the raw frontier have yielded to stories of American conquest and oppression, complexity and pluralism, and cautionary tales of ecological disaster, yet still within a national context.[8] A field of comparative studies, also concerned with the question of national identity, has long analyzed Canadian and American societies as similar yet distinct new world creations. Louis Hartz's 1955 critique of what he called the "tyrannical compulsion" of Americans toward a Lockean liberal consensus, still has appeal. Hartz argued that the hold of Lockean liberalism on the American national identity has made Americans unable to fully understand or tolerate anything else, including unconquered Indians, revolutionary communism, and, eventually, to our credit, slavery. Others, particularly Canadians, have further distinguished between Hartz's new world European "fragments," particularly Canada's Burkean political tradition which, despite British North America's own internal quarrels and its pressures toward greater independence from Britain, has long held a deep distrust of American liberalism.[9]

From these dramatic ideas have descended the pallid, if valid, homilies of social scientists, such as Seymour Martin Lipset's in *Continental Divide* on the distinct "values and institutions of the United States and Canada." Lipset's statistically backed generalizations are valuable starting-points for discussion, but they are not compelling history. We may nod when Lipset tells us that Americans are individualistic, antistatist, ideological, and egalitarian, whereas Canadians are respectful of authority, a traditional organic society, and, ironically it would seem, more concerned than Americans about the poor and outcast. Or we may nod off.[10]

History written by historians is a far messier reality. Nations, as Benedict Anderson has described them, are, among other things, "imagined communities."[11] A national identity, as another writer put it, is an imaginative stance toward the world, a question of feeling at home, or, as Eric Hobsbawm has argued, something that local people partly control.[12] A national boundary must be created—first as a centrally imposed political border, but, more important, it must gradually become a social construct, defining "us" and "them," "friend" and "enemy," in the minds of the people who live along it.[13] On one side of the cactus-pocked forty-ninth parallel, then, people were supposed to think Canadian, on the other, American. Turner himself, however, recognized in one of his earlier essays that "[i]deas, commodities even," and certainly history, "refuse the bounds of a nation." Recent historians, mucking around in the details of the past and noting the fragility of modern nation-states and new forms of globalization, have coined the term "transnational" history, or history in which shared phenomena across nations can matter as much as differences between them—where continuities of people and the natural environment can matter as much as political boundaries and the distinctions those boundaries evoke.[14]

Although the nation-state will undoubtedly persist as the central organizing principle of history and society for a good long while, this essay argues that national boundaries should not determine the boundaries of historical inquiry. Transnational and national histories must fold into a larger pluralisitic narrative. The West, for example, is often best viewed from a continental perspective. On the high plains borderland, the last North American agricultural frontier, we find the converging struggle of two capitalist democracies and many native nations to live on an unforgiving landscape. It was a struggle that, in the wake of the American Civil War, escalating native-white conflict,

and the making of an independent Canada, aroused familiar and often nationalistic visions of land and freedom. Yet for borderland residents, identity
was fluid and historically specific. Where they were and who they wanted to
become was often more important than who they had been, and neither always had to do with nations or nationalities. The forces of nature were so
strong, and the populations so similarly diverse and intermingling, that between 1890, shortly after parallel American and Canadian railroads came
through, and 1920, when the farmers' exodus began, the borderland was a
place where telling an American citizen from a Canadian became increasingly
difficult. Through the various and diverse forms of public life—baseball, picnics, or church and community associations—we find another lens through
which identity crosses, and sometimes ignores, borders.

For anyone expecting notable national differences along this border,
George VandeVen is happy to disabuse them of the idea. His readiest memories
of cross-border familiarity involve baseball, particularly the homesteaders vs.
townies rivalry. "We beat Chinook so bad they didn't even know they was on the
same field," he chuckled, still proud of the homesteaders' mighty pitching and
hitting. Another game pitted homesteaders against homesteaders, drawn from
both sides of the boundary line. One of the players was a Mountie.[15]

Nothing signified the increasing unity of the borderland's newcomers
better than baseball. By the 1890s, many Americans would have described
baseball as the "American game."[16] And certainly the American side of the
border was enthusiastic about the sport. The Chinook newspaper published
regular reports of the town team's games and related items, including a list of
"baseball proverbs" for the philosophical fan. The game was played in every
school district, from the Missouri River benchlands to the border.[17]

Moreover, baseball has long been an arena in which Canadians measure
their relative independence from American influence, a debate that was heat-
ing up during the Maple Creek–Chinook settlement period. A "southern in-
truder," a disgusted Toronto *Globe* writer called the sport in 1905, against
which "cricket fights an uphill battle to preserve old world culture on the
frontier."[18] Baseball, for many Canadians, was a symptom of creeping Americanization. Yet Canada had its own claims on the sport, dating at least from
the occasion King George's birthday in Beachville, Ontario, in 1838, at which
some form of baseball was the game of choice to celebrate the king's victory
over Ontario's democracy-minded Rebellion of 1837. This was one year before
the apocryphal "invention" of baseball in Cooperstown, New York. Long before the Canadian Pacific Railway penetrated the prairie in 1883, baseball in
its many nineteenth-century forms was popular in Ontario and along the Red

River. And the Canadian West embraced the sport with enthusiasm. By 1917, Climax, Saskatchewan, and Corral Coulee, Montana, two tiny communities that had sprung up between Chinook and Maple Creek, played "hotly contested games every weekend." In June 1919 a baseball tournament in nearby Shaunavon included teams from Havre and Chinook south of the border, as well as Maple Creek, Moose Jaw, and six other Saskatchewan towns. Along the border, Americans had no monopoly on the "national sport."[19]

Records from southwest Saskatchewan reveal not only who was playing baseball—Americans, native Canadians, and immigrants alike—but suggest that people loved it. They played it at every picnic, at every sports day, at every nationalist Canadian celebration. Often there were doubleheaders.[20] On Victoria Day 1909, "The Fat Men vs. Lean" game in Maple Creek prompted the liveliest reportage: "Bill Green, weighing 253½ pounds without his suspenders, stepped into the pitchers box with due dignity, took a fore and aft reef in his trousers, spat on the ball, swung his glass arm around two or three times, and then looked 'Dink,' who was behind the bat, square in the eye. 'Dink' rubbed his right [hand] over the place where his hair ought to have been and gave the signal for an out-drop. . . . For the hungry tribe the 'Swede' in the box looked handsome but harmless."[21]

In a small community where everyone knew everyone else, such name-calling and exaggeration were the stuff of close association based on mutual respect and understanding. In the informal setting of the district picnic, baseball was a democratic affair. Everyone played—men, women, and children. "In the summer there were ball games on Sunday afternoons," recalled a woman from near the border, "where everybody was welcome and everybody who wished to play did so, it never mattered how many were on the teams."[22]

Eastend, south of Maple Creek, eventually became a curling town, but baseball played an important part in its history. The first person ever buried in Eastend was killed in a baseball game, and as there was no cemetery, his death necessitated one. The player was Anton Rustad, hit by a pitch in a game between the hamlets of Lowell and Eastbrook in May 1914. Eastend at the time was little more than a ranch with pretensions, but the trauma of Rustad's death allegedly resulted in a ban on baseball "for some time," according to the local history book. If there was a ban, it was quickly lifted. By June the Eastend team was practicing three times a week. In 1915 local businesses closed for two hours to see their team lose 9–7, to Antelope Butte.[23]

One afternoon in the tiny town of Govenlock a few miles above the U.S. border, a man named Jack Hoffman discovered the magic of baseball. As George Shepherd tells it, Jack was in a game between the married men and the bachelors. Jack was playing for the bachelors, but everyone was soon in for a surprise. Midgame, Jack's abandoned wife from Montana arrived in Govenlock seeking her long-lost husband. "The game proceeded," Shepherd continues, "with Jack in the married men's team and the bachelors so demoralized that the married men won the game." Though "Mrs. Hoffman stayed and we came to like her a lot," in a game freighted with the metaphors of "going home" and being "safe," Jack Hoffman had literally sought a change of identity, a new beginning as a freer man. An old homesteader from the Missouri River benchlands, expressing a last wish, longed for nothing but baseball:

> The time is here about or when
> Our ages are past three score and ten.
> I hope when we cross that great divide
> We can play base ball on the other side.[24]

"We can play base ball on the other side." The writer meant in heaven, but the phrase described the borderland itself, and its promise of freedom and new beginnings. Baseball, says George VandeVen, knew no border.[25]

Nor did many of the local relationships. George likes to describe the area's transborder cosmopolitanism in another brief sketch of his childhood days on the Montana side of the line north of Chinook. As a toddler in the mid-1910s, George spent all his time at his father's coal mine, meeting the people who came to the tiny Dutch settlement of Hollandville from a wide surrounding area to buy the VandeVen's coal. They came from the new settlements and homesteads that since 1910 had filled the dry, flat borderland between the Cypress Hills and Chinook. "A lot of them," he recalled, were from the Canadian side of the line: Germans, Mennonites, Scandinavians, Russians, Dutch, Swiss, Belgians, English, Irish. They would line up and set out flared grain boxes, narrower on the bottom, to be filled. Some were returning from Chinook with a truck or wagon piled with groceries and supplies, which they'd empty out to fill with coal. A donkey pulled coal carts up a railroad track out of the mine. "It was quite a place to grow up because at one time I could speak about five languages," he said. "I could swear in five languages, too," he added with amusement—a level of erudition of which his mother was not terribly fond. The newcomers were only continuing the kind of cultural mixing that had gone on since the early settlement period in the 1890s, but now their relationships, interethnic as well as interracial, stretched increasingly across the border.[26]

With contact came composite identity—people of mixed race and ethnicity, familiar with and somewhat tolerant of the ways of others. Residents such as Mable Horse Man or Enemy Girl Jones were of mixed ancestry. Others, such as George VandeVen and artist Charlie Russell, were pluralists by desire and experience. During his youth as the most arcadian of cowboy idealists, Charlie Russell lived with the Canadian Blackfeet for six months in the 1880s (a "tough time," he admitted) and later became an advocate for the homeless Canadian Cree in northern Montana. He did not claim to understand Indian cultures fully, but visibly admired them: his artwork is filled with them, his regular dress included a Metis-style sash, and he and his friends frequently donned Indian costumes, escaping in their imaginations from an increasingly populated and complex world.[27] "The robe will be spred and the pipe lit," he would write to more than one friend; "when the grass grows long in the trails betwine our camps it is not good."[28] With Indian metaphors he would draw his white culture back toward arcadia and personal freedom.

Even as the fluidity of the border created individuals and occasions of mixed culture, on neither side of the border did all this mixing create what we would call a "multicultural" society, where groups were considered equally entitled to power, wealth, or social acceptance. This is hardly surprising, given the racial prejudices and tensions of the United States and Canada at the time. Post–Civil War American race relations had reached a new nadir in the early twentieth century, between whites and blacks as well as among ethnic groups. World War I heightened British Canadian racism against French Canada and the immigrants whom they called "enemy aliens." On the northern plains one had to look no further than native groups to find grave social imbalances. Indians at Fort Belknap, the reservation near Chinook, lived with the strange duality of physical segregation and the expectation of cultural assimilation. Indians often worked for whites as ranch laborers, but whites never worked for Indians, except as the emissaries of white culture on the reservation. Metis were accepted jockeys, scouts, musicians, shingle mill operators, and were thought worthy of listings in local histories, yet were not exempt from racial slurs. "This Metis friend had many good qualities," we learn of Isador Laframboise in the Maple Creek history book, "tho at times dimmed by lesser ones learned from other races." Canadians, by reputation more tolerant of differences and less demanding of ideological uniformity, committed their sins against difference, too. A dominant Anglo-Canadian-American culture reigned, influenced but not overtaken by myriad mingling cultures.[29]

Nonetheless, if anyplace bore out Alexis de Tocqueville's maxim that Americans were "forever forming associations," the borderland was one of these. "In the city men shake hands and call each other friends," wrote Russell in one of his prairie aphorisms, "but its the lonesome places that ties their hearts together." In Maple Creek, Chinook, and Eastend alike, the divisions born of pluralism diminished with associations, created less for ideological reasons than to provide escape from the isolation of ranch and homestead life. Between 1890 and 1920 the borderland sprouted clubs, organizations, and affiliations assiduously. In one nineteen-month period the town of East-end organized more than twelve voluntary organizations. Even on the Canadian side of the line, government was no substitute for camaraderie.[30]

Some were business organizations formed for commercial advantages. Their names filled the local newspapers. In the Chinook area cooperative irrigation projects mushroomed along the Milk River, along with an early-day small rancher's Stockgrowers' Association, Chinook Business Men's Association, Commercial Club, cooperative Farmers' Round-up Association, and North Chouteau County Wool Grower's Association.[31] The Maple Creek area produced the early-day Whitemud Pool Round Up association, and later, partly under the aegis of the provincial government's Co-operative Organization Branch, there was a Southern Saskatchewan Wool Growers' Association, Stockgrowers' Association of Saskatchewan, Maple Creek Creamery Association, a hospital board, Board of Trade, and a Public Works Commission. Wheat pool cooperatives attracted members in the 1910s and burgeoned after World War I on both sides of the line—in Saskatchewan under the guidance of American organizer Aaron Sapiro.[32]

These organizations were proof that the old frontier mythology of self-reliance and individualism was deeply embedded in an increasingly collective society in the North American West. The progressive political movement toward social justice that took hold in the 1890s across the Atlantic world had for Canadians and Americans a common origin in Europe, which led the language and ideas of social change. Moreover, views of modernity and self-reliance straddled the border. American and Canadian attitudes toward the twentieth century's shifting social and political agendas were singularly divided between conservative individualists and progressives who welcomed a new society. Rube Gilchrist, a lanky Nova Scotian who arrived in the Cypress Hills in the spring of 1900, seemed more like a dissenting American individualist when he described his neighbors as "hardy, self-reliant descendants of the original pioneers, who are very capable of looking after themselves; we don't like people from the outside coming into the hills to try and look after us."[33] Meanwhile, on the American side of the line, the Chinook prophet of cooperatives welcomed the collectivism that was transforming the dispersed and localized society on which the Western American myth of self-reliance was based: "Combined interest is the coming rule of the day," wrote the

Chinook prophet of cooperatives, W. M. Wooldridge, in 1903, and he was right, though it was not to come for twenty-odd years.[34]

Most organizations, though, were purely social—the stuff of small-town novels. A list of Chinook and Maple Creek clubs 1910 to 1915, invites a comparison of the people who formed them:[35]

Chinook	Maple Creek
Literary Society	[Robert] Burns Club
Opera House	Opera House
Chinook orchestra	Maple Creek Brass Band
Coming Men of America	Old Timers' Society
Modern Woodmen of America	Modern Woodmen of America
Ancient, Free, & Accepted Masons	Ancient, Free, & Accepted Masons
Willing Workers Society	Quadrille Club
Independent Order of Oddfellows	Independent Order of Oddfellows
Eastern Star of Montana	Canadian Order of Foresters
Ladies' Aid Society	Ladies' Aid societies
Episcopal Ladies' Guild	Horse Breeder's Association
Laurel Lodge of the Daughters of Rebecca	Maple Creek Curling Club
Chinook Baseball Team	Maple Creek Baseball Club
Gun Club	Maple Creek Dramatic Company
Royal Neighbors of America Knights of Fidelity	Maple Creek Agricultural Society
Chinook Equal Suffrage Club	A. O. U. W.
Society of Montana Pioneers (statewide)	International Brotherhood of Maintenance of Way
Commercial Club	Pioneer L. O. Lodge
St. Timothy's Guild	Royal Templars of Temperance Lodge
Chinook Aerie of Eagles	Women's Total Abstinence Society (including a "babies' league")
Democratic Party	Lacrosse Club
Republican Party	Medicine Hat Brotherhood of Trainmen (affiliations)
	Women's Hospital Aide Society
	Skating Rink Company
	Orange Lodge
	Overseas Club
	Maple Creek Boy Scouts
	Maple Creek Club
	Board of Trade
	Liberal Party
	Conservative Party

Canadians, too, were apparently "forever forming associations." The Canadian town has a distinct Scots flavor, with its Orange Lodge and Robert Burns and curling clubs. Its Quadrille and Overseas clubs suggest a European-minded populace, as does the sport of tennis, played and reported in local news.[36] The "Maple Creek Club," fashioned after an English gentlemen's club, complete with a reading room and electric lights, had no genteel counterpart among Chinook's saloons.[37] The Chinook Commercial Club had its twin in Maple Creek's Board of Trade. The egalitarian Equal Suffrage Club strikes the note of classic American reform, yet Saskatchewan granted women the vote in 1916, only sixteen months after Montana.[38] Other evidence, too, runs contrary to national stereotypes. Maple Creek's Total Abstinence Society drew public criticism from one area Scotsman who wished to "guard against the curtailing of liberty and freedom" and, in the language of Toryism or classical republicanism, advocated simple "self control" over drink.[39] Judging from this list, Chinookites appear to be nineteenth-century associative townspeople emerging into the corporate interests of a new twentieth-century society, whereas Maple Creek residents seem to be British Empire, acquiring a mixture of collectivist twentieth-century interests and American laissez-faire liberalism.

This organizational impulse in southwest Saskatchewan may have been an outgrowth of the American Progressive movement toward collective activity and reform, and thus a sign of "Americanization." (Foreign investment in Canada was at this time rapidly becoming more American than British.) It may also have been the class association that fit easily into the British and Canadian political tradition. Clearly both influences were at work in both a local and international context of social and economic transformation.

Religious affiliation was another remarkably neutral meeting ground. To paraphrase writer Norman Maclean's line that "there was no clear line between religion and fly fishing" in his Montana Scots Presbyterian family, there was no clear line between religion and socializing in this corner of the Northern Plains.[40] Religion had the aura of a social occasion, comfortable as a feather mattress; it started out that way by necessity. An itinerant Baptist preacher packed the Chinook town hall in 1890, despite a dearth of Baptists. In what seemed a proverb of regional worship, the same Baptist preacher found himself dining at a table in the Montana Hotel with a Congregationalist minister and a Catholic priest. Like it or not, people of different faiths found themselves sharing not only dinner tables but church services and rooms to hold them in. "The Scandinavians, Germans, Ontario men, Englishmen, and run-of-the-mine Americans, even the Syrian grocer and his family, became Presbyterians because that was where the only social action was," recalled novelist Wallace Stegner of the Eastend religious community he knew as a boy. While some isolated themselves from this easy-going mingling—the Mennonite communities, for example—what another early resident recalled as an "ecumenical spirit" characterized the region throughout the settlement period.[41]

At the same time, ecumenicism had its limits on both sides of the line. Missionaries to the Indians had arrived early, and native religion was suppressed at Fort Belknap. Reservation superintendents advocated "eliminat[ing] any doubtful features" of ceremonial dances that suggested "anything more than innocent amusement," generally "curtailed" the frequency and duration of dances, and tolerated no "tortures" or "sun dances." Occasional religious tensions existed among new settlers as well. Even the game of baseball could not overcome a disappointing incident in the 1920s when a Cypress Hills teacher recalled that her "four Catholics were not allowed to go to a Protestant picnic" to play ball.[42]

The hub of the area's social life, however, was neither religion nor voluntary association, but picnics—an age-old custom of rural life. "What kept these people going?" asked a chronicler of one local family history. "It wasn't religion; I never saw any of them in church." It was picnics, he suggests. On both sides of the border every neighborhood or school district held picnics, drawing from populations across thirty square miles or more. They ranged from outdoor feasts and religious meetings, to weekly winter dances with midnight "lunches" that went on until dawn, ball games, food down by a swimming hole, and full-blown rodeos. "Box socials," annual "stampedes" or rodeos, "sports days," Christmas pageants: these were the chief outlets for people's passions, the backbone of their self-image. "When a storm hit enroute to someone's home for a dance," wrote one veteran of southwest Saskatchewan social events, "no one turned back for home, but each one of the men in the sleigh would take turns walking ahead of the horses to make sure they were on the right road." He recalled attending thirty-two dances in a single winter.[43] "We would rather dance than eat," wrote one participant, high praise considering how high eating was on the list of activities in border country. There was no "age gap," no "element of social status," but great "camarad[er]ie," recalled another.[44]

If picnics were occasions at which folks could learn to accept other cultures, they were also opportunities for citizens to become explicitly nationalized—turned into Canadians or Americans. Official celebrations such as Victoria Day and Dominion Day in Canada and the Fourth of July in the United States were big events, sometimes lasting two days. By about 1910, however, the patriotic content of these events was almost beside the point. With Americans eagerly attending Victoria Day picnics, such gatherings became a forum for powerful local interests. Prominent community members occasionally threw big holiday dance parties—the Gaff family's rancher-farmer dance of 1913, for example—that people recalled with immediacy fifty years after the fact. By 1907, as sheep began to overtake cattle on local ranges and the area's wealthiest citizens tended to be sheep ranchers, Chinook held the annual "Non-Ah Float Ball," a two-day affair of dances, orations, food, and baseball to celebrate the close of the wool season. The Murraydale Stampede and Picnic in the Cypress Hills became a showcase for the best international rodeo competitors, and an ardent interest of many residents.[45]

Minority groups participated in large public celebrations, as if confirming that these were occasions at which the bonds of nationhood or community were formed among diverse people. In footraces, the "Indian race" preceded the "cowboy race" at the Victoria Day celebration at Maple Creek in 1910, for example (there was no mention of Indians who were also cowboys), and an "Indian pow-wow" was incorporated into the annual Murraydale Stampede.[46] Yet minority groups also held their own gatherings. The Chinese celebrated Chinese New Year, a week-long occasion during which they greeted other townspeople with "gong gay fa toy," or "happy new year." The Indians held Sun or Grass Dances (despite reservation agents' efforts to prohibit or curtail them) which, like rodeos or ball games, were transborder events. White observers remember watching wagon trains of Indians from the Nikaneet reservation in the Cypress Hills headed south to Fort Belknap, returning three weeks later trailing out for what seemed a mile or more with additional hangers-on and dozens of dogs.[47]

Such tribal or cross-tribal gatherings were bittersweet. They reminded Indians of their losses even as they revived their sense of identity. "My heart is sad," said Chief Little Bear, a Cree from Canada, at a Ft. Belknap Grass Dance gathering in 1903; "I see my people that were once as numerous as the mosquito and whose sting was as sharp as the buffalo gnat have fallen like the leaves shaken from the dry branch of the cottonwood tree." He continued in such striking similes, describing Indians he saw before him as emblems of a tragic loss of identity, who sat "like a death-feigning opossum, too drunk to know whether this is a grass dance or a ping-pong party."[48] In the 1870s and 1880s, before the railroads and new settlement, native groups had played a kind of political border game with the U.S. army and the mounted police. The border, which they called the "medicine line" for its power to protect them from danger on the other side, had given them asylum and hope. But after thirty years, in a time when many sources of identity competed with nationalism, many Indians believed that they were no one at all.

By the 1910s borderland residents even used national identity to promote a broader international sense of community. In 1916, when the young Canadian town of Eastend was still founding clubs at fantastic rate, a large group of area residents formed the Minnesota Society. Competing for membership with everything from the Dauntless Society (for Christian charity and benevolence) to the baseball team and the Kennel Club, its appeal was uncertain. But the Minnesota Society drew considerable attention. At its first annual banquet and dance, the 125 guests included "not only a reunion of the Minnesota people" but the "whole community" in order to "enhan[ce] the social welfare and stimulat[e] the sentiment of good feeling which has always prevailed here," reported the newspaper. They toasted the king; they toasted their adopted land; they toasted Canadian citizenship.[49]

Like Bill Helgeson, it seemed that many wanted to be Canadians *and* Americans. A Norwegian immigrant who worked for a time in Saskatchewan, and then twenty miles northeast of Chinook from 1912 to 1914, Helgeson described assimilation as a form of wisdom given him by a Norwegian-American on the boat to America: "'Get away and stay away from the Norwegians as soon as you can and have nothing to do with them. They will just keep you as long as they can, work you hard and pay you as little as they can get by with. . . . Go to work for Americans or anybody else, and see how they or other people live and work.'" Once on the Northern Plains, Helgeson lived by this dictum. "By staying away from Norwegians, I learned how to talk English fast as the Sutherlands [his first employers], and learned American ways and customs." The fact that he was in southern Saskatchewan at the time did not seem to matter. Canada and the United States were for him one general English-speaking culture. In fact, he felt "more like a Canadian or American" than a Norwegian, he wrote proudly. As another Chinook-area resident later put it, "The Canadians are Americans too."[50]

To match the complex and multilayered private identities and public life of these borderlanders, the history of the West would benefit from a more fully imagined North American West. If Frederick Jackson Turner's oversimplified scheme of a single American culture forged by wilderness has long gone by the wayside, so should the enduring nationalist lens that ignores the continuity of social, economic, and ecological regions. Generalizing about this West will not be easy. Local environments and who happened to be in them make for many different stories. What happened on this borderland is not what happened in Alberta and Wyoming ranch country. Nevertheless, this history presents a world in which the parallel Canadian and American railroads that pushed across the northern prairie in the 1880s, the natives they displaced, and the settlements they spawned, are parts of a single story. The time has come for a transnational lens, more specific than that of just capitalism or democratic societies, or a generalized "wilderness"—a lens through which we can compare shared populations and environments. Nationalism is still a faith position among historians. But as George VandeVen knows, it is time we made it part of the pluralistic view of history—just one factor among many.

When in 1914, World War I suddenly lay across the cross-border culture like a fuse, the old "medicine line" abruptly reemerged. Children became aware of affiliations they "hadn't really known we had." "Here's to the American eagle," the Canadian boys taunted American-born boys; "He flies over mountain and ditch, But we don't want the turd of your goddamn bird, You American son of a bitch." Nationalism, particularly anti-German and antiethnic sentiments, occasionally verged on hysteria, as when Chinook townspeople threatened to hang an "old rancher named Herman Boldt . . . but instead they made him get down on his knees in front of the court house and kiss the flag."[51]

But strong nationalist feelings proved neither divisive nor long lived. Compared to the American southwest, where nationalist and assimilationist sentiments exacerbated Anglo-Hispanic tensions, this borderland retained a friendlier atmosphere, simply because its population, though diverse, did not divide along a clear fault line of linguistic and racial differences. Nor was the region a timeless and ancient rural heartland common in Asian or European typology, preserving authentic age-old values against a tide of modernity.[52] For most people in the region identity was complex—a blend, often self-conscious, of where they were at the moment and who they had been before. In this harshest of physical environments, they all wanted to achieve what one Eastend French aristocrat called "la vie libre," to *become* something and still retain part of where they had come from. In the lives on the borderland, the real divide was not the border. It was the line that divided past from future—the line of hope—and, as in baseball, a game without a clock, it seemed to stretch into infinity.

NOTES

Some of this material appeared previously in different form in *The Medicine Line: Life and Death on a North American Borderland* (New York: Routledge, 2001.)

    1. *Eastend Enterprise,* December 7, 1916.

2. *Maple Creek News*, May 26, 1910; *Chinook Opinion*, August 6, 1903; June 6, 1901; May 30, 1901.

3. Wallace Stegner, *Wolf Willow: A History, a Story, and a Memory of the Last Plains Frontier* (Lincoln: University of Nebraska Press), 84–85; *Chinook Opinion*, April 23, 1903; *Eastend Enterprise*, March 4, 1920; Ann Saville, ed., *Between and Beyond the Benches: Ravenscrag* (Eastend, Sask.: Ravenscrag History Book Committee, 1983), 242–43.

4. Frederick Jackson Turner, "The Significance of the Frontier in American History," in *The Frontier in American History* (Tucson: University of Arizona Press, 1986), 3, 12. Richard Hofstadter, *The Progressive Historians* (Chicago: University of Chicago Press, 1968), pt. 2, chap. 4, "The Frontier as an Explanation," is still one of the most insightful of myriad Turner critiques. Two recent reevaluations are Patricia Nelson Limerick, *The Legacy of Conquest: The Unbroken Past of the American West* (New York: W. W. Norton, 1987), 20–27, and William Cronon, *Nature's Metropolis: Chicago and the Great West* (New York: W. W. Norton, 1991), 31, 46–54, 402 n.115.

5. Lucien Febvre, "*Frontière:* The Word and the Concept," in *A New Kind of History: From the Writings of Lucien Febvre*, ed. Peter Burke, trans. K. Folca (New York: Harper & Row, 1973), 208–11; Fernand Braudel, *The Identity of France*, vol 1., *History and Environment*, trans. Sian Reynolds (New York: Harper & Row, 1989), 310.

6. Turner, "Significance of the Frontier," 3.

7. Febvre, "*Frontière,*" 214–15; Peter Sahlins, "Natural Frontiers Revisited: France's Boundaries since the Seventeenth Century," *American Historical Review* 95 (December 1990): 1441; Turner, "Significance of the Frontier," passim. On Canada, see John Conway, "An Adapted Organic Tradition," *Daedalus* 117 (fall 1988): 4, 383.

8. The most influential of these historians and their works are Limerick, *Legacy of Conquest;* Donald Worster, *Rivers of Empire: Water, Aridity, and the Growth of the American West* (New York: Pantheon Books, 1985); Richard White, "*It's Your Misfortune and None of My Own*": *A New History of the American West* (Norman: University of Oklahoma Press, 1991); and Cronon, *Nature's Metropolis.*

9. Louis Hartz, *The Liberal Tradition in America: An Interpretation of American Political Thought since the Revolution* (New York: Harcourt, Brace, 1955), 12, and *The Founding of New Societies: Studies in the History of the United States, Latin America, South Africa, Canada, and Australia* (New York: Harcourt, Brace, 1964), 93–95, 114, 118. Classic works discussing Canadian national character are Frank Underhill, *In Search of Canadian Liberalism* (Toronto: Macmillan of Canada, 1960), and W. L. Morton, *The Canadian Identity* (Madison: University of Wisconsin Press, 1961).

10. Seymour Martin Lipset, *Continental Divide: The Values and Institutions of the United States and Canada* (New York: Routledge, 1990), 2.

11. Benedict Anderson, *Imagined Communities: Reflections on the Origins and Spread of Nationalism* (London: Verso, 1983), 15.

12. D. J. Jones, *Butterfly on Rock* (Toronto: University of Toronto Press, 1970), 4, quoted in A. B. McKillip, *Contours of Canadian Thought* (Toronto: University of Toronto

Press, 1987), 17; E. J. Hobsbawm, *Nations and Nationalism since 1780: Programme, Myth, Reality* (Cambridge: Cambridge University Press, 1990), 10–11.

13. Peter Sahlins, *Boundaries: The Making of France and Spain in the Pyrenees* (Berkeley: University of California Press, 1989), 8, 270–71.

14. On Turner's global perspective, see Thomas Bender's introduction to *Rethinking American History in a Global Age*, ed. Thomas Bender (Berkeley: University of California Press, 2002), 2–5. He takes the Turner quotation from Frederick Jackson Turner, "The Significance of History," in *Frontier and Section: Selected Essays* (Englewood Cliffs, N. J.: Prentice-Hall, 1961), 20–21. Transnational history demotes the nation-state to one more factor in the turbulent, pluralist variety of people, interests, institutions, and ideas, both new and persisting, that are the central premise of Morton Keller's work. See especially his portrait of how modern American society emerged in *Affairs of State: Public Life in Late Nineteenth Century America* (Cambridge: Harvard University Press, 1977) and *Regulating a New Economy: Public Policy and Economic Change in America, 1900–1933* (Cambridge: Harvard University Press, 1990). On transnationalism, see the essays in Bender, *Rethinking American History;* "The National and Beyond: Transnational Perspective on United States History," a special issue of the *Journal of American History* 86 (December 1999), esp. David Thelen, "The Nation and Beyond: Transnational Perspectives on United States History," 965–75, Richard White, "The Nationalization of Nature," 976–86, and Ian Tyrrell, "Making Nations/ Making States: American Historians in the Context of Empire," 1015–44; and also a periodization of the transnational into a "borderlands" stage of development in Jeremy Adelman and Stephen Aron, "From Borderlands to Border: Empires, Nation-States, and the Peoples in Between in North American History," *American Historical Review* 103 (June 1999), and responses to their article in *American Historical Review* 104 (October 1999).

15. Author interview with George VandeVen, Chinook, Montana, August 6, 1998.

16. By the 1890s Walt Whitman had described baseball as "America's game," with the "snap, go, fling of the American atmosphere," and Mark Twain remarked that it was "the very symbol . . . of the drive, and push, and rush" of the nineteenth century. Nicholas Dawidoff, ed., *Baseball: A Literary Anthology* (New York: Library of America, 2002), 5.

17. *Chinook Opinion*, April 25 and May 23, 1901. Wayne Westover, "Time Keeps Passing," 1964, MS., Blaine County Public Library, Chinook, Montana.

18. William Humber, *Cheering for the Home Team: The Story of Baseball in Canada* (Erin, Ont.: Boston Mills Press, 1983), 15.

19. Humber, *Cheering for the Home Team*, 12–13; anonymous, "North Country Ball," *Chinook Opinion Golden Jubilee edition*, 1964; *Eastend Enterprise*, June 26, 1919.

20. See *Maple Creek News*, May 26 and July 7, 1910, or *Ranching News*, May 27, 1909, reporting two baseball games played on Victoria Day, May 24.

21. *Ranching News*, May 27, 1909.

22. Gladys (Baynton) Perrin, "John and Evelyn (Reed) Baynton," *Between and Beyond*, 374.

23. Anonymous, "Riverside Cemetery," *Range Riders and 'Sodbusters'* (North Battleford, Sask., 1984), 119. *Eastend Enterprise*, July 1, 1915.

24. Westover, "Time Keeps Passing."

25. George Shepherd, *West of Yesterday*, ed. John H. Archer (Toronto: McClelland and Stewart, 1965), 87.

26. VandeVen interview, August 6, 1998; "Interview with George Vandeven," June 28, 1984, Montana Historical Society, OH 796, tape 1 of 2, interviewer Laurie Mercier.

27. Brian Dippie, *Charles M. Russell, Word Painter: Letters, 1887–1926* (Fort Worth, Tex.: Amon Carter Museum, 1993), 25, 47, 121–122.

28. Charles M. Russell letter to Churchill B. Mehard, October 1916, and letter to Maynard Dixon and Frank B. Hoffman, August 21, 1917, in Dippie, *Charles M. Russell*, 229, 240.

29. Keller, *Regulating a New Economy*, 251, 282; Gerald Friesen, *The Canadian Prairies: A History* (Lincoln: University of Nebraska Press, 1984), 354; "Nikaneet Indian Reserve," *Between and Beyond*, 301–6; Gwen Pollock, comp., *Our Pioneers* (Maple Creek, Sask.: Southwestern Saskatchewan Old Timers' Association), 61–62.

30. Alexis de Tocqueville, *Democracy in America*, ed. J. P. Mayer, trans. George Lawrence (1848; Garden City, N. Y.: Doubleday, 1966), 513; Charles M. Russell letter to Tom Conway, March 24, 1917, in Dippie, *Charles M. Russell*, 233–34; *Eastend Enterprise*, 1914–16.

31. Janet Allison, *Trial and Triumph: 101 Years in North Central Montana* (Chinook, Mont.: North Central Montana CowBelles, 1968), 20, 18; *Chinook Opinion*, February 26, March 5, 1903, May 23, 1901; Bonifas, "Curtain Going Up," MS., Blaine County Public Library.

32. Saskatchewan Department of Agriculture, "Historical Outline of Agriculture in Saskatchewan as Reflected in Reports of the Department" (Regina: Saskatchewan Archives Board, 1955), vi; anonymous, "Ranching in the Cypress Hills and Area," MS., Saskatoon Archives Division, Canada Department of Agriculture Publication 1133, Saskatchewan Archives Board, M85.1.102; *Ranching News*, May 19, 1904, *Maple Creek News*, February 10 and September 15, 1910, and November 20, 1913. On Sapiro's efforts in the United States, see Keller, *Regulating a New Economy*, 154–56.

33. Harold Longman, "Rube Gilchrist," *Leader Post*, August 23, 1954, in Saskatchewan Archives Board.

34. On Europe's leading role in the "highly complex web of international institutions and influences" that constituted what Daniel T. Rogers calls the Atlantic world's "age of social politics" (1890–1940), see Daniel T. Rogers, "An Age of Social Politics," in Bender, *Rethinking American History*, 258, 261. *Chinook Opinion*, March 5, 1903, reprinted from the *National Homemaker*, January 1903.

35. *Chinook Opinion*, 1901–8; Bonifas, "Curtain Going Up," MS.; *Maple Creek Ranching News*, 1903–1904, *Maple Creek News*, 1909–1914; John Bennett, *Northern Plainsmen: Adaptive Strategy and Agrarian Life* (Chicago: Aldine, 1969).

36. C. Blytheman's provincial tennis career is followed in the *Maple Creek News,* 1909–11.

37. *Maple Creek News,* February 8, 1912.

38. John Archer, *Saskatchewan: A History* (Saskatoon, Sask.: Western Producer Prairie Books, 1980), 176; Michael Malone and Richard B. Roeder, *Montana: A History of Two Centuries* (Seattle: University of Washington Press, 1976), 202–3.

39. Letter from Thomas C. Armstrong, *Maple Creek News,* December 1, 1910. A "Thomas Armstrong," born in Scotland in 1879, immigrated to Canada in 1889 and is listed in the *Fourth Census of Canada, 1901,* The Territories, 204, Assiniboia West, Maple Creek, p. 11.

40. Norman Maclean, *A River Runs Through It and Other Stories* (Chicago: University of Chicago Press, 1976), 1.

41. *Chinook Opinion,* June 26, 1890; "History of Blaine County Churches," *Chinook Opinion Jubilee Edition,* 1964; *Chinook Opinion,* May 29, 1890; Stegner, "Finding the Place: A Migrant Childhood," in Clarus Backes, ed., *Growing Up Western* (New York: Harper Collins, 1991), reprinted in *Where the Bluebird Sings to the Lemonade Springs: Living and Writing in the West* (New York: Random House, 1992), 7. On Mennonites, see Caroline Erbacher, "Minnesota Settlement," and Ann Schroeder, "Hydro," MS., 1964, Blaine County Public Library.

42. Narrative annual reports for 1911, 1915, 1916, and 1920, Fort Belknap Agency, BIA Superintendent's Annual Narrative and Statistical Reports, 1907–8, microfilm roll 45, National Archives of the United States. Memories of Emma G. Robinson in "Teachers at Fairwell Creek School District," *Between and Beyond,* 251.

43. See Henry Louis Gates Jr., *Colored People* (New York: Alfred A. Knopf, 1994), 211–16; Jack Shepherd, "The Jack Shepherd Story," in *From Sage to Timber: A History of the Fort Walsh, Cypress Hills (West Block), Merryflat, and Battle Creek Areas* (Maple Creek, Sask.: Merry Battlers Ladies Club, 1993), 210; Arne Svennes, *Between and Beyond,* 111.

44. Rachel (Newton) Decrane, "Reminiscing," *Between and Beyond,* 12.

45. Shepherd, *West of Yesterday,* 73; Lillian Miller, "I Remember Montana," reminiscence, MS. (Montana Historical Society, Helena, Mont.), 204–6; "R. L. Polk & Co.'s Directory," 1909–10 and 1915–16; *Chinook Opinion,* August 1, 1907; *Between and Beyond,* 174.

46. *Maple Creek News,* May 26, 1910.

47. *Chinook Opinion,* February 18, 1904; Superintendent's Annual Narrative and Statistical Report 1915, Ft. Belknap Agency, BIA, roll. 45; "Nikaneet Indian Reserve," *Between and Beyond,* 304.

48. "Grass Dance Is Celebrated," reprinted from the *Havre Plain Dealer* in the *Chinook Opinion,* July 2, 1903.

49. *Eastend Enterprise,* September 24 and October 29, 1914, February 25, June 10, July 1, and August 12, 1915, and January 6 and 20, February 3 and 24, and March 9 and 16, 1916.

50. Bill Helgeson, "Homesteading on the Big Flat," MS. (Blaine Country Public Library, Chinook, Mont.), 1–2; VandeVen interview, August 6, 1998.

51. Dan Cushman, *Plenty of Room and Air* (Great Falls, Mont.: Stay Away Joe Publishers, 1975), 191.

52. Sarah Deutsch, *No Separate Refuge: Culture, Class, and Gender on an Anglo-Hispanic Frontier in the American Southwest, 1880–1940* (New York: Oxford University Press, 1987), 118–19. Prasenjit Duara, "Transnationalism and the Challenge to National Histories" in Bender, *Rethinking American History*, 34.

A Successful Defense of Yesterday

Hoyt Moore and the Administration of the Steel Code under the National Industrial Recovery Act

Charles W. Cheape

As centerpieces of the early New Deal, the National Industrial Recovery Act (NIRA) and the National Recovery Administration (NRA), which was created in 1933 to administer the law, have been much analyzed by historians. Led by Arthur Schlesinger Jr., a traditional interpretation described the program as a major, well-intentioned, but ultimately unsuccessful attempt at integrated public-private planning for economic recovery.[1] In this view the legislation involved a significant expansion of the state's role that failed in the face of sometimes contentious opposition from private interests, especially the business community, before the law was declared unconstitutional by the U.S. Supreme Court in May 1935.

In a familiar fashion, a revisionist interpretation emerged in the 1960s and 1970s. Ellis Hawley's masterful study highlighted the failure or frustration of all parties to the process, including central planners, economic reformers, big and small business, and organized labor.[2] Many revisionists went further to explain the NRA's failure by focusing on its ineffectiveness and its efforts to accommodate big business in order to establish a corporatist, associational economy.[3] Recently, a more nuanced, postrevisionist study has pictured the NRA as a transition case. In this version the New Deal program helped awaken initially hostile or indifferent big businessmen to the advantages of cooperation with government in order to reduce state regulation and provide more industry control and stability, although the results were sometimes disappointing.[4]

As a central factor in the American economy and as the epitome of big business, the steel industry has usually been seen by various historians of the NIRA as behaving in accordance with their larger interpretive patterns. The traditional view described the struggles by top regulators and the White House to compel industry captains like Myron Taylor and W. A. Irvin at U.S. Steel and Charles Schwab and Eugene Grace at Bethlehem Steel to get in line.[5] Revisionists have pointed out the steel industry's support for and control over its NRA code, which was abetted by poor judgment and weak oversight within government itself.[6] Postrevisionists have said that despite steel's early, reluctant cooperation with the NRA, by 1935 the industry recognized the agency's value for its own ends and sought an active response from the Roosevelt administration after the Supreme Court struck down the NIRA.[7]

However, a close study of the inner workings of the steel code challenges all three interpretive schools. The industry's experience with the NIRA instead reflects an extension of the patterns of U.S. political economy in the Gilded Age and Progressive Era charted by Morton Keller. Public policy evolved not through any single dominant pattern of causation but in an untidy process involving contingency, the persistence of past forces in the face of change, and the interaction of numerous, diverse factions.[8] In a similar fashion, the papers of Hoyt Moore, chief counsel and architect of the steel code, show that steel men were consistently fearful, defensive, and adversarial toward the NIRA and the NRA from beginning to end.[9]

Moreover, the episode reflects Moore's dominant role in the process. In this crisis for the nation and the steel industry, leadership fell not to high-profile executives like Schwab and Grace but to a veteran specialist in corporate law, who not only administered but also shaped, wrote, and interpreted policy. As an expert in opposition to the expansion of state power and the concomitant rise of organized labor, he amply reflected the suspicion and hostility of the industry leaders who were his nominal bosses. He also skillfully and effectively devised, implemented, and directed the means to express and sustain that resistance in order to preserve virtually autonomous private enterprise. For a key national industry, he blunted the application of the largest and most controversial program of public intervention in the early New Deal.

Establishing Control

Hoyt Moore's control of the actual operation of the Steel Code Authority emerged during its formation, which has been described elsewhere and needs only brief review.[10] Part of his power naturally resulted from the external forces necessitating the code. The Great Depression left the steel industry in desperate straits, running at 25 percent of capacity between 1931 and 1933. Then the NIRA mandated a series of individual industry codes produced jointly by representatives of the NRA, owners, and workers and focused on trade practices and labor relations. Commercial provisions were to set and regulate standards for production and selling. Labor portions called for a shortened work week, a minimum hourly wage, and recognition of workers' rights to organize and bargain collectively.

Contrary to revisionist and postrevisionist versions, the steel industry deeply feared the new program's expansion of government and labor power. At the first meeting of the American Iron and Steel Institute (AISI) to consider the NIRA, executives obsessed over labor issues and virtually ignored trade clauses that offered the chance to control price and production. Hysterical industry leaders even refused to attend a session when government officials invited William Green, president of the American Federation of Labor.

Simultaneously fighting the nation's worst depression and the increasing threat of government intrusion and organized labor and hampered by the weak AISI which had little authority or expertise, steel men almost inevitably turned to Hoyt Moore. They badly needed someone with specialized knowledge, independence, negotiating skills for dealing with government administrators and fiercely autonomous business leaders, and appreciation for the power conferred by the creation of the Steel Code Authority. No steel executive qualified, but Moore had all the essentials. Born in 1870, he was a senior partner in the prominent corporate law firm of Cravath, Degersdorff, Swaine and Wood (later renamed Cravath, Swaine and Moore). He was a veteran in business-government relations, having worked for nearly three decades as a committed supporter of private enterprise in appearances before the Federal Trade Commission (FTC), in negotiations with the U.S. Department of Justice, and in filing briefs with the U.S. Supreme Court.

Moore was especially attractive for his long association with the steel industry. Bethlehem Steel Corporation had been his major client for more than twenty years, and one Cravath partner aptly noted that "no lawyer ever unreservedly gave more of himself to a client than Hoyt Moore has given to

Bethlehem." Moore's dedication, mastery, and success earned the complete trust and confidence of Charles Schwab, Bethlehem's founder, and Eugene Grace, its long-time president, who nominated the attorney as chief counsel of the AISI to first draft and then administer the steel code. While their support assured his appointment, their industry-wide respect and leadership and Moore's position as an independent attorney offset any fears that he would simply be a Bethlehem man.

Building on his ability, expertise, and impressive backing, Moore quickly consolidated and extended his power and influence by creating an extensive network of experts and executives in key positions. Eight Cravath partners and associates worked for the steel code, including his assistant, Chester McLain. In drafting the code Moore worked closely with two former Cravath lawyers, Robert McMath and Kenneth Halstead, who had become powerful senior executives at Bethlehem and U.S. Steel respectively. As his key steel man, the attorney had Walter Tower, a nine-year manager of commercial research at Bethlehem, who with the backing of Schwab and Grace would become the code's chief administrator.

Despite a potential rivalry between the lawyer and the steel man, Moore's edge in age, experience, and authority made him the dominant partner in a smooth relationship. Tower, whose career blossomed in the 1920s (almost two decades after Moore appeared), was a modern manager comfortable with bureaucracy and collective action. Unlike the steel man and younger corporate and New Deal lawyers who were similarly inclined and who believed in expanded public power through cooperation or coercion, the sixty-three-year-old Moore was a feisty nineteenth-century conservative who vigorously espoused private enterprise, the open shop, limited government, and individual rights.[11]

For him, as for Schwab, Grace, and most other senior steel executives and owners, the Steel Code Authority was not an entry into some corporatist framework uniting business and the state. An unavoidable program mandated by (then) popular public policy, it had to be designed to blunt the intrusion of government power. Moore's shared vision with steel leaders and critical expertise in law and business-government relations assured his leadership. His prior personal relationship with Tower (whose son had married the attorney's daughter) helped promote harmony as the two experts reinforced each other's efforts. In fact, Tower probably owed his position as much to Moore as to Schwab and Grace.

Finally and fundamentally, Moore's administrative power resulted from his design and drafting of the steel code itself in the summer of 1933. Far more than a legal technocrat translating top managers' and owners' ideas into legal language, he was a leader, an interpreter, and a policy maker. His first version set the agenda for all subsequent discussions and with only minor changes became the final code, justifying his later boast that "I planned the code in that way." He and McLain skillfully garnered unqualified written assent to the new code authority from the often captious heads of fractious, competing firms. In addition, he served as the industry's central link in successful negotiations with the federal government.

Moore's single greatest innovation for the steel code was his application of the rule of private contract, simultaneously binding members together by force of law, minimizing the federal government's role, and exalting his own power as the chief counsel for the Steel Code Authority who was inevitably and frequently consulted about the interpretation and enforcement of the contract. That provision, which was apparently unique among all the NRA codes, gave Moore extraordinary flexibility and power.

On the one hand, his document centralized authority over code members and enforced tightly regulated trade practices to regulate price and production and to restore profit margins. It reduced competitive discretion by requiring all members to sell at a delivered price that had two essential, standardized components—base pricing and all-rail transportation costs. Several dozen basing (or origination) points were defined near major centers of steel manufacture, and each producer had to list prices publicly for each of his products at the nearest basing point in order to assure uniform calculation of shipping charges. A ten-day period for implementation precluded rapid, competitive changes, and open pricing promoted the homogenization of quotations. Actual transportation charges were set by all-rail published prices from the basing point and not from the actual place of production.

On the other hand, the contract allowed Moore to pursue a decentralized approach to labor relations that preserved company autonomy and compelled the federal government to pursue individual firms for any transgressions. Although the code restated the language of Section 7(a) of the NIRA calling for workers' rights to organize and bargain collectively, industry leaders simultaneously asserted their unswerving devotion to the open shop and the promotion of company unions to discourage independent organized labor. To evade NRA attempts at national labor standards, the steel code created twenty-one labor districts with differing minimum wages. Instead of a forty-hour week, member firms only had to average forty hours per week over a six-month period.

Thus the code's labor provisions insulated the code authority from any requirements to participate in or enforce matters not stipulated in the contract itself. Moore cleverly realized that he was creating an instrument that centralized power over the steel industry as required and approved by the federal government. As he planned it, the use of contract law reflected his and most steel leaders' deep commitment to unfettered private enterprise and prevented the government from using the Steel Code Authority to further extend its own power over the industry.

President Franklin Roosevelt approved the steel code in August 1933, confirming Moore's leading role. He had written a document that won the industry's enthusiastic endorsement. At first, 184 companies assented, and eventually 250 of the estimated 350 eligible firms signed the agreement. Nonsigners, though considerable in number, represented only marginal concerns, for early supporters accounted for more than 93 percent of ingot capacity and 84 percent of the industry's sales in 1932. At the same time Moore had so well planned and tightly drawn the code that officials in the NRA and in the Roosevelt administration found it virtually impervious to serious modification. Nevertheless, in their anxiety to launch the high-profile program, they accepted it. As one envious government advocate ruefully observed, "The battle went to the strong."

Exercising Control

Given Moore's dominance in creating of the steel code, his central role in its administration followed logically. Within the industry Moore confirmed that leadership at the first official meeting, on August 29, 1933, of the AISI's board of directors acting as the code authority. He prepared to control events even before the session began, first designating the compelling problems to be faced and then making them the formal agenda. In most cases he also prepared resolutions for such issues as jobber definition and status, discount policy, transportation rules, and the determination of voting power by members according to their sales volume. The minutes indicate that he ran much of the day-long meeting, smoothly covering his full agenda and easily obtaining passage of his proposals with little significant disagreement or modification.[12]

Besides confronting immediate industry concerns, Moore's resolutions reinforced the centralized structure of the Steel Code Authority that the lawyer had first planted in the code itself, making the AISI's board of directors and not the larger trade association the authority's top body. The attorney could more easily oversee the thirty-man board (later expanded to thirty-two), for it was of course much smaller and many of its members were well known to Moore as he was to them. As he noted later, "We gave a great deal of thought to the question of how the Board should operate." The creation of four functional committees at the first meeting (which were eventually increased to seven) maintained the tight focus by retaining final authority in the board itself and by appointing board members to chair five of the seven bodies.[13]

Such an organization made it even easier for Moore and his group to dominate the operation of the code. President Robert Lamont and Secretary George Charls of the AISI soon resigned to be formally replaced by Tower as executive secretary and Moore as counsel, which allowed the lawyer to bring in his team of attorneys from the Cravath firm, including L. V. Collings, who succeeded Charls as operating secretary. Moore and Tower quickly tripled the AISI staff to sixty-two, fifty of whom worked for the code authority.[14] Because the board met only monthly and its executive committee (actually called the general administrative committee) convened only biweekly, Moore and Tower and their associates became the core of the code authority. Only they could provide full-time, continuous, and expert management, and unlike the committee members they owed no allegiance to any individual steel company.

Moore played a surprisingly active, ongoing part in the code's operation though as counsel he would normally have been only a consultant. The statistics committee quickly made gathering data routine, but in the areas of rule making, interpretation, and enforcement—the essence of the code authority's activities—Hoyt Moore was at the center as he had planned. His design had made the steel code itself comprehensive but very difficult to amend. As a result, the interpretation and application of its general provisions depended on a series of commercial resolutions and regulations, usually drafted by Moore or reviewed by him if proposed by a functional committee. In effect, the document embodying the steel code was a constitution and the subsequent rules were laws. Having written the constitution, the lawyer now helped compose the laws.

The process kept rule making out of the hands of meddling politicians, government officials, and steel makers alike. For example, because the determination of basing points was such a contentious issue for both steel manufacturers and their customers, Moore insisted that their locations should be specifically included in the code. As he explained the arrangement to one steel man, "I planned the Code in that way because I was fearful that, if it were made easy to amend the basing point schedule, there would be pressure from all sides, particularly from Washington which as you know, desires to have all basing points cut out and to have the products sold either f.o.b. mill or f.o.b. destination." When powerful interests raised substantive complaints about errors or omissions in the list, commercial resolutions provided corrections.

Thus, in October 1933, commercial resolution thirteen compensated Detroit, which was not listed as a basing point, with special advantages in the calculation of transportation costs in order to assuage the outcry from General Motors, Chrysler, and their supporters.[15]

The code authority employed this technique frequently and fairly effectively. Although the steel code called for the calculation of transportation costs using railroad rates, some fourteen resolutions and regulations were passed to allow adjustments for water and truck transport. Though the document permitted jobber discounts (at Moore's insistence), eleven different rules were enacted to define and refine jobber status.[16] At the first meeting of the authority, Moore pushed through two regulations to define jobber qualifications while avoiding quantity discounts that would complicate record keeping and encourage evasion of the code's delivered-price formula.[17]

Naturally such proposals did not originate entirely with Hoyt Moore. As suggested by his use of "we" in describing the choice of the AISI's board of directors to head the code and by his occasional presentation of an issue as an open question, he consulted carefully with knowledgeable and powerful industry officials outside his own group of experts, most often with Eugene Grace with whom he had long been associated. However, on issues that he considered vital to the code's enforcement and the preservation of the steel contract, he successfully fought even owner-operators to get his way.

When H. L. Hughes, assistant to the president of U.S. Steel, and K. B. Halstead, counsel for the same firm, proposed in commercial resolution eight that purchasers be charged for the cheapest water rate available even if they later shipped by rail, Moore forced them to back down and require that products be shipped as sold. Hughes complained bitterly to no avail that such a demand "would be impracticable for such a seller to make such an investigation and at the same time have any chance of securing the business." The steel men's optional approach created a loophole for a bigger private discount, which directly threatened the orderly system of delivered prices that the code promised.[18] To preserve the enforcement powers of the code authority, the manufacturers had to surrender.

At the same time Moore demonstrated a political astuteness that escaped most steel makers. In the face of criticism that the NIRA negated the nation's antitrust laws, Hugh Johnson, the head of the NRA, had argued vociferously that industry codes should not penalize small firms. Given this continuing and emotional public concern, Moore thought it "inadvisable" to have jobber discounts based on quantity, which would disadvantage little enterprises. In this case at least, political concerns reinforced the lawyer's desire for a simplified pricing process that was easily overseen.[19]

In a similar vein, Moore and his Cravath associates often wrote or reviewed Tower's drafts of letters responding to criticisms about code provisions from complainants both within and without the industry. The lawyer was certainly no public relations expert, and he was often abrupt, fussy, and obscure. However, his long career in dealing with government bodies made him more sensitive to public opinion than most steel makers. Furthermore, his reviews and drafts assured strict adherence to the legal complexities and details of the steel code in order to maintain the contract's power and effectiveness in preserving the industry's autonomy. Indeed, his exquisitely precise explanations in numbing legal language often must have left critics disarmed or confused.[20]

In the area of actual implementation, Moore's role was more indirect because the code authority created its own enforcement division and process, if somewhat belatedly and incrementally. Overwhelmed at the start by the immensity of its tasks, the authority did not at first review all of its members' contracts, but concentrated instead on examining preexisting long-term and consignment agreements, which offered the biggest opportunity for deviation from the code's formula for delivered prices. Much of this work was done by a team of Cravath lawyers brought in by Moore. In December 1933, nearly four months after the code's enactment, the board of directors created an enforcement division, which eventually had a team of fifteen people.[21]

The enforcement division faced a huge challenge, for in conforming with the code, members filed more than 20,000 base prices and thousands of contracts, including more than 5,300 jobber agreements. To facilitate implementation the division published the jobber agreements, inviting criticism from competitors. Publication brought more than six hundred protests, resulting in the cancellation of fifty agreements and the modification of selling terms for specific products in a quarter of the other cases.[22]

The system worked reasonably well, especially given the code authority's newness and inexperience and the expected resistance to such investigations and discipline from previously autonomous firms that had answered to no one in their pricing and sales practices. Total fines levied were surprisingly low, totaling only $21,709 as of January 1935, which an NRA report judged "negligible" in the face of thousands of contracts totaling hundreds of millions of dollars. The remarkable rate of compliance reflected a combination of steel makers' support for Moore's code and the threat of substantial fines, which were assessed at ten dollars per ton, about one quarter of the composite price of steel.[23]

In the area of labor, the part played by Moore and his team was smaller because, as noted earlier, the lawyer intentionally planned to minimize the code's role and leave as much responsibility as possible to the individual firms in order to thwart any intrusion by the federal government or organized labor. This limited effect applied not only to labor relations, which were left entirely to member firms and the NRA, but to issues involving minimum wage and maximum hours provisions, which were included in the code. The Steel Code Authority's statistics committee gathered and reported requisite data on wages and hours to the NRA. The authority's labor committee and enforcement divisions made cursory investigations of complaints, which amounted to little more than seeking explanations from the companies involved.[24]

Because the code did not provide for penalties after verifying violations, Walter Tower explained to the federal administrator overseeing the steel industry that "the most that it [the board of directors] can do" was to report the incidents to the NRA. Nor did the authority expect to find any problems. An astounded Kenneth Simpson, one of two NRA representatives on the AISI's board of directors, reported that when he asked about labor infractions in early 1935, he "was informed by various directors and, in particular by the Chairman, Mr. Grace, that no violations of the labor portion of the Code had occurred within the last twelve months."[25]

Besides those issues in which Moore and his team wanted no part, there were of course conflicts that suggested the limits to their power. Perhaps as many as one hundred eligible companies refused to join the code, even after being informed of their opportunity and duty to do so. Most were marginal enterprises that could be easily ignored, but some, like the South Chester Tube Company, raised problems for the code authority. South Chester persistently undersold its competitors, and despite its small size and dated technology, it did unsettle the steel pipe industry.[26]

At times the challenges were defined geographically. A report by the chairman of the code's traffic committee lamented that "it is difficult to conceive of a more chaotic situation or a more flagrant disregard of the Code than now prevails in the State of Texas. . . . In many situations our committee was convinced that jobbers were being encouraged, if not actually aided and abetted, in some practices [by code members]." Texas had long been a chaotic dumping ground for low-priced products, and even after eighteen months of

the steel code, powerful jobbers, intransigent steel manufacturers, an un-
friendly Texas Railroad Commission, and aggressive truckers were in no
mood to accept any system of delivered prices.[27]

Nevertheless, there were virtually no major challenges to Moore and his
team from within the industry, and the lawyer effectively quashed the one serious exception within the code's first six months. A network of product committees comprised of middle-level managers from major companies colluded
to stabilize production and fix prices in violation of the nation's antitrust
laws, mocking Moore's plan of delivered prices openly arrived at and seriously jeopardizing the code's support in the NRA and at the White House.[28]
When the FTC, which was bitterly hostile to the Steel Code Authority and to
the NRA, exposed the practices in early 1934, Moore swiftly moved to end
them and break the committees' power.[29] Within a few weeks he had the
product managers removed from the code authority's commercial committee
and the product committees banished from any role in the steel code.[30]

Except for a few specific and narrow challenges like the South Chester
case, Moore and his team dominated the Steel Code Authority from this
point on. He had always had the backing of top executives, like Eugene Grace,
W. A. Irvin, Tom Girdler, and Ernest Weir. He had long shared their ideas
about private enterprise and limited government, and the code authority as
conceptualized by Moore had effectively articulated and implemented those
beliefs while insulating industry and individual company practices from
government intrusion. Moreover, for similar reasons he had broad support
among the leaders of most medium and many small companies as well. Although the industry code imposed an unprecedented centralized authority
over such competitive, independent firms, it did so with familiar techniques
and traditional appeals like the basing point system, delivered prices, an
equal opportunity to compete for business, and decentralized control over
labor relations. Finally, of course, no one could replace the attorney's expertise and experience.

The entire industry's enthusiasm for Moore's work was twice demonstrated by its members' overwhelming assent to the code in votes taken in the
summer of 1933 and again in the late spring of 1934, when companies representing more than 90 percent of industry capacity, endorsed the plan. In addition, the steel code was remarkable for the very few complaints against it
from within the industry itself.[31] In short, the major challenges to the authority
of Moore and his team of experts came from the very government that had
required the code in the first place.

Marginalizing Government

For Hoyt Moore, and very possibly for Walter Tower as well, the Steel Code Authority's major task was to deal with and usually combat the NRA and other parts of the federal government. Although Tower signed much of the correspondence from the code authority to the NRA, he consulted Moore on all key issues, and in many cases the lawyer was the steel industry's voice. Thus, he recommended that code members not respond to a seemingly innocuous survey by the NRA about future relations between the steel industry and the federal government, arguing that the questions were too broad to be answered accurately and that imprecise replies might unknowingly commit the industry in detrimental ways.[32]

At the same time Moore and Tower had to be circumspect in accepting the right of powerful owner-operators to voice their opinions. However unwise these sentiments might be, such top men could not be muzzled or ignored. In some cases the cooperation came naturally, as when Moore accompanied Eugene Grace to the office of Joseph Eastman, federal coordinator of transportation, to urge that railroads buy their steel only from code members, even if at a higher price than that quoted by nonmembers. Moore and Grace had long worked together, and Grace was often viewed by outsiders as the industry's spokesman.[33] In other cases Moore and Tower had to surrender control. For example, E. T. Weir promptly censured the two men for their "presumptuous" usurpation of the right of individual expression in instructing code members not to respond to the NRA survey mentioned above. Tower apologized and Moore agreed that the issue was best dropped.[34]

Nevertheless, although Moore and Tower compromised in a few cases, they served as code spokesmen simply because only they had the knowledge, the expertise, and the continuous, full-time focus essential for handling the complex problems of government regulation, sometimes involving federal agencies in conflict with the NRA itself. Thus, Moore supplanted H. E. Graham of the Jones and Laughlin Steel Company to negotiate with Comptroller General J. R. McCarl on the ticklish issue of pricing bids for U.S. government projects. McCarl naturally insisted on the lowest possible quotations, even if they violated code formulas for delivered prices and contradicted NRA policies for economic recovery. Despite repeated argument and appeals to the NRA itself, Moore lost this case, for even a Cravath colleague pointed out the futility of seeking NRA sanction of the federal government for disobeying the code.[35]

In other instances Moore was more successful. He used the contacts of Cravath's Washington office to monitor a hostile investigation by the FTC and to acquire secretly an advance copy of its report. He effectively negotiated with representatives of the Southern Hardware Association and with the U.S. Department of Justice (via Cravath's Washington office) in order to free the organization from a 1926 antitrust decree so that its members could negotiate jobber contracts consistent with code provisions. And he diplomatically but firmly quashed a blundering attempt by General Thomas S. Hammond, chief of the Trade Associations Division of the NRA, to have his body and the Department of Commerce certify the code's authority to handle trade practices and employee relations.[36]

As industry voices, Moore and Tower occasionally found it useful to work with the NRA. They appealed with some success to R. W. Shannon, the NRA's deputy administrator of the steel code, for exemptions for steel firms from overlapping codes in printing, engineering, construction, and electrical work. Initially, steel manufacturers retained oversight of employees in already existing operations in those areas, while regulation of any new work went to the other codes, but by 1935 the NRA had generally terminated steel's exemptions from overlapping codes.[37]

Cooperation with the NRA for mutual self-interest was especially useful in dealing with other branches of the federal government. Exploiting the NRA's antagonistic relationship with the FTC, Moore sent an advance copy of that agency's hostile report on the steel code in March 1934 to Blackwell Smith, Assistant General Counsel of the NRA, apparently at Smith's request. This action preceded a meeting of the AISI's board of directors with NRA head Hugh Johnson to complain about the FTC's inaccuracies and biases, which prompted Johnson to have Moore and Tower to prepare a statement that the NRA could use to answer the document.[38]

Moore's most important use of the NRA helped undermine an investigation by the National Recovery Review Board in the spring of 1934. The board, a political creation of severe NRA critics like U.S. Senators Gerald Nye and William Borah, amply reflected the hostility of its chairman, Clarence Darrow, toward big business in general and U.S. Steel in particular.[39] Its interrogation of the Steel Code Authority occurred shortly after the FTC's March 1934 report, and its near certain condemnation of the Steel Code Authority raised serious problems. The steel code was simultaneously being reviewed by the NRA for renewal by President Roosevelt, and another effective public attack might well lead FDR to insist on major modifications that would sharply curtail the industry's autonomy.

Moore then turned to Donald Richberg, general counsel of the NRA, to help bail out the steel manufacturers and simultaneously blunt the NRA's own critics. In the Darrow hearings the review board insisted on accepting the FTC report as a basic source of evidence for the steel industry and refused to let the contentious Moore mount an extended counterattack. Moore quickly withdrew the Steel Code Authority from the hearings and, after winning Richberg's approval (which Hugh Johnson seconded), he adamantly rejected the review board's demand that it return.[40]

Lacking the power of subpoena and anxious to avoid delay, the Darrow group backed down and did not make a public issue of the withdrawal, even though Moore and Tower denied the board's later attempt to see code authority papers. Its subsequent, hostile report apparently had little effect on the renewal of the steel code (though it did help strengthen critics of the NRA), and the critical momentum against the steel code faded.[41]

However, cooperation with the NRA was neither comprehensive nor enthusiastic nor typical of Moore, Tower, and the Steel Code Authority. It occurred in those relatively few instances of mutuality of interests, and it was necessitated by the steel men's need to insulate themselves from the emergence of a more active state. For their part there was no vision of a corporatist society that depended on the integration of the public and private sectors and their elites so as to assure a stable order.[42] Even in the case of the Darrow board, Moore's agitation and personal appeal to Richberg at home indicated a hurried, unplanned, and temporary alliance. The steel lawyer and the Steel Code Authority were responding to events instead of directing them.

Like Eugene Grace, Tom Girdler, E. T. Weir, and others for whom he worked, Moore extolled a laissez-faire approach in which businessmen worked out their problems among themselves. He bitterly condemned owners who ran to government to resolve problems of private enterprise. When a warehouse firm in St. Paul, Minnesota, complained directly to the NRA about a code regulation, Moore growled that "it does seem to me a pity that [their protests] cannot be written directly to the Institute or to some member of the Code so that a satisfactory answer will be made and Washington kept out of the matter. I cannot refrain from wondering what Nichols, Dean, & Gregg would think if someone should go to Washington complaining as to their prices."[43] Moore was sure that "such men do not think of the consequences to result from the clear implication of their action that they are desirous of having governmental interference with business."[44]

This mistrust of government in general was applied specifically to the NRA from the outset as demonstrated by Hoyt Moore's design of the Steel Code Authority and its contract. Furthermore, after a year's experience under the New Deal–mandated arrangement, Moore remained unyielding in his opposition to the NRA, even though he recognized the obvious benefits to the steel industry. He wrote privately to Gilbert Montague, a fellow elite corporation lawyer active in the formation of several codes, that "as you know, personally I am entirely out of sympathy with the principle underlying [the] codes and I believe that the sooner they are gotten rid of the better. I say this realizing that they have given some freedom from the antitrust laws, but I believe the remedy is worse than the disease."[45]

Under Moore's and Tower's direction, then, the code authority normally pursued an adversarial relationship with the NRA to restrict any state infringement of private enterprise, a spirit that pervades Moore's papers. Government representatives on the code authority's board of directors often found themselves ignored or stymied. Kenneth Simpson, the original NRA division administrator for the steel code and thus a member of the AISI board, complained that the code authority made little serious effort to answer NRA criticisms or to respond to its request for changes: "I have said many times in the past to them, that they must take some action on these important matters, otherwise, the action will be taken for them by the Administration. I endeavored to make this statement as emphatic as possible." On the other side, Moore counseled Tower to beware of R. W. Shannon, Simpson's deputy and successor in overseeing the code. "It would seem that he is holding out on you for some purpose."[46]

The Steel Code Authority frequently seemed to go out of its way to resist the NRA as the result not only of the steel men's hostility to government but also because of Moore's closely related concern that the contract embodying the code authority be punctiliously observed in order to preserve its viability. Thus, when the NRA asked each code to establish a standardized trade practices committee in order to facilitate the handling of interindustry problems, the steel authority failed to do so, leaving the issue to its commercial committee, and did not bother to report its inaction until questioned.[47] In another case, for more than a year the code authority refused to grant the Metropolitan Water District of Los Angeles the right to use much lower land-grant railroad rates in calculating the transportation charges for its steel, although such rates were allowed to the federal government and the New Deal's Reconstruction Finance Corporation was financing the project.[48]

Moore's team was especially uncooperative on labor matters, as the lawyer had intended. When R. W. Shannon learned that workers at Bethlehem Steel's plant at Sparrow Point received their pay in two-week intervals after they had earned it, he asked Walter Tower to investigate the situation for possible "unnecessary hardship" on the workers. Tower refused to act because this complaint was not a code matter of minimum wages and maximum hours according to the contract. He argued that it was not an issue covered by the code "in any sense" and was "entirely a matter of contract or understanding between employer and the individual employee."[49]

Subsequently, the NRA asked all codes to add a few simple rules about the method of payment to their industry's workers, but Moore urged Tower to skirt the issue. The executive secretary was to write Shannon that he could not predict what the directors would do until they were presented with the question. Meanwhile, he was to tell Shannon, "I have filed your letter in such a manner that it will come to my attention again if and when amendments to the Code shall come up for consideration." Moore privately wrote Tower that "it does not seem to me that Mr. Shannon's letter calls for serious attention at the present time."[50]

Such entrenched resistance even led to defiance of President Roosevelt. When cooperatives like the Ohio Equity [Flower] Exchange Company and the American Fruit Growers, Inc., complained that they lost customary discounts because they did not receive jobber status under the steel code, Shannon asked Moore and Tower to reclassify the two enterprises. He cited FDR's executive orders of October 23, 1933, and February 17, 1934, that removed code burdens from cooperatives and referred to the opinion of NRA counsel, who had participated in drafting the February order and who insisted that it was created especially "to cut squarely across this particular code."[51]

Moore ignored the request, pointing out that neither firm met code authority standards for jobber status. He went on to assert that the executive order was an unconstitutional attempt to modify the steel code contract to which the president had already assented. When Shannon and NRA counsel persisted, the ever suspicious Moore advised Tower that Shannon wanted a showdown, which would be unwise. Instead, he suggested simply acknowledging the deputy administrator's letter while advising code members that they could not give jobber discounts to unqualified cooperatives. In March 1935, more than a year after the conflict had begun, neither cooperative was listed among the industry's jobbers.[52]

Moore and Tower's unrelenting, contentious approach generated little reprisal and in fact achieved remarkable success. The Steel Code Authority persisted in its autonomy, and in mid-1934, nine months after its enactment, FDR, who was anxious to sustain the NRA's momentum, renewed the code with no serious modifications. The radical reforms urged by the FTC and the Darrow board, including the abolition of the basing point system, were ignored as were labor leaders' complaints and reformers' requests for public hearings. In fact, the process was settled by negotiations between an NRA group headed by the already sympathetic Donald Richberg and an AISI group including Moore and top owner-operators like Grace, Irvin, Weir, and Girdler. As in the 1933 creation of the code, the steel lawyer was at the center, interpreting, recasting and even initiating language.[53]

Most of the specific changes implemented were embodied in recommendations formally made by the Steel Code Authority. An eight-hour day became mandatory immediately, no longer requiring the industry to reach 60 percent capacity, but that practice was already the industry norm and the forty-hour week could still be averaged over a six-months period. Tying members' dues directly to sales in place of a flat charge for all firms with less than $500,000 annual gross did not significantly strengthen the voting power of small companies (as reformers had hoped), and Moore readily agreed to the change. A ten-day interval for filing price changes was abolished, but the practice of published prices was retained. The code authority surrendered its power to set minimum prices, which it had never used. It also allowed the use of cheaper transportation by water and truck but reserved the power to set terms.[54]

The two most significant changes were only potential ones that were never used. FDR ordered the NRA and the FTC to recommend alterations in the basing point system, but the two bickering agencies made separate studies that appeared only shortly before the NIRA was declared unconstitutional. In the other case, the NRA's head was empowered to suspend any action by the AISI's board of directors that improperly amended the code. That change did place a theoretical limit on the board's power to interpret the rigid code, as Moore had planned, but the amendment was never employed. In sum, the alterations were so meek that even the NRA admitted that there was little effect, and enthusiastic code members endorsed the revisions by a 92 percent vote.[55]

Resisting to the End

The renewal left intact the basic tenets of the code as well as the industry's fundamentally hostile attitude toward the NRA. It is hardly surprising, then, that the steel industry exhibited little desire to extend the code or to embrace some other form of government cooperation and regulation when the U.S. Supreme Court ruled the National Industrial Recovery Act unconstitutional in the Schechter case in late May 1935.[56] Prior to that decision, code authority leaders did begin maneuvering to deal with the renewal of the NIRA, which they apparently thought likely. They demonstrated no enthusiasm but reacted reluctantly to conform outwardly to public policy as they had two years earlier at the NRA's birth. Furthermore, Moore and Tower showed no interest in joining other firms and industries lobbying for extension.[57]

The Schechter decision declaring the NIRA unconstitutional freed Moore, Tower, and the steel manufacturers from any public expectations about civic duty and cooperation with the federal government. They immediately made clear that they had no intention of working with the NRA or of seeking its reenactment, for the adversarial relationship between the code authority and the federal agency had worsened since the steel code's extension a year earlier.

Since 1933 R. W. Shannon and other NRA officials had repeatedly sought to have the code authority oversee nonmembers from the steel industry to ensure their conformity to the code and to relieve the burden on the NRA's own overworked enforcement division. Throughout 1934 and early 1935, Moore and Tower resisted tenaciously, first by denying any authority and responsibility and then by half-truths, evasion, and inaction. However, their weakening position by March 1935 was troubling, for the stakes were considerable. Nonmembers often underpriced code members, and by ignoring them the code authority avoided publishing the dissenters' lower rates with the rest of the industry's basing point prices.[58] Perhaps even more important was Moore's determination to restrict the code to the precise limits of the contract itself. To extend the code authority's power to cover outsiders would fundamentally compromise its carefully constructed function as a private agent of the steel industry and make it vulnerable to external control as an instrument of the NRA and the federal government.

Although Moore's delay and obfuscation on the nonmember issue repeatedly exasperated Shannon and the NRA, a year-long battle on the printing of a labor poster left Moore and Tower even angrier and more hostile and confirmed all their suspicions about the inevitable creeping intrusion of government power. When FDR asked the NRA to make rules about informing workers of their rights, the agency produced a poster that gratuitously added the president's remarks about employees' right to vote for collective bargaining, made when Roosevelt extended the steel code in June 1934.[59]

At a time of very bitter labor relations in the steel industry, any additional references to worker organization incensed Moore, who then successfully appealed to Donald Richberg's assistant, Blackwell Smith, to have the extra wording struck off. However, AFL President William Green, a member of the NRA's Labor Advisory Board, persuaded Hugh Johnson to reverse Smith's decision. The equally determined Moore then convinced Donald Richberg that he should again strike off the offending language, but when the steel lawyer returned from a two-month vacation in the fall of 1934, Richberg had added new material from FDR's order creating a special National Steel Labor Relations Board, which the frustrated Moore thought even worse. In early 1935 he angrily persuaded the NRA to once again remove the extra wording and to have the Steel Code Authority added to the list of bodies to which workers could complain. That action once more set off the prolabor forces in the NRA, who in April moved to have the AISI struck off the poster and to reinstate additional language about worker rights.[60]

By this point the contentious relationship had begun to lose even the veneer of formal civility. During the poster case Moore had angrily harangued Richberg that "I cannot see the slightest excuse for keeping always before employees this constant urge to stir up trouble. What we need is peace, not more unrest among employees, but the more there is of this kind of thing the more unrest there will be." An equally frustrated Shannon had abandoned his even-handed, trusting approach toward the Steel Code Authority by early 1935 and accused Walter Tower of "endeavoring, innocently, no doubt, to confuse the issues." Moore's and Tower's delays and evasions so goaded Shannon that over the minor issue of special billet prices he abruptly and without warning threatened to recommend that the NRA suspend an action by the AISI's board. The attack ignited the already hostile Tower, who in this case at least was acting properly. He charged Shannon with automatically assuming that the AISI board "consciously acts to the contrary purpose" and with having an attitude that generated "conditions that appear at times to approach friction." Shannon fired back that any such claim was "utterly at variance with fact of which your knowledge is equal to mine."[61]

In this sullen atmosphere, cooperation between the Steel Code Authority and the NRA fell to a new low, and prospects for preserving the steel industry's autonomy looked very gloomy. Shannon chided his close associate Malcolm Sharp for thinking "that the Steel Industry is more inclined toward industrial statesmanship than my experiences reveal." Even the normally sympathetic Richberg told the AISI's directors that "in the present temper of the public mind there [was] no possible chance for their industry, or indeed any industry, to proceed under any privately formed or operated agreement of a cartel nature. The only choice [was] between a return to the conditions of the status quo ante or operations under a code involving a high degree of cooperation with and participation by the Administration."[62] Meanwhile, the NRA steadily worked toward a significant modification of the basing point system into a group mill plan and continued pushing the code authority toward accepting oversight of nonmembers with the resulting publication of their prices.[63]

As the NRA became more rigorous in its regulation of the industrial codes and the relationship between the steel industry and the agency deteriorated, Moore reacted by helping to draft the plaintiff's brief against the U.S. government in the Schechter case that eliminated the NRA. The historian of elite corporate lawyers during the New Deal has argued that they were ambiguous about the constitutionality of New Deal legislation and especially of the NIRA. This confusion resulted in part because of their business clients' support for a program that the companies so dominated. However, such uncertainty never bothered Hoyt Moore because, as we have seen, he had skillfully and effectively avoided cooperation when possible and insulated his clients from the interference of the active state by using existing contract law. Likewise, as the future of the steel industry's private contract dimmed, he represented steel makers' interests by attacking the NRA's constitutionality.[64]

Immediately following the Schechter decision, then, the steel industry happily severed relations with the NRA and looked toward a return to Richberg's status quo ante. The AISI's board of directors quickly stopped operating as the head of the code authority. The contract ceased with the termination of the code, and the authority no longer received or published basing point prices or collected damages for violations. Later in the summer, at Moore's direction the AISI made its final statement about the NIRA and the preservation of private enterprise by refusing to surrender its code records as the NRA requested.[65]

The industry's only continuing interest in using government centered on the unlikely possibility that existing legislation might somehow permit the reinstitution of a private industry contract to regulate trade without antitrust liability, a forlorn hope that soon died. One week following the Schechter decision, the AISI's board of directors voted for self-regulation to uphold the old code rules with no enforcement provisions. Three days later at a meeting of AISI members, about 150 steel companies, representing more than 90 percent of ingot capacity, unanimously agreed to maintain "individually and voluntarily" practices of fair competition, prevailing wages and hours standards, and rights of collective bargaining (meaning company unions).[66]

Steel men offered no evidence that they missed the NIRA or longed for its return. As a sop to public opinion they agreed to report violations to the NRA, if any appeared. Not unexpectedly, the industry never needed to make any such statements and otherwise behaved as it had prior to 1933 and the Steel Code Authority. For example, even without the official controls of Moore's contract, the system of multiple basing points and delivered prices continued to operate informally, just as it had before the NRA, until antitrust enforcement ended it in 1948.[67]

In addition, the steel manufacturers' determined opposition to organized labor persisted despite the passage of the National Labor Relations Act in 1935, which the U.S. Supreme Court upheld in the Jones and Laughlin decision in 1937.[68] In one major exception, Myron Taylor of U.S. Steel signed a contract with the Steel Workers Organizing Committee in 1937. But Taylor had little contact with the Steel Code Authority and acted for his own reasons that were unrelated to the NRA experience. Bethlehem accepted unions only after a bitter strike and prosecution under the National Labor Relations Act in a case defended by Hoyt Moore. The resistance of Tom Girdler's Republic Steel Company to unionization produced a vicious strike that ended in ten deaths in the famous Memorial Day massacre of 1937.[69]

The record of the steel code creates serious problems for all major interpretations of the NIRA. Contrary to the traditional view, on both sides the battle was not fought by top leaders like Schwab, Grace, Roosevelt, and Johnson, but in the trenches by relatively unknown men like Moore, Tower, Shannon, and Simpson. Furthermore, the code's history flatly contradicts any corporatist interpretation by revisionists or postrevisionists. The steel industry maintained throughout its experience with the National Industrial Recovery Act a remarkably sustained, adversarial relationship toward the NRA and any effort at government regulation. It did not seek the NIRA; it did not work willingly with the NRA; and it did not lament the passing of the law and its enforcement agency. Indeed, by 1935 the relationship between steel and the government had worsened. The industry's case simply offers no evidence for a cooperative, corporatist vision depending on the integration of mutual government and business interests to achieve harmony and stability.

Steel's experience should encourage future analysts of the NIRA to apply Morton Keller's more nuanced historical approach instead of searching for some single pattern of causation. His work on late-nineteenth and early-twentieth-century America has convincingly portrayed a political economy that is variegated, complex, and inconsistent as the forces of persistence and pluralism interacted with change.[70] The ample repetition of such patterns in the steel code's history points the way to a more complete and persuasive study of the entire NIRA.

In particular, steel's record reflects the linkage between continuity and contingency. A single remarkable attorney led the determined preservation of steel leaders' entrenched preferences for private enterprise and a limited state. Like many conservatives, including the more famous contemporary lawyer and politician James Beck, Hoyt Moore vigorously opposed the New Deal.[71] Unlike Beck, who railed fruitlessly about constitutional abstractions,

Moore battled effectively through the creative and continuing application of his legal expertise. Although he led a team of experts and established a powerful hierarchy to control the industry, Moore was not the harbinger of a new corporatist society. Unlike New Deal lawyers and some more accommodating corporate attorneys, he had scant use for bureaucracy, expert administration, and regulation through public-private cooperation or government coercion. He happily oversaw the rapid disbanding of the Steel Code Authority and its team of experts and returned to his independent practice as Bethlehem Steel's counsel.[72] As an advocate of private power, strict constructionism, and individual rights, he chose to destroy a strong centralized organization that could be eventually co-opted by growing federal authority.

Ironically, of course, his very success in protecting the steel industry's intransigence and autonomy only sharpened the fears of opponents of big business and eventually produced a far more intrusive regulatory state. However, as of 1935 such changes were still being debated. For the first three years of the New Deal, Hoyt Moore led a remarkably successful defense of yesterday.

NOTES

1. Arthur M. Schlesinger Jr., *The Age of Roosevelt,* vol. 2, *The Coming of the New Deal* (Boston: Houghton Mifflin, 1965), 87–176.

2. Ellis W. Hawley, *The New Deal and the Problem of Monopoly: A Study in Economic Ambivalence* (Princeton, N.J.: Princeton University Press, 1966), 19–146; Pamela Pennock, "The National Recovery Administration and the Rubber Tire Industry, 1933–1935," *Business History Review* 71 (winter 1997): 543–68; Jason Taylor, "Cartels or Fair Competition? The Economics of the National Industrial Recovery Act," *Essays in Economic and Business History* 17 (1999): 215–28.

3. Bernard Bellush, *The Failure of the NRA* (New York: Norton, 1975); Robert F. Himmelberg, *The Origins of the National Recovery Administration: Business, Government, and the Trade Association Issue* (New York: Fordham University Press, 1976).

4. Colin Gordon, *New Deals: Business, Labor, and Politics in America, 1920–1935* (New York: Cambridge University Press, 1994), 166–203.

5. Schlesinger, *Age of Roosevelt,* 2:116–17.

6. Jesse C. Moody, "The Steel Industry and the National Recovery Administration: An Experiment in Industrial Self-Government" (Ph. D. diss., University of Oklahoma, 1965); Bellush, *Failure of the NRA,* 52–53.

7. Donald R. Brand, *Corporatism and the Rule of Law: A Study of the National Recovery Act* (Ithaca, N.Y.: Cornell University Press, 1988), 207–26; Gordon, *New Deals,* 201.

8. Morton Keller, *Affairs of State: Public Life in Late Nineteenth Century America* (Cambridge: Harvard University Press, 1977), esp. chaps. 9–11, and *Regulating a New Economy: Public Policy and Economic Change in America, 1900–1933* (Cambridge: Harvard University Press, 1990).

9. Hoyt Moore's records constitute the bulk of the collection of the American Iron and Steel Institute at the Hagley Museum and Library in Wilmington, Delaware, and subsequent citations to them will be identified as the AISI Collection.

10. Charles Cheape, "Tradition, Innovation, and Expertise: Writing the Steel Code for the National Recovery Administration," *Business and Economic History* 25 (winter 1996): 69–88. Unless otherwise noted, this article provides the sources for the remainder of this section.

11. Daniel Ernst, *Lawyers Against Labor: From Individual Rights to Corporate Liberalism* (Urbana: University of Illinois Press, 1995); Peter Irons, *New Deal Lawyers* (Princeton, N.J.: Princeton University Press, 1982). For the study of an attorney who corresponded to Moore, see Sidney Fine, *"Without Blare of Trumpets": Walter Drew, The National Erectors Association, and the Open Shop Movement, 1903–1957* (Ann Arbor: University of Michigan Press, 1995).

12. E.F. Broun, "Notes on First Meeting of Board of Directors . . . August 29, 1933," August 30, 1933, in Memoranda of Fact, vol. 1, box 60, AISI Collection.

13. Hoyt Moore to L.V. Collings, March 29, 1934, correspondence file, vol. 5, box 54, AISI Collection; Walter Tower, "The Operation of the Steel Code," May 24, 1934, box 59, AISI Collection.

14. Tower, "Operation of the Steel Code."

15. Hoyt Moore to L.F. Rains, September 7, 1933, correspondence file, vol. 1, box 54, AISI Collection; H.C. Crawford's undated, unsigned memorandum on steel code transportation policy, attached to Walter S. Tower to Hoyt Moore, December 31, 1934, correspondence file, vol. 9, box 55, AISI Collection.

16. A.G. White, "Preliminary Report on the Iron and Steel Industry," March 1935, 34–35, box 3, entry 33, Code Administrative Studies, Records of the National Recovery Administration, Record Group 9, National Archives, Washington, D.C. Subsequent citations will be identified as NRA, RG9.

17. Broun, "Notes on First Meeting . . . August 29, 1933."

18. Hoyt Moore to H.L. Hughes, September 7, 1933, and H.L. Hughes to Hoyt Moore, September 7, 1933, correspondence file, vol. 1, box 54, AISI Collection; Commercial Resolution no. 8, in Office File re Commercial Resolutions and Regulations, box 57, AISI Collection.

19. Hoyt Moore, memorandum for Mr. McLain, January 4, 1934, in Memoranda of Fact, vol. 1, box 60, AISI Collection.

20. See, e.g., Walter Tower/Hoyt Moore to Arthur D. Whiteside, 8 January 1934, in Price Fixing file, box 67, AISI Collection; Hoyt Moore to Frank Cobourn, April 28, 1934, and Hoyt Moore to Edwin J. Marshall, April 30, 1934, correspondence file, vol. 6, box 54, AISI Collection.

21. E. F. Broun, "Memorandum: Resolutions Regarding Enforcement of Steel Code," September 26, 1934, in Memoranda of Law, vol. 1, box 58, AISI Collection; Hoyt Moore to Donald S. Richberg, November 17, 1934, correspondence file, vol. 9, box 55, AISI Collection.

22. Tower, "Operation of the Steel Code;" C. W. King to Walter S. Tower, June 26, 1934, in Memoranda of Fact, vol. 2, box 60, AISI Collection.

23. White, "Preliminary Report," 48; Code of Fair Competition for the Iron and Steel Industry, art. 10, sec. 2, and art. 12, sec. 1; "1932's Steel Losses," *Iron Age* (June 16, 1933): 445.

24. For five such cases, see Grover C. Brown to Chester McLain, October 28, 1933, and attachments, correspondence file, vol. 2, box 54, AISI Collection.

25. Walter S. Tower to R. W. Shannon, October 23, 1934, folder 7, box 2972, and Kenneth Simpson to R. W. Shannon, February 15, 1935, folder 1, box 2964, entry 25, Consolidated Code Industry Files: Iron and Steel, NRA, RG9.

26. See, e.g., "South Chester Tube Company, In Re: Iron and Steel Industry," [March 1934], correspondence file, vol. 5, box 54, AISI Collection; Walter S. Tower to Hoyt Moore, January 7, 1935, correspondence file, vol. 10, box 55, AISI Collection; W. A. Irvin to Hoyt Moore, January 25, 1934, correspondence file, vol. 4, box 54, AISI Collection.

27. H. C. Crawford to Benjamin Fairless, February 6, 1935, correspondence file, vol. 10, box 55, AISI Collection.

28. Hoyt Moore to L. V. Collings, March 29, 1934, correspondence file, vol. 5, box 54, AISI Collection; files of National Tube Company, Inland Steel Company, Corrigan, McKinney Steel Company, Columbia Steel and Shafting Company, Crucible Steel Company of America, and American Steel and Wire Company in box 66, AISI Collection.

29. Hoyt Moore to L. V. Collings, March 29, 1934; U.S. Federal Trade Commission, *Practices of the Steel Industry Under the Code,* March 20, 1934, 5–9.

30. Hoyt Moore to L. V. Collings, March 29, 1934; "Resolution Regarding the Committee on Commercial Matters . . . March 15, 1934," correspondence file, vol. 5, box 54, AISI Collection.

31. AISI, minutes of meeting of July 13, 1933, correspondence file, vol. 1, box 54; L. V. Collings to R. W. Shannon, July 23, 1934, folder 8, box 2972, entry 25, Consolidated Code Industry Files: Iron and Steel, NRA, RG9; White, "Preliminary Report," 32.

32. Hoyt Moore to J. C. Argetsinger, October 29, 1934, and Chester McLain to Walter S. Tower, October 29, 1934, correspondence file, vol. 1, box 55, AISI Collection.

33. Hoyt Moore to Eugene Grace, December 23, 1933, correspondence file, vol. 3, box 54, AISI Collection.

34. E. T. Weir to Walter Tower, November 2, 1934, Walter Tower to E. T. Weir, November 6, 1934, and Hoyt Moore to Walter Tower, November 13 and 19, 1934, correspondence file, vol. 9, box 55, AISI Collection.

35. Richard Wilmer to Hoyt Moore, December 29, 1933, correspondence file, vol. 3, box 54, AISI Collection.

36. Hoyt Moore to Richard Wilmer, February 11, 1934, correspondence file, vol. 4, box 54, AISI Collection; Hoyt Moore to Walter Tower, March 8, 1934, correspondence file, vol. 5, box 54, and Nelson B. Gaskill to Hoyt Moore, October 26, 1934, Southern Hardware Jobbers Association file, box 58, AISI Collection; Hoyt Moore to Walter Tower, November 29, 1933 and Walter Tower/Hoyt Moore to General Thomas S. Hammond, December 1933 [sic], correspondence file, vol. 3, box 54, AISI Collection.

37. Walter Tower/Chester McLain to R. W. Shannon [October 31, 1934], correspondence file, vol. 8, and Chester McLain to Walter Tower, February 26, 1935, correspondence file, vol. 11, box 55, AISI Collection.

38. Hoyt Moore to Blackwell Smith, March 24, 1934, and Hoyt Moore to Raoul Desvernine, April 14, 1934, correspondence file, vol. 5, box 54, AISI Collection.

39. Schlesinger, *Age of Roosevelt*, 2:132–34; Hawley, *New Deal*, 84–85, 95–97.

40. National Recovery Review Board, "Stenographic Report of Hearing Held in the Matter of the Steel Industry," April 20–21, 1934, box 67, AISI Collection; Hoyt Moore, "Steel Code: Re Hearing before Darrow Board," April 21, 1934, in file on National Recovery Review Board, box 67, AISI Collection.

41. Schlesinger, *Age of Roosevelt*, 2:133–34; Hawley, *New Deal*, 95–97, 478; Lowell B. Mason, "Darrow vs. Johnson," *North American Review* 238 (December 1934): 530.

42. For a definition of corporatism, see Michael J. Hogan, "Explaining the History of American Foreign Relations: Corporatism," *Journal of American History* 77 (June 1990): 154.

43. Hoyt Moore to Walter Tower, December 30, 1933, correspondence file, vol. 3, box 54, AISI Collection.

44. Hoyt Moore to Walter Tower, March 24, 1934, correspondence file, vol. 5, box 54, AISI Collection.

45. Hoyt Moore to Gilbert Montague, July 31, 1934, correspondence file, vol. 7, box 55, AISI Collection.

46. Kenneth Simpson to R. W. Shannon, April 13, 1934, folder 1, box 2964, entry 25, Consolidated Code Industry Files: Iron and Steel, NRA, RG9; Hoyt Moore to Walter Tower, March 24, 1934, correspondence file, vol. 5, box 54, AISI Collection.

47. Walter Tower to R. W. Shannon, December 27, 1934, folder 5, box 2965, entry 25, Consolidated Code Industry Files: Iron and Steel, NRA, RG9.

48. A. F. Faber, "Memorandum on the Metropolitan Water District: Steel Code Exemption," February 6, 1935, correspondence file, vol. 10, box 55, AISI Collection.

49. Walter Tower to R. W. Shannon, December 18, 1934, correspondence file, vol. 9, box 55, AISI Collection.

50. Walter Tower/Hoyt Moore to R. W. Shannon, February 1935 [sic], and Hoyt Moore to Walter Tower, February 13, 1935, correspondence file, vol. 10, box 55, AISI Collection.

51. Burr Tracy Ansell to R. W. Shannon, April 9, 1934, correspondence file, vol. 5, box 54, AISI Collection.

52. Hoyt Moore to R. W. Shannon, April 28, 1934, and Hoyt Moore to Walter Tower, June 16, 1934, correspondence file, vol. 6, box 54, AISI Collection. The jobber list is attached to Walter Tower's memorandum to the steel industry, March 18, 1935, Office File Re Commercial Resolutions and Regulations, vol. 1, box 57, AISI Collection.

53. Moody, "Steel Industry," 139, 297–99; Hoyt Moore to R. E. McMath, May 19, 1934, and to Donald Richberg, May 19, 1934, correspondence file, vol. 6, box 54, AISI Collection.

54. Hugh Johnson et al. to the President, May 29, 1934, and "Report of the Board of Directors of American Iron and Steel Institute . . . May 29, 1934," folder 2, box 2964, entry 25, Consolidated Code Industry Files: Iron and Steel, NRA, RG9; "Effect on the Industry of the Amendment," in "Digest of Excerpts Taken from the Iron and Steel Code History Prepared by Messrs. Shannon, Liske and Dally," folder 13, box 2976, entry 25, Consolidated Code Industry Files: Iron and Steel, NRA, RG9.

55. "Effect on the Industry of the Amendment"; L. V. Collings to R. W. Shannon, July 23, 1934, folder 8, box 2972, entry 25, Consolidated Code Industry Files: Iron and Steel, NRA, RG9.

56. *A.L.A. Schechter Poultry Corp. et al. v. United States*, 295 U.S. 495.

57. Walter Tower to Hoyt Moore, May 18, 1935, and Hoyt Moore to Walter Tower, May 18, 1935, correspondence file, vol. 13, box 55, AISI Collection.

58. See, e.g., Hoyt Moore to Walter Tower, February 3, 1935, correspondence file, vol. 10, and Hoyt Moore to R. W. Shannon, February 11, 1935, and R. W. Shannon to Hoyt Moore, March 6, 1935, correspondence file, vol. 11 and Hoyt Moore to R. W. Shannon, March 21, 1935, correspondence file, vol. 12, box 55, AISI Collection; Walter Tower to R. W. Shannon, February 1, 1935, folder 7, box 2971, entry 25, Consolidated Industry Files: Iron and Steel, NRA, RG9.

59. Moody, "Steel Industry," 261–63.

60. W. M. Duvall to A. C. C. Hill, September 21, 1934, Henry L. Collins to Dr. Gustav Peck, December 5, 1934, L. J. Bernard to Jack Garrett Scott, December 27, 1934, and Walter Tower to R. W. Shannon, April 29, 1935, folder 16, box 2978, entry 25, Consolidated Code Industry Files, Iron and Steel, NRA, RG9.

61. Hoyt Moore to Donald Richberg, November 17, 1934, correspondence file, vol. 9, and R. W. Shannon to Walter Tower, January 23, 1935, correspondence file, vol. 10, and Walter Tower to R. W. Shannon, February 12, 1935, and R. W. Shannon to Walter Tower, February 19, 1935, correspondence file, vol. 11, box 55, AISI Collection.

62. R. W. Shannon to Malcolm Sharp, March 7, 1935, folder 11, box 2974, entry 25, Consolidated Code Industry Files: Iron and Steel, NRA, RG9; Kenneth Simpson to R. W. Shannon, March 15, 1935, folder 1, box 2964, entry 25, Consolidated Code Industry Files: Iron and Steel, NRA, RG9.

63. National Recovery Administration, "Summary of the Report of the National Industrial Recovery Board," March 15, 1935, folder 20, box 2987, entry 25,

Consolidated Code Industry Files: Iron and Steel, NRA, RG9; Robert T. Swaine, *The Cravath Firm and Its Predecessors, 1819–1947*, 3 vols. (New York: private printing, 1946–48), 2:557–58.

64. Swaine, *Cravath Firm*, 2:557–58; Ronen Shamir, *Managing Legal Uncertainty: Elite Lawyers in the New Deal* (Durham, N.C.: Duke University Press, 1995), chaps. 1–2.

65. Walter Tower to R. W. Shannon, June 8, 1935, folder 5, box 2965, entry 25, Consolidated Code Industry Files: Iron and Steel, NRA, RG9.

66. "Memorandum with Regard to Questions Arising in Connection with the Steel Code," June 29, 1935, in Memoranda of Fact, vol. 4, box 60, AISI Collection; Walter Tower to R. W. Shannon, June 11, 1935, and "Resolution Adopted by Members of Iron and Steel Industry," June 6, 1935, folder 25, box 3018, entry 25, Consolidated Code Industry Files: Iron and Steel, NRA, RG9; "Steel Institute Leads Wide Move to Retain NRA Rules Voluntarily," *New York Times*, June 7, 1935, 1, 16.

67. Walter Tower to R. W. Shannon, June 11, 1935, folder 25, box 3018, entry 25, Consolidated Code Industry Files: Iron and Steel, NRA, RG9; Moody, "Steel Industry," 195.

68. *NLRB v. Jones and Laughlin Steel Corp.*, 301 U.S. 1.

69. Irving Bernstein, *Turbulent Years: A History of the American Worker, 1933–1941* (Boston: Houghton Mifflin, 1970), 467–70, 480–90, 727–29; Paul A. Tiffany, *The Decline of American Steel: How Management, Labor, and Government Went Wrong* (New York: Oxford University Press, 1988), 14–16.

70. Keller, *Affairs of State* and *Regulating a New Economy*.

71. Morton Keller, *In Defense of Yesterday: James M. Beck and the Politics of Conservatism, 1861–1936* (New York: Coward-McCann, 1958), chap. 10.

72. Walter Tower, who was much more the modern professional manager, would remain with the AISI to help revivify it as industry spokesman and publicist. Tiffany, *Decline of American Steel*, 21–22, 30–31, 43–44, 100, 121, 128, 172, 181.

PART THREE

Institutional Experiences

TEN

"A Protected Childhood"

The Emergence of Child Protection in America

Michael Grossberg

In 1910 New York charity leader Edward T. Devine declared that young Americans must have a "protected childhood."[1] His demand expressed the central goal of almost forty years of agitation on behalf of the nation's children. Beginning in the 1870s more and more Americans began to dwell on the escalating dangers facing the republic's children and conversely the threat that delinquent, neglected, abandoned, and abused children posed to the society. These dual concerns generated a broad-based movement to save American children. Campaigns ranged from crusades to ban child labor to drives to lower infant mortality. Amid the welter of child-saving efforts, protection became the primary way of reformulating the fundamental responsibility of American society to its youngest members. It captured the dual concerns of the era by expressing both the need to assist the young and the need to guard against potentially dangerous youths. In this way the idea of protecting children provided a powerful and persuasive rationale for new policies and practices.

Recent historical scholarship on the social welfare battles of the late nineteenth and early twentieth century helps us understand the centrality of child protection to child saving in industrial America. It has avoided the reductionism of past answers that explained activism as the product of either benevolence or social control and that ignored the agency of recipients and others drawn into reform struggles. Instead, historians have shown that altruism and self-interest affected all social welfare efforts and that recipients and other interested parties responded interactively not passively to them. Similarly, they have made it clear how important it is to place the social reforms of the era within a broad framework of state reconstruction that occurred throughout North America and Western Europe, particularly the rise of a maternalist idea of state welfare responsibilities.[2] To this work must be added an understanding of the power of what historian Morton Keller has called the forces of persistence—localism, antistatism, and individualism—and a recognition that the collision of persistence and change in state creation had complex and ambiguous consequences.[3] Finally, the emergence of children and childhood as distinct subjects of historical inquiry has revealed the importance of examining the place of children in the era's social reform movements. It has demonstrated how changing conceptions of children propelled many of the reforms of the era.[4] Consequently, the emergence of child protection can be now be understood by relating it to the changing notions of public and private authority, new ideas about children and the family, and lingering commitments to family autonomy and limited government that dominated the American republic during the late nineteenth century and initial decades of the twentieth. From such a perspective it becomes clear that finding a way to legitimate piercing the veil of family privacy was the fundamental challenge confronting child savers.

Child protection became the primary way of meeting that challenge. It arose out of a reconceptualization of the relationship between strangers that expanded the boundaries of individual and collective moral responsibility and initiated a wave of American humanitarian reform that begin in the 1870s and lasted into the 1920s. An earlier wave in the antebellum America had found expression in a host of mass movements from abolitionism and women's rights to campaigns against corporal punishment and alcoholism.[5] The second wave also found numerous expressions, but differences between the two movements are far more revealing than commonalties. Most significantly, the second wave of American humanitarianism evidenced much less faith in both privatism—especially self-policing—and individual and family autonomy, and, conversely, a much greater faith in public authority and the authority of experts. It also produced cadres of child protectors, who became part of what French theorists Michel Foucault and Jacques Donzelot have labeled "discursive movements." By that they mean that at particular times new ways of perceiving social conditions give rise to new forms of knowledge, and that knowledge compels attempts to apply it. Though the motivations and resulting efforts vary significantly, those who respond to such developments form a discursive movement because of shared priorities, assumptions, and tactics.[6] Child protection was just such a discursive movement. Equally important, like the first, the second wave of humanitarian reform was a trans-Atlantic movement of shared ideas, concerns, and practices. Modernity, whether in London, Paris, or New York, threatened the young and threatened them with similar perils.[7] As a result, social reforms like child protection became subjects of international debate and agitation. Nevertheless, each child protection movement like other social reforms in North America and Western Europe was distinctive as well and can be understood only by recovering the way it constructed and deployed its version of child saving. American child protectors were distinguished by their reliance on the law and the intermingling of public and private authority.

The distinctively American approach is evident in the ideas and actions of the movement's key actors: child protectors. As the creators, propagandists, and implementers of child protection, they helped construct a new idea of public life in America. Their achievements emerged out of the collision of general developments with specific events. Each must be identified and explained to understand how and why child protectors made protection the new standard for determining how Americans fulfilled their basic responsibilities to their children.

Social Knowledge

Recovering the time-bound creation of what anthropologist call "social knowledge" is critical to understanding why cadres of child protectors entered the lists to protect America's children. In this case that means determining what reformers "knew" about children and how they learned it. That knowledge spurred them into action and shaped their particular approaches.[8] Though the era's social knowledge about children had multiple, interconnected, and trans-Atlantic sources, four were critical to the emergence of child protection in the United States.

First, late-nineteenth-century Western Europeans and North American learned to fear for their families. Evidence of family failure seemed to be everywhere: rising divorce rates, increased participation of women in the workforce, low marriage rates among educated women, falling birth rates among the middle and upper classes coupled with high birth rates among working class and immigrant families, growing poverty, rising juvenile delinquency, and on and on. Looking back, family problems and changes clearly were the product of massive structural changes in the economy and society tied to industrial capitalism, urbanization, and immigration. At the time, though, the general diagnosis among much of the middle and upper classes that formed the recruiting grounds for child protectors was less fundamental. Though points of emphasis shifted between heredity and environment, working-class and immigrant families and neighborhoods were labeled a contagion that threatened the rest of society; they were increasingly feared as breeding grounds of crime, disease, pauperism, and sexual immorality.[9] Equally important, unlike the first humanitarian movement, knowledge of the ever-present diversity of American families in this era bred intolerance and demands for uniformity, which in turn forced a collision between the persistent commitment to family autonomy and new claims of the public interests in household affairs. In short, a sense of family crisis led to a deepening understanding of the dire plight of many families and to fears that their troubles might undermine the society itself. As President Theodore Roosevelt thundered to a conference of churches, "Questions like the tariff and the currency are of literally no consequence whatsoever compared with the vital question of having the unit of our social life, the home, preserved."[10]

A redefinition of childhood also altered the social knowledge of the era. Throughout the European world a new understanding of child development encouraged an ever more refined conception of children as separate and distinct individuals with their own needs and interests and a conception of childhood as a special time for study, growth, and play. Age itself became more and more important as a marker of individual identity and status.[11] These new ideas found numerous expressions in the era, most notably what sociologist Viviana Zelizer has called the sacralization of childhood—the seemingly paradoxical development of children gaining greater emotional value to their parents at the same time that their economic worth declined.[12] These developments led to the conviction that the young would grow to be productive and responsible adults only if they enjoyed a proper childhood. And that belief in turn encouraged a new sense of the vulnerability, needs, and dependence of the young as well as a determination to create space for a childhood in children's lives by extending the years of youthful dependence and excluding the young as much as possible from the market and public life. It also compelled a redefinition of parenting roles that emphasized parental obligations over parental rights and led legal scholar Ernst Freund to assert in 1904 that parental authority was "a power in trust. . . . The authority to control the child is not the natural right of the parent; it emanates from the State."[13] The redefinition of childhood and parenting, in turn, made information about working class and immigrant children even more alarming and encouraged the conclusion that proper childhood must be imposed if it was not embraced. Indeed the identification of children without a childhood as a problem in need of remediation was accompanied by and to an extent caused by a declining confidence in the abilities of families to rear their children properly.

An expansion of civil society in America also added to the social knowledge of the era. Civil society describes the social space between the family and state—a space of public discourse and action carried on by individuals who band together in non-governmental or quasi-governmental organizations, institutions, and movements. Ideas and policies developed by these groups are broadcast through newspapers, magazines, journals, books, conferences, professional associations, and the other mediums of the public sphere.[14] Over the course of the nineteenth century the United States, with its relatively weak governmental state and decentralized and underdeveloped bureaucracy, became a fertile host for an expansive and expanding civil society.[15]

By the end of the century two critical developments combined to make children a central concern of American civil society. First, women took an increasingly prominent role in civil society. The weak American state created greater opportunities for women's political and civil activities than was possible in most European countries.[16] Women's activism challenged a male monopoly on public discourse and opened it up to discussions of private values and well being, particularly that of children and families. As Mary Mumford declared in 1894: "The experiences of the woman's narrow sphere are the same on a wider plane. If she follows her broom into the street, she is confronted with a problem upon which she has been at work for centuries."[17] Second, philanthropy and the professions assumed a greater role in the public sphere. Philanthropists and the organizations that they created and staffed became ever more powerful actors in the discussion and implementation of vital public policies. And organized experts donned the mantle of professionalism to carve out their own space in the public sphere based on claims of disinterested expertise. The home is "to social science what the atom is to physics and the cell is to biology," the sociologist and minister Samuel W. Dike mused in 1904. "The home contains within it the great secret of all the social sciences."[18] At times allies and other times adversaries, philanthropists like Laura Spelman Rockefeller and professionals like Edith Abbot became critical sources of information and action about children and the family.[19]

Finally, social and economic change forced a reevaluation of the role of the public authority in all sectors of American life that also altered social knowledge. The persistent American embrace of antistatism in general and the deference to family autonomy in particular fell under new scrutiny. Activists demanded a new balance between public and private interests. Their demand sprang from the widespread conclusion throughout European society that greater governmental action was required because only the state commanded the resources and authority to police families more vigorously. Consequently, unlike the reliance of first humanitarian movement on moral suasion and nonstatist solutions, the second discounted the possibility of individual self-reformation and turned to the coercive authority of the state to construct a just society. In the United States that power was exercised primarily at the local and state level since those governmental units retained primary jurisdiction over children and families. And inevitably it clashed with the persistent resistance to state intervention into the nation's homes. The collision led activists to the law. The appeal of the law in its many guises—statutes, common law, and administrative rules as well as the ideology of legalism with its commitment to adversarial solutions and rights—was not just instrumental but also constitutive. It became a means to legitimate as well as a tool to construct a new balance in family policy.[20]

Pulling these strands together, the new social knowledge produced by changes in popular and professional conceptions of families and children, extensions of civil society, and increased acceptance of state power led to an enlarged sense of individual and collective moral responsibility for children that propelled many women and men to try and save the nation's young. Though built on the actions of previous reformers, the new child savers far exceeded those earlier efforts. "Throughout America's past, Americans cared for their own children's welfare," historian Hamilton Cravens observes. "Since the 1870s, however, Americans have invented child saving as a closely related series of public issues, thus creating an organized child-saving movement in politics, society, and culture. Only in modern times, then, have Americans asked public entities, whether governmental or not, to assume more and more responsibility for various social goals."[21]

Protection was at the center of child saving. It became the primary way to conceptualize a new sense of the public responsibility to the nation's young. The appeal of protection lay in its simultaneous expression of a specific duty to come to the aid of children and of a clear recognition that only extraordinary circumstances warranted interventions into the nation's homes. In that way it legitimated a new balance between public interests and family autonomy while encouraging a host of child-saving campaigns that would rearrange the relationships between children, parents, the state, and civil society. It thus became a rhetorical trump in social reform controversies. Protection also became an appealing ideal because it contained a dual meaning and thus expressed without resolving the tension between protecting children from society and protecting society from children. These clashing meanings and their consequences emerged as child protectors, children, parents, philanthropists, and child welfare professionals clashed over specific forms of child protection.

Three Examples

The new social knowledge of the late nineteenth century provides a necessary but not a sufficient reason why child protection emerged in the late nineteenth century. It had to be acted upon. Child protection crusades erupted in America when a spark ignited the now combustible environment. Stories of unprotected children produced that spark. Three tales that led to child protection campaigns illustrate the range and complexity of the new movement.

Cruelty

The first American child protection story was the tragic tale of Mary Ellen. Born illegitimate in 1864, poor relief officials indentured the infant to a New York couple. They could not support her and without telling local authorities passed Mary Ellen on to her natural father and his second wife. When her father died she remained in a New York City tenement with her stepmother and the stepmother's second husband. Local officials lost track of her until 1874, when rumors of mistreatment began circulating. After a charity worker found Mary Ellen dressed in rags, malnourished, and covered with bruises, she tried to have to the child removed but had no success until she persuaded the head of the recently formed Society for the Prevention of Cruelty to Animals to investigate. SPCA counsel Elbridge T. Gerry documented the charges of child cruelty and had a writ issued to bring the girl into a courtroom where a weeping Mary Ellen told a tale of constant beatings, starvation, and being kept locked in closet and never allowed out to attend school or play. The court found her stepmother guilty of assault and battery and sentenced her to a year in prison at hard labor. The judge sent Mary Ellen to an orphanage.[22]

The story burst like a thunderstorm over the city and the nation, forcing the knowledge of a particular social evil onto a shocked society. Like most child protection issues, physical cruelty toward children was not a new problem. However, in late-nineteenth-century Western Europe and North America a new understanding of child abuse emerged. Its sources lay in the fusion of the general developments promoting child protection with a growing moral aversion to physical pain that developed over the course of the nineteenth century into what historian James Turner has called "the Victorian revulsion from suffering."[23] These sentiments fed the conviction that freedom from physical coercion and deliberately inflicted pain was an essential human right, one that even children could claim. However, labeling child cruelty as a specific crime challenged the distribution of power between families and the state through a direct assertion of the separate interests and rights of the young. Thus it needed more than simply the emergence of a supporting context, it needed a galvanizing event. Mary Ellen's story was that event.

In the reactions to Mary Ellen's story much was made of the fact that societies existed to protect animals but not children. Gerry and his allies responded by gathering together a group of elite New Yorkers to create the New York Society for the Prevention of Cruelty to Children. They all shared his concern about the city's children and his fears about the social disorder caused by child problems.[24] The idea of preventing cruelty to children quickly took hold in the republic. In two years seven more societies were founded; there were 200 by 1910, and the numbers kept growing.[25] Rapid expansion occurred because Mary Ellen's story made the child, and especially an abused girl, a broad cultural symbol of victimization and redemption that could be used to trigger compassion and legitimate challenges to the rights of some parents.[26] The societies made child cruelty the most extreme violation of children's emerging right to a childhood.

The power of Mary Ellen's story to ignite action demonstrated the significance of narratives in child protection. Such tales turned abstract problems facing children into specific dramas that humanized complex issues like the redefinition of children's status and parental rights. In this way stories transferred social knowledge to larger groups and made problems like child abuse understandable to all, and actionable to some. At the same time, the way stories like Mary Ellen's were told framed the way a problem like child cruelty would be understood. In this case, storytelling meant that child cruelty would be understood as a social problem attributable to failed immigrant and working-class parents because in this era there was no understanding of child abuse as a problem confronting children and families in all classes as there would be in the subsequent late-twentieth-century child abuse crusade. As a result, child cruelty quickly became a charge in the indictment against working-class and immigrant homes and additional evidence of their pathology.[27]

To battle cruelty, American child protectors seized upon the law. They conceived of child protection primarily as an issue of legal enforcement. Their reliance on the law stemmed in part from a series of judicial decisions that had begun to curb the traditional common law parental right of chastisement by redefining cruel punishment as something less than endangering a child's life. The Illinois Supreme Court expressed the new conviction in 1869 when it insisted that parental authority must be exercised "within the bounds of reason and humanity." The justices declared unequivocally: "it is monstrous to hold that under the pretense of sustaining parental authority, children must be left, without the protection of the law, at the mercy of depraved men or women, with liberty to inflict any species of barbarity short of the actual taking of life."[28] Gerry and his allies acted on these new convictions by securing statutes and establishing procedures that made child cruelty a separate and distinct form of parental mistreatment and grounds for taking a child from its home and punishing the parent. Significantly, they used the law not only as a coercive force but also as a constitutive one to give children rights separate from those of their parents and thus an individual claim to protection. Our aim, as Gerry declared, is "to aid suffering childhood, through the law, by the law, and under the law. It is the hand of the law, the fingers of which trace charges of injury to children and fasten the grasp of the law upon the offender." And he legitimated this form of child protection with an appeal to children's rights by claiming that it was a fundamental "axiom that at the present day in this country, children have some rights which even parents are bound to respect."[29]

At the same time child protectors tried to make freedom from abuse a right of childhood, they also had to defer to the tradition of parental control over children and quiet fears that the new anticruelty statutes would launch a wholesale invasion of the nation's homes. They did so by emphasizing that they were concerned only with failed families and by trumpeting their acceptance of corporal punishment and the right of parents to chastise their offspring in a reasonable fashion. Even so, by elevating protection from cruelty to a right, Gerry and his allies sought to create standards for evaluating punishment that reduced the deference accorded parental authority.

Anticruelty campaigners could rely on the law because they created quasi-public—quasi-private organizations. Like Anthony Comstock and his minions, who served as both federal postal agents and also as officials of local antivice agencies as they policed abortion, contraception, and other actions newly banned as obscene, private agents like Gerry served as private officials granted public power to determine which abusers would be prosecuted and which would not. They did so because local authorities granted societies like his the right to investigate charges of child abuse, issue warnings or summons to parents, and, if necessary, remove children from abusive families.[30] By blurring public and private authority, child protectors created a precedent of private agencies as creators and enforcers of public policy. Such institutional hybridization reveals that the emerging American variant of the Western European welfare state retained a lingering uneasiness with public power. Instead of significantly expanding public bureaucracy, it relied on allocative strategies that used tax incentives, public subsidies, and dispersed authority to check the growth of the state by fostering a vibrant and powerful public sphere filled with private agencies authorized to tackle public problems. As Cravens notes, "the United States was the only nation in the industrialized world to create a national welfare state without a national bureaucracy to administer it. As Americans used the State—meaning any level of government, but especially the states and the federal government—increasingly in modern times to address social problems, it was always with an eye to keeping state bureaucracy and machinery on as parsimonious a level of functioning as possible."[31]

As the societies tackled the problem of child abuse they expanded their definitions of cruelty. From bans on buying cigarettes to prohibitions against performing in burlesque theaters, child protectors secured legislation that used cruelty protection to limit children's access to the social and commercial life of industrial America by filling states codes with new regulations that substantially enlarged the legal definition of risks facing children. Each addition, from bans on entering dance halls or skating rinks to prohibitions against joining the circus or purchasing alcohol to specific criminal penalties against child abuse or neglect represented a risk that now had to be proscribed. Each was premised on the assumption that childhood was a distinctive and vulnerable stage of life and that public regulation of childrearing had to be expanded to protect the young.[32]

But child protectors could not impose their policies unilaterally. Instead they had to both interact with recipients and confront differences in their own ranks. A wide, perhaps a widening, variety of families with conflicting needs, interests, and internal differences ensured that parents and children were not just passive recipients of the new policies. On the contrary, they helped determine the meaning and use of anticruelty. Clearly many parents grew to fear "the Cruelty" as the SPCCs were known. Evocatively, a deathly ill mother in Edward W. Townsend's 1895 novel *A Daughter of the Tenements* feared that if she went to hospital the NYSPCC would take her daughter. She pleaded with a friend: "Go to my room and take Carminella before they get her. Hide her!" [33] Nevertheless some family members turned the anticruelty laws to their own ends. Parents would use the Cruelty to threaten or punish children they could not control; children would report parents. For example, in 1920, after acceding to her dying mother's request that she leave school and care for her four younger brothers and sisters, a young woman turned to the Massachusetts Society for the Prevention of Cruelty to Children when she could not prevent her father from beating her and her brothers. When nothing changed, she left the house, got a job, and helped support her siblings. Two years later, though, the next oldest girl in the family sought the society's help to stop the beatings. Then in 1922 the children hired a lawyer who accused the father of incest with the girls as well as the beatings. Finally he was convicted and sentenced to 8 to 10 years in prison; and the younger children were put in the care of the Boston welfare department.[34] Such actions suggest that rather than simply a chronicle of new levels of surveillance, campaigns against child cruelty renegotiated power and decision making between some families and the state and within some families. Equally important, unintended consequences led to a split in the movement as societies like the MSPCC discarded the legalistic model created by Gerry for a social welfare one that emphasized the provision of social services. Such schisms demonstrate how experiences with enforcing anticruelty statutes made child protection a broad and increasingly diverse movement as child savers simultaneously tried to aid children and guard society.[35]

Mary Ellen's story made child cruelty the first major child protection drive with its own balance of altruism and self-interest. Anticruelty reformers used protection to establish a new threshold of humane treatment of children by reshaping the public concept of child suffering from being an inevitable part of the human condition to being a problem that could and should be solved. In doing so they redefined the balance between parental and children's rights and made family violence a major public issue. Consequently, as historian Susan Tiffin concludes, "the decision as to whether punishment was moderate or not was increasingly felt to be one that parents themselves could not take but had to be measured by an external standard."[36] And yet, they also institutionalized without resolving a fundamental uncertainty about child cruelty: locating the line between legitimate parental punishment and child abuse. That was their legacy as well.[37]

The campaign against child cruelty established child protection as a new rationale for saving the nation's young. It spurred the creation of more and more campaigns to protect children. Though they were all interconnected in critical ways, the particularities of each form of child protection are critical to understanding the broadening goals and changing consequences of child protection. Two forms of child protection—morals policing and protective institutions—illustrate the nature and range of the movement. Though each spawned a distinctive child protection campaign, they shared a common trajectory: a problem burst into public consciousness with a galvanizing story, the story generated controversy and action, and the actions led to new policies that helped redefine the place of the young in America and reframe contests over child protection.

Immorality

On July 4, 1885, William T. Stead, a noted British journalist and reformer, published "The Maiden Tribute to Modern Babylon" in London's *Pall Mall Gazette*. His exposé revealed how he had easily purchased a thirteen-year-old, white, working-class girl for the explicit purpose of prostitution by paying her mother just five pounds. Stead acted at the behest of British purity crusaders who were trying to restrict prostitution, or white slavery as they and others called it. They were particularly worried about tales of girls being abducted off the streets and forced into a life of prostitution. When lobbying failed to get Parliament to attack white slavery by raising the age of consent from thirteen years of age to sixteen, they turned to Stead and storytelling. His story produced an immediate response. Two hundred and fifty thousand people gathered in Hyde Park to demand legislative protection for young girls; shortly thereafter Parliament passed a new age of consent law.[38]

In a vivid example of the trans-Atlantic character of child protection, Stead's story circulated widely in America and earned him title of the John Brown of white slavery. "The Maiden Tribute to Modern Babylon" sent such strong shock waves of public concern and anxiety that it caused a moral panic in the United States as it had Britain.[39] Almost immediately campaigns for higher age of consent laws were launched as child protection efforts. Age of consent restrictions dictate the age at which a person can legally consent to sexual relations; they are based on the assumption that below a certain age children are incapable of sufficiently understanding the nature of sexual intercourse to consent to it. Like many family law regulations, enforcement had relied primarily on self-policing. Age of consent laws became a child protection issue because Stead's story forced a public debate about whether that policy should continue given the era's changing knowledge of childhood, especially the emerging conviction that childhood must be prolonged by increasing the years of sexual inaction and ignorance. The movement also followed from a fearful view of the adult world, one filled with sexual predators and the specter of prostitution, and the efforts of women's rights advocates and social purity campaigners to eliminate the sexual double standard and the privileges it gave men.[40]

The Women's Christian Temperance Union led the movement. Founded in 1874 as an antidrink organization, the WTCU developed a comprehensive agenda for social reformation that sought to put the interest of girls and women at the center of public consciousness.[41] Higher age of consent laws became part of the organization's efforts to protect young women and to change male behavior. The WTCU gathered information showing that most states set the age of consent far too low to protect young women. The average age was the traditional common law one of 10, though some states had raised it to 12 and Delaware had lowered it to 7.[42] The WTCU used this addition to the social knowledge of children, and the panic produced by Stead's story, to launch campaigns to make sexual relations with young women a criminal offense by raising the age of consent in each state.[43] Helen Gardener informed readers of *Arena* that the "need of a vigorous crusade, in behalf of exposed girlhood and in the interest of public morality, against such shameful legislation, should be obvious to all."[44]

At the heart of the age of consent campaign, was yet another a turn to the coercive and constitutive authority of the law. Much like the WTCU's rejection of the antebellum antidrink tactic of temperance for the postbellum one of prohibition, the organization rejected self-policing for state regulation. WTCU's leader Frances Willard declared: "Reforms are good, but law is better. Reformers spend years in trying to alleviate the misery caused by evil institutions and practices, evils which law with its iron hand could crush in a day."[45]

Criminalizing sex with underage girls fit the larger agenda of child protection. Age of consent reform offered middle-class women reformers a means of policing working-class youths, redefining the appropriate code of moral conduct for the young and for men, and countering the temptations of the commercial culture of industrial America with its teeming factories, offices, stores, street life, theaters, and amusement parks. Though policing the morals of young women was not new to this age, as historian Mary Odem explains, "What was new in the late nineteenth and early twentieth centuries, however, was the broadened scope of the campaigns and the mounting demands for state regulation of the problem. Public anxiety about the morality of young women greatly intensified and spread to all regions of the country during this period of rapid urban and industrial growth. Instead of the religious and voluntary efforts pursued earlier, moral reformers now began to insist on a forceful response from the state." [46] Morals protection thus became another form of child protection. It ranged from censorship drives to prevent the young from reading obscene books to bans on the young entering dance halls.[47]

However, the age of consent campaign did not go unopposed. Critics illustrate the range of participants in the debates over child protection. The most vociferous opponents argued that young men needed protection not just young women. They tended to view young women quite differently than did the reformers. Instead of virtuous girls in need of aid, they raised the specter of conniving and immoral young harlots who used the law to blackmail inexperienced boys. Their fear of laws turned into tools of avarice and vengeance by designing young women echoed contemporary concerns about the continued legitimacy of breach of marriage suits.[48] Thus a Nebraska newspaper editorialized: "Have these clamorous women no sons? Protect our sons as well as daughters!"[49]

Resistance to higher ages of consent forced child protectors and the public alike to confront age distinctions among children and notions of sexuality latent in the child protection movement. In particular, it raised questions about the legal and social meaning of puberty. Public discussion of physical development as an issue of child protection reinforced the emerging tendency to segment childhood into developmental stages fostered by the growing influence of the child study movement, particularly the work of psychologist G. Stanley Hall. Hall advanced a scientific rationale for identifying childhood as a separate stage of life and for considering adolescence as a particular period of childhood. He described adolescence as a turbulent period of physical, emotional, and sexual development during which youths needed to be shielded from adult duties and expectations. Moreover, as Jeffrey P. Moran has recently argued, sexuality was at the heart of the new idea of adolescence and policing it a fundamental concern.[50] These new understandings of child development encouraged the prolongation of youthful dependence and the segregation of youths from the world and the pressures and temptations of adulthood. [51] Adolescence thus became a scientific way to legitimate the need to protect young women. Child protectors used the information to make the age of consent a double boundary: it separated adolescent girls from their younger sisters and from adult women.[52]

Reformers employed these distinctions among children to overcome their opponents. By 1900 almost all states had raised the age to 16, some to 18, and a few to only 14. [53] The new codes also created the crime of "statutory rape," which penalized sexual relations with girls newly designated as adolescents, whether the young women consented or not. By making it a separate crime with lesser penalties than rape, statutory rape implicitly recognized the possibility of volition on the part of teenage girls while still classifying them as victims. Age of consent reform as child protection thus tried to penalize those who illegally crossed the new statutory line between childhood and adulthood. Its objective was to protect young women from sexual exploitation. But like all child protection measures, it also had unintended consequences as the new policies spurred complex responses. Two of these illustrate some of the dynamics and consequences of the child protection movement.

First, the fate of the new protections lay with an emerging system of child welfare and juvenile justice increasingly dominated by social workers, psychologists, probation officers, and juvenile court judges. These new institutional actors altered the focus of sexual protection from the immorality of men and victimization of young women that had been the basic concern of the WTCU and its allies to policing young moral offenders, particularly adolescent girls. They did so in part because many of them thought that young women were often willing participants in sexual encounters and not necessarily the victims of male predators that the reformers had assumed them to be. Accordingly, judges and other court officials created the feminine juvenile offense that Steven Schlossman and Stephanie Wallach have termed "precocious sexuality": "girls were prosecuted almost exclusively for 'immoral' conduct, a very broad category that defined all sexual exploration as fundamentally perverse and predictive of future promiscuity, perhaps even prostitution. But although girls, unlike boys, were almost never accused of violating criminal statutes, they received stiffer legal penalties."[54] The results were evident in statutory rape cases where female chastity often became the critical issue. Typically a California prosecutor asserted in the case of a nineteen-year-old boy and a pregnant, fifteen-year-old girl: "The boy is pretty respectable boy. The girl has been running around with many people, judge. It is one of those cases where it is too bad that any complaint had been filed at all."[55] Consequently in its guise of treatment not punishment, juvenile courts created a policy of preventing underage sex by policing girls much more strictly than boys or men. In this way Willard's fears came to pass as judges ensured that child sexual protection would continue to have gender distinctions and indeed institutionalize a new double standard.

Second, working-class and immigrant parents found the new laws an appealing means of policing their own daughters. Their desire to do so stemmed from a different family crisis than the one spurring child protectors into action. In this case, generational conflicts erupted within American homes over clashing family values, particularly young women seeking greater social and sexual freedom. Many parents feared their daughters were becoming sexually active and wanted to control the consequences of their daughters' conduct. And thus in an unforeseen interaction between reform and response, the new protections sparked a protection movement by parents. They seized upon the laws as a means of restraining their daughters by calling on the state to enforce parental edicts from commands to stop dating certain boys to complaints about late night dancing. Parents also used the laws to force boys to marry their pregnant daughters or face prosecution.[56] Sometimes parents succeeded; sometimes they did not. For example, Mr. and Mrs. Alberti turned to the Los Angeles Juvenile Court when they could not control their sixteen-year-old daughter, Patricia. Her father told court referee Miriam Van Waters that Patricia "goes out about seven or eight and comes back at twelve and sometimes twelve thirty and I don't know where she goes." He also complained that she also disobeyed them by wearing makeup and refusing to let her older brother act as a chaperon. Van Waters negotiated a settlement in which Patricia agreed to stay away from dance halls, let brother be her chaperon, stop using makeup, and obey her parents in exchange for the right to continue going out. And the whole family had to agree to let a probation officer monitor their conduct. [57] In this way child protection became a vehicle for increased parental supervision of children and for higher levels of state surveillance of households both of which compelled new negotiations between parents and children and between families and public officials.

Statutory reform succeeded in creating new ways of protecting young women from sexual exploitation even though it did not produce the more uniform sexual standard the age of consent activists had sought. As a result, the new age of consent laws and the debate and actions that they instigated balanced altruism and self-interest by legitimizing the policing of sexuality of adolescents as a specific form of child protection. Its prime legacy was the creation of status offenses: crimes because of the age of the offender not the act itself. In this way, policing morals as a form of child protection fostered new struggles among child protectors, court officials, and family members while it also provided another means of defining and promoting a prolonged childhood.

Feeblemindedness

Robert L. Dugdale published *The Jukes: A Study in Crime, Pauperism, Disease, and Heredity* in 1877. A merchant turned welfare reformer, Dugdale learned of the Jukes while on an inspection tour in rural New York for the state prison association. He found six of the family in jail, and wondered why. That question led him to research, which in turn led him to Max, an eighteenth-century backwoodsman and progenitor of the family. Dugdale followed the family tree to uncover information on 708 of Max's descendants. Mixing environmental and hereditary arguments, his family history of the Jukes told how disease, criminality, poverty, drunkenness, and mental defects had afflicted generation after generation. And he tallied up the social costs of the family— $1.3 million over seventy-five years. The Jukes quickly entered professional and popular lore as dire evidence of family pathology and the threat that mental retardation posed to American society.[58]

Like the other stories, *The Jukes* altered public knowledge and spurred demands for action that expanded the domain of child protection. As reformer Frank Gidden noted in a preface to a 1910 edition of the book: "*The Jukes* has long been known as one of these important books that exert an influence out of all proportion to their bulk."[59] Dugdale's book helped make children suffering from mental retardation a child protection cause. Again like the others, dealing with the young afflicted by mental deficiencies was not a new problem; once more, what was new was both a sense of crisis and the particular social construction given the problem during this era. Amid a broad concern about all children with disabilities, retarded children were singled out as the most disabled and thus the most important target of protection. An earlier mixed set of views, including a sense of retarded individuals as harmless burdens on society, was replaced by what came to be called the "menace of the feebleminded."[60] This dramatic shift revealed the growing power of science, particularly medical science, in child protection beliefs and practices.[61] Doctors and medical researchers made retarded children a singular concern of those fearful of the feebleminded. Henry Goddard, director of research at the Vineland School for the Feebleminded in New Jersey and one of America's leading applied social scientists, complained that so many paupers and criminals were "of such a high grade of defectiveness that they never get into court and yet have feeble-minded children. We cannot touch these adults. We must somehow get a hold of their children." Those sentiments ensured that retarded children would be subjected to their own form of protected childhood.

The movement to protect these children was dominated by members of organized groups of institution managers, especially the National Conference of Charities and Corrections and the Association of Medical Officers of American Institutions for Idiots and Feebleminded Persons. The success of these organizations in crafting new forms of protection for feebleminded children highlights the ability of nongovernmental agencies to dominate social policies toward the young. They authorized study after study that documented how retardation undermined social stability and order by propagating prostitution, delinquency, pauperism, alcoholism, and other social maladies. The solution seemed obvious to them and obviously a child protection issue: abandon toleration, self-policing, and autonomous family decision making; replace them whenever possible and necessary with state-mandated sequestration, beginning with the young.[62]

And, once more, law stood as an appealing policy tool for child protection. Isaac Kerlin, superintendent of a Pennsylvania training school and an intellectual leader of the movement, demanded that the state assume the relation of parent to retarded children, "abridging personal liberty where its exercise is attended with a crusade against the rights of the peaceable." He called for the creation of "villages of the simple," where the retarded would live separate from society and barred from marriage and thus sexual relations.[63] Similarly, Goddard implored: "What we want is protection for society. If we wish to save our teachers from the possibility of being murdered by their pupils or our daughters from being killed by their wooers or businessmen from being struck down by the blows of feebleminded boys, we must be on the watch for symptoms of feebleminded in our school children." Such demands illustrate what historian Edward Dickinson argues were the clashing impulses emerging in both European and North American child welfare: democratic and integrative strategies that coexisted uneasily with authoritarian and repressive ones. "For those who seemed willing and able to become productive, well-adjusted members of society," he contends, "progressive reforms offered assistance, support, and opportunities. For those who seemed unwilling to be integrated into the ideal of organic society, welfare programs were less benign. Rising standards of health and vocational competence meant that some children and young people gained substantial benefits from vocational training, from child support payments brought in by professional legal guardians, or from infant welfare programs; but they also meant that other young people faced repression, stigmatization, and institutional confinement."[64] The determination to use the law to compel the segregation of retarded children also revealed the flip side of the rights talk used to legitimate calls for state intervention to protect children: the right of other children to be protected from the contagion of feeblemindedness as yet another balance of altruism and self-interest being crafted by child protectors.

Campaigns to protect society from retarded children through institutionalization achieved significant success even though most child welfare advocates had begun to question the effectiveness of institutionalization and to urge that children be kept in their families whenever possible. But instead of arguing that retarded children should remain in their homes and be monitored by truant officers or probation officers like other children labeled as deviants, child protectors championed institutionalization as the first not the last resort for these children. The superintendent of a North Carolina institution made the goals of that policy quite clear: "The ultimate aim of the school is the elimination of feeblemindedness from the race by segregation." As a result, institution populations grew throughout the era in both real numbers and as a percentage of the population. According to historian Steven Noll, "In 1904, 17.3 feeble-minded persons per 100,000 of the general public had been institutionalized. By 1923, this figure had climbed to 46.7."[65] Growing institutionalization exposed the basic logic of protection for retarded children: they could be saved only by being treated as perpetual children. In 1920 the superintendent of a South Carolina training school expressed that new understanding: "the inmates of this institution are commonly referred to as children regardless of their ages. The term is used both to enable us to avoid the use of the term inmate and also to serve as a reminder that our charges are entitled to the tactful and affectionate treatment that all young children require."[66] Permanent custodial care made these self-fulfilling prophecies and created a very particular kind of protected childhood.

Segregation of a different sort occurred in response to the continued presence of many mildly retarded children in the community. It did so as a result of another child protection effort of the era, compulsory school laws. Compulsory education laws institutionalized the conviction that schooling would cure social problems from poverty to crime, train children for successful futures, and extended childhood by ensuring that the young would be in classrooms for much of the first part of their lives. They also expressed the growing conviction that families should no longer be able to decide unilaterally how much schooling a child needed. By 1930 most states required that children stay in school until they were at least fourteen years old, and many decreed sixteen.[67] However, mandatory school attendance for all children also meant that more retarded children would be sitting in classrooms alongside other students in a now captive student body and would stay there year after year.

Another European import, special education classes, seemed the most appealing way to resolve this unintended problem. James Van Sickle, superintendent of the Baltimore Public Schools, acknowledged that special classes would cost more than mainstreaming retarded children into regular classrooms, but he contended that "the presence in a class of one or two mentally or morally defective children so absorbs the energies of the teacher and makes so imperative a claim upon her attention that she cannot under these circumstances properly instruct the number commonly enrolled in a class. School authorities must therefore greatly reduce this number, employ many more teachers, and build many more schoolrooms to accommodate these unfortunates who impede the regular progress of normal children." Thankfully, he concluded, the "plan of segregation is now fairly well established in large cities, and superintendents and teachers are working on the problem of classification, so that they make the best of this imperfect material."[68]

Special education served dual purposes. It balanced care and protection by providing a humane environment and appropriate training for retarded children while controlling them and making sure they would not disrupt or threaten the normal children. Though Goddard and other leaders of the movement preferred complete segregation in residential institutions, they accepted the reality that all retarded children simply could not be placed in institutions. And on this basis, special education spread throughout the nation through statute and administrative order. By 1934 more than 427 communities had created special education classes.[69] Though child protectors never succeeded in getting all noninstitutionalized retarded children into special classes, their campaign ensured that segregation and integration, institutionalization and deinstitutionalization would be persistent child protection issues as they were in all policies dealing with the mentally ill and others labeled deviants.

Tellingly, there was less resistance to the segregationist policies applied to retarded children than to other forms of child protection. Except for individual challenges, the new policies were generally met with silent acceptance.[70] However neither the permanent segregation of the most retarded children nor special education classes for the rest were considered sufficient protection from the contagion of feeblemindedness. Like age of consent campaigners, reformers and others worried about retarded young women. An official of the Russell Sage Foundation contended that the "feebleminded girl is vastly more dangerous to the community than the feebleminded boy. This arises partly from the fact that the feeble-minded woman is unable to protect herself, and partly from the fact that she is not affected by the moral restraints or the regard for consequences which restrain normal women."[71] States like Virginia and North Carolina responded to such fears by passing legislation that kept women in institutions during their childbearing years. Nevertheless, even more protection was demanded. Another trans-Atlantic movement, eugenics, seemed the only answer. Eugenicists promised to end the hereditary sources of unwanted social behavior through sterilization. And they proclaimed it too as a right of children: the right to be well born. They legitimated their demands by using the therapeutic ideals of the age and claims that the rights of community must be considered over those of the individual.

Indiana passed the first sterilization act in 1907. By 1917 fifteen states enacted the policy and by 1930 twenty-four had done so. By that date 6,000 operations had been conducted, four times the number in the rest of world combined.[72] Sterilization had a mixed judicial reception until 1927 when Supreme Court Justice Oliver Wendell Holmes Jr. upheld the sterilization of eighteen-year-old Carrie Buck by affirming the right of society to "prevent those who are manifestly unfit from continuing their kind." And he voiced the sentiments of this form of child protection by declaring, "three generations of imbeciles is enough!"[73]

The application of child protection to retarded children demonstrates how similar logic could have very different results with different groups of children. With no cure possible, those classified as feebleminded simply could not perform the role of moral reformation assigned to children as the inhabitants of the future. So others had to be protected from them. The protection campaign also revealed the depth of the segregation impulse in the era. Segregation was not just a racial policy; separation was instead a pervasive response to the growing diversity of industrial America. It found numerous expressions from ethnically restrictive covenants and zoning laws to the founding of private clubs and schools. And all of its forms were dependent on law. Segregating the retarded stands as one of the most extreme form of this widespread impulse. And protecting these children also meant that the feebleminded would be the most marked and excluded children, the most separated from the rest of society, and thus the most protected.

Conclusion

By making their fellow citizens hear what reformer John Spargo called "the bitter cry of the children," child protectors succeeded in making a protected childhood a central concern of American society.[74] They did so by turning the child into a powerful icon of reform through galvanizing stories that tugged at collective heartstrings and provoked crises over the fate of children in families deemed failures. With the endangered child as their legitimating symbol, reformers chronicled the threats posed by modern society and then attacked each one. As they did, they ensured that protection expressed the ambivalent belief that children were both at risk in America and a risk to America and thus legitimated the right of the public to intervene to save them. And they institutionalized their solutions in statutes, judicial decisions, administrative policies, agencies, and organizations that created the new ideal of a protected childhood and lingered on long after their initial reforming zeal had dissipated. Those institutionalized solutions and the reconstructed child on which they were based became an integral part of an emerging American welfare state that retained a fundamental ambivalence about the legitimacy and effectiveness of public authority and a fundamental faith in family privatism.

In their campaigns for a protected childhood, child protectors influenced both their time and the future. Their actions made the child a tool for legitimating American social policy throughout the twentieth century. Indeed they succeeded in turning *protection* into a keyword of American political culture and making *child protection* a trumping phrase of American political discourse. In 1899 philosopher John Dewey aptly captured the intent of child protection with the declaration: "What the best and wisest parent wants for his own child, that must the community want for all its children."[75] Those stirring words inevitably masked conflicts, contradictions, and confusion, but they come down to us as a vivid reminder of the fundamental assumptions and goals of this movement to create a protected childhood.

NOTES

1. Devine cited in R. A. Meckel, *Save the Babies: American Public Health Reform and the Prevention of Infant Mortality, 1850–1929* (Baltimore: Johns Hopkins University Press, 1990), 103.

2. And for the most significant of these studies, see Leroy Ashby, *Endangered Children: Dependency, Neglect, and Abuse in American History* (New York: Twyne Publishers, 1997); Linda Gordon, *Heroes of Their Own Lives: The Politics and History of Family Violence in Boston, 1880–1960* (New York: Penguin Press, 1988); Timothy A. Hacsi, *Second Home: Orphan Asylums and Poor Families in America* (Cambridge: Harvard University Press, 1997); Molly Ladd-Taylor, *Mother-Work: Women, Child Welfare, and the State, 1890–1930* (Urbana: University of Illinois Press, 1994); Gwendolyn Mink, *The Wages of Motherhood: Inequality in the Welfare State* (Ithaca, N.Y.: Cornell University Press, 1995); Mary E. Odem, *Delinquent Daughters: Protecting and Policing Adolescent Female Sexuality in the United States, 1885–1920* (Chapel Hill: University of North Carolina Press, 1995); Elizabeth Pleck, *Domestic Tyranny: The Making of Social Policy against Family Violence from Colonial Times to the Present* (New York: Oxford University Press, 1987); Andrew Polsky, *The Rise of the Therapeutic State* (Princeton, N.J.: Princeton University Press, 1991); Theda Skocpol, *Protecting Soldiers and Mothers: The Political Origins of Social Policy in the United States* (Cambridge: Harvard University Press, 1992).

For an insightful overview of this literature, see Felicia A. Kornbluh, "The New Literature on Gender and the Welfare State: The U.S. Case," *Feminist Studies* 22 (1996): 171–97; and see, e.g, Seth Koven and Sonya Michel, eds., *Mothers of a New World: Maternalist Politics and the Origins of Welfare States* (New York: Routledge Press, 1993).

3. Morton Keller, *Regulating a New Society: Public Policy and Social Change in America, 1900–1933* (Cambridge: Harvard University Press, 1994).

4. For the nature and possibilities of this literature, see Hugh Cunningham, "Review Essay: Histories of Childhood," *American Historical Review* 103 (1998): 1195–1208.

5. For an insightful discussion of these issues, see Thomas Haskell, "Capitalism and the Origins of the Humanitarian Sensibility," *American Historical Review* 90 (1985): 339–61, 547–66.

6. Michel Foucault, *Power/Knowledge: Selected Interviews and Other Writings, 1972–1977*, ed. Colin Gordon (New York: Pantheon Books, 1980); Jacques Donzelot, *The Policing of Families* (New York: Pantheon Books, 1979). For an application of this approach, see Polsky, *Rise of the Therapeutic State.*

7. Daniel Rodgers, *Atlantic Crossings: Social Politics in a Progressive Age* (Cambridge: Harvard University Press, 1998), chaps. 1–4; see also Keller, *Regulating a New Society,* 2.

8. For a general discussion of changing understandings about children and childhood in this era, see Hugh Cunningham, *Children and Childhood in Western Society since 1500* (New York: Longman, 1995), chaps. 4, 6.

9. For an overview of the American version of this family crisis, see Michael Grossberg, "Balancing Acts: Crisis, Change, and Continuity in American Family Law, 1890–1990," *Indiana Law Journal* 28 (1995): 273–308; and Susan Tiffin, *In Whose Best Interests? Child Welfare Reform in the Progressive Era* (Westport, Conn.: Greenwood Press, 1982), chap. 5.

10. Quoted in Michael Willrich, "Home Slackers: Men, the State, and Welfare in Modern America," *Journal of American History* 87 (2000): 465.

11. Howard Chudacoff, *How Old Are You? Age Consciousness in American Culture* (Princeton, N. J.: Princeton University Press, 1989), chaps. 1–4.

12. Vivian A. Zelizer, *Pricing the Priceless Child: The Changing Social Value of Children* (New York: Basic Books, 1985), 11.

13. Ernst Freund, *The Police Powers* (Chicago: Callaghan, 1904), 248.

14. For a general discussion of civil society, see Adam Seligman, *The Idea of Civil Society* (New York: Free Press, 1992).

15. Gary G. Hamilton and John R. Sutton, "The Problem of Control in the Weak State: Domination in the United States, 1880–1920," *Theory and Society* 18 (1989): 1–46; Kathryn Kish Sklar, "The Historical Foundations of Women's Power in the Creation of the American Welfare States," in Koven and Michel, *Mothers of a New World,* 43–93.

16. Koven and Michel, "Introduction," *Mothers of a New World,* 20, and see 2, 24–25; Tiffin, *In Whose Best Interest?* 49–53.

17. Mary Mumford, "The Place of Woman in Municipal Reform," *Outlook* 49 (1894): 587.

18. Cited in Willrich, "Home Slackers," 464.

19. For discussions of these various issues, see Cunningham, *Children and Childhood*, 137, 152–59; Seth Koven and Sonya Michel, "Womanly Duties: Maternalist Politics and the Origins of Welfare States in France, Germany, Great Britain, and the United States, 1880–1920," *American Historical Review* 95 (1990): 1076–1108; Ellen Fitzpatrick, *Endless Crusade: Women Social Scientists and Progressive Reform* (New York: Oxford University Press, 1990).

20. See Grossberg, "Balancing Acts," 275–89.

21. Hamilton Cravens, "Child Saving in Modern America, 1870s-1990s," in *Children at Risk in America: History, Concepts, and Public Policy*, ed. Roberta Wollons (Albany: State University of New York Press, 1993), 4; and see Lela B. Costin, Howard Jacob Karger, and David Stoesz, *The Politics of Child Abuse in America* (New York: Oxford University Press, 1996), 50.

22. Etta Angel Wheeler, "The Story of Mary Ellen, Which Started the Child Saving Crusade through the World," reprinted in *National Humane Review* (January–February 1962): 16–17. And for a critical assessment of the story, see Lela B. Costin, "Unraveling the Mary Ellen Legend: Origins of the 'Cruelty' Movement," *Social Service Review* 65 (1991): 203–23. For newspaper accounts, see the *New York Times*, April 10, 11, 14, and 22 and December 27, 1874.

23. *Reckoning with the Beast: Animals, Pain, and Humanity in the Victorian Mind* (Baltimore: Johns Hopkins University Press, 1980), 1; and for a discussion of the origins of this new sensibility about physical suffering, see Elizabeth B. Clark, "'The Sacred Rights of the Weak': Pain, Suffering, and the Culture of Individual Rights in Antebellum America," *Journal of American History* 82 (1995): 463–93.

24. For analyses of the founding of the NYSPCC, see Joyce Antler and Stephen Antler, "From Child Rescue to Family Protection: The Evolution of the Child Protection Movement in the United States," *Children and Youth Services Review* 1 (1979): 177–204; Pleck, *Domestic Tyranny*, chap. 4.

25. N. Ray Hiner, "Children's Rights, Corporal Punishment, and Child Abuse, Changing American Attitudes, 1870–1920," *Bulletin of the Menninger Clinic* 43 (1979): 235; and see Homer Folks, "Societies for the Prevention of Cruelty to Children," *Charities Review* 10 (1900): 43–45.

26. For a discussion of these points, see Costin, Karger, and Stoesz, *Politics of Child Abuse*, 57–75.

27. For a fuller discussion of the role of legal narratives, see Michael Grossberg, *A Judgment for Solomon: The d'Hauteville Case and Legal Experience in Antebellum America* (New York: Cambridge University Press, 1996); and for an assessment of the use of stories in contemporary child abuse cases, see Barbara J. Nelson, *Making an Issue of Child Abuse: Political Agenda Setting* (Chicago: University of Chicago Press, 1984).

28. *People v. Fletcher,* 52 Illinois 395. A year later in another case Illinois Justice Anthony Thurston added: "Even the power of the parent must be exercised with moderation. He may use correction and restraint, but in a reasonable manner. He has the right to enforce only such discipline, as may be necessary to the discharge of his sacred trust; only moderate correction and temporary confinement." *People v. Turner,* 55 Illinois (1870), 280, 284. And see Pleck, *Domestic Tyranny,* 76–77.

29. Elbridge Gerry, "The Relation of Societies for the Prevention of Cruelty to Children to Child-Saving Work," *Proceedings of the National Conference of Charities and Corrections* (1882), 9:129. For a general discussion of children's rights in this era, see Michael Grossberg, "Children's Legal Rights? A Historical Look at a Legal Paradox," in Wollons, *Children at Risk in America,* 119–26.

30. See, e.g., the "Act of the Incorporation of Societies for the Prevention of Cruelty to Children," *Laws of NY,* 1875, chap. 130, p. 114; 1881, chap. 130, p. 114. For an analysis of the links between morals policing and child protection, see Nicola Beisel, *Imperiled Innocents: Anthony Comstock and Family Reproduction in Victorian America* (Princeton, N.J.: Princeton University Press, 1997).

31. Cravens, "Child Saving," 4

32. "Abandonment and Other Acts of Cruelty to Children," *Laws of NY,* 1881, chap. 676, vol. 2, pp. 69–72.

33. Edward Townsend, *A Daughter of the Tenements* (New York: Lovell, Coryell, 1895), 12.

34. Cited in Gordon, *Heroes of Their Own Lives,* 228–29.

35. For a critique of the NYSPCC, see Homer Folks, *Care of Destitute, Dependent, and Delinquent Children* (New York: Macmillan, 1902), 173–75; Roswell C. McCrea, *The Humane Movement:, A Descriptive Survey* (New York: Columbia University Press, 1910), 138–46; Antler and Antler, "From Child Rescue to Family Protection," 183–99.

36. Tiffin, *In Whose Best Interest?* 146–47.

37. Pleck, *Domestic Tyranny,* 76

38. For an analysis of the story and its impact, see Judith Walkowitz, *City of Dreadful Delight: Narratives of Sexual Danger in Late-Victorian London* (Chicago: University of Chicago Press, 1992), 70–82.

39. For an initial presentation of the concept of moral panics, see Stanley Cohen, *Folk Devils and Moral Panic* (London: MacGibbon and Kee, 1972).

40. For a general discussion of the context of age of consent laws, see Michael Grossberg, *Governing the Hearth: Law and the Family in Nineteenth-Century America* (Chapel Hill: University of North Carolina Press, 1985), chap. 3.

41. For a general assessment of the WTCU's goals, see Jane Larson, "'Even A Worm Will Turn at Last': Rape Reform in Late-Nineteenth-Century America," *Yale Journal of Law & the Humanities* 9 (1997): 21–33. Sklar, " Historical Foundations of Women's Power," 61.

42. Helen H. Gardener, "The Shame of America: The Age of Consent Laws in the United States," *Arena* 11 (1895): 192–215.

43. For general discussions of the role of the WTCU in the age of consent campaigns, see Jane Larson, "'Even A Worm Will Turn at Last'"; and Odem, *Delinquent Daughters*, chap. 1.

44. Gardener, "Shame of America," 192.

45. Frances E. Willard, "The World Moves on and With it Women," *Woman's Magazine* 10 (1987): 137.

46. Odem, *Delinquent Daughters*, 1, and see 9–11.

47. Keller, *Regulating a New Society*, 109–10.

48. For a discussion of opposition to breach of marriage promise suits, see Grossberg, *Governing the Hearth*, 51–63.

49. Cited in Helen H. Gardener, "A Battle for Sound Morality, or the History of Recent Age-of-Consent Legislation, Part II," *Arena* 14 (1895): 21. For assessments of the opposition to higher age of consent statutes, see Odem, *Delinquent Daughters*, 31–34; Larson, "'Even A Worm Will Turn at Last,'" 53–63.

50. Jeffrey P. Moran, *Teaching Sex: The Shaping of Adolescence in the Twentieth Century* (Cambridge: Harvard University Press, 2000), chap. 1.

51. G. Stanley Hall, *Adolescence: Its Psychology and Its Relations to Physiology, Anthropology, Sociology, Sex, Crime, Religion, and Education* (New York: Appleton, 1904); G. Stanley Hall, *Youth: Its Education, Regimen, and Hygiene* (New York: Appleton, 1907); and see Dorothy R. Ross, *G. Stanley Hall: The Psychologist as Prophet* (Chicago: University of Chicago Press, 1972), chaps. 3–4; Chudakoff, *How Old Are You?* chap. 4.

52. For a particularly insightful analysis of the role of sexuality in the anti-cruelty movement, see Stephen Murray Robertson, "Sexuality through the Prism of Age: Modern Culture and Sexual Violence in New York City, 1880–1950" (Ph. D. diss., Rutgers, The State University of New Jersey, 1998), chaps. 1–6.

53. Odem, *Delinquent Daughters*, 33–37.

54. Cited in Steven Schlossman and Stephanie Wallach, "The Crime of Precocious Sexuality: Female Juvenile Delinquency in the Progressive Era," *Harvard Educational Review* 48 (1968): 68.

55. Quoted in Odem, *Delinquent Daughters*, 71. For other cases see ibid, chap. 3.

56. Odem, 43–45, 49–52; Robertson, "Sexuality through the Prism of Age," 14, 164, 177, 198.

57. The case is described in Odem, *Delinquent Daughters*, 160–62.

58. Robert L. Dugdale, *The Jukes: A Study in Crime, Pauperism, Disease, and Heredity* (New York: Putnam, 1877); and see James W. Trent Jr., *Inventing the Feeble Mind: A History of Mental Retardation in the United States* (Berkeley and Los Angeles: University of California Press, 1994), 70–72.

59. "Introduction," *The Jukes*, 4th ed. (New York: Putnam, 1910); and see Trent, *Inventing the Feeble Mind*, 70–72.

60. For a discussion of the "menace of the feebleminded," see Mark Haller, *Eugenics: Hereditarian Attitudes in American Thought* (New Brunswick, N. J.: Rutgers University Press, 1963); Trent, *Inventing the Feeble Mind*, esp. chap. 5; Steven Noll, *Feeble-*

minded in Our Midst (Chapel Hill: University of North Carolina Press, 1995); and Patrick J. Ryan, "Unnatural Selection: Intelligence Testing, Eugenics, and American Political Cultures," *Journal of Social History* 30 (1997): 669–85.

61. Edward Dickinson, *The Politics of German Child Welfare from the Empire to the Federal Republic* (Cambridge: Harvard University Press, 1996), 60.

62. Peter L. Tyor and Leland V. Bell, *Caring for the Retarded in America: A History* (Westport, Conn.: Greenwood Press, 1983).

63. "Report of the Standing Committee: Provision for Idiots," *National Conference of Corrections and Charities* 12 (1885): 174.

64. Dickinson, *Politics of German Child Welfare*, 60–61.

65. These numbers are cited in Steven Noll, *Feeble-minded in Our Midst*, 4.

66. Cited in Tyor and Bell, *Caring for the Retarded*, 108.

67. Tiffin, *In Whose Best Interest?* 144–46; Michael B. Katz, *In the Shadow of the Poorhouse: A Social History of Welfare in America* (New York: Basic Books, 1986), 130–31.

68. Quoted in Seymour B. Sarason and John Doris, *Educational Handicap, Public Policy, and Social History: A Broadened Perspective on Mental Retardation* (New York: Free Press, 1979), 268–67; and see Philip L. Safford and Elizabeth J. Safford, *A History of Childhood and Disability* (New York: Teachers College Press, 1996), 179–87.

69. Safford and Safford, *History of Childhood and Disability*, 184; Trent, *Inventing the Feeble Mind*, 144–55; and see Jeffrey Khana, "Special Education: A Historical Review of the Massachusetts Experience, 1823–1940," paper in author's possession.

70. See, e.g., *Doren v. Fleming*, 6 Ohio Circuit Court Reports, n.s. (1905), 81, which chronicles the failed attempt of a child to get out of an institution for the retarded.

71. Quoted in Haller, *Eugenics*, 45.

72. See Grossberg, "Balancing Acts," 280–81.

73. *Buck v. Bell*, 274 U.S. 200, 207 (1927); and see Keller, *Regulating a New Society*, 33–37.

74. John Spargo, *The Bitter Cry of the Children* (1906; Chicago: Quadrangle Books, 1968).

75. Dewey is cited in Grace Abbott, *The Child and the State* (Chicago: University of Chicago Press, 1938), 2:612.

ELEVEN

Kluxing the Eighteenth Amendment

The Anti-Saloon League, the Ku Klux Klan, and the Fate of Prohibition in the 1920s

Thomas R. Pegram

In 1924, Wayne Wheeler, the imperious general counsel and legislative strong-man of the Anti-Saloon League learned that South Carolina's ASL superintendent had devoted "considerable . . . time" to organizing Ku Klux Klan locals in the Palmetto State. Wheeler immediately contacted the league's pliant national superintendent, F. Scott McBride, and informed him that any association between the ASL and the Klan, then at the height of its power and notoriety, would be "very detrimental" to the league and its cause of prohibition. McBride quickly chastised the hapless South Carolinian and sent all superintendents a letter restating the league policy of single-minded attention to prohibition and reminding them to "withhold our public activities from organizations over whose official acts we have no control and over which we have no authority."[1]

Despite warnings from the league hierarchy, local officials and operatives of the ASL in the mid-1920s frequently collaborated with Klansmen in grass-roots efforts to enforce prohibition. Hampered by internal disagreement at the highest levels, the league had not followed up its legislative triumphs with a clear enforcement policy. Indecision from the national ASL and lax efforts by judges, politicians, and police pushed frustrated local ASL agents to seek help from dry church and community leaders. Many such local prohibition enthusiasts had been caught up in the recruiting surge of the Klan, drawn in by the Invisible Empire's denunciation of political corruption and lawbreaking. Together, ASL officials and Klansmen pressured lawmen and prosecutors, gathered evidence against bootleggers, joined raiding parties into liquor and gambling dives, and generally operated in the shadowland between law enforcement and vigilantism. Thus local conditions and the decisions of numerous low-level ASL operatives undercut the official separation between the respectable dry activism of the Anti-Saloon League and the secret operations of masked Klansmen.

Informed observers routinely noted connections between the league, the Klan, and the defense of prohibition. "If [the Klan] is not literally a part of the Anti-Saloon League," charged the *Baltimore Evening Sun* in 1924, "it is at least so close an ally as to be almost indistinguishable from it in many parts of the country."[2] Imperial Wizard Hiram W. Evans suggested several months earlier that "in actual operation . . . the Klan functions along the same lines as the Anti-Saloon League."[3] Press reports linked the two organizations, especially as parallel scandals between 1924 and 1927 decimated popular support for the Klan and undermined the ASL's reputation for probity and effectiveness. Historians of the Klan stress the shared outlook and frequent local collaboration between the Klan and the league.

Still, recent historians of alcohol reform have matched Wheeler's eagerness to separate the Anti-Saloon League, the agent of modern, bureaucratic temperance activism, from the persistent images of vigilante brutality and intolerance that cling to the 1920s Klan. For a generation, temperance historians struggled to establish prohibition as a flawed yet genuine reform, rather than a repressive curtailment of liberty, a sour rejection of cultural pluralism, or an ill-considered experiment in social control. Prohibition, temperance historians contend, was rooted in the Progressive drive to improve public health, to regulate business enterprise that harmed the public interest, and to forge social cohesion through legislative means. The Anti-Saloon League, in turn, embodied the organizational revolution that reshaped the nineteenth-century nation of courts, parties, and island communities into a modern society of large institutional structures and bureaucratic mechanisms.[4]

The league's identity as a professional, efficient, and politically sophisticated pressure group was central to this interpretation. The league's reform efforts, one supporter explained, had "no need of fanaticism. There is no need for the business man or church member to make street speeches for temperance."[5] From its founding in 1893, the Protestant ministers and attorneys who controlled the league used publicity and thorough organization to build a powerful dry sentiment in the Protestant churches, then steadily pressured legislators to enact local option restrictions on alcohol sales, county and state prohibition laws, and, ultimately, national prohibition through the ratification of the eighteenth amendment. The league's methods, structure, and sensibility were distinctly modern, and therefore seemed far removed from the Klan's secretive rituals, ludicrous nomenclature and costumes, hate-filled rhetoric, and spasms of violence. The framework of the organizational synthesis that informs temperance historians concealed the interplay between the Klan and the ASL in the 1920s.

Ironically, the organizational interpretation that led temperance historians to overlook the Klan's role in prohibition enforcement is also central to new assessments of the 1920s Klan. Rejecting traditional interpretations of the Klan as a violent fringe group, new studies present the Invisible Empire as part of the modern, associational civic ethos of the new era. More tied to Progressivism than to the issues of Reconstruction, motivated more by local politics than by the racist, anti-Catholic theatrics of Klan leaders, the hooded figures of the new Klan historiography appear as fit associates of the Anti-Saloon League. Yet, images of modern Klansmen and prohibitionists alike are overdrawn and in need of revision. The revised image of the 1920s Klan too easily glides past contemporary criticism of the masked order, the everyday bigotry of Klan politics and boycotts, and the persistent stain of violence that complicated the Klan's relationship to the social and political mainstream of the 1920s. On the other hand, historians who emphasize the bureaucratic innovations of prohibition reformers downplay the extent to which prohibitionists were motivated by cultural intolerance, anti-Catholicism, and commitments to Anglo-Saxon superiority.

For all its explanatory power, the organizational synthesis lacks the fluidity necessary to capture the inconsistencies and fluctuating dynamics of 1920s public policy controversies. Unexpected and unlikely alliances like that of the Klan and the ASL formed and fell away in ways that confound streamlined explanations. For instance, American Legionnaires and other "100 percent American" opponents of 1920s history textbooks that reflected new critical perspectives were surprisingly joined in their patriotic objections by numerous ethnic leaders anxious to place their heroes into the traditional American narrative. Many nativist Protestants, in strange reaction to ethnic patriotism, defended uncomfortable scholars and their critical works. Defined by its prosperity, devotion to business, and mass popular culture on the one hand, and effectively portrayed, on the other, as a deeply divided "discontented

America" struggling with the legacies of World War I, 1920s society over-matches the sleek determinism of the organizational synthesis.[6]

A better approach to the interpretive challenges posed by the Anti-Saloon League and the Ku Klux Klan, one that accounts for contingency and complexity in the 1920s, is provided by Morton Keller's analysis of the variegated contours of social movements and the public policies they produced. In an exhaustive survey of American public policy between 1900 and 1933, Keller identified three central factors at work in creating social policy. First, the Progressive generation of reformers advocated "policies designed to restore an American social cohesion whose loss they regarded as a major casualty of modern times." These policies often promoted "a better-organized, more uniform, more efficient social order." Implementation of policies intended to ensure greater "unity and efficiency" were countered by a second powerful force, "the fact of American pluralism." Racial, ethnic, cultural, and class differences resisted and reshaped the Progressive campaign for social cohesion. Finally, another powerful countercurrent, "the persistence—even the strengthening—of traditional social values and beliefs" further influenced public policy formation.[7] Keller's formula of Progressivism, pluralism, and persistence clarifies the complex reality underlying the contradictory historical images of the Klan and the ASL. Both organizations reflected diverse and inconsistent influences. Rank-and-file concerns sometimes trumped organizational directives. Despite differences, the two groups also cooperated. Similar tensions and dynamics influenced prohibition as a public policy and, as historians increasingly recognize, shaped 1920s society. By challenging the organizational synthesis, the dominant historical construct encasing current interpretations of the Klan and the ASL, a more complex yet fuller and more satisfying assessment of the social movements and public policies of the 1920s becomes possible.

The Ku Klux Klan in 1920s Society

When national prohibition commenced in 1920, the Anti-Saloon League had been active in Protestant churches and in politics for a generation. By contrast, the sudden resurgence of the Ku Klux Klan, which attracted between three and six million white-sheeted enthusiasts by mid-decade, had just begun. The second Klan, named after the masked band of southern night riders who violently resisted the federal government and political rights for black southerners during Reconstruction, was founded in 1915 by William J. Simmons, an

Alabama-born former minister given to dramatic gestures and obsessed with the arcane world of white, Protestant fraternalism. The rapid national growth of the Klan between 1920 and 1925 owed little to the efficiency of its leadership, however. Simmons was ousted as imperial wizard in 1922 by Hiram Evans, a Dallas dentist, prompting a numbing procession of lawsuits over the control of the Klan, which was matched at the state level by repeated battles over turf, rank, and money.[8]

More important in explaining the Klan's burst of popularity was the hooded order's alignment with three prominent forces in the public culture of the 1920s: entertainment and popular amusement; the power of advertising and lure of voluntary associations, both linked to the business boom of the period; and the noisy identification with "100 percent Americanism" that emerged after World War I. The search for amusement and the thrill of spectacle were clearly part of Klan's appeal. Despite the Invisible Empire's supposed distaste for modern cultural styles, the Klan embraced new forms of mass entertainment to build its membership. Initial interest in the revived order was tied to the 1915 release of D. W. Griffith's epic film, *The Birth of a Nation*, which romanticized the Reconstruction Klan. Soon after, Klansmen offered their own work in the new medium. Ohio Klansmen produced a recruiting film, *The Toll of Justice*, which featured aerial acrobatics, a Hollywood-style romance, and a "picked squad of the Columbus Police Force" as elements in its tale of daring Klansmen foiling criminal bootleggers and drug smugglers. Beyond its uplifting moral lessons, Klan promotional material claimed the film would deliver "suspense that grips" and "love that throbs." Oregon Klansmen hoped the appeal of a double feature of "thrilling" Klan-made movies would compel potential members to endure the recruiting lecture that preceded the entertainment. Radio broadcasts featuring Klansmen aired in Denver. Indiana music stores advertised Klan-produced records. The Klan clearly intended to exploit modern mass culture as well as to regulate it.[9]

The KKK also offered an abundance of traditional entertainment. At the height of its influence, local Klans sponsored parades, picnics, fairs, and other community gatherings for white Protestants. One Klan barbecue in Valparaiso, Indiana, in 1923 promised "20 Brass Bands . . . High, Tight Wire Walking, 100 Feet in the Air—Wild Broncho-Busting [*sic*] . . . Imported Texas Cowboys" and fireworks to end the day.[10] At other rallies Klansmen soared aloft in hot air balloons. Outdoor settings and solemn rituals created excitement at large Klan meetings, with particular anticipation reserved for the cross burnings that were their highlight. Eyewitness accounts of Klan meetings almost universally noted the great enthusiasm that accompanied these fiery displays. As one historian acknowledged, "it was fun to be a Klansman."[11] For those who were not targets of its intolerant rhetoric and political thrusts, the Klan provided fellowship and entertainment similar to that which accompanied the great nineteenth-century wave of popular reforms and enthusiasms.

More central to the Klan's expansion after 1920 was its ability to profit from advertising and the associational impulse of the new era. The prominence of 1920s mass-market advertising and corporate associations fostered a popular culture of salesmen and joiners. A hard-charging marketing campaign advertising the Klan as a men's voluntary association aided its growth. In 1920 Simmons hired two public relations agents, Elizabeth Tyler and Edward Young Clarke, to promote the then-sickly Klan. Tyler and Clarke sent Klan recruiters (called kleagles) into the lodges of the South, then nationally, drumming up support for what they called a patriotic fraternal body dedicated to law and order. Earning a portion of each membership fee, kleagles gathered thousands of recruits, a process known as kluxing. In an age of voluntary associations, the Klan was unusually successful in attracting and organizing followers, despite strong press criticism of the revived order. So closely was the Invisible Empire identified with 1920s associational life that the use of "kluxing" as a shorthand term for "the vociferous rounding up of the populace," enjoyed a brief vogue during the period.[12]

More fundamental than the excitement, entertainment, business contacts, and fraternal fellowship that the Klan offered was its ideology of racial, ethnic, and religious chauvinism and exclusivity. Described by scholars as white Protestant nationalism or reactionary populism, the Klan's outlook attributed progress, order, freedom, and democracy to the ascendancy of native-born, white, Protestant Americans.[13] The Klan hierarchy loudly and repeatedly charged that African Americans were racially incapable of becoming full-fledged American citizens, that Jews refused to assimilate into American society, and that immigrants, especially Catholics, by maintaining their loyalty to foreign lands and an alien, undemocratic Church, endangered the republic. "The Roman Church," contended Evans, "is, fundamentally and irredeemably, in its leadership, in politics, in thought, and largely in membership, actually and actively alien, un-American and usually anti-American." Beset by foreign designs, unaided by a shabby liberalism that had "excused" rather than resisted "the alien invasion," Evans melodramatically insisted that "the Klan is literally once more the embattled American farmer and artisan, coordinated into a disciplined and growing army, and launched upon a definite crusade for Americanism!"[14]

The Klan's bigotry and anti-Catholicism was not simply a rhetorical flourish of its leaders, as some historians suggest, but was a central component of "Klannishness." Minutes of KKK meetings reveal that conversations within local klaverns (lodges) were regularly punctuated by derogatory references to blacks, Jews, foreigners, and, most consistently, Catholics. Complaints about "caseys" (a term derived from the initials of the Knights of Columbus, a Catholic fraternal order), rumors of arsenals buried under Catholic churches, and speculation concerning Rome's design to infiltrate the United States government were staples of Klan discussion. Intolerant sentiments took concrete form in boycotts organized by Klansmen in many communities against Catholic, Jewish, and immigrant merchants. Finally, the Klan took its campaign against Catholic public power—and parochial schools—into politics. Klansmen rallied against Catholic candidates, urged that school boards cast out Catholic officials and teachers, and, in Oregon, championed a law requiring students to attend public schools.[15]

The ugliness of Klan bigotry and reports of shootings, savage beatings, and intimidation by masked Klansmen led many contemporary observers and generations of historians to view the 1920s Klan as a violent, repressive, fringe group. Recent "populist" studies, however, attempt to place the hooded order within the mainstream of 1920s American society. Focusing on local or state Klans outside the South, these Klan "community studies" downplay the centrality of vigilante violence and repression of minorities in the 1920s Klan movement, stressing instead the conformity between the Klan's views and those of America's white, Protestant majority.[16] In Indiana, the nation's most thoroughly organized realm, Leonard J. Moore found that Klansmen rejected violence as a strategy and largely ignored the African American, immigrant, and Catholic residents of the state. Elsewhere, victims of Klan floggings tended to be fellow white Protestants who violated moral codes by patronizing bootleggers, conducting extramarital sexual affairs, or mistreating their families. Northern Klans were more often on the receiving end of violence, as vigorous anti-Klan rallies sometimes ended in stonings and gunfire.[17]

While acknowledging the virulently bigoted language and attitudes of the Klan, the new Klan historians contend that during what John Higham called "the tribal twenties"—an era marked by immigration restriction, the prosecution of Sacco and Vanzetti and the hounding of other radicals, white resentment of the "New Negro," and vigorous debates about the suitability of Catholic candidates for high political office—neither the language nor the attitudes of the Klan was out of step with prevailing white, Protestant opinion.[18]

Contemporary appraisals of the Klan support elements of this view. In a generally critical assessment of the Klan, *Outlook* nevertheless professed that the "disintegrating forces" of "alien ideas" worried Americans. "Many of the very people who come to this country because it is great and rich and strong and free," it continued, "have done their utmost to belittle all that has made it such, and some of these have agitated and organized to destroy the institutions on which the present strength and freedom of America rest."[19]

Still, the Klan was far from a representative presence in 1920s America. The willingness of Klansmen to undertake extralegal means in defense of law and morality was sharply criticized by contemporaries. Condemnation of the Klan's closed membership lists, secret proceedings, and masks was widespread throughout the 1920s. Even though the Invisible Empire's racial, ethnic, and religious bigotry reflected popular American prejudices, the stridency with which Klan officials pronounced it was deemed offensive even by the insensitive standards of the decade. Many observers who were untroubled by the Klan's assertion of white Protestant superiority nevertheless considered the hooded order an extremist group because of its whips, masks, and clandestine operations.

The populist Klan historians have more effectively dismantled the image of the Invisible Empire as the refuge of marginalized rural fanatics. The Indiana Klan, for example, enrolled between one-quarter and one-third of the state's white, male Protestants: drawing from all economic strata except the very highest business and professional group (although most consistently from the clerks and shopkeepers at the fringes of white-collar status and skilled workers); from residents of city, town, and country; and from all Protestant denominations (except the apolitical Fundamentalists). Some contemporaries of the Klan reached similar conclusions. In Oregon, reported one journalist, "not the bad people of the State, but the good people—the very good people—are largely responsible for the transformation of the ... commonwealth into an invisible empire."[20] Another keen observer believed the Klan attracted "the good, solid, middle-class citizens, the 'backbone of the Nation.'"[21] Despite bizarre, repugnant qualities that justifiably placed the Klan outside the mainstream of American behavior and belief, the social profile of its members, its willingness to appropriate the mechanisms of modern popular culture, and much of its fraternal and political activity reflected dominant rather than marginal themes of 1920s America. The appeal as well as the menace of the Invisible Empire embodied the mixed patterns of optimism and uncertainty, conflict and community that characterized the "discontented America" of the 1920s.

Even within the Klan, the ideology of native, white, Protestant cultural supremacy deferred slightly to the reality of American pluralism. German Lutherans, proud of their ethnic heritage and in many cases with at least one immigrant parent, were welcome in the midwestern realms. The Klan eventually created an affiliated organization, the American Krusaders, for foreign-born citizens desiring to participate in Klan activities. In Indiana, the hooded order awkwardly invited African American Protestants to join the anti-Catholic crusade. Occasionally, as with Idaho Klansmen who invited their town's only Jewish family to KKK celebrations, official Klan doctrines were set aside to accommodate local desires. Similarly, some klaverns showed little interest in nativist or anti-Catholic pursuits. Like most Americans, Klansmen sometimes differed among themselves or contradicted their own professed views.[22]

The forces of persistence and pluralism—traditional values and practices confronting ethnic, racial, and religious diversity—that Keller placed at the center of social change and public policy early in the twentieth century clearly figured in the development of the second Klan. But contemporaries and historians also found strains of Keller's third category—Progressivism—in the Klan movement. Reporters drew on the imagery of insurgent Progressivism to describe the atmosphere of Klan rallies. Robert Duffus, a strong critic of the Invisible Empire, asserted that the "bronzed, homely, good-natured" crowd at a large Klan gathering in Indiana in 1923 "would have seemed perfectly at home eleven years ago in a Progressive party rally." Stanley Frost went further, contending that "a large proportion" of Hoosier Klansmen "had been Bull Moosers, some having leaned to La Folletteism," and that nationally, the hooded fraternity bore a noticeable likeness to elements of the Progressive Party. The Klan "contains about the same basic elements of partly dissatisfied and partly idealistic middle-class folk, as well as the same fringes," he argued. "Its gatherings give the same appearance and feeling. It is strong in about the same parts of the country, and it sings 'Onward Christian Soldiers' just as indefatigably as the Bull Moosers did."[23]

Populist Klan historians emphasize the importance of Progressive themes in understanding the second Klan's popularity. Within its restrictive Protestant white supremacist framework, the 1920s Klan promoted civic activism and political reform. Beyond fighting to repress parochial schools and remove Catholic influence from public instruction, the Klan advocated less controversial improvements to public education. The Women of the Ku Klux Klan, a separate organization for white Protestant women, became a vehicle for activism on behalf of white women's political rights and gender equality, as well as for white, Protestant domination. Resistance to new business and politi-

cal elites, whose rise had disrupted community social structures, characterized Klan activism in many localities. Most of all, grassroots support for the
Klan in the early 1920s united behind a drive to end corruption in politics, reverse government inattention to lawbreaking, and reform what many Klan
supporters saw as a dangerous culture of criminality and moral laxity that
threatened social cohesion and civic improvement. Those concerns swept
Klan-backed political candidates into office in Oregon, Colorado, Texas, Indiana, and other states. "The Klan movement was triggered, in good part,"
Moore asserted, "not by disillusionment with progressivism, but by a yearn-
ing to fill the void left by its demise." Among the moral issues that motivated
Klansmen, he continued, "the great symbol of that desire was Prohibition."[24]

The Perils of a Dry Alliance

Enthusiasm for prohibition enforcement emerged from the grassroots of Klandom, rather than from Evans' Atlanta headquarters. Nativism and anti-Catholicism dominated the attention of the imperial wizard until Al Smith's political
ascent in the late 1920s (and falling Klan membership) led Evans to assign prohibition equal prominence in his denunciations of the New York Democrat. But
in such Klan strongholds as Texas, Oklahoma, Indiana, Ohio, and Oregon, as
well as among pockets of Klansmen in New Jersey and New York, prohibition
support was a defining issue from the outset of the early 1920s Klan movement.
Raw conditions in southwestern oil towns and the refusal of state and local authorities to interfere with illegal drinking, gambling, and prostitution generated
an atmosphere of moral crisis that produced the Klan movement in Texas, Oklahoma, and Arkansas. For northern and western Klansmen, enforcing prohibition and wresting control of public schools from Catholic and alien influences
were primary policy objectives. Klansmen joined police or launched their own
vigilante raids on illegal saloons, pushed for tough prosecution of liquor law vio-
lators, occasionally tried to stack juries against bootleggers, and, nearly everywhere after 1923, demanded stronger federal and state enforcement measures.

But just as prohibition sentiment occupied on awkward place in progressive reform, exposing the coercive underside of the progressive campaign for
rationality, cohesion, and improvement, so, too, did the Ku Klux Klan's support for enforcement of the Volstead Act and its local equivalents create ambivalence within dry ranks. The Invisible Empire pursued wets with both
efficient political organization and vigilante brutality. In Oklahoma, hooded
knights traded gunfire with criminal bootleggers. Southwestern Klansmen

kidnapped and flogged suspected bootleggers and some drinkers. Yet a reporter commended the Oregon Klan's "discretion in its choice of victims."[25] Both the success and the excess of the Klan in enforcing prohibition complicated matters for the Anti-Saloon League.

On the one hand, by 1924 the Klan was potentially a valuable ally in the losing battle to enforce national prohibition. Since the ratification of the eighteenth amendment, contributions to the league had dwindled and popular enthusiasm for its cause had flagged. The ASL maintained a headlock on Congress and most state legislatures, but the problem for dry forces centered on the enforcement of existing statutes rather than legislative fine-tuning. The federal Prohibition Bureau was significantly undermanned and underfunded, hampered by corruption, and overwhelmed by widespread, although by no means universal, defiance of the liquor ban. States provided little, if any, funding for concurrent prohibition enforcement, which had been a fundamental component of dry strategy. Salaries for league representatives were in arrears and morale was slipping. Finally, ASL leaders disagreed over enforcement policies. A group backing Ernest Cherrington, a key policy maker and director of league publications, favored a lengthy temperance education campaign to build up cultural support for prohibition among wets, rather than antagonizing them with aggressive increases in fines and arrests. Wheeler's faction demanded sterner legislation to buttress law enforcement. Yet even Wheeler resisted turning the league into a "detective agency."[26]

The Klan could have become the missing arm of the dry movement. Like the league, the Klan was firmly entrenched in Protestant churches. "The United Brethren preachers in Kansas are practically all Klansmen," confided one ASL informant.[27] Churches furnished the members of Klan-directed law enforcement committees that led local prohibition efforts. The Klan also modeled its crisp mobilization of voters on ASL practices—with one vital distinction. Frost reported in 1924 that the Indiana realm "follows the tactics of the Anti-Saloon League, with the difference that, while the League operates openly, the Klan prefers to keep its hand covered, and to veil both its actions and its power with as much secrecy as possible."[28] Sharing a constituency with the ASL, supported by a membership that numbered into the millions, intimidating in presence and mysterious in operation, and eager to rout the bootleggers and illegal drinkers—the Klan could have become an influential partner in sustaining the struggle of the faltering Anti-Saloon League. Indeed, Evans later boasted that the Klan "completed a reorganization and revivification of the dry forces of the nation, following the decay that fell upon the Anti-Saloon League with the achievement of its primary purpose."[29]

Yet the league had sound reasons for avoiding any conspicuous contact with the Invisible Empire. League doctrine barred affiliation with other organizations or issues aside from prohibition. The league's operational "Blue Book" stressed that the ASL "refuses to be distracted from its main object. It is not an anti-vice association, a purity crusade or a mere law enforcement bureau."[30] Nor did the league want to cut itself off from possible allies in a pluralistic society. The Klan's open espousal of racist, nativist, and anti-Catholic sentiments contradicted the league's policy of welcoming all support for prohibition and resisting only the liquor trade.

But the Klan worried the league for deeper reasons. As Evans' braggadocio indicated, the Klan was a rival to the ASL for the allegiance of Protestant churches. Alert churchgoers may have noted that whereas the league visited Protestant churches to raise funds, the Klan made it a practice to donate money to congregations. More damaging was the temptation posed by the Klan's ideology. Since the adoption of national prohibition and its subsequent fitful enforcement, ASL leaders had struggled to keep the anti-immigrant and anti-Catholic animosities of its own officials from bubbling to the surface. Already in 1920, William Anderson, the rough and tumble New York superintendent (and "Blue Book" author) had ignited a controversy by accusing the Catholic Church and the Tammany political machine with conspiring to overturn prohibition.[31] Public identification of the league with the Klan could destroy the ASL's image as a legitimate, lawful political force.

Highly publicized episodes of Klan violence and vigilantism along with widespread criticism of the hooded order's hidden membership lists and secret operations intensified the Anti-Saloon League's unwillingness to work with the Klan. Tales of murder and evasion of justice by Louisiana Klansmen were reported in 1923. Combat in Illinois's Williamson County, pitting Klansmen against bootlegging gangs and wayward lawmen, and a brutal riot in Niles, Ohio, between the Klan and a coalition of bootleggers and immigrant working-class clubs required the intervention of national guard troops in 1924. The press denounced the Klan's role in continuing violence and were joined by political and business elites, along with higher-status service clubs such as Kiwanis and Rotary, in opposing the masks, secret ceremonies, and stealthy politics of the Invisible Empire. The ASL, wooing the anti-Klan groups to the dry cause and feeling itself superior to the Klan, officially remained distant from the hooded order. Even Anderson, the ASL official reporters considered closest to the Klan, rebuked Klan secrecy with the defiant assertion, "it has never been necessary to look under cover to find me."[32]

Yet, driven by necessity or conviction, influenced by the same streams of persistence, pluralism, and progressivism that stoked the social current of the 1920s, numerous state and local ASL officials waded into troubled waters and made common effort with the Klan. Then scandals and political setbacks from 1924 until 1927 swept through both organizations, devastating the Klan and the league and leaving prohibition without effective defenders.

Falling Together

Public revelations of cooperation between the Invisible Empire and the Anti-Saloon League appeared at a pivotal stage in the meteoric career of the 1920s Klan. In 1924 the Klan was at the height of its popularity and political influence. Klan-influenced votes had seemingly secured political control of Oregon, Indiana, and Colorado; an attempt to condemn the hooded order at the 1924 Democratic convention had failed; and more recruits appeared ready for initiation into the mysteries of the Invisible Empire. But a succession of reversals that resembled the Anti-Saloon League's troubles after achieving national prohibition deflated the political promise of the Klan by 1925. In Oregon, courts struck down the Klan's public school law and patronage conflicts fractured the relationship between the KKK and state government. In Colorado, experienced politicians easily thwarted Klan-backed legislators and the grand dragon of the Colorado realm was jailed for income tax evasion.[33]

The Klan's fall in its Indiana stronghold was more shocking and destructive to the Klan movement. Hoosier Klandom was presided over by a swaggering opportunist named D.C. Stephenson, who exaggerated his authority by means of huge rallies and repeated references to what he claimed was a direct telephone connection between his office and the White House. Stephenson sparred with Imperial Wizard Evans and, on the eve of the Indiana realm's great success in the 1924 election, Evans expelled "the Old Man" from the Klan. Defiantly, Stephenson dragged down the Klan and its Republican political allies within a year. The last in a string of groping, mauling assaults on women by Stephenson ended in the suicide of his final victim and a murder conviction for the erstwhile "law in Indiana." When his expected pardon did not come, Stephenson revealed the bribes that had lashed Indiana politicians to the Klan. The scandal, along with revelations of Stephenson's drunken, hedonistic conduct while grand dragon, led defenders of law and order within the Klan to desert in droves. Klan influence quickly receded from midwestern and western states and shrank back to its original southern base.[34]

As this swift transition in the fortunes of the Klan unfolded, the ASL was forming numerous small alliances with hooded drys. The Klan and the league worked at the local level in informal law enforcement groups or in state politics as members of dry, conservative coalitions. In New Jersey a mixed body of Protestant laypeople and Klansmen in Asbury Park, acting on information provided by an ASL agent, launched an antivice campaign against prominent local figures. Meanwhile, both the Klan and the ASL vigorously opposed the 1924 reelection of the wet Republican senator Walter J. Edge. New Jersey league superintendent James K. Shields was so intent on defeating Edge that he seriously considered entering the race himself. In rarer cases ASL officials either openly or involuntarily revealed close attachments to the Invisible Empire. Alabama superintendent J. Bibb Mills, a veteran ASL worker, publicly helped defeat an antimask bill aimed at the Klan in 1927. A stolen Klan membership list in Buffalo in 1924 revealed that George Fowler, western New York district superintendent of the ASL, had joined the Invisible Empire the year before.[35]

Increasingly, dalliances with the Klan worsened internal controversies that embarrassed and damaged the Anti-Saloon League. In 1925 a Milwaukee ASL worker seeking to undermine the state superintendent met with Klansmen to form an independent law enforcement agency using the league's name. When the arrangement soured, dissatisfied Klansmen leaked the story. This airing of dirty laundry was particularly troublesome because the rebellious Milwaukee official was the brother of a prominent league superintendent and his superior was general superintendent McBride's younger brother.[36]

Klan-tinged scandals in Texas, where the Klan issue had disrupted state politics, and in Kansas hurt the league more deeply. Charges leveled by a national ASL official that the Texas superintendent had endorsed a Klansman for governor, drew a Klan salary, and invited Klan participation at the state ASL convention tore apart the prohibition alliance in Texas and nearly caused the Lone Star ASL to sever relations with the national organization. News that the Kansas superintendent had skimmed money from prohibition enforcement groups, including angry Klansmen, led the national press to highlight the "Anti-Saloon League's Lost Virtue" in this midwestern stronghold of temperance. The temporary replacement for the disgraced superintendent turned out to be a former Klansman who had once "lighted the flaming cross in his church" and was considered by Kansas league insiders to be more loyal to the Invisible Empire than to the ASL.[37] "So acute is the situation in Kansas that we cannot have the Klan name or influence save in a friendly way," confided a nervous league official as the scandal unfolded. "We can't be klan or anti-klan."[38]

Given the disabling effect of the Klan on Anti-Saloon League activities, the mild measures taken against league officials who were active with the Klan indicates ambivalence in the ASL hierarchy concerning the Invisible Empire. "It would be better not to have a state superintendent who is a Klansman," suggested McBride, yet he believed the Kansas Klansman could be effective as a lesser ASL official.[39] McBride also recommended the Buffalo district superintendent who had joined the Klan as a "high-class, aggressive young man" who could "make a good state superintendent."[40] McBride ultimately sided with the Klan-connected Texas superintendent and offered the disruptive Milwaukee agent a league job in Arizona until the man's "spasmodic mental gyrations" spun him out of the Anti-Saloon League altogether.[41] Desperate to keep the faltering league operational, ASL leaders only required their Klannish officials to camouflage themselves modestly.

Nevertheless, when top league figures fell into scandals, the Anti-Saloon League became fatally tied to the Invisible Empire's corrupt descent. Perhaps the most crippling blow to the reputation of the ASL and prohibition was the downfall of William Anderson, the outspoken New York superintendent. Anderson was a gifted propagandist for the dry cause and one of the league's toughest legislative experts. He was assigned the superintendent's job in such challenging wet bastions as Illinois, Maryland, and New York, where he indulged his taste for the give and take of bruising political combat. Anderson's talent and candor, along with his self-promotion, made him a press favorite. *Outlook* judged him to be "perhaps, the most outstanding figure in the group of men who removed the stigma of amateurishness from the prohibition movement." In 1919 the *Literary Digest* extravagantly described him as "the man who made America dry," an icon of the Anti-Saloon League and even of prohibition itself.[42]

By 1923, however, Anderson's name suggested corruption, anti-Catholicism, and the Ku Klux Klan. Previously, his searing criticism of New York governor Al Smith, Tammany Hall, and the Catholic hierarchy had barely been contained by his professionalism. But after wet forces publicized Anderson's diversion of slender league funds to cover personal expenses and presented an indictment for forgery against him, the cornered superintendent left caution behind. He roared that Tammany's unpatriotic actions pushed good people into the Klan. New York wets, he claimed, hoped "to tie the Anti-Saloon League and the Klan up together, tie one rock to their two necks and push them overboard at the same time." Throughout his tirade, an eyewitness noted, "he spoke in [the Klan's] defense in the friendliest manner conceivable."[43] Anderson, who steadfastly denied Klan sympathies, had done more than anyone to bind the league to the Invisible Empire.

The resulting trial and conviction of Anderson for third degree forgery shook the ASL. Press reports emphasized the New York league's secrecy, lack of candor, and blustering threats during the proceedings. "Prohibition has suffered much from its advocates," concluded the *Nation*.[44] The national ASL abandoned Anderson, publicly stating that he had not "intentionally" broken the law, but privately noting that Anderson's behavior as "an individual player rather than a team worker" led him astray. Anderson quit the ASL, and after a short term in prison, formed the American Protestant Alliance, a frankly nativist, anti-Catholic association.[45]

If the Anderson scandal had not thoroughly "ku kluxed" the Anti-Saloon League's image, the public linking of the Indiana ASL and the disintegrating Hoosier Klan finished the process by 1927. Despite professions from Indiana superintendent Edward Shumaker that the league was "not working with [the Klan] in either an official or unofficial way," both organizations carried out liquor raids under the authority of the Horse Thief Detective Association, a frontier-era holdover that allowed citizens to assume police functions. Klan pressure also helped enact Shumaker's "bone-dry" bill, a strict ban on liquor possession that surpassed federal regulations in severity.[46]

The Stephenson scandal that toppled the Indiana Klan uprooted the Hoosier ASL as well. Although the sybaritic Stephenson was uninterested in prohibition, journalists probing his downfall stressed the league's role in building the Indiana Klan. Duffus reported that "Indianans think that Shumaker and his league prepared the way for the Klan by drilling their followers to take orders and to apply the single test of wetness or dryness to candidates for public office." According to Duffus, "without taking over the league or making an open alliance with it, [Klan organizers] adopted it as their model" and drew on its constituency of activists.[47]

Shumaker furthered the linkage between the faltering Klan and the ASL by following Stephenson into jail. After Shumaker denounced state authorities for failing to uphold dry laws, attorney general Arthur Gilliom, a prominent opponent of the KKK, prosecuted the surprised superintendent for contempt of court. As Shumaker began a sixty-day sentence, reporter Louis Budenz (later a renowned ex-communist informer) proclaimed the hapless superintendent "a close publicity rival to that of his fellow Hoosier celebrity, ex-Grand Dragon D.C. Stephenson."[48] The forces of persistence, pluralism, and Progressivism that shaped the Klan and the ASL also drew them into a fatal public embrace.

The Ku Klux Klan and the Anti-Saloon League were in retreat by 1927. The Invisible Empire's advocacy of morality and improvement had been badly undercut by the misdeeds of its leaders, its legislative bungling, and a renewed surge of masked violence and bigoted rhetoric. Support for the Klan, so enthusiastic only three years before, melted away. The ASL had also suffered reversals. Battered by scandals, unable to rally support to national prohibition (the Federal Council of Churches in a devastating 1925 report declared the league's approach to prohibition enforcement an utter failure), and weakened by the sudden death of Wayne Wheeler, the league was but a shell of the once-vigorous body that had forced prohibition onto the national political agenda.[49]

In 1928 the Klan briefly rebounded as anti-Catholic opposition to the presidential candidacy of Al Smith, the Catholic Democrat from New York, swept sections of the country. The Anti-Saloon League also mobilized against Smith and, once more, the robes of the Klan tripped the league and caused it to stumble. James Cannon, the Southern Methodist bishop who was the leading Democratic lobbyist in the ASL, launched a bitter, fruitless campaign of opposition to Smith among Democrats. Cannon's fulminations against "Romanism" closely aligned with the Klan's position, reminding Americans of the ASL's troubling proximity to the now-despised hooded order. His attempt to uproot Democratic allegiances also reinforced charges that the league had become a front for the Republican Party. Then scandal engulfed Cannon as charges ranging from wartime flour hoarding and stock fraud to adultery tarnished the Virginian's reputation as a religious leader and political activist.[50]

The shared history of the ASL and the Invisible Empire in the 1920s cannot by itself explain the failure of prohibition as a social policy. But the relationship of prohibition to the complicated interaction of the Klan and the league furnishes historians a valuable lesson in the interpretation of social movements. More precisely, it reveals the perils of using overarching analytical models to make sense of discrete, contingent, and sometimes contradictory historical relationships. The connections between prohibition, the ASL, and the Klan have been misdiagnosed in two ways. First, an interpretive tradition running from Repeal into the 1960s diminished the Progressive, reformist strains in prohibition, the league, and even the Klan. Guided by a civil libertarian distaste for dry interventionism, sickened by the violence and racist venom of the revived Klan then active as the terroristic wing of southern "massive resistance" to the civil rights movement, and informed by a historical understanding of the 1920s as a decade of misplaced faith in business, government inactivity, and antimodern convulsions, historians emphasized the repressive, reactionary elements in prohibition reform and the 1920s Klan movement. In a terse summary of this viewpoint, Richard Hofstadter dismissed prohibition as a "pseudo reform" undeserving of inclusion in the catalog of progressive achievements.[51] Neither prohibition nor the Klan movement of the 1920s seemed to offer much for understanding the expansion of American reform.

Historians influenced by the organizational synthesis then reinserted prohibition into the reform mainstream and deemed the 1920s Klan a significant social movement worthy of patient study. Propelled by the belief that bureaucratic mechanisms and associational activity were the wellsprings of modern American development, historians looked with new respect at the efficient interest-group activism of the ASL and the civic associationalism of klaverns. But in the zero-sum game of historiographical monopoly, the new insights came at the expense of a second set of misperceptions. Temperance historians, pressing the forward-looking credentials of league activists, neglected to investigate cooperation between the ASL and what they still considered a reactionary, semicriminal Klan movement. Complicating evidence of bigotry, repression, and even violence among Klansmen was similarly downplayed by populist Klan historians.

Keller's challenge to accept the complexity of the past has obvious merit in analyzing the Klan and the prohibition movements of the 1920s. His insistence on the interplay of Progressivism, pluralism, and persistence in 1920s social policy formation cautions historians not to mistake any one of the numerous social crosscurrents of that period for the main pulse of society. As we have seen, the complex pulls of modern forms and traditional beliefs, racist assumptions and Progressive hopes, bigoted exclusion and community-building were present in both the Klan and the Anti-Saloon League, and they influenced the two groups' shared interest in prohibition and their complicated relationship to one another. The rapid shifting of the league and the Klan from positions of influence to marginality, from the mainstream to the extreme also suggests that political styles and orientations, as well as cultural beliefs and social structures, were complex and multidimensional in the early twentieth century, subject to the ebbs and flows that characterize Keller's analysis of modern American public life. There are broad patterns evident in 1920s society and governance, but sustained attention to smaller questions of cause and effect is necessary for them to be discerned. If historians are to comprehend the discontented 1920s, they cannot further ignore the tangled, reluctant partnership of the Klan and the Anti-Saloon League in futile defense of prohibition.

NOTES

1. Wayne Wheeler to F. Scott McBride, July 12, 1924 (first quote), McBride to Wheeler, July 21, 1924, reel 10, F. Scott McBride Papers, microfilm edition of Temperance and Prohibition Papers, Ohio Historical Society, Columbus (hereafter MP, reel number); McBride to Rev. E. M. Lightfoot, July 21, 1924, E. J. Moore to Lightfoot, July 22, 1924 (second quote), MP 5. For confirmation that the proscribed "organization" was the Klan, see McBride to Rev. F. L. Watkins, August 5, 1924, MP 9.

2. *Baltimore Evening Sun,* August 28, 1924.

3. Stanley Frost, "When the Klan Rules: The Crusade of the Fiery Cross," *Outlook* 136 (January 9, 1924): 66.

4. K. Austin Kerr, *Organized for Prohibition: A New History of the Anti-Saloon League* (New Haven, Conn.: Yale University Press, 1985); Norman Clark, *Deliver Us from Evil: An Interpretation of American Prohibition* (New York: Norton, 1976); John C. Burnham, "New Perspectives on the Prohibition 'Experiment' of the 1920s," *Journal of Social History* 2 (fall 1968): 51–68.

5. *American Issue* 17 (October 30, 1909): 14.

6. Jonathan Zimmerman, "Each 'Race' Could Have Its Heroes Sung: Ethnicity and the History Wars in the 1920s," *Journal of American History* 87 (June 2000): 92–111; David J. Goldberg, *Discontented America: The United States in the 1920s* (Baltimore: Johns Hopkins University Press, 1999).

7. Morton Keller, *Regulating a New Society: Public Policy and Social Change in America, 1900–1933* (Cambridge: Harvard University Press, 1994), 4–5.

8. David M. Chalmers, *Hooded Americanism: The History of the Ku Klux Klan,* 3d ed. (Durham, N.C.: Duke University Press, 1987), 28–38, 100–108; "The Rise and Fall of the K. K. K." *New Republic* 53 (November 30, 1927): 34.

9. "Wilbert Pictures Co. Presents 'The Toll of Justice,'" 1924, author's collection; Shawn Lay, ed., *The Invisible Empire in the West: Toward a New Historical Appraisal of the Ku Klux Klan of the 1920s* (Urbana: University of Illinois Press, 1992), 153, 57; Kathleen Blee, *Women of the Klan* (Berkeley: University of California Press, 1991), 169.

10. Leonard J. Moore, *Citizen Klansmen: The Ku Klux Klan in Indiana, 1921–1928* (Chapel Hill: University of North Carolina Press, 1991), 99.

11. Lynn Dumenil, *The Modern Temper: American Culture and Society in the 1920s* (New York: Hill and Wang, 1995), 238.

12. Stanley Frost, "When the Klan Rules: The Business of 'Kluxing,'" *Outlook* 136 (January 23, 1924): 144; Robert L. Duffus, "Salesmen of Hate: The Ku Klux Klan," *World's Work* 46 (May 1923): 31–38.

13. Moore, *Citizen Klansmen,* 13–43, Nancy MacLean, *Behind the Mask of Chivalry: The Making of the Second Ku Klux Klan* (New York: Oxford University Press, 1994), xiii–xiv.

14. Evans, "The Klan's Fight for Americanism," *North American Review* 223 (March 1926): 45, 42, and 49.

15. David A. Horowitz, ed., *Inside the Klavern: The Secret History of a Ku Klux Klan of the 1920s* (Carbondale: Southern Illinois University Press, 1999); Lowell Mellett, "Klan and Church," *Atlantic Monthly* 132 (November 1923): 586–92; Frank Bohn, "The Ku Klux Klan Interpreted," *American Journal of Sociology* 30 (January 1925): 387–89; Frost, "'Kluxing,'" 145–47; Waldo Roberts, "The Ku-Kluxing of Oregon," *Outlook* 133 (March 14, 1923): 491; "Intolerance in Oregon," *Survey* 49 (October 15, 1922): 77.

16. The new Klan scholarship is summarized in Lay, *Invisible Empire in the West*. Important works include Moore, *Citizen Klansmen;* Lay, *Hooded Nights on the Niagara: The Ku Klux Klan in Buffalo, New York* (New York: New York University Press, 1995), and William D. Jenkins, *Steel Valley Klan: The Ku Klux Klan in Ohio's Mahoning Valley* (Kent, Ohio: Kent State University Press, 1990). Two recent studies that emphasize Klan violence and repression of minorities focus on southern Klans: MacLean, *Behind the Mask of Chivalry;* and Glenn Feldman, *Politics, Society, and the Klan in Alabama, 1915–1949* (Tuscaloosa: University of Alabama Press, 1999).

17. Moore, *Citizen Klansmen,* 22–25; Edward T. Devine, "More About the Klan," *Survey* 48 (April 8, 1922): 42; Stanley Frost, "When the Klan Rules: The Lure of the White Masks," *Outlook* 136 (January 30, 1924): 185; Charles C. Alexander, *The Ku Klux Klan in the Southwest* (Lexington: University of Kentucky Press, 1966), 23–24, 58–82; David J. Goldberg, "Unmasking the Ku Klux Klan: The Northern Movement against the KKK," *Journal of American Ethnic History* 15 (summer 1996): 42–44; Chalmers, *Hooded Americanism,* 238, 272–74; "Even the Klan Has Rights," *Nation* 115 (December 13, 1922): 654.

18. John Higham, *Strangers in the Land: Patterns of American Nativism, 1860–1925* (New York: Atheneum, 1970), 264.

19. "K. K. K." *Outlook* 136 (January 9, 1924): 51. For similar sentiments from a well-informed journalist, see Stanley Frost, "When the Klan Rules: The Giant in the White Hood," *Outlook* 135 (December 19, 1923): 675.

20. Roberts, "Ku-Kluxing of Oregon," 491; Moore, *Citizen Klansmen,* 44–75.

21. Frost, "Giant in White Hood," 674.

22. Moore, *Citizen Klansmen,* 47–52; Chalmers, *Hooded Americanism,* 217–19; Blee, *Women of Klan,* 169.

23. Robert L. Duffus, "Ancestry and End of the Ku Klux Klan," *World's Work* 46 (September 1923): 528; Stanley Frost, "The Klan Shows Its Hand in Indiana," *Outlook* 137 (June 4, 1924): 188; Stanley Frost, "When the Klan Rules: The Giant Begins to Rule Us," *Outlook* 136 (February 20, 1924): 309.

24. Moore, *Citizen Klansmen,* 191; Blee, *Women of the Klan,* 51–57. For a more ambivalent appraisal of women's rights and the Klan, see MacLean, *Behind the Mask of Chivalry,* 115–17.

25. Roberts, "Ku-Kluxing of Oregon," 491; Charles P. Sweeney, "The Great Bigotry Merger," *Nation* 115 (July 5, 1922): 9; Stanley Frost, "Night-Riding Reformers: The Regeneration of Oklahoma," *Outlook* 135 (November 14, 1923): 439; Edward T. Devine, "The Klan in Texas," *Survey* 48 (April 1, 1922): 10–11. For rare episodes of

Klan support for bootleggers, see Sweeney, "Bigotry Merger," and Robert A. Goldberg, *Hooded Empire: The Ku Klux Klan in Colorado* (Urbana: University of Illinois Press, 1981), 149–62.

26. McBride to D. W. Hutton, June 27, 1925, MP 4; Kerr, *Organized for Prohibition*, 211–35, 246–48.

27. Julius Smith to McBride, September 26, 1925, MP 8.

28. Frost, "Klan Shows Its Hand," 188. For examples of vigilante law enforcement action and political activism in support of prohibition by Klansmen, see MacLean, *Behind the Mask of Chivalry*, 106–7; Lay, *Hooded Knights*, 70–76; and Jenkins, *Steel Valley Klan*, 34–38.

29. Evans, "The Ballots Behind the Ku Klux Klan," *World's Work* 55 (January 1928): 247.

30. William H. Anderson, *The Church in Action against the Saloon* (Westerville, Ohio: Anti-Saloon League of America, 1906), 15.

31. "Catholics and Prohibition," *Literary Digest* 65 (April 10, 1920): 44–45, 125–26. For Klan church visits, see Chalmers, *Hooded Americanism*, 34–35, and Alexander, *Klan in Southwest*, 87–88.

32. "Anderson Talks of Ku Klux Klan," *New York Times*, September 9, 1923; Leonard Lanson Cline, "In Darkest Louisiana," *Nation* 116 (March 14, 1923): 292–93; Robert L. Duffus, "How the Ku Klux Klan Sells Hate, II," *World's Work* 46 (June 1923): 174–78; Chalmers, *Hooded Americanism*, 185–88; Jenkins, *Steel Valley Klan*, 117–39; Jeffrey A. Charles, *Service Clubs in American Society: Rotary, Kiwanis, and Lions* (Urbana: University of Illinois Press, 1993), 30–31.

33. Horowitz, *Inside the Klavern*, 143–46; Robert A. Goldberg, "Denver: Queen City of the Colorado Realm," in Lay, *Invisible Empire*, 57–60.

34. M. William Lutholtz, *Grand Dragon: D.C. Stephenson and the Ku Klux Klan in Indiana* (West Lafayette, Ind.: Purdue University Press, 1991); Moore, *Citizen Klansmen*, 8–9, 14–19, 185–86; Morton Harrison, "Gentlemen from Indiana," *Atlantic Monthly* 141 (May 1928): 676–86; Alva W. Taylor, "What the Klan Did in Indiana," *New Republic* 52 (November 16, 1927): 330–32.

35. Chalmers, *Hooded Americanism*, 247–48; James K. Shields to McBride, August 13, 19, and October 7, 1924, MP 8; Feldman, *Klan in Alabama*, 138–39; Lay, *Hooded Knights*, 68–69, 122–23.

36. *Milwaukee Sentinel*, August 7, 1925; D. W. Hutton to David L. McBride, June 25, 1925; David L. McBride to F. Scott McBride, October 29, 1925, MP 6; F. Scott McBride to D. W. Hutton, June 27, 1925; R. P. Hutton to F. Scott McBride, September 10, 17, 1925; F. Scott McBride to R. P. Hutton, September 15, 1925, MP 4; F. Scott McBride to Wayne Wheeler, October 24, 1925, MP 10.

37. W. G. Clugston, "The Anti-Saloon League's Lost Virtue," *Nation* 122 (February 24, 1926): 203–5; McBride to Julius Smith, October 21, 1925, MP 8; Joseph A. McClelland to McBride, December 20, 1925, MP 5.

38. Julius Smith to McBride, September 16, 1925, MP 8.

39. McBride to Julius Smith, October 21, 1925, MP 8.

40. McBride to George B. Safford, October 2, 1925, MP 8.

41. F. Scott McBride to David L. McBride, June 5, 1925; David L. McBride to F. Scott McBride, June 26, 1925 ("gyrations"), MP 6; for Texas, see McBride to Wheeler, September 18, 1924, MP 10.

42. "Not a Case Against Prohibition," *Outlook* 136 (February 13, 1924): 252; "'The Man Who Made America Dry' Tells Why and How," *Literary Digest* 62 (August 16, 1919): 48, 50; "Prohibition—Anderson Answers Pertinent Questions on the Battle Against Alcohol," *Forum* 62 (July 1919): 68–82.

43. *New York Times*, September 9, 1923.

44. "Reformers Must Reform," *Nation* 118 (February 13, 1924): 155; "Frankness Is an Asset," *Outlook* 133 (March 28, 1923): 564–65; "A Threat Worse than a Blunder," *Outlook* 134 (August 8, 1923): 536–37.

45. F. Scott McBride to R. H. Scott, July 15, 1924, MP 8; "Report of General Superintendent F. Scott McBride, September 30th, 1925," 7–9, MP 6; *The Reminiscences of William H. Anderson* (1950), 37–57, 64–66, in the Oral History Collection of Columbia University.

46. Edward S. Shumaker to McBride, July 25, 1924, MP 8; Louis Francis Budenz, "Indiana's Anti-Saloon League Goes to Jail," *Nation* 125 (August 24, 1927): 178; Moore, *Citizen Klansmen*, 123, 181.

47. Robert L. Duffus, "A Political Volcano Seethes in Indiana," *New York Times*, October 2, 1927.

48. Budenz, "League Goes to Jail," 177; Louis Francis Budenz, "There's Mud on Indiana's White Robes," *Nation* 125 (July 27, 1927): 81–82; Arthur Gilliom to Trustees of the Indiana Anti-Saloon League, February 25, 1926; Shumaker to McBride, July 20, 1926, MP 14.

49. Kerr, *Organized for Prohibition*, 239, 249.

50. Robert A. Hohner, *Prohibition and Politics: The Life of Bishop James Cannon, Jr.* (Columbia: University of South Carolina Press, 1999), 215–90.

51. Richard Hofstadter, *The Age of Reform: From Bryan to F.D.R.* (New York: Vintage Books, 1955), 289–93.

TWELVE

The Public Storm

Hurricanes and the State in Twentieth-Century America

Raymond Arsenault

On August 16, 1888, a powerful hurricane struck the coast of southeastern Florida. The storm's maximum sustained winds may have exceeded 100, or even 125, miles per hour, but no one knows for sure. The storm originated as a tropical depression somewhere in the Atlantic Ocean sometime in late July or early August. The earliest recorded human encounter with the storm occurred on August 14, a few miles off the northern coast of Haiti, but inhabitants of more easterly Caribbean islands may have experienced the storm's high winds and water even earlier. On August 15, the storm battered several of the lower Bahama Islands, inflicting considerable damage and loss of life, but no one in Florida knew about the Bahamians' plight. The Bahamians themselves had only a vague notion of what had just happened, and authorities in Nassau were never able to come up with an exact count of the dead and injured. When the outer winds of the storm began to buffet the coast of Florida on the evening of the fifteenth, some savvy inhabitants may have suspected that a major hurricane was headed their way. But no one knew for sure. At that point, no one in Florida, or anywhere else for that matter, had any hard evidence about the size, shape, strength, history, or direction of the hurricane. As the fury of the storm became evident the next morning, the residents of Dade County, where the eye first made landfall, scrambled for their lives. Understandably, no one had the time, the inclination, or the expertise, to measure the barometric pressure, wind speed, eye configuration, or any other aspect of the roaring natural monster that was threatening their community. One local man claimed that the tidal surge at the mouth of the Miami River reached 14 feet, but no one ever verified his claim, perhaps because in all of Dade County there was not a single newspaper reporter or meteorologist, amateur or professional.

As the scattered inhabitants of southeastern Florida began to emerge from the rubble, the hurricane swept across the peninsula, sideswiping the village of Fort Myers before continuing west into the Gulf of Mexico. No one tracked the hurricane's exact path across the Gulf, but on August 19 it struck the Louisiana coast somewhere west of New Orleans. In the Louisiana interior the storm lost strength and fragmented before passing into history unnamed and unknowable. Here, as in Florida, the survivors managed the best they could, burying their dead, rebuilding their homes, and simply carrying on—all without government assistance or media coverage. In the end, the storm left changed lives and vivid memories, but little data and almost no public scrutiny.[1]

A little more than a century later, on August 24, 1992, Dade County experienced Hurricane Andrew. The full force of the storm struck the Florida coast at Homestead, at 4:30 in the morning. By that time few individuals in Homestead or anywhere else regarded Andrew as a stranger. Anyone with access to television, radio, or a morning newspaper already knew something about the character and potential of what some were calling "the storm of the century." A broad array of government officials, both domestic and international, had gathered a wealth of sophisticated data on Andrew, tracking the storm's evolution from its origins as a small tropical depression near the Cape Verde Islands on August 17, to its designation as a tropical storm by the National Weather Bureau on August 18, to its upgrade to hurricane status on August 23, to its classification as a category 4 storm on the Saffir-Simpson scale on August 24. Radar-generated images produced by satellite, aviation, and maritime surveillance provided government officials and the public with the exact latitude and longitude of the storm, as well as the changing shape and intensity of the wind and rain. Hourly updates on the Cable News Network, the Weather Channel, and other networks allowed the public to monitor every twist and turn in Andrew's journey across the Atlantic, in full color with running commentary from a host of meteorological experts. Moreover, during the last week of August nearly every newspaper in the Western Hemisphere ran a daily, front-page story profiling the storm. Even those who lived thousands of miles from the storm's path had the opportunity to experience the storm vicariously. Indeed, they could hardly avoid doing so.

All of this attention gave Andrew a distinct public personality and a "personal" history defined and documented by a precise set of measurements: peak winds of 175 miles per hour; maximum sustained winds of 145 miles per hour; a maximum recorded gust of 212 miles per hour; a maximum wind radius of 12.5 miles; a minimum barometric pressure of 922 millibars or 27.23 inches at the time of landfall, the third lowest ever recorded in North America; a 16.89 foot storm surge at Miami; a death toll of 51; 80,000 homes and 15,000 pleasure boats in the Dade County area badly damaged or destroyed; 1.4 million Dade County homes without electricity; 35 million tons of debris; more than $30 billion dollars in damages. The list could go on and on, and often did in the various narratives constructed by government officials and journalists.[2]

The stark contrast between these two accounts, one vague and incomplete and the other precise and comprehensive, is revealing. These two storms, one private and one public, separated by a century of technological innovation, bureaucratic development, and evolving public consciousness, demonstrate that the character and meaning of hurricanes changed dramatically in the twentieth century. Before 1900, the connection between hurricanes and human societies was essentially private; public agencies rarely became involved in individual or communal struggles for survival, and the press paid only fleeting attention to storms large or small. So-called acts of God came and went, and no one held out much hope that human vulnerability to such "natural disasters" could be eliminated. Weathering fierce storms was part of life, plain and simple. Only in the twentieth century, after years of governmental activism, did such resignation give way.[3]

As the account of Hurricane Andrew suggests, by the 1990s a sprawling bureaucracy had turned hurricanes into public events of the first order, bringing the expectation and the promise that government agencies would do everything in their power to protect private citizens and private property from the ravages of cyclonic fury. Working in conjunction with state and local authorities, and buttressed by thousands of print and electronic media sources, federal officials drew on an elaborate network of tracking and warning systems, research facilities, educational publications, evacuation plans, relief efforts, and emergency management teams. All of this activity promoted a sense of administrative mastery and technological control that stood in sharp contrast to the acknowledged unpredictability and vulnerability of earlier eras. Although this sense of mastery and control proved to be somewhat illusory in the case of Andrew's magnitude, few observers questioned the attempt to "manage" the storm. For better or for worse, the shared experience of the "public storm" had become an inescapable part of modern American life.

The evolution of the public storm phenomenon offers historians an interesting case study in institutional development. In recent years, several innovative scholars, including Morton Keller and Theda Skocpol, have deepened our understanding of the transformation and mobilization of governmental institutions in response to changing perceptions of social reality and the function of the state. Even though there has been a great deal of continuity in the nature of the problems addressed during the twentieth century, the scope and scale of governmental activism and regulation have reached levels that would have been unthinkable at the beginning of the century. These shifts in public policy have come in fits and starts, as the pace of change has responded to all manner of contingencies and alternating surges of public expectation and "persistent antistatism," to use Keller's term. When applied to the expanding role of government in the "management" of hurricanes, this new approach to institutional history reveals a complex interplay among bureaucratic structures, technological change, and popular culture.[4] Regrettably, there is little sense of this interplay in the existing literature on hurricanes, most of which offers a narrowly focused, technology-driven view of the subject. Written by ex-bureaucrats or popular science enthusiasts, these tales of wind and water and "Yankee ingenuity" tell us relatively little about the nature of change, the multiple factors influencing public policy, or the larger context of American culture. One notable exception is Ted Steinberg's illuminating and sophisticated recent study, *Acts of God: The Unnatural History of Natural Disaster in America*. Steinberg's interdisciplinary analysis of governmental and public complicity in "natural" disasters such as floods, earthquakes, tornadoes, and hurricanes complements the present study and should encourage other scholars to explore this neglected area of environmental-political history.

As an expression of the ethos of mastery and management, the saga of the public storm is primarily a story of post–World War II America. But there is an earlier story of less purposeful development that helps to explain why the institutionalization of the public storm took so long to mature. For more than a century the dominant pattern was one of institutional drift, an inertial legacy that, according to the eminent legal historian J. Willard Hurst, was characteristic of the American experience before the second half of the twentieth century.[5] Thus, for a full understanding of the historical evolution and public policy implications of the public storm, we need to pay some attention to the early history of the connections between American meteorology and bureaucracy.

During the colonial and early national eras, official governmental involvement in tracking, predicting, and responding to tropical storms was negligible. Early hurricane research, like the broader study of weather, was a private affair conducted by self-trained meteorologists such as Benjamin Franklin. In the 1740s Franklin offered the novel hypothesis that dynamic storm systems, not surface winds, determined the movement of tropical storms. Later researchers, including Thomas Jefferson, tried to extend Franklin's insights, but government officials did not offer much assistance until 1814, when the surgeon general ordered daily weather observations at all army posts and hospitals. Three years later, Joseph Meigs, the commissioner of the General Land Office, asked local land-office registrars to keep daily weather records, but military physicians remained the backbone of the national meteorological effort until after the Civil War. The army's data proved useful to scientists such as William Redfield, who published an important series of papers on hurricanes in the 1830s and 1840s. One of the first researchers to understand the basic structure of tropical storms, Redfield concluded that such storms involved a large mass of cyclonic winds rotating around a center. He was also the first observer to attempt to trace the paths of hurricanes as they moved from the Caribbean region to the American mainland. Unfortunately, since the American government showed no interest in Caribbean meteorology, he had to rely on other sources to fill out his tracking charts. One such source was Lt. Col. William Reid of the British Royal Engineers, who began a systematic study of hurricanes in Barbados in 1831. Reid not only plotted storm tracks but also devised a general "law of storms," which included a list of rules for storm-threatened mariners. In 1847 he initiated what may have been the world's first hurricane warning system, displaying a series of flags that announced the rise and fall of barometric pressure.[6]

By that time the American meteorological effort had a new look: in 1842 President John Tyler appointed James P. Espy, the author of *Philosophy of Storms,* an influential treatise on thunderstorms, as the federal government's first official meteorologist; and four years later the newly created Smithsonian Institution began to collect weather records while forming a national network of voluntary meteorological observers. In 1849, Joseph Henry, the first secretary of the Smithsonian, announced the creation of a telegraphic warning system that "would solve the problems of American storms." Despite Henry's enthusiasm, none of this had much effect on the ability of ordinary citizens to deal with the annual spate of hurricanes. During the 1850s and 1860s tropical storms came and went with little or no warning, and few, if any, American citizens expected this state of affairs to change anytime soon.[7]

The first real breakthrough came in 1870 when an unlikely combination of events raised hurricane tracking to a new level of sophistication and promise. In February a congressional resolution endorsed by President Grant authorized the Secretary of War to institute a national weather service. Two months later the War Department assigned the task to the Army Signal Service, which in November created a new bureau, the Division of Telegrams and Reports for the Benefit of Commerce. Despite its cumbersome title, this division soon presided over a national network of meteorological reporting stations.[8] The second event took place in Havana, Cuba, where Father Benito Vines, the new director of the Jesuit College of Belén, turned his attention to tropical storm research and the need for a reliable hurricane warning system. The most knowledgeable and imaginative hurricane researcher of his day, Father Vines was the first forecaster to base his calculations on observations of both the lower and upper atmosphere and the first to analyze the seasonal trajectory of tropical storm activity. Largely in place by 1873, his warning system ultimately "utilized hundreds of volunteer observers, gathered ship reports, issued telegraph warnings to nearby islands, and even developed a "pony express" between isolated villages to warn residents of approaching hurricanes."[9]

Recognizing the significance of Vines's work, the Signal Service contracted to receive daily cable reports from weather stations in Havana, Santiago de Cuba, and Kingston, Jamaica. The reports began in early August 1873, allowing the service to issue the nation's first official tropical storm warning on August 23. Other reports and warnings followed, but insufficient funding stymied efforts to expand the reporting system to Puerto Rico, Barbados, and Guadeloupe. Without additional Caribbean reporting stations, the system provided little protection to Americans living on or near the Atlantic or Gulf coasts, a perilous reality that became all too apparent in September 1875 when an unexpected hurricane nearly wiped out the town of Indianola, Texas. This and later disasters added to the public clamor for a more comprehensive reporting system, and by 1880 the Signal Service was receiving daily cables from six Caribbean stations. Even so, the government's commitment to the system remained tenuous; indeed, for several months in 1881 all Caribbean reports were suspended pending the determination of "the legality of spending any part of the appropriations in maintaining a station outside the limits of the United States." In 1882 the reports resumed, and by the end of the decade the newly organized Cuban Meteorological Service was acting as a clearinghouse for hurricane data from several islands, including Antigua and Puerto Rico. But even this expanded warning system inspired little enthusiasm among Gilded Age politicians and bureaucrats. No one in the federal government, it seems, was ready to acknowledge the nation's responsibility to protect its citizens from destructive tropical storms. As late as 1889 Father Vines's makeshift warning system still received most of its operating funds from private sources, primarily shipping concerns, insurance companies, and merchant associations.[10]

Fortunately, change was in the air—or more literally in the snowdrifts and floodwaters of the American heartland. The traditional grumbling about the Signal Service's lack of professionalism and administrative mismanagement turned into a rousing chorus of criticism after the service failed to predict the record-setting blizzards of 1886 and 1887 and the devastating Johnstown, Pennsylvania, flood of 1889. As public dissatisfaction with the Signal Service's weather reporting reached new heights, Congress responded by transferring the government's meteorological duties to civilian control, creating the United States Weather Bureau within the Department of Agriculture. Under the direction of Mark Harrington, a distinguished academic and the founding editor of the *American Meteorological Journal*, the new agency opened its doors in July 1891, just in time for the annual hurricane season. To Harrington's relief, the 1891 hurricane season was relatively uneventful, as was the 1892 season. But his luck ran out the following year when six hurricanes struck the American mainland. Two of the hurricanes were unusually powerful storms that left death and devastation on a massive scale; together they were responsible for more than four thousand deaths, largely because Americans had little or no warning that the storms were approaching. The 1893 hurricane season was "the second most deadly in the United States since record keeping began," a sobering fact that cast serious doubt on the new agency's capacity to protect the public from nature's fury. The Weather Bureau fared somewhat better in 1894, when its timely warning of a hurricane approaching the southern coast of Rhode Island was credited with saving hundreds of lives among the fishermen of Narragansett Bay. But, in general, the bureau's early efforts to track and forecast tropical storms did not inspire public confidence. By 1896 the bureau had greatly expanded the number of official meteorological reporting stations, including nearly fifty in Florida, but the new system, which had only limited connections to Caribbean reporting stations, brought little relief to coastal residents, who invariably bore the brunt of tropical storm damage. To cite one example, when a fast-moving and powerful hurricane roared across the Gulf of Mexico and struck Cedar Key, Florida, in September 1896, the residents of the tiny Gulf community—and the Weather Bureau—were caught completely off guard.[11]

The Cedar Key storm, which eventually killed 114 people and left a trail of destruction from Florida to Pennsylvania, made a great impression on the

American public, including presidential candidate William McKinley. Following America's declaration of war against Spain in 1898, McKinley claimed that he feared hurricanes far more than he feared the Spanish navy. Accordingly, he urged Congress to authorize the creation of a comprehensive hurricane warning system that would protect the Caribbean operations of American military and merchant vessels. The resulting legislation, passed in July 1898, led to the establishment of a Weather Bureau forecasting center at Kingston, Jamaica, and official reporting stations in Cuba, Santo Domingo, Trinidad, Curacao, St. Kitts, and Barbados. Following the end of hostilities, the acquisition of territorial possessions in the Caribbean prompted the bureau to open additional stations in Puerto Rico and Dominica and to transfer the forecasting center to Havana. Persuading host nations or colonies to accept Weather Bureau personnel required diplomatic tact, the promise that American meteorologists would disseminate their findings throughout the Caribbean region, and a plan to train local weather observers who would eventually replace American observers. By 1902 the localization of the staff was virtually complete, as all but one of the Weather Bureau's American-born employees had returned to the United States. Following the onset of Cuban independence in May 1902, the bureau moved the hurricane forecast center from Havana to Washington, where it would remain until 1935. According to Weather Bureau chief Willis Moore, this qualified withdrawal from the Caribbean served the cause of diplomacy and uplifted the morale of bureau employees, who were less than enthusiastic about extended tours of duty in the disease-infested tropics. But, as historian Erik Larson recently pointed out, this simple explanation masked a complex story of imperial condescension and bureaucratic cover-up.[12]

Moving the hurricane forecast office from Havana to Washington was actually a calculated effort to avoid a public relations disaster in the wake of the great Galveston, Texas, storm of September 1900. As Larson and other scholars have demonstrated, the Weather Bureau's complicity in the Galveston tragedy—where more than 6,000 citizens perished in less than twenty-four hours—is clear: despite repeated observations and bulletins by the College of Belén's tracking stations, no hurricane warning ever reached the city of Galveston, primarily because the Weather Bureau had temporarily banned the cable transmission of Cuban weather reports (ostensibly to prevent "the transmission over Government lines of irresponsible weather information"). To make matters worse, Isaac Cline, the longtime director of the Weather Bureau's Galveston station, had repeatedly assured local residents that the notion that the city could be destroyed by a hurricane was an "absurd delusion." After Cline lost his wife, and nearly lost his daughter, in the storm, Moore tried to deflect criticism of the bureau by portraying Cline as a courageous martyr, "one of the heroic spirits of that awful hour." And sometime later, after Cuban authorities pointed out that they had tried to warn uncooperative American officials about the impending storm, the Weather Bureau chief concocted a diabolical Cuban plot to discredit his agency. As he explained in a plaintive letter to the secretary of agriculture, "I know that there have been many secret influences at work to embarrass the Weather Bureau. . . . It is apparent to me and to every ranking officer . . . in the West Indies that the people do not appreciate our service, that the only thing they want is to kick us and say good-bye." In an age when America was coming to terms with its imperialist urges, Moore's self-serving, anti-Cuban scapegoating found a receptive audience in Washington. Aside from a few War Department leaders who had served in Cuba and who knew enough about the situation to revoke the ban on Cuban weather reports, government officials rallied behind the bureau, which, despite the Galveston fiasco, conducted business as usual until Moore's retirement in 1913.[13]

The inability of Moore and other Weather Bureau officials to work with their Cuban counterparts, unquestionably the most experienced and sophisticated hurricane trackers in the world, had profound consequences, inhibiting scientific advancement and threatening public safety for at least a generation. In 1919 the bureau opened a second hurricane forecast center in San Juan, Puerto Rico, and the proliferation of aviation and radio technology brought some improvement in the bureau's storm warning capabilities by the early 1920s. But the Progressive Era and its immediate aftermath did not witness any major changes in public expectations or governmental involvement in storm forecasting or management. Tropical storms came and went, usually with little warning, and the government's role was still limited to data collection by the Weather Bureau, the flood-control efforts of the Army Corps of Engineers, and the activities of special military detachments assigned to law enforcement or clean-up duty. Although both the science of meteorology and the scope of the federal government had experienced dramatic advancements since the turn of the century, the fundamental notion that hurricanes were an unpredictable and uncontrollable natural force remained unchallenged.[14]

Interestingly enough, when the challenge did come, its primary catalysts were not science or government, but demography and nature. Beginning in 1926, a series of powerful hurricanes disrupted the great Florida Boom, causing extensive damage and loss of life in an area that had been all but uninhabited a generation earlier. On the morning of September 20, 1926, a major storm packing peak winds of 138 miles per hour roared into Miami, propelling a thirteen-foot storm surge into Biscayne Bay. As the eye passed directly over the city, northern transplants who had never experienced a hurricane before emerged from their battered dwellings only to discover a few minutes later that the worst was yet to come. By the end of the day, the death toll was more than 200, and much of the city was in ruins. The first hurricane to strike the city in twenty years, "the big blow of '26" cost an estimated $1.4 billion in property damage, a staggering figure that exceeded the losses attributed to the great Galveston storm of 1900. It also received more press coverage than any storm since the Galveston hurricane. Much of the coverage was sharply critical of the Weather Bureau, which had a lot of explaining to do in the days and weeks following the storm. Reporters and survivors alike wanted to know why Richard W. Gray, the chief meteorologist at the bureau's Miami office, waited until 11:30 P.M. on the nineteenth, less than eight hours before the peak winds struck the city, before issuing an official hurricane warning. Was this the best that the Weather Bureau could do? Some observers feared that it was and argued that federal government should stop wasting tax money on a worthless hurricane warning system. But others took a different tack, suggesting that the time had come for the federal government to assume the responsibility of protecting its citizens from natural disasters. If a mixture of technology and governmental organization could cut a canal through the isthmus of Panama and put military aviators in the air, why couldn't the same combination bring a measure of relief from the ravages of tropical storms?[15]

Such speculation became even more common after the proverbial "flood of the century" inundated the entire Mississippi River region in the spring of 1927. John Barry, the author of *Rising Tide: The Great Mississippi Flood of 1927 and How It Changed America*, has argued that the sheer magnitude of the 1927 flood prompted a revolution in American attitudes toward disaster relief and federal responsibility, and perhaps he is right. But if he had looked eastward to Florida—if he had gazed upon the ruins of the Miami boom—he would have realized that the great Mississippi flood was not the only natural force propelling this revolution. Indeed, Florida provided a second thrust in this direction in 1928, when a devastating hurricane struck the coast near Palm Beach before sweeping across the northern edge of the Everglades. Palm Beach itself escaped the worst ravages of the storm, but the residents of the inland Lake Okeechobee region were not so fortunate. Although the Weather Bureau office in Miami was aware that the storm had already struck Grand Bahama Island, killing more than a thousand Bahamians, the bureau issued its first hurricane warning less than twelve hours before the eye reached the Florida coast. By that time it was too late to get word to the isolated farmers living in the lowlands south and west of the lake. At Belle Glade, where hundreds of migrant workers perished, a low earthen dam quickly gave way to a raging fifteen-foot storm surge, and other nearby communities suffered a similar fate. The official Florida death count was 1,836, but the actual toll was much higher. Years later farmers were still "plowing up bones" in the blood-drenched soil of the Okeechobee basin. Although the realization that most of the victims were black migrants tempered the public response to the tragedy, the pressure on the government to do something, anything, about killer storms mounted as the disaster-ridden decade drew to a close.[16]

The first meaningful step toward increased governmental responsibility, the Mississippi Flood Control Act of 1928, had little to do with hurricanes. But a second piece of legislation, the River and Harbors Act of 1930, expanded the notion that the government could use preventive measures to limit the effects of tropical storms. Among other things, the River and Harbors Act authorized the construction of the Hoover Dike, a massive 35- to 45-foot-high concrete ring around Lake Okeechobee. The Army Corps of Engineers completed the first phase of the dike in 1937, the same year Zora Neale Hurston immortalized the victims of the 1928 storm with her searing novel *Their Eyes Were Watching God*. By that time Franklin Roosevelt's New Deal had undertaken several massive projects designed to tame or harness the forces of nature, including the Tennessee Valley Authority and the Grand Coulee Dam.[17] In this context of rising technological expectations, adopting a more aggressive approach to the hurricane problem seemed logical and fitting. At the same time, in keeping with the New Deal's commitment to governmental innovation, the national hurricane forecast center in Washington underwent a complete reorganization in early 1935. The Washington office was replaced with two regional centers, a primary office in Jacksonville, Florida, and a secondary office in New Orleans. Headquartering the forecasters in population centers that actually experienced tropical storms signaled a renewed dedication among Weather Bureau officials, who promised a new era in hurricane forecasting and protection.[18]

Regrettably, the new era did not come soon enough for the 408 Americans who perished in the Great Labor Day Hurricane of September 1935. One of the most powerful storms in recorded history, the 1935 hurricane carried peak winds approaching 250 miles per hour and a minimum barometric pressure of 26.35 inches, at the time the lowest pressure ever recorded in the Western Hemisphere. The storm struck the Florida Keys just south of Key Largo, where hundreds of World War I Bonus Marchers and Civilian Conservation Corps workers were constructing a highway parallel to the Florida East Coast Railway. The workers had been brought in by the Federal Emergency Relief Agency in 1934 to complete the final forty miles of the highway link to Key West. Housed in small tents and flimsy shacks, they had virtually no chance to withstand a direct hit from even a minor hurricane. In the end, this vulnerability—and a lack of warning—sealed their fate. Less than 24 hours before the hurricane hit the Keys, the Weather Bureau characterized the storm as a minor tropical disturbance with "shifting gales and probably winds of hurricane force." Later, after the bureau discovered that the storm was strengthening, government officials hurriedly dispatched a relief train from Homestead. But the ill-fated train never reached the stranded workers; when a 20–foot storm surge washed over Long and Upper Matecumbe Keys, the train and 41 miles of tracks and trestles were swept into the sea. The tragic drowning of hundreds of workers who had survived the Hoover Administration's repression of the Bonus March and the worst ravages of the Great Depression was a bitter irony that shocked and angered many Americans, including Ernest Hemingway, who was then living in Key West. After helping to bury the dead, Hemingway penned a biting essay titled "Who Murdered the Vets?" "Who sent nearly a thousand war veterans, many of them husky, hard-working and simply out of luck, but many of them close to the border of pathological cases, to live in the frame shacks on the Florida Keys, in the hurricane months?" he asked plaintively. Surely, he added, "the clearing of the Anacostia Flats is going to seem an act of kindness compared to the clearing of Upper and Lower Matecumbe."[19]

Weather Bureau officials were relieved that Hemingway did not emphasize their complicity in the workers' deaths. But they also knew that, in the wake of the tragic 1935 storm, hurricane trackers and other government officials would be under increased pressure to protect the public from killer storms To some the 1935 Labor Day fiasco provided further proof of nature's uncontrollable power and the futility of governmental attempts to brook that power. But to most Americans the government's involvement in the episode reinforced the growing expectation that public officials should play an active role in disaster avoidance and relief. Although this expectation would not be fully satisfied or institutionalized until the 1970s, the combination of expanding governmental authority during World War II and a series of unusually active hurricane seasons during the 1940s raised the "public storm" concept to a new level by midcentury.

Recognizing the public's rising expectations, New Deal officials reorganized the Weather Bureau in June 1940, moving it from the Department of Agriculture to the Department of Commerce. Though largely cosmetic, this bureaucratic shuffle raised the profile of government meteorologists, presaging the new responsibilities that would soon descend upon them. The proliferation of military installations in Florida and Texas during the war inevitably linked tropical storm forecasting with national security, prompting the relocation of the forecast office to Miami in 1943. President Roosevelt placed the Miami office under the joint control of the Army Air Corps and the U.S. Navy for the duration of the war, a development which allowed hurricane forecasters to take full advantage of new military-related technologies such as radar and advanced aviation reconnaissance. On July 27, 1943, Army Air Corps Colonel Joseph Duckworth became the first pilot to fly deliberately into the eye of a hurricane. Encountering the storm off the coast of Galveston, he made two flights into the eye—a daring feat that made him an instant folk hero. The romantic era of the "hurricane hunter" had arrived, and by the end of the war hurricane penetration flights by Air Corps and Navy aircraft had become almost routine, especially in the Pacific where massive typhoons inflicted heavy damage on American naval vessels in 1944 and 1945.[20]

The war years also witnessed the rise of Grady Norton, a folksy Alabaman who became the first hurricane forecaster to achieve semicelebrity status. Norton began working for the Weather Bureau in 1915 and became the bureau's chief hurricane forecaster in 1935, but it was in the 1940s that he revolutionized the art and science of storm forecasting. Following the "development of radar and radio direction-finding equipment," which facilitated the observation and measurement of winds throughout the troposphere, Norton "developed a theory that hurricanes moved with the wind flow in the upper troposphere," rather than around a surface high-pressure area. To prove his point, he predicted the path of an October 1944 storm with astonishing accuracy. This feat assured his legendary status among hurricane forecasters, but to most Floridians he was simply the man with the calm, reassuring voice, the oracle who filled the airwaves with dependable warnings and practical advice, first on the radio and later on television. Foreshadowing future generations of weather celebrities, this self-described "wind jammer" from "Fleahop, Alabama" died in folk-hero fashion in October 1954, following a grueling 12-hour session plotting Hurricane Hazel's path across the Caribbean.[21]

Under Norton's leadership, the hurricane forecast office evolved into a highly visible public agency and an icon of popular culture. An important milestone in this evolution was the decision to provide each hurricane with a name. Attaching anthropomorphic qualities to tropical storms was hardly new. The unpredictable nature of tropical storms, and the uniqueness of each storm, inspired a natural and widespread appreciation for the "personality" and "character" of individual hurricanes. But with the official naming of hurricane "Able" in August 1950, public officials ushered in a new age of meteorological anthropomorphism. In alphabetic fashion, "Able" gave way to "Baker," and so on, as the 1950 storm season worked its way through ten hurricanes, ending with a powerful mid-October storm aptly named "King." For three seasons the Weather Bureau employed traditional military code words as storm names, but in 1953 bureau officials decided to use an alphabetic series of women's names.[22]

The official feminization of hurricanes, following a long tradition of references to "Mother Nature" and other feminized natural entities, quickly caught on with the public and the press. Punctuating hurricane coverage with gendered story lines and language was common practice by the mid-1950s, as reporters described a succession of unruly "women." "The weathermen weren't unaware of the name's meaning," explained a *Miami News* reporter covering Hurricane Donna in 1960, "scientists can be romantics, too. They knew that Donna in the Italian tongue means 'lady.' And like all hurricanes, they spoke of her as 'she.' She was their Donna, their lady." In 1965 the *Miami News* special edition on Hurricane Betsy opened with the phrase "The Lady was a Tramp!" One reporter referred to Betsy as "one of Nature's angry ballet dancers," the purveyor of a "furious dance" who "unfurls her great skirts and pirouettes before us." In similar fashion a *Tampa Tribune* story referred to Betsy as a "giddy, oversized maiden." Weather Bureau officials encouraged such rhetoric and frequently cited the unpredictability of hurricanes as a legitimate rationale for feminine designation. "Hurricanes are like the women they're named for," head forecaster Gordon Dunn stated in 1960. "We never outguess them completely."[23]

Such tongue-in-cheek quips were relatively rare for Dunn, a no-nonsense scientist whose professional demeanor complemented the rising sophistication and bureaucratization of hurricane forecasting. After assuming the directorship in 1954, following Grady Norton's death, Dunn guided a major expansion of the Miami forecasting office, which was renamed the National Hurricane Center (NHC) in 1955. A year later, in anticipation of the International Geophysical Year (1957–58), he and other Weather Bureau officials initiated the National Hurricane Research Project (NHRP), an ambitious investigation of the structure of hurricanes. With the age of space capsules and astronauts looming on the horizon, the NHC did not want to be left behind in the high-stakes game of government-sponsored technology. In 1956 the NHC reequipped its Air Force hurricane hunters with WB-50s, replacing the outmoded WB-29s that had been used since 1946. Not to be outdone, the U.S. Navy's hurricane hunter squadron was soon using highly sophisticated, four-engine Super Constellations, which propelled hurricane reconnaissance and research into a new era. Utilizing elaborate Doppler radar systems, these flying laboratories quickly became the stuff of legend, inspiring a spate of admiring newspaper and magazine articles, plus several action novels and documentary films. Following the shock of the Soviet Union's 1957 *Sputnik* launch, the hurricane hunters' exploits were welcome news in a nation desperate for signs of American technological achievement.[24]

In April 1961 the cosmonaut Yuri Gagarin's celebrated journey into space, accomplished nearly a month ahead of American astronaut Alan Shepard's space flight, further deflated American confidence. The National Aeronautics and Space Administration (NASA) eventually eclipsed the Soviet space program, but in the meantime Americans were forced to look elsewhere for technological dominance.[25] One potential area of dominance was meteorological research, especially the new science of weather modification. In 1962 the National Hurricane Center launched Project Stormfury, the first extended effort to lessen the frequency and intensity of tropical storms. The idea of physically altering the structure of hurricanes received serious attention as early as the 1940s, when a series of severe hurricane seasons inspired a call for desperate measures, including a proposal to destroy or divert hurricanes with atomic weapons. Following the explosions at Hiroshima and Nagasaki in August 1945, the enterprising county commissioners of Lee County, Florida, offered several thousand acres of land to the Army for a proving ground where the effects of atomic energy on hurricanes could be tested.[26]

The Army never took Lee County up on its offer, but in 1947 a Navy "hurricane hunter" aircraft seeded a hurricane with silver iodide crystals after the storm passed over the Florida peninsula and headed into the open waters of the North Atlantic. Government officials made no claim that the seeding, known as Project Cirrus, had any effect on the storm, but the 1947 hurricane's erratic behavior became a subject of controversy when the NHC resumed seeding experiments in the late 1950s. According to one suspicious Miami journalist, following the 1947 seeding "the hurricane stalled, reformed and then swung back to slash at Savannah, Ga., and the South Carolina coast doing heavy damage."[27] The seeding of Daisy in 1958, Esther in 1961, and Beulah in 1963 produced no measurable effect, but these failures did not calm the fears of conspiracy theorists or deter Project Stormfury scientists from trying again. In September 1965, in the immediate aftermath of Hurricane Betsy, Secretary of Commerce John T. Connor called for "a vigorous national program" to test the feasibility of weather modification. This produced new expectations and additional funding, but little happened until 1969, when the NHC "bombed" Hurricane Debbie with a massive dose of silver iodide crystals. According to project director R. Cecil Gentry, "scientists hoped to freeze Debbie to death. Theoretically, water should form around the crystals sowed in the clouds around the hurricane's eye. The water would freeze around the crystals . . . and rob the storm of its heat and energy." Unfortunately for Gentry and Project Stormfury, Hurricane Debbie "barely twitched" under the "massive chemical barrage," leading even Gentry to question the likelihood of major storm modification in the foreseeable future. "Do not look for a breakthrough tomorrow," he warned, a prediction confirmed by the modification project's demise in 1971.[28]

Project Stormfury proved to be a scientific disappointment and a public relations fiasco. But the NHC fared much better in other areas of technological advancement. The completion of the WSR-57 coastal radar warning system in the early 1960s provided the NHC and the American public with nearly continuous surveillance of storm tracks within 150 miles of the East and Gulf Coasts. And by the early 1970s an extensive network of oceanic buoys gave storm analysts access to direct measurements of oceanic surface conditions. This integrated system of radars and buoys produced an unprecedented mass of data, the utility of which depended on sophisticated computerization. It would be several decades before computer technology harnessed the full potential of the new tracking and warning system. In the meantime NHC scientists consoled themselves with the wonders of satellite technology.[29]

With the launching of TIROS-I, America's first experimental weather satellite, in April 1960, the science of storm tracking entered a new age. The earliest images from space were crude and difficult to interpret, but NHC scientists soon demonstrated the usefulness of satellite-generated photographs. In the fall of 1961 television images beamed down from TIROS 3 allowed government forecasters to issue an early warning of Hurricane Carla's impending assault on the Texas coast. The warning, which produced the first large-scale hurricane evacuation in American history, reportedly saved hundreds of lives, spurring new interest and investment in weather satellite technology. As the decade progressed, weather satellites became increasingly sophisticated: in 1964 NIMBUS-1 provided the first infrared night photographs from space; in early 1966 ESSA-1 and ESSA-2, equipped with wide-angle television cameras, became the nation's first fully operational weather satellites; and later in the same year ATS added "spin-scan" capability to the science of satellite photography. In the mid-1970s geosynchronous satellites gave way to the geostationary models of the GOES (Geostationary Operational Environmental Satellite) series, which produced broad-scale hemispheric photographs at 30-minute intervals.

Full utilization of weather satellites as research tools awaited advances in computer technology. But the problem of unused data did little to offset the conceptual impact of the spectacular image generated by space-based cameras. For the first time, NHC scientists and others could see the full, awe-inspiring outlines of cyclonic power. The shape or body of the storm had become real, transcending and objectifying what earlier had been only an imaginative construct. Photographic and computer-enhanced representations of swirling winds reinforced the anthropomorphic and "personal" nature of tropical storms, giving them life in a new way. This was especially true following the development of McIDAS (Man-computer Interactive Data Access System) software, created at the University of Wisconsin in the mid-1970s, which literally "put the pictures in motion."[30]

All of this technology took on added cultural significance with the proliferation and maturation of television news. From the mid-1960s on, local and national storm reports featured vivid images of approaching hurricanes, which complemented the steady stream of data provided by the NHC. Videotape technology allowed television editors and reporters to create riveting narratives of storm activity. By splicing satellite photographs, interviews with NHC forecasters, and on-location reporter updates filmed against a backdrop of rising wind and water, television coverage became an integral part of the "public storm" experience. Television, and to a lesser extent print-media graphics, transformed and deepened the vicarious participation of citizens far removed from the storm's path. Hurricanes had become a source of national crisis and concern, a shared experience that engaged and transfixed millions of Americans.[31]

The technological innovations and media advances of the 1960s brought heightened public expectations and increased pressure in Washington. At the same time a general resurgence of political activism underscored the government's responsibility for "managing" the environment, especially in the context of the Great Society initiatives of the Johnson Administration. Accordingly, in July 1965, the National Hurricane Center, along with the rest of the National Weather Bureau, became part of a new agency, the Environmental Sciences Services Administration (ESSA). With this bureaucratic reshuffling the NHC entered an era of unprecedented expansion and activity. In the fall of 1965 ESSA officials created a 21-person Tropical Analysis Center at the NHC and gave NHC director Gordon Dunn the added responsibility of directing the National Hurricane Warning Service for the entire Atlantic basin. This reorganization concentrated authority in the Miami office and downgraded the responsibilities of the hurricane forecast offices in Boston, New

Orleans, Washington, and San Juan, Puerto Rico. By the time Gordon Dunn retired in 1967, the NHC staff had grown to 83, and the public visibility of the Miami office had reached new heights.[32]

Dunn's successor, Robert H. Simpson, expanded the NHC staff to well over 100 during his six-year tenure (1968–73), primarily through an increased emphasis on research and development. In 1970 Congress transferred oversight of the NHC to the National Oceanic and Atmospheric Administration (NOAA), a new agency that signified the federal government's growing commitment to meteorological science. Under NOAA's administration Simpson enhanced the NHC's scientific reputation, creating a Satellite Applications Unit (SAU) and introducing the Saffir-Simpson scale, a categorization scheme that ranks hurricanes according to wind speed and destructive potential. The introduction of the five-point Saffir-Simpson scale in 1975 gave the public a convenient means of classifying individual hurricanes and systematized differential levels of expectation and preparedness. Identifying an approaching storm as a potentially catastrophic category 3 or 4 hurricane gave added force and specificity to the NHC's hurricane watches and warnings, underscored the scientific legitimacy of hurricane forecasting, and focused public attention on the NHC. For some hurricane buffs it also added to the lore of experience and survival, in the manner of a sports statistic or superlative. As an official government ranking system, the Saffir-Simpson scale had the power to authenticate danger and risk, and to reinforce the profiling of individual storms. Who could resist the gathering drama of an approaching category 3 or 4 storm, or the tales of damage, loss, and survival that were sure to follow?[33]

The Saffir-Simpson scale was, of course, only one element of a broad set of public policies that encouraged America's growing fascination with hurricanes. During the late 1970s the federal government's efforts to measure and track tropical storms, aided by the mass media's willingness to disseminate such information, evolved into a comprehensive program of storm "management." In March 1979 President Jimmy Carter issued an executive order creating the Federal Emergency Management Agency (FEMA), the first federal agency empowered to oversee all aspects of disaster prevention and assistance. In the long history of American disaster relief, no governmental authority had ever assumed so much control or responsibility. Before the 1930s, state and local authorities shouldered almost all of the burden, although intermittent examples of federal relief began as early as 1803, when an act of Congress provided aid to a fire-ravaged New Hampshire town. During the Great Depression, the Reconstruction Finance Corporation, the Bureau of Public Roads, and the Army Corps of Engineers provided some assistance to stricken communities, but federal efforts remained limited and haphazard until the 1960s, when a series of catastrophic disasters prompted calls for federalization on an unprecedented scale. In 1964 President Lyndon Johnson initiated the practice of designating hard-hit communities as national disaster areas eligible for special federal assistance, and four years later Congress passed the National Flood Insurance Act and created the Office of Emergency Preparedness, an underfunded agency that provided a symbolic focus for federal relief efforts but little more. The devastating effects of Hurricane Camille in 1969 and Hurricane Agnes in 1972 added to the growing public pressure for federal disaster assistance, prompting the Nixon Administration to establish the Federal Disaster Assistance Administration (FDAA) as part of the Department of Housing and Urban Development (HUD) in 1973. A year later the Disaster Relief Act codified the process of national disaster area declarations, replacing an ad hoc system that had been plagued by insufficient follow-through and undue political influence.

Thus, by the mid-1970s federal responsibility for disaster assistance was a given. Washington's contribution involved more than 100 federal agencies, a testament to the scope, if not the efficiency, of the government's efforts. Unfortunately, these agencies often worked independently or even at cross-purposes, and their activities and policies frequently conflicted with the parallel efforts of state and local authorities. This state of confusion became a major concern of the National Governors Association, which urged President Carter to streamline the federal government's disaster assistance programs. The creation of FEMA went a long way toward solving this problem by merging a number of overlapping federal agencies, including the Federal Insurance Administration, the National Fire Prevention and Control Administration, the National Weather Service Community Preparedness Program, the Federal Disaster Assistance Administration, and the Federal Preparedness Agency of the General Services Administration. FEMA's first director, John Macy, made a concerted effort to coordinate his agency's efforts with those of state and local officials, some of whom were understandably wary of the new mega-agency. He also instituted "an all-hazards approach" to emergency management that emphasized "direction, control and warning systems which are common to the full range of emergencies from small isolated events to the ultimate emergency—war." This flexible approach proved useful during FEMA's first decade, which witnessed a wide range of major disasters, including the toxic chemical contamination of Love Canal, the refugee crisis following the 1980 Mariel boatlift, the nuclear accident at Three Mile Island, and the devastation of Hurricane Hugo.[34]

FEMA's myriad activities—from the formulation of evacuation plans to the dispensing of relief funds—helped to publicize and legitimize the goal of storm management. Working in close cooperation with the NHC and NOAA, FEMA served as a central clearinghouse for information, advice, and regulation. It did so, in part, by encouraging the development of a professional subculture of hurricane experts. In May 1979 the agency cosponsored a national conference on "Hurricanes and Coastal Storms: Awareness, Evacuation, and Mitigation." Held in Orlando, the three-day meeting brought together an unusual mix of academics and public administrators and became a model for the annual conferences that followed. During the 1980s and 1990s the national hurricane conferences grew in size and influence, signifying the rising academic and professional interest in tropical storms. In 1983 Professor William Gray of Colorado State University issued his first annual hurricane prediction profile, which he derived from measurements of sea temperature, upper-level wind direction, West African rainfall, and a periodic meteorological phenomenon known as "El Niño." Gray's predictions drew considerable publicity, inspiring other meteorological researchers to turn their attention to the mysteries of tropical storms. Indeed, a massive proliferation of hurricane research projects, technical papers, government grants, and local and regional conferences testified to the expansion and professionalization of what some observers were beginning to call "the hurricane business."[35]

Much of this activity was conducted beyond public view, but this became less true in the 1980s as FEMA, along with the NHC, assumed a mediating role between the professional world of hurricane specialists and American popular culture. FEMA and NHC officials presided over an elaborate system of official hurricane "watches" and "warnings" that gave them the power to order the evacuation of millions of citizens. Both before and after storms, the enforcement of public policy and the mobilization of volunteers and resources required communication links that placed government officials in the public eye. Working with the press had become an integral part of storm management. With the approach of the fall hurricane season, many newspapers offered special hurricane preparedness sections that relayed storm emergency procedures, evacuation routes, survival tips, and other words of wisdom from government authorities. Later, when the hurricanes actually materialized, televised storm reports featured regular updates from the NHC. During the 1980s, NHC director Neil Frank became a familiar face to the millions of Americans who listened to his pronouncements on CNN, the Weather Channel, and other networks. Frank's successors—Robert Sheets, Jerry Jarrell, and Max Mayfield—continued this tradition, and after his appointment as

FEMA director in 1993, James L. Witt joined the list of hurricane media stars. Though something less than folk heroes, these men cultivated a familiarity that accentuated the "public storm" phenomenon.[36]

In doing so, they discovered that turning scientific and organizational expertise into public awareness can be a difficult task. In the public mind, the gospels of prevention and technological sophistication often shaded into expectations of mitigation and decreased risk. Professional hurricane experts knew all too well that storm management could only go so far, but this did not stop some citizens from expecting and demanding near invulnerability to tropical storms.

Throughout his long tenure at the NHC, Neil Frank strained to control a revolution of rising public expectations. In 1985, in trying to counter criticism of a new prediction-evacuation system that provided "'odds' on where a storm will strike," Frank freely admitted that "two-thirds to three-fourths of the people who evacuate with 24–hour lead time are going to do so unnecessarily. . . . for every four times we tell you to evacuate, only one will be necessary." And "we're not going to get any better," he explained, ". . . the atmosphere is very complex. . . . We're going to continue to have meteorological surprises." Such admissions did not sit well with some observers. "Despite having at his disposal millions of dollars worth of sophisticated technology, a trained staff, and 20 years experience in South Florida," one Miami reporter complained, "Frank still can't tell people exactly what they want to know: where will the storm hit, when will it hit, and when should we run? Frank can only warn and worry." Another reporter characterized Frank as "a sincere prophet of doom and horror," and still another blanched at his "ominous storm warnings" and sharp criticism of "the federal flood-insurance program, which encourages people to develop in coastal areas where they shouldn't be."[37]

NOAA and FEMA officials often echoed Frank's warnings, but the sheer size of the government's forecasting and emergency apparatus communicated a different message, one of control and technological mastery.[38] Periodic demonstrations of nature's fury, such as the catastrophic destruction of Hurricane Andrew in 1992, reminded Americans of their continued vulnerability.[39] But, as the twentieth century drew to a close, such demonstrations often became lost in the mystique of the "public storm." In conjunction with broad technological change—especially the increasing sophistication and scope of mass media—a century of governmental expansion, from Progressivism and the New Deal to the Cold War and the Great Society, had created an institutional context that sustained and deepened this mystique. The same national state that spawned social security, Medicare, and the military-industrial complex redefined hurricanes as threats to national security, producing a social construct that placed powerful restraints on environmental and political consciousness. Far removed from the hurricanes of past centuries—when natural disasters straddled the separate spheres of private risk and governmental indifference—the storms of today occupy a central place in American political and popular culture. From the marble corridors of Washington to the barrier islands of Florida, Texas, and the Carolinas, the "public storm" rages on.

NOTES

1. Jay Barnes, *Florida's Hurricane History* (Chapel Hill: University of North Carolina Press, 1998), 73; John M. Williams and Iver W. Duedall, *Florida Hurricanes and Tropical Storms*, rev. ed. (Gainesville: University Press of Florida, 1997), 71, pl. 2; National Oceanic and Atmospheric Administration (NOAA), *Tropical Cyclones of the North Atlantic Ocean, 1871–1986*, Historical Climatology Series 6–2 (Asheville, N.C.: National Climatic Center, 1987).

2. Barnes, *Florida's Hurricane History*, 261–84, 312–14; Williams and Duedall, *Florida Hurricanes and Tropical Storms*, 1–4, 13, 16, 37–42, 82, 102–7, 139; *Miami Herald*, August 10–September 15, 1992; *St. Petersburg Times*, August 18–20, 2002; James B. Elsner and A. Birol Kara, *Hurricanes of the North Atlantic: Climate and Society* (New York: Oxford University Press, 1999), 414–22. See also Walter Gillis Peacock, Betty Hearn Morrow, and Hugh Gladwin, *Hurricane Andrew: Ethnicity, Gender, and the Sociology of Disaster* (London: Routledge, 1997); Eugene F. Provenzo, *Hurricane Andrew, the Public Schools, and the Rebuilding of Community* (Albany: State University of New York Press, 1995); Eugene F. Provenzo and Asterie Baker Provenzo, *In the Eye of Hurricane Andrew* (Gainesville: University Press of Florida, 2002); Roger A. Pielke, *Hurricane Andrew in South Florida: Mesoscale Weather and Societal Responses* (Boulder, Colo.: National Center for Atmospheric Research, 1995); United States Department of Interior, National Park Service, *Hurricane Andrew: The National Park Service Response in South Florida* (Denver: National Park Service, 1994).

3. See John C. Burnham's appeal for additional research in "A Neglected Field: The History of Natural Disasters," *Perspectives* (American Historical Association Newsletter) (April 1988): 22–24. Although Burnham's suggestions are well taken, the historical literature on "natural disasters" in the United States is actually extensive. See especially: Donald Worster, *Dust Bowl: The Southern Plains in the 1930s* (New York: Oxford University Press, 1979); David McCullough, *The Johnstown Flood* (New York: Simon and Schuster, 1968); Kai T. Erikson, *Everything in Its Path: Destruction of Community in the Buffalo Creek Flood* (New York: Simon and Schuster, 1976); Pete Daniel, *Deep'n As It Come: The 1927 Mississippi River Flood* (New York: Oxford University Press, 1977); John M. Barry, *Rising Tide: The Great Mississippi Flood of 1927 and How It*

Changed America (New York: Simon and Schuster, 1997); Steven Biel, *Down with the Old Canoe: A Cultural History of the Titanic Disaster* (New York: Norton, 1996); Mike Davis, *Ecology of Fear: Los Angeles and the Imagination of Disaster* (New York: Henry Holt, 1998); and Ted Steinberg, *Acts of God: The Unnatural History of Natural Disaster in America* (New York: Oxford University Press, 2000). On hurricanes, see Isaac R. Tannehill, *Hurricanes: Their Nature and History* (Princeton, N. J.: Princeton University Press, 1938); Marjory Stoneman Douglas, *Hurricane* (New York: Rinehart, 1958); David M. Ludlum, *Early American Hurricanes, 1492–1970* (Boston: American Meteorological Society, 1963); Gordon E. Dunn and Banner I. Miller, *Atlantic Hurricanes*, rev. ed. (Baton Rouge: Louisiana State University Press, 1964); Thomas Helm, *Hurricanes: Weather at Its Worst* (New York: Dodd, Mead, 1967); Jerry Rosenfeld, *Eye of the Storm: Inside the World's Deadliest Hurricanes, Tornadoes, and Blizzards* (New York: Plenum, 1999); Erik Larson, *Isaac's Storm: A Man, A Time, and the Deadliest Hurricane in History* (New York: Crown, 1999); Peter Davies, *Inside the Hurricane: Face to Face with Nature's Deadliest Storms* (New York: Henry Holt, 2000); and Elsner and Kara, *Hurricanes of the North Atlantic*. See also Sebastian Junger, *The Perfect Storm: A True Story of Men and the Sea* (New York: Norton, 1997).

4. See Morton Keller's groundbreaking trilogy: *Affairs of State: Public Life in Late Nineteenth Century America* (Cambridge: Harvard University Press, 1977); *Regulating a New Society: Public Policy and Social Change in America, 1900–1933* (Cambridge: Harvard University Press, 1979); and *Regulating a New Economy: Public Policy and Economic Change in America, 1900–1933* (Cambridge: Harvard University Press, 1990). See also Theda Skocpol, *Protecting Soldiers and Mothers: The Political Origins of Social Policy in the United States* (Cambridge: Harvard University Press, 1992). Peter Evans, Dietrich Rueschmeyer, and Theda Skocpol, eds., *Bringing the State Back In* (New York: Cambridge University Press, 1985).

5. J. Willard Hurst, *Law and the Conditions of Freedom in the Nineteenth-Century United States* (Madison: University of Wisconsin Press, 1964).

6. Robert C. Sheets, "The National Hurricane Center—Past, Present, and Future," *Weather and Forecasting* 5 (June 1990): 189–90; Larson, *Isaac's Storm*, 37–53, 121–22; Mark Monmonier, *Air Apparent: How Meteorologists Learned To Map, Predict, and Dramatize Weather* (Chicago: University of Chicago Press, 1999), 18–42; James Rodger Fleming, *Meteorology in America, 1800–1870* (Baltimore: Johns Hopkins University Press, 1990), 23–73; Donald R. Whitnah, *A History of the United States Weather Bureau* (Urbana: University of Illinois Press, 1961), 1–13; Patrick Hughes, *A Century of Weather Service: A History of the Birth and Growth of the National Weather Service, 1870–1970* (New York: Gordon and Breach, 1970), 3–16, 189–90; Douglas, *Hurricane*, 217–226; Gizela Kutzbach, *The Thermal Theory of Cyclones: A History of Meteorological Thought in the Nineteenth Century* (Boston: American Meteorological Society, 1979); Barnes, *Florida's Hurricane History*, 33; Edgar B. Calvert, "The Hurricane Warning Service and Its Reorganization," *Monthly Weather Review* 63 (April 1935): 85; William C. Redfield, "Remarks on the Prevailing Storms of the Atlantic Coast, of the Northeast-

ern States," *American Journal of Science* 20 (1831): 17–51; William C. Redfield, "On Three Several Hurricanes of the American Seas and Their Relations to the Northers, So Called, of the Gulf of Mexico, and the Bay of Honduras, with Charts Illustrating the Same," *American Journal of Science*, 2d series, 2 (1846): 311–34; Lt. Col. William Reid, *An Attempt to Develop the Law of Storms* (London: John Weale, 1946). See also Ludlum, *Early American Hurricanes, 1492–1870*; and Dunn and Miller, *Atlantic Hurricanes*, 137–40.

7. Monmonier, *Air Apparent*, 32–54; Fleming, *Meteorology in America, 1800–1870*, 23–81, 142–43; Hughes, *Century of Weather Service*, 4–5, 16–19; Whitnah, *History of the United States Weather Bureau*, 12–15; Douglas, *Hurricane*, 224–30; Marcus Benjamin, "Meteorology," in *The Smithsonian Institution, 1846–1896: The History of Its First Half Century*, ed. George Brown Goode (Washington, D.C.: Smithonian Institution, 1897), 647–78; Maxime Bocher, "The Meteorological Labors of Dove, Redfield, and Espy," *American Meteorological Journal* 5 (1888): 1–13; James P. Espy, *The Philosophy of Storms* (Boston: Little and Brown, 1841); James P. Espy, *First Report on Meteorology to the Surgeon General of the United States Army* (Washington, D.C., 1843).

8. U.S. Congress, *Congressional Globe*, 41st Congress, 2d Session, 42, Part 2 (February 9, 1870), 1160; U.S. Army Signal Service, *Report of the Chief Signal Officer to the Secretary of War for the Year 1872* (Washington, D.C., 1872); Whitnah, *History of the United States Weather Bureau*, 19–58; Hughes, *Century of Weather Service*, 19–23; Sheets, "National Hurricane Center," 190; Calvert, "Hurricane Warning Service," 85; Monmonier, *Air Apparent*, 7–8, 12, 48–53, 158–59.

9. Barnes, *Florida's Hurricane History*, 33, 67; Calvert, "Hurricane Warning Service," 85; Larson, *Isaac's Storm*, 102–3; Douglas, *Hurricane*, 230–36; Rosenfeld, *Eye of the Storm*, 230–32; Dunn and Miller, *Atlantic Hurricanes*, 140–42; Benito Vines, *Investigation of the Cyclonic Circulation and the Translatory Movement of West Indian Hurricanes* (Washington, D.C.: U.S. Weather Bureau, 1898); Benito Vines, *Practical Hints about West Indian Hurricanes* (Washington, D.C.: U.S. Weather Bureau, 1885). See also Louis A. Perez, *Winds of Change: Hurricanes and the Transformation of Nineteenth-Century Cuba* (Chapel Hill: University of North Carolina Press, 2001).

10. Calvert, "Hurricane Warning Service," 85–86; Barnes, *Florida's Hurricane History*, 67–68; Sheets, "National Hurricane Center," 190; Hughes, *Century of Weather Service*, 23–28, 192–93; Dunn and Miller, *Atlantic Hurricanes*, 140–42; Douglas, *Hurricane*, 230–46.

11. Whitnah, *History of the United States Weather Bureau*, 22–100; Hughes, *Century of Weather Service*, 26–28, 34, 36–38; Monmonier, *Air Apparent*, 53, 164; Larson, *Isaac's Storm*, 69–72; Barnes, *Florida's Hurricane History*, 74. On the Johnstown flood, see McCullough, *Johnstown Flood*.

12. Calvert, "Hurricane Warning Service," 86; Larson, *Isaac's Storm*, 72–74, 102–8; Sheets, "National Hurricane Center," 194; Gordon E. Dunn, "A Brief History of the United States Hurricane Warning Service," *Muse News* 3 (1971): 140–43; Hughes, *Century of Weather Service*, 42; Douglas, *Hurricane*, 249–53.

13. Larson, *Isaac's Storm*, 100–142, 230–58, 267–72; Douglas, *Hurricane*, 253–58; Willis Moore to Secretary of Agriculture, September 21, 1900, box 1475, General Correspondence, Department of Agriculture, National Archives, Washington, D.C. For other accounts of the 1900 Galveston hurricane, see Isaac Cline, "Special Report on the Galveston Hurricane of September 8, 1900," *Monthly Weather Review* (November 16, 1900): 372–74; Joseph L. Cline, *When the Heavens Frowned* (Dallas: Mathias, Van Nort, 1946); Gary Cartwright, "The Big Blow," *Texas Monthly* (August 1990): 76–81; John Coulter, ed., *The Complete Story of the Galveston Horror* (Chicago: J. H. Moore, 1900); David G. McComb, *Galveston: A History* (Austin: University of Texas Press, 1986); and David Ballingrud, "Without Warning," *St. Petersburg Times*, May 28, 2000, 1A, 12A–14A. On Moore's controversial career, see Whitnah, *History of the United States Weather Bureau*, 82–130, 178.

14. Whitnah, *History of the United States Weather Bureau*, 131–200; Sheets, "National Hurricane Center," 194; Calvert, "Hurricane Warning Service," 86; Hughes, *Century of Weather Service*, 44–68; Dunn, "Brief History," 141–43. Voluminous information on the activities and administration of the National Weather Bureau during these years can be found in records of the Weather Bureau, record group 27, sections 5.1 and 5.2, National Archives, Washington, D.C. On the flood-control activities of the Army Corps of Engineers in the early twentieth century, see Barry, *Rising Tide*, 115, 157–60, 165–68; and John Ferrell, *From Single to Multi-Purpose Planning: The Role of the Army Engineers in River Development Policy, 1824–1930* (Washington, D.C.: U.S. Army Corps of Engineers, 1976).

15. *Miami Herald*, September 16–30, 1926; *Miami News*, September 16–30, 1926; Barnes, *Florida's Hurricane History*, 111–26; Steinberg, *Acts of God*, 51–61; Williams and Duedall, *Florida Hurricanes and Tropical Storms*, 14–15, 75, pl. 6; Douglas, *Hurricane*, 258–67; Howard Kleinberg and L. F. Reardon, *The Florida Hurricane and Disaster, 1926* (Miami: Centennial Press, 1992); *The Florida Hurricane Which Devastated Miami, Hollywood, Ft. Lauderdale, . . .* (Chicago: American Autochrome, 1926); Joseph Hugh Reese, *Florida's Great Hurricane* (Miami: L. E. Fesler, 1926); Garnet Varner Walsh, *Hurricane, 1926* (Chicago: Petit Oiseau Press, 1958). See also Clarence Walker Barron, *Lessons from Florida Winds* (New York: *Wall Street Journal* reprint, 1927); and *Lessons of the Storm* (Pittsburgh: Jones and Laughlin Steel, 1926).

16. Barry, *Rising Tide*, 363–426; Lawrence E. Will, *Okeechobee Hurricane and the Hoover Dike*, 2d ed. (St. Petersburg, Fla.: Great Outdoors, 1967); Barnes, *Florida's Hurricane History*, 127–40; Douglas, *Hurricane*, 267–71; Steinberg, *Acts of God*, 59–63. The most comprehensive study of the 1928 Okeechobee hurricane is Eric L. Gross, "Somebody Got Drowned: Florida and the Great Okeechobee Hurricane Disaster of 1928" (Ph. D. thesis, Florida State University, 1995). See also William Fox, "The Night 2,000 Died," *St. Petersburg Times*, September 14, 1986; and Jeff Klinkenberg, "A Storm of Memories," *St. Petersburg Times*, July 12, 1992.

17. Barry, *Rising Tide*, 399–407; Will, *Okeechobee Hurricane*, 179–93; Gross, "Somebody Got Drowned"; Alfred Jackson Hanna and Kathryn Abbey Hanna, *Lake*

Okeechobee: Wellspring of the Everglades (Indianapolis: Bobbs-Merrill, 1948); Julie Hauserman, "Welcome to Dike Okeechobee," *St. Petersburg Times*, May 31, 2000; Zora Neale Hurston, *Their Eyes Were Watching God* (Philadelphia: J. B. Lippincott, 1937); Marc Reisner, *Cadillac Desert: The American West and Its Disappearing Water*, rev. ed. (New York: Penguin, 1993), 135–68; Fredrick J. Dobney, *River Engineers on the Middle Mississippi: A History of the St. Louis District, U.S. Army Corps of Engineers* (Washington, D.C.: GPO, 1978).

18. U.S. Weather Bureau, *Annual Report, 1934–35* (Washington, D.C.: GPO, 1935), 9–10; Sheets, "National Hurricane Center," 195–96; Calvert, "Hurricane Center," 87–88; Dunn, "Brief History," 141–42; Whitnah, *History of the United States Weather Bureau*, 135–36; Robert W. Burpee, "Grady Norton: Hurricane Forecaster and Communicator Extraordinaire," *Weather Forecasting* 3 (September 1988): 247–50.

19. W. F. McDonald, "The Hurricane of 31 August to 6 September 1935," *Monthly Weather Review* 63 (September 1935): 269–71; Barnes, *Florida's Hurricane History*, 144–59; Douglas, *Hurricane*, 271–279; Steinberg, *Acts of God*, 63–68; Rodman Bethel, *Flagler's Folly: The Railroad That Went to Sea and Was Blown Away* (Key West, Fla.: R. Bethel, 1987); Whitnah, *History of the United States Weather Bureau*, 136; Burpee, "Grady Norton," 247–48; Ernest Hemingway, "Who Killed the Vets?" *New Masses* (September 17, 1935), 9–10. See also U.S. Congress, *Hearings on H.R. 9486 Before the House Committee on World War Veterans' Legislation*, 74th Congress, 2nd Session (1936); Gary Dean Best, *FDR and the Bonus Marchers, 1933–35* (Westport, Conn.: Praeger, 1992); and Les Standiford, *Last Train to Paradise: Henry Flagler and the Spectacular Rise and Fall of the Railroad That Crossed an Ocean* (New York: Crown, 2002).

20. Sheets, "National Hurricane Center," 196, 199–200; Douglas, *Hurricane*, 352–55; Whitnah, *History of the United States Weather Bureau*, 201–16; Barnes, *Florida's Hurricane History*, 34; Helm, *Hurricanes*, 51–63; Elsner and Kara, *Hurricanes of the North Atlantic*, 41–42; Rosenfeld, *Eye of the Storm*, 238–39; Dunn and Miller, *Atlantic Hurricanes*, 145, 156; Davies, *Inside the Hurricane*, 79–82.

21. Burpee, "Grady Norton," 247–53; Sheets, "National Hurricane Center," 196; Dunn and Miller, *Atlantic Hurricanes*, 136, 145, 183, 202, 236, 269; Douglas, *Hurricane*, 292–93, 300; Grady Norton, "Hurricane Forecasting (A Soliloquy)," MS. (1947), National Hurricane Center Library, Miami, Florida.

22. "Alice to Wallis," *Time* (June 15, 1953), 102; Barnes, *Florida's Hurricane History*, 35–38; Helm, *Hurricanes*, 104; Douglas, *Hurricane*, 293; Steinberg, *Acts of God*, 67–68. The idea of using women's names to identify hurricanes appeared as early as 1941 in George Stewart's novel *Storm* (New York: Random House, 1941).

23. Dunn and Miller, *Atlantic Hurricanes*, 8–9. Barnes, *Florida's Hurricane History*, 38, notes: "Air force and navy meteorologists who tracked the movements of typhoons across the wide expanses of the Pacific frequently assigned female names to storms. This system became official in 1953, when the Weather Bureau began using female names for storms in the Atlantic. It continued through the late 1970s, until women's groups and several countries lobbied the World Meteorological Organization

to change the naming system. In 1979 men's names and names of international origin were added to the lists." *Miami News*, September 16, 1960, September 8, 11, 1965; *Tampa Tribune*, September 10, 1965; *Miami Herald*, September 11, 1960. The newspaper accounts cited above, and hundreds of others, can be found in scrapbooks located at the National Hurricane Center Library in Miami. See especially the scrapbook labeled "Newspaper Articles on Hurricane Donna, Hurricane Cleo, and other Hurricanes from *The Miami Herald* and *The Miami News* from 1960 to 1964" (hereafter cited as NHC Scrapbook 1960–64). See also "Another Sexist Bastion Falls," *New York Times*, May 13, 1978.

24. Sheets, "National Hurricane Center," 196, 199–201, 204; Douglas, *Hurricane*, 355–58; Davies, *Inside the Hurricane*, 80–82; Helm, *Hurricanes*, 50–63, 128–29; Rosenfeld, *Eye of the Storm*, 238–41; Isaac Tannehill, *Hurricane Hunters* (New York: Dodd, Mead, 1954); *Miami Herald*, September 3, 1977, August 10, September 3, 1978, *Miami News*, August 29, 1979, August 4, 1980, August 17, 1983, NHC Scrapbook 1950–85, National Hurricane Center Library, Miami . See also R. M. Markus, N. F. Halbiesen, and J. F. Fuller, *Air Weather Service, Our Heritage, 1937–1987* (Scott Air Force Base, Ill.: Military Airlift Command, U.S. Air Force, 1987); and the novel by former Air Force pilot and hurricane hunter William C. Anderson: *Hurricane Hunters* (New York: Crown, 1972). On the International Geophysical Year, see Walter Sullivan, *Assault on the Unknown: The International Geophysical Year* (New York: McGraw-Hill, 1961).

25. For an overview of the "space race" between the United States and the Soviet Union, see James Schefter, *The Race: The Uncensored Story of How America Beat Russia to the Moon* (New York: Doubleday, 1999).

26. *Bradenton Herald*, August 21, 1945; *Tampa Daily Times*, August 9, 1945.

27. *Miami News*, August 19, 28, 1969 (quotation), *Ft. Lauderdale News*, September 12, 1965, in NHC Scrapbook 1966–69; Rosenfeld, *Eye of the Storm*, 136; Elsner and Kara, *Hurricanes of the North Atlantic*, 380; Dunn and Miller, *Atlantic Hurricanes*, 294; Douglas, *Hurricane*, 292; Barnes, *Florida's Hurricane History*, 177–80; Davies, *Inside the Hurricane*, 82–86.

28. *Miami Herald*, August 30, 1964, NHC Scrapbook 1960–64; *Miami Herald*, September 15, 1965 (Connor quote), NHC Scrapbook 1966–69; *Miami Herald*, June 20, 1972, August 1–2, 1978; *Ft. Lauderdale News*, September 12, 1965, August 24, 1969 (Gentry quote); *Miami News*, August 18–19, 1969, all in NHC Scrapbook 1950–85. See also the following NHC Scrapbook 1950–85 clippings: "Gov't Weather Tampering Is Causing World Floods," *National Tattler*, December 24, 1972; and "Rainmaking on Protests 'Ridiculous,'" *Hollywood Sun-Tattler*, August 24, 1972, which reported the National Weather Service's denial "that it seeded clouds over Miami Beach to bring down rain on protesters outside the Republican National Convention." On Project Stormfury, see Robert C. Gentry, "Hurricane Modification," in *Weather and Climate*, ed. W. N. Hess (New York: John Wiley and Sons, 1974); Robert Sheets, "Tropical Cyclone Modification: The Project Stormfury Hypothesis," NOAA Technical Report ERL 414–AOML 30 (1981), 1–52; Sheets, "National Hurricane Center," 200; Dunn

and Miller, *Atlantic Hurricanes*, 294–96; Rosenfeld, *Eye of the Storm*, 245–48; Davies, *Inside the Hurricane*, 79–102; Elsner and Kara, *Hurricanes of the North Atlantic*, 380; Hughes, *Century of Weather Service*, 181, 200; and Barnes, *Florida's Hurricane History*, 229–30. On the emerging science of weather modification, see U.S. Congress, Senate Committee on Foreign Relations, *Weather Modification*, 93rd Cong., 2nd session, 1974; Frederick Sargent, "A Dangerous Game: Taming the Weather," *Bulletin of the American Meteorological Society* 48 (1967): 452–58; W. R. Derrick Sewell, ed., *Human Dimensions of Weather Modification* (Chicago: University of Chicago Press, 1966); Robert G. Fleagle, ed., *Weather Modification: Science and Public Policy* (Seattle: University of Washington Press, 1969); National Research Council, *Weather and Climate Modification: Problems and Progress* (Washington: National Academy of Sciences, 1973); Steinberg, *Acts of God*, 127–47; and the *Journal of Weather Modification* (1969–).

29. Sheets, "National Hurricane Center," 197–99, 204–5; NOAA, Federal Coordinator for Meteorological Services and Supporting Research, *National Hurricane Operations Plan, 1972* (Washington: U.S. Department of Commerce, 1972), FCM 72–2.

30. James F. W. Purdom and W. Paul Menzel, "Evolution of Satellite Observations in the United States and Their Use in Meteorology," in *Historical Essays on Meteorology, 1919–1995*, ed. James Rodger Fleming (Boston: American Meteorological Society, 1996), 103–17; J. D. Johnson, F. C. Parmenter, and R. Anderson, "Environmental Satellites: Systems, Data Interpretation, and Applications," *NOAA NESS* (October 1976), NOAA S/T 76–241); Sheets, "National Hurricane Center," 197–99, 201–4; Dunn and Miller, *Atlantic Hurricanes*, 291–94; Elsner and Kara, *Hurricanes of the North Atlantic*, 42–43; Rosenfeld, *Eye of the Storm*, 236–38; and E. A. Smith, "The McIDAS System," *IEEE Transactions: Geosciences* (GE-13) (1975): 123–28. See also E. C. Barrett and D. W. Martin, *The Use of Satellite Data in Rainfall Monitoring* (New York: Academic Press, 1981). See also *Miami News*, August 26, 1964, NHC Scrapbook 1960–64; and *Miami Herald*, November 22, 1975, May 26, July 19, 1982, August 29, 1984, and c.1974 *Herald* clipping "Machines Speed Weather Data," all in NHC Scrapbook 1950–85.

31. On the maturation of television news, see Erik Barnouw, *Tube of Plenty: The Evolution of American Television*, 2d rev. ed. (New York: Oxford University Press, 1990); David Schoenbrun, *On and Off the Air: An Informal History of CBS News* (New York: E. P. Dutton, 1989); and the 6–part documentary video series *Dawn of the Eye* (Princeton, N. J.: Films for the Humanities and Social Sciences, 1997), esp. pt. 4, "The Powers That Be, 1960–75," and pt. 5, "The Electronic Battalions, 1975–88."

32. Sheets, "National Hurricane Center," 196–97; National Weather Bureau, Office of the Federal Coordinator, *Report of the 1966 Interdepartmental Hurricane Warning Conference, Atlantic* (Washington, D.C.: GPO, 1966), 1–49. See also the voluminous clippings in the NHC Scrapbook 1966–69, esp. *Miami News*, September 8, 1965.

33. Sheets, "National Hurricane Center," 197; Elsner and Kara, *Hurricanes of the North Atlantic*, 21–24, 44, 137–38, 382; Barnes, *Florida's Hurricane History*, 13–14; Rosenfeld, *Eye of the Storm*, 18–19, 239–41, 249. On Simpson's tenure as NHC director, see *Miami News*, August 27–28, 1969; *Miami Herald*, August 27, 1969, NHC Scrapbook

1966–69; *Miami Herald,* August 22, 1969, May 30, 1974; *U.S. News and World Report* (September 8, 1969): 33, NHC Scrapbook 1950–85. See also Robert H. Simpson and H. Riehl, *The Hurricane and Its Impact* (Baton Rouge: Louisiana State University Press, 1980).

34. For a history of FEMA and its predecessors, see "History of the Federal Emergency Management Agency," available from World Wide Web (*fema.gov/about/ history.htm*); Peter J. May, *Recovering from Catastrophes: Federal Disaster Relief Policy and Politics* (Westport, Conn.: Greenwood, 1985); and Steinberg, *Acts of God,* 106–14, 173–95. See also *Miami Herald,* September 10, 12, 1965, *Ft. Lauderdale News,* September 16, 1965, *Miami News,* June 7, 1966, NHC Scapbook 1966–69; Ron Sachs, "Storm Target Areas Urged to Obey Warnings Quickly," *Miami Herald,* September 1974; *Miami Herald,* May 30, June 1, 1982; L. Erik Calonius, "Hurricane Experts Say the State of Their Art Can't Avert a Disaster,"*Wall Street Journal,* October 14, 1983, all in NHC Scrapbook 1950–85; Douglas C. Dacy and Howard Kunreuther, *The Economics of Natural Disasters: Implications for Federal Policy* (New York: Free Press, 1969); U.S. General Accounting Office, *Federal Disaster Assistance: What Should the Policy Be?* (Washington: GAO, 1980); U.S. General Accounting Office, *Requests for Federal Disaster Assistance Need Better Evaluation: Report to the Congress* (Washington, D.C.: GAO, 1981); Federal Emergency Management Agency, *This Is the Federal Emergency Management Agency* (Washington, D.C.: FEMA, 1982); U.S. General Accounting Office, *Consolidation of Federal Assistance Resources Will Enhance the Federal-State Emergency Management Effort: Summary: Report* (Washington: GAO, 1983); House Committee on Government Operations, *Federal Assistance to States and Communities for Hurricane Preparedness Planning: Twentieth Report* (Washington, D.C.: GPO, 1983); U.S. Congress, Senate, Committee on Appropriations, Subcommittee on HUD-Independent Agencies, *Federal Flood Insurance Program: Hearing before a Subcommittee of the Committee on Appropriations, United States Senate, Ninety-seventh Congress, First Session: Special Hearing, Federal Emergency Management Agency, Nondepartmental Witnesses* (Washington, D.C.: GPO, 1981).

35. Earl J. Baker, ed., *Hurricanes and Coastal Storms: Awareness, Evacuation, and Mitigation,* Florida Sea Grant College, Report 33 (Gainesville: Florida Sea Grant and Marine Advisory Program, 1980); Lawrence S. Tait, ed., *Hurricanes . . . Different Faces in Different Places,* 17th Annual National Hurricane Conference, Atlantic City, N.J, April 11–14, 1995 (Tallahassee, Fla.: National Hurricane Conference, 1995). On the evolution of hurricane research in the 1980s and 1990s, see Elsner and Kara, *Hurricanes of the North Atlantic,* passim; Sheets, "National Hurricane Center," 207–30; and the periodic technical reports published by the NHC and NOAA. On William Gray, see Elsner and Kara, *Hurricanes of the North Atlantic,* 334, 344; William M. Gray, "Global View of the Origins of Tropical Disturbances and Storms," *Monthly Weather Review* 96 (1968): 669–700; Gray, "Hurricanes: Their Formation, Structure, and Likely Role in the Tropical Circulation," in D. B. Shaw, ed., *Meteorology Over the Tropical Oceans* (London: Royal Meteorological Society, 1979), 155–218; Gray, "Atlantic Seasonal Hurricane Frequency: Part I: El Nino and 30 mb Quasi Biennial Oscillation

Influences," and "Atlantic Seasonal Hurricane Frequency: Part II: Forecasting Its Variability," *Monthly Weather Review* 112 (1984): 1649–83; Gray and C. W. Landsea, "African Rainfall as a Precursor of Hurricane-Related Destruction on the U.S. East Coast," *Bulletin of the American Meteorological Society* 73 (1992): 1352–64; Gray et al., *Summary of Atlantic Tropical Cyclone Activity and Verification of Authors' Seasonal Prediction* (Fort Collins: Colorado State University, 1995); *St. Petersburg Times*, August 9, 1998; and Gray's Web site: *(www.tropical.atmos.colostate.edu/forecasts/index.html)*. On El Niño, see Cesar N. Caviedes, *El Niño in History: Storming Through the Ages* (Gainesville: University Press of Florida, 2001).

36. Frank served as NHC director from 1973 to 1987, when he was replaced by Robert C. Sheets. See Neil L. Frank, "The Hard Facts About Hurricanes," *NOAA Magazine* 4 (1974): 4–9; and various clippings in the NHC Scrapbook 1950–85, esp. *Miami News*, May 29, 1982, *Miami Herald*, September 24, 1975, May 29, 1976, June 1, 1980, June 1, 6, July 29, November 20, 25, 1982, September 12, 1984, March 10, 1985, and K. Demaret, "Hurricane Expert Dr. Neil Frank Issues an Ominous Warning for Millions of Americans," *People* 20 (August 29, 1983): 87–88. On the growing celebrity status of hurricane forecasters, see the series of profiles by Mike Clary in the *Miami Herald*, March 5, June 6, July 29, June 3, 1984; and Al Burt, "The Calm Before," *Miami Herald*, March 10, 1985, all in the NHC Scrapbook 1950–85. For examples of the special "hurricane sections" issued by many major newspapers, see *Miami Herald*, June 27, 1982, July 28, 1983, NHC Scrapbook 1950–85; and "Hurricane Guide," *St. Petersburg Times*, May 28, 2000. On Witt's tenure at FEMA, see Steinberg, *Acts of God*, 190–95.

37. Demaret, "Hurricane Expert," 87–88; Burt, "Calm Before," *Miami Herald*, March 10, 1985; *Miami Herald*, June 1, 1980; all in NHC Scrapbook 1950–85. In a September 24, 1975, *Miami Herald* story by Sam Jacobs, "She Was Surprise to Most," Frank stated: "I know people find it hard to believe that we can send a rocket to the moon and have it land just a few feet from where we planned it to and then I say that I can only predict a hurricane to within 50 miles, but it's true." A year later NHC forecaster Gilbert Clark confessed: "We're the first to admit we can't predict what they'll do. They can move so crazily, wobble as much as 50 miles in either direction. It's almost like their alive." *Miami Herald*, August 9, 1976, NHC Scrapbook 1950–85.

38. *Miami News*, May 31, 1979, May 29, 1981, *Miami Herald*, May 26, 30, June 1, 1982, July 28, 1983, *Sun Reporter*, May 29, 1982, Calonius, "Hurricane Experts Say," all in NHC Scrapbook 1950–85; Erik Larson, "Waiting for Hurricane X," *Time* 152 (September 7, 1998): 62–66.

39. See Pielke, *Hurricane Andrew in South Florida;* Roger A. Pielke, "Reframing the U.S. Hurricane Problem," *Society and Natural Resources* 10 (1997): 485–99; Provenzo and Provenzo, *In the Eye of Hurricane Andrew; St. Petersburg Times*, August 18–20, 2002; Roger M. Wakimoto and Peter G. Black, "Damage Survey of Hurricane Andrew and Its Relationship to the Eyewall," *Bulletin of the American Meteorological Society* (February 1994): 189–200; Hugh E. Willoughby and Peter G. Black, "Hurricane Andrew in Florida: Dynamics of a Disaster," *Bulletin of the American Meteorological Society*

(March 1996): 543–49; and Congress, Senate, Committee on Governmental Affairs, *Rebuilding FEMA: Preparing for the Next Disaster: Hearing before the Committee on Governmental Affairs, United States Senate, One Hundred Third Congress, First Session, May 18, 1993* (Washington, D.C.: GPO, 1994). During the past decade several important studies have explored recent trends in the politics and culture of "natural" disasters. See especially Andrew Ross, *Strange Weather: Culture, Science, and Technology in the Age of Limits* (London: Verso, 1991); Rutherford H. Platt, *Disasters and Democracy: The Politics of Extreme Natural Events* (Washington, D.C.: Island Press, 1999); Davis, *Ecology of Fear;* and Steinberg, *Acts of God.*

The Multiplicity of
American Public Life

Ellen Fitzpatrick

The essays in this volume belong to a rich and lively tradition in American historiography. For as long as American history has been written, whether by amateurs or professional historians, public life has been a vital and compelling element of intellectual inquiry and analysis. Indeed, in the earliest years of the discipline, many students of the American past considered the nation's history to be nothing more than "past politics." That idea has met a vigorous challenge among contemporary scholars who have insisted on a more textured and pluralistic history. Yet the debate over the proper focus of historical study itself reveals how central politics and public life have been to the field of American history.

The wish to capture the essence of the American national experience accounts for much of the enduring fascination of political history. By focusing on public life, historians not only recount crucial moments in the American past, they reflect on the broader meaning of our society, its institutions, laws, values, and cultural practices. Even in the nineteenth century, when the view of history as past politics held, perhaps, its greatest sway, students of the American past struggled to fashion out of their examination of United States history something more than an account of government and statecraft. Amateur historians who lavished attention on the formal political life of the nation acknowledged that the essence of America's history could not be easily captured by a catalog of presidents and laws. Rather, they imagined a grander and more expansive vision of the American past—one in which a young nation realized in extraordinary ways the ideals of liberal democracy.[1]

Nineteenth-century public life exemplified for patrician historians the sources of American exceptionalism. As Tocqueville long ago observed of the United States, "there society governs itself for itself." That American passion for engagement stood at the center of heroic nineteenth-century historical narratives. In this sense, politics and the public sphere constituted the very lifeblood of American history. From these interests and origins emerged a tradition of historical writing that soon dominated the discipline.[2]

The intellectual tradition crafted by patrician historians persisted into the twentieth century, even as their celebratory accounts gave way to a more critical perspective on the American past in the Progressive years. Amid a wave of historical revisionism, politics and public life remained the axis around which historical debate and discussion turned in the early twentieth century. Scholars such as Charles Beard, who sought to reveal the true forces shaping the evolution of American democracy, nonetheless kept the focus on political power even as they challenged romantic interpretations of the nation's Revolutionary history. Growing attention to economic and social history rendered more complex a narrative still dominated by a preoccupation with political history.[3]

As history's intellectual domain expanded even further in the interwar years, with growing attention to social and economic class and the experience of "ordinary" Americans, public life remained of central concern to the maturing discipline of history. World War II and the events of the immediate postwar years only heightened these preoccupations among historians. The lure of American exceptionalism remained strong in the Cold War era as historians sought to trace political stability and economic abundance to the nation's distinctive "liberal tradition."

Then came the vigorous revival of social history in the 1960s and 1970s, a development that at first glance seemed to dislodge politics from its place atop the intellectual pyramid of history. In fact, historical study of politics and public life expanded at a tremendous pace in the late twentieth century. Political history was deeply enriched and enlivened by a growing insistence on previously ignored groups and fresh categories of analysis as essential components of a "new political history." A more expansive vision of public life ultimately allowed political history not only to survive the challenge posed by social history but to sink stronger and deeper roots in the discipline.[4]

This outcome wasn't the inevitable result of political history's staying power. Rather, it was an intellectual achievement—one that owed much to the imagination of individual historians such as Morton Keller. Keller and other historians of his generation, who devoted their careers to making a new place for politics, law, and public life in the story of the American past, did much to ensure the continued intellectual vitality and appeal of American political history.

Many did so at a time when scholars and citizens increasingly viewed government, law, and politicians with, at best, a searching skepticism. The civil rights crusade, the growing critique of American foreign policy, sharp attacks on the persistence of social and economic inequality, the rise of liberation movements, campus protests, civil disobedience, and antigovernment protests shook the foundations of American political life in the 1960s and early 1970s. The sanctity of law, the essential fairness of American institutions, faith in politicians, and the centrality of formal politics and elections were all challenged by critics during these turbulent years.

The uproar likewise changed American intellectual life, and altered the disciplines. History especially seemed to reflect the full range of conflict within the larger society, as younger scholars insisted that the time had come for a "new history"—one that rejected a traditional preoccupation with politics, government, and elites. African Americans, women, ethnic and religious minorities, the working class, poor Americans, immigrants, and the other "have-nots" of society deserved, many scholars insisted, a central place in a new narrative of American history. Yet this was not to be simply a matter of including overlooked groups in a reconfigured historical narrative. Rather, the call was for a history that looked beyond formal politics to social, economic, cultural, and ideological forces as crucial determinants of change and continuity.[5]

For many of us who studied with Morton Keller during these tumultuous years, the challenge was to realize in our own work such fresh approaches to historical study while retaining our interest in the realm of politics, public life, law, and ideas. Keller provided his students with a rewarding example of how this might be achieved. For in his teaching and in his research, Keller demonstrated the ways in which historical study could be continually reinvigorated by new ideas and yet carefully connected to a longer tradition in American historiography.

Part of Keller's lesson involved a way of reimagining public life that emphasized not simply formal politics but the "polity"—that arena in which government and the people interacted and thereby shaped national life in profound and often lasting ways. Within this space Keller offered a pluralistic vision of American society. It was a place populated by men and women, of divergent religious, ethnic, and racial groups, shaped by countless associations, defined and debated by diverging social critics, changed by constantly shifting coalitions, historical actors, and agents, altered by the force of law and the machinery of government, and most of all, joined to generations that had come before and those who were yet to follow by what was accomplished and what was left undone.

In surveying this vibrant scene Keller emphasized the notion of multiplicity. Among American society's most compelling characteristics were varieties of belief, perspective, conviction, and experience. Public life reflected and was forced to mediate these essential elements of diversity. That it often did so half-heartedly, or in ways that seemed contradictory, was an essential ingredient of American politics and society. Keller urged his students to look for the variations, listen to the full range of voices, respect the contradictions, and capture the wide spectrum of experience and belief. That imperative also necessitated a look beyond American national boundaries to the historical experience of other countries. Such counsel provided an especially effective compass for historians who were seeking to chart the dramatic and fast-moving currents of late-nineteenth and early-twentieth-century history.

It is not easy to convey how powerful this subtle and nuanced approach to public life, to legal and political history, was in the context of the late 1960s and 1970s, especially. The discipline of history then reflected deep conflict over the proper focus and most useful ways of understanding the American past; interpretations often turned around polarities. Was Progressive reform best understood as a genuine and humanitarian crusade for social reform or was it more truly a hard-nosed, carefully conceived, and determined effort to exert social control? As graduate students it was tempting to divide everything we read into one of these two hostile camps. The idea that elements of social reform and social control could be intertwined in a single individual, association, movement, law, program, or ideology seemed a rather anemic response to the intellectual blood sport of the period. Yet Keller urged his students to consider the possibility. And from that quiet insistence came, as the foregoing essays demonstrate, a genuine and often illuminating way of reimagining the character of modern American politics and society that recognized the coexistence of "ambitions and anxieties."[6]

That public life could be understood through careful study of a compelling individual, evocative moment, unusual event, through the sometimes-tedious workings of an institution, by reference to region, race, or religion was another crucial aspect of Keller's teaching. There was no single method-ology or uniquely praiseworthy way of grasping the variegated elements of American history. A good historian must use whatever methods offered the best possible view of the past in all its complexity. No one source or approach would do. By his own example, Keller demonstrated to all of us that essential truths about American political life might be found in a Thomas Nast car-toon, the intricate workings of a life insurance company, in a judicial opinion, or buried in the huge periodical literature that flourished in the late nine-teenth and early twentieth centuries.

It is not surprising that this openness to breadth of subject and approach led Keller's students to examine diverse aspects of American historical expe-rience. In the essays presented here alone, murder, hurricanes, New Deal agencies, jurisprudence, women's and Native American experience, Progres-sive reform, regionalism, the Ku Klux Klan, and pluralism itself illuminate in all their particularity remarkably broad dimensions of American public life in the modern period. But more than range of subject, these studies reflect Keller's influence in their repeated insistence that the truth of the past can be found at the intersection of change and continuity. As Keller expressed it, to describe the "complex interplay between old and new is the major challenge facing historians of twentieth-century America."[7]

This appreciation for the complexity, variety, and contradictions of Ameri-can public life constitute, perhaps, Morton Keller's most enduring legacy to his students. Another is the personal example of a human being who pos-sesses and has worked to impart a strong belief in nation and history. Keller urged his students to engage the American past with respect for the world in-habited by previous generations but with an equally rigorous honesty. To study the past on its own terms, but in ways that accent the enduring significance of history to modern American society exemplified Keller's mandate for the study of history. In an age when respect for the past, a commitment to deter-mining knowable truths, and a capacity to temper honesty with understanding seem old-fashioned virtues indeed, it is a message that remains of compelling significance for the discipline of history.

NOTES

1. Richard Hofstadter, *The Progressive Historians* (New York: Vintage, 1970); Peter Novick, *That Noble Dream: The Objectivity Question and the American Historical Profes-sion* (Cambridge: Cambridge University Press, 1988); John Higham, *History: Professional*

Scholarship in America (Baltimore: Johns Hopkins University Press, 1965); Ellen Fitzpatrick, *History's Memory: Writing America's Past, 1880–1980* (Cambridge: Harvard University Press, 2002); Dorothy Ross, "Grand Narrative in American Historical Writing: From Romance to Uncertainty," *American Historical Review* 100, 3 (June 1995); Robert Allen Skotheim, *American Intellectual Histories and Historians* (Princeton, N.J.: Princeton University Press, 1966); Mark Leff, "Revisioning U.S. Political History," *American Historical Review* 100, 3 (June 1995).

2. Alexis de Tocqueville, *Democracy in America*, vol. 1 (New York: Vintage Books, 1945), 59.

3. There is a large literature on the Progressive historians; see esp. Hofstadter, *Progressive Historians;* Ernest Breisach, *American Progressive History* (Chicago: University of Chicago Press, 1993); Dorothy Ross, *The Origins of American Social Science* (Cambridge: Cambridge University Press, 1991); Novick, *That Noble Dream;* Higham, *History;* Cushing Strout, *The Pragmatic Revolt in American History* (New Haven, Conn.: Yale University Press, 1958); Morton White, *The Revolt Against Formalism* (New York: Viking, 1949); Ellen Nore, *Charles A. Beard* (Carbondale: Southern Illinois University Press, 1983); Nancy Cott, *A Woman Making History* (New Haven, Conn.: Yale University Press, 1991).

4. Louis Hartz, *The Liberal Tradition in America* (New York: Harcourt, Brace, 1955); Fitzpatrick, *History's Memory;* Eric Foner, ed., *The New American History* (Philadelphia: Temple University Press, 1990); Joyce Appleby, Lynn Hunt, and Margaret Jacob, *Telling the Truth About History* (New York: W.W. Norton, 1994); Leff, "Revisioning U.S. Political History."

5. Foner, *New American History;* Appleby, Hunt and Jacob, *Telling the Truth About History;* Paul Buhle, *History and the New Left* (Philadelphia: Temple University Press, 1990); Lawrence Levine, *The Opening of the American Mind* (Boston: Beacon Press, 1996).

6. Morton Keller, *Affairs of State: Public Life in Late Nineteenth Century America* (Cambridge: Harvard University Press, 1977), 598.

7. Morton Keller, *Regulating a New Economy: Public Policy and Economic Change in America, 1900–1933* (Cambridge: Harvard University Press, 1990).